FORD
AUSTRALIA

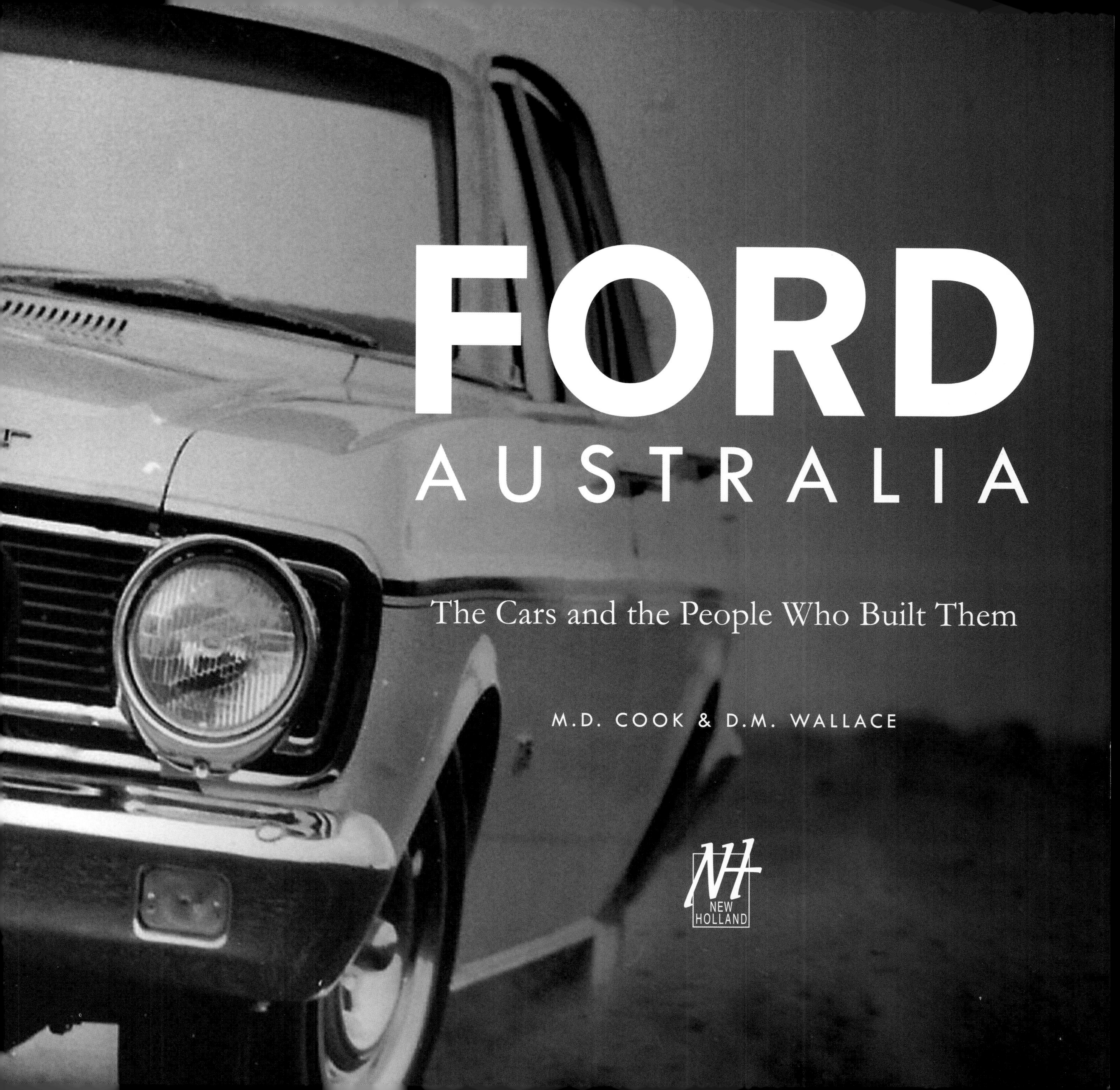

FORD AUSTRALIA

The Cars and the People Who Built Them

M.D. COOK & D.M. WALLACE

NEW HOLLAND

OFFICIAL TRACK CAR
FORD
JTV-847
03953-H

CONTENTS

FOREWORD

The automotive industry attracts people passionate about vehicles. In fact, you could say you don't survive in the industry unless you are. Whatever your passion, the automotive industry is a broad church, demanding a wide range of skills and disciplines. You can take pride that the results of your efforts are visible every day, on the road. This passion can take many forms; some like to build cars, some to collect and possess them. Others like to restore old cars, some to race new ones, others may admire good design (or deplore bad). Some people just like to drive cars, kick tires or smell rubber.

Sometime during the 1990s, Adrian Ryan, part of the Public Affairs Department of Ford Australia, began gathering old records, brochures, documents and memorabilia of the company, with the aid of another archival tragic, Les Drayton. Their passion was to preserve the history of the company and its people. Very quickly the volume of documents and objects outgrew its original location at R.J. Pound, then the Discovery Centre, later at the Broadmeadows Assembly Plant, before developing into the Adrian Ryan archives located in the basement of the old Head Office building in Broadmeadows. Before his retirement, Adrian enlisted another long serving Ford employee, Michele Cook, to succeed him. As well as special projects, the archives provide an information service within the organisation, as well as the community outside the company, media, enthusiasts, and a wide range of researchers, authors, scholars and students. One such special project was the transcribing and digitizing of production records from 1925 to the present day, a three-year project undertaken by Michele and another long serving Ford retiree, Doug Wallace.

The announcement by Ford of the cessation of manufacturing was met with disbelief and dismay. The decision was made that the efforts of those many thousands of Ford employees, over many years, should not go unrecognised. And so this book was born; a book for those who worked at Ford, Ford owners and car enthusiasts.

While researching the extensive archives of Ford Australia, interviewing past employees, renewing acquaintances, sharing memories and having a good laugh, all the material was there. Finally, after nearly eighteen months, the book came together. A book that was about Ford Australia, the cars, and the people who built them.

Writing the book was not difficult. The story told itself, with the enthusiastic assistance of the nearly eighty Ford retirees and 'blue bloods', who unstintingly gave their time and advice, told their stories, related anecdotes and generally allowed the authors into their lives. For those who also volunteered but could not be interviewed because of distance or time constraints, they apologise. To comply with the libel laws of the country, some of the anecdotes, amusing as they were, could not be included while others, omitted due to space, might make it into another book. The problem was selecting the images. Over 6,000 images were originally selected, then culled to 1,200. Agonising choices followed to reduce the number down to the approximately 600 finally selected.

We hope you enjoy the story of *Ford Australia: The Cars and the People Who Built Them.*

Michele and Doug

VIC
AFV-563

17 47

CHAPTER 1
BEGINNINGS

THE FORD YEARS 1863—1929

1863: Henry Ford born on July 30 at Dearbornville, Springfield Township, Wayne County, near Detroit, Michigan.

1893: Edsel Bryant Ford born November 6 to Henry and Clara Ford.

1896: Henry builds his first car (essentially a frame fitted with four bicycle wheels) the Quadricycle in Detroit.

1903: Ford motor Company incorporated in Detroit June 16.

1904: First Ford, a model A, imported to Australia.

1905–1925: Ford vehicles imported by agents and distributors through Ford Canada.

1908: Model T first produced in Detroit.

1909: R.J. Durance and his wife arrive to establish a Ford branch office and dealerships in Australia.

1913: First moving automotive assembly line at Ford Highland Park Assembly Plant, speeding assembly almost eight times.

1917–1918: First Ford truck, the TT, produced in Detroit. Henry Ford II born to Eleanor and Edsel Ford. First Fordson tractors in Australia.

1923: Hubert French and Mel Brooks arrive in Australia to review Australian operations.

1924: Hubert French and others arrive in Australia to establish manufacturing.

1925: Ford Motor Company of Australia and Ford Manufacturing Company of Australia incorporated March 31 and rent premises from Dalgety Wool Company in Geelong. Production of Model T range commences in Dalgety building July 1, 1925. Ford purchases land at Norlane in Geelong, Eagle Farm in Brisbane, Granville in Sydney, and rents premises at Adelaide, Brisbane, Freemantle, Hobart and Sydney. Plans announced to construct assembly plants at Geelong, Adelaide, Brisbane and Fremantle.

1925–1927: Assembly plants commence operations in Geelong, Adelaide, Brisbane, Fremantle, Hobart and Sydney. New Manufacturing plant opens in Geelong.

1928: Introduction of Model A range of vehicles in Australia. Assembly plant in Hobart, Tasmania closed due to low volumes.

The word Distributor has come to mean nothing more or less than a bunch of easy-living, luxury-loving, and opulent Directors, whose only thought is to squeeze more profits out of the business without the vestige of a thought of the future welfare of the Ford Motor Company. A band of vultures who will stoop to anything to satisfy their greedy hunger for profits. I do not believe that there is a place in our organisation for men of this character, either directly or indirectly…distributors' petty thieveries are so numerous that it is almost hopeless to attempt to correct them all. [1]

Early in November 1923, Ford representatives Hubert French and Mel Brooks arrived from Canada via New Zealand for a five-month tour of Australia, to review the operation of the Ford Australian Distributors and their sub-dealers. For many months, rumours had circulated in Australia that Ford, and perhaps General Motors, would soon begin local manufacture of vehicle bodies and chassis in Australia. The timing was right. During the First World War, the Australian Government, concerned with the limited shipping space available for goods essential to the war effort, had considered prohibiting the import of all motor vehicles, but compromised on banning only vehicle bodies; allowing chassis to be imported. As a result the body building industry was small and fragmented, a cottage industry. The policy was somewhat relaxed after the war, the ban replaced by a high import protective tariff on vehicle bodies, strongly supported by the distributors

LEFT A Ford Model A, shown here as part of a promotion used in the 1920s, was the first Ford vehicle to land in Australia

RIGHT Harley Tarrant in a Tarrant Ford

and body builders, often one and the same, who dominated the automotive market. A multitude of manufacturers from England, France, Italy, America and of course Ford, through Ford Canada, a member of the British Commonwealth, supplied these distributors. Australian body builders constructed the bodies, sometimes to the customer's specification, often to suit themselves. The result was a market of multiple makes and models, a variety of styles, and no standardisation, resulting in a higher retail price than other countries. A few distributors and importers, dominated the market; Ford alone had six major distributors who were also body builders. They built virtually what they wanted and charged accordingly. Increasingly customer correspondence back to Ford Canada complained of a lack of support, little stock, high prices for spare parts and, more concerning, the poor quality. W.C. Campbell, Managing Director of Ford of Canada was reportedly furious at the exorbitant prices charged and profits made by the distributors. He wrote to Edsel Ford on September 24, 1923 pointing this out, suggesting that after twenty years, the time was right to develop 'a more adequate and economical system for serving the Australian public.' Edsel had agreed.[2] Campbell chose French and Brooks, charging them with assessing the performance of the Australian distributors, their dealers, their after-sales servicing of vehicles, the size of the market and ultimately, to make recommendations as to the feasibility of manufacturing in Australia.

Hubert Charles French was an American by birth, a Canadian by choice and naturalisation, born at Battle Creek, Michigan in 1882. Taller than average and weighing 108 kg, educated and with a towering intellect, he was an imposing figure. Graduating from the Michigan College of Law, with degrees in Law and Civil Engineering in 1903, at twenty-one he became a partner in a Canadian contracting company, working all over Canada. The tough construction industry was no place for those who shied from conflict and French fitted in well. He had a keen business sense, was blunt in manner and speech, a heavy smoker, liked a drink and betting on racehorses—a habit he only stopped when it threatened his marriage. After his first wife died in 1910, he married Mildred Gillespie in 1911 in Toronto. Like Henry Ford, he was interested in all things mechanical. He left the contracting industry after ten years, in 1913, to follow this passion, building and racing speedboats. This business failed and like Henry, French was bankrupted. He spent some time managing a Canadian building supply company before joining Ford Canada in 1919, an industry also known for its tough and competitive nature. He would have got on well with Henry: an almost puritanical approach to life and work, an engineer who liked to tinker. At Ford, his straight talking, fair dealing and ability to achieve sales targets resulted in his appointment as assistant sales manager for Ford Canada by 1922. Naturalised as a Canadian in 1920, his ambition, business and analytical skills, as well as his background in contracting, construction and sales made him an obvious choice for Campbell. French was to review the manufacturing, distribution and sales, Brooks the service and spare parts supply operations.

French and Brooks' arrival in Australia was anticipated; en route to Australia they had stopped in Auckland, New Zealand, to conduct a similar survey of the Ford dealerships and were reasonably satisfied with the management of the operation. While in New Zealand, quite by chance, they met G.V. Cornwell, the manager of Tarrant Motors and Ford's Victorian distributor, who was there on holiday. Cornwell cabled Davies and Davies, the NSW distributor, requesting accommodation arrangements be made for French and Brooks on their arrival, and the trio sailed together from Auckland to Sydney; French was impressed with Cornwell's attitude and commitment to the Ford Motor Company and the potential value he brought to Ford. On their arrival in Sydney, they separated, Cornwell to travel on to Melbourne, with arrangements to meet them later, and to travel with French and Brooks when they visited the Tarrant sub-dealers.

Compared to the amiability of Cornwell, the reception of French and Brooks in Sydney could not have been more stark. Neither of the NSW distributor principals, brothers Lewis and Arthur Davies, was at the wharf to greet them. Instead, they were met by a clerk from the Davies' office, who escorted them to their hotel by taxi—no company vehicle. There they found their request for a suite of rooms, as befits senior executives of an international company planning to use their suite as accommodation and office, had been ignored. Lew Davies had booked them into a single room with twin beds.

If the Davies brothers had wanted to antagonise French, a man they had not met, they succeeded magnificently. Worse was

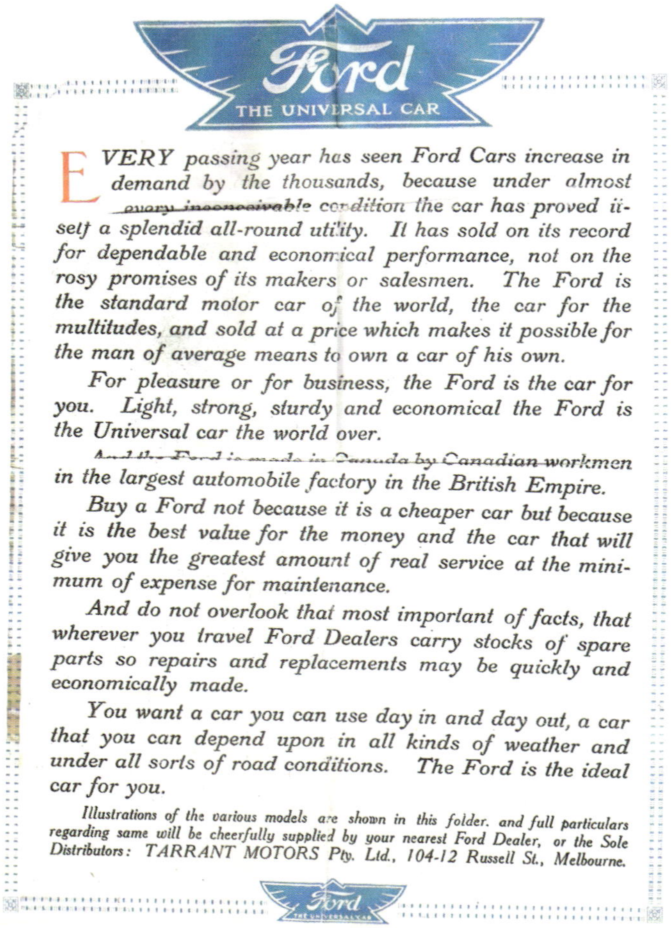

Ford
THE UNIVERSAL CAR

EVERY passing year has seen Ford Cars increase in demand by the thousands, because under almost every inconceivable condition the car has proved itself a splendid all-round utility. It has sold on its record for dependable and economical performance, not on the rosy promises of its makers or salesmen. The Ford is the standard motor car of the world, the car for the multitudes, and sold at a price which makes it possible for the man of average means to own a car of his own.

For pleasure or for business, the Ford is the car for you. Light, strong, sturdy and economical the Ford is the Universal car the world over.

And the Ford is made in Canada by Canadian workmen in the largest automobile factory in the British Empire.

Buy a Ford not because it is a cheaper car but because it is the best value for the money and the car that will give you the greatest amount of real service at the minimum of expense for maintenance.

And do not overlook that most important of facts, that wherever you travel Ford Dealers carry stocks of spare parts so repairs and replacements may be quickly and economically made.

You want a car you can use day in and day out, a car that you can depend upon in all kinds of weather and under all sorts of road conditions. The Ford is the ideal car for you.

Illustrations of the various models are shown in this folder, and full particulars regarding same will be cheerfully supplied by your nearest Ford Dealer, or the Sole Distributors: TARRANT MOTORS Pty. Ltd., 104-12 Russell St., Melbourne.

LEFT 1920s Tarrant's brochure promoting the reliability and virtues of the Ford car

to come. After French re-arranged their hotel booking to his satisfaction, they dismissed the offer of another taxi to the Davies and Davies offices, also located in George Street, and walked there instead, enjoying the sunshine and warm weather. They had to wait for some time, cooling their heels in the reception area before being eventually ushered into Managing Director Lew Davies' office to meet him and his brother, Arthur. This first meeting was decidedly frosty on both sides and Lew Davies introduced their General Manager, a Mr. Lock, assigned to assist them. French later wrote that Lock, in the U.S. 'might make a reasonable Branch Analyst'. [3] We are not party to what transpired at that meeting but French later wrote:

> *...before the end of the day he (Lewis Davies) began to get a glimpse of the great white light of understanding.* [4]

That night, French and Brooks attended a dinner at the home of Arthur Davies, and French's poor first impressions of the Davies brothers continued. They dined alone, not meeting the Davies family. He later wrote in his report:

> *Dinner at Arthur Davies home, he is extremely wealthy. Arthur Davies is raw, crude, and without the slightest vestige of desire to be of service either to his community or his country.* [5]

French also added that he believed Lew Davies had engineered their poor reception.

French and Brooks continued a series of meetings over the next three days but were hampered repeatedly by the Davies' refusal to give them access to their accounts, or other details of their business. According to Davies, district organisers visited regional dealers about once a month and he considered their territory, all of NSW, capably represented by them. The dealers refuted this, one Sydney dealer revealing a Davies representative had only visited him twice in ten years.

As their vehicle from Canada had not arrived, French procured a T Model Tourer from Davies and Davies for them to commence the first leg of their journey, to travel from Sydney to Brisbane. Their plan was to visit and interview as many dealers in Australia as they could, and assess their capability as Ford representatives, as well as assess the performance of the Distributors. Accompanied by Davies and Davies' northern region manager and two service managers, they departed Sydney on November 6 for Brisbane. According to French, 'the Davies attitude has undergone a complete change,' [6] but with French and Brooks giving nothing away, they left Sydney with speculation rife as to their intentions.

The task of visiting all dealers between Sydney and Brisbane, let alone all dealers within Australia, must have been a daunting one. Even in the twenty-first century, the trip from Sydney to Brisbane, without stops, can take two days, given the state of the highway. To stop as many as three or four times a day, zig-zagging their way through the Hunter Valley and the northern New South Wales regions, and reach Brisbane in seven days is impressive, given the road conditions of the time. Their first stop was at Parramatta, then Windsor, before overnighting in Maitland. They continued over the next few days visiting in turn, Taree, Kempsey, Coffs Harbour, Grafton and Lismore, arriving in Brisbane on November 19, 1923.

The dealer visits were enlightening. According to French, the quality of dealers ranged from the well run, with showrooms and a service department, to one whom merely acted as a selling broker, with the service department outsourced to a garage, in reality a blacksmith shop and a carriage painting shop. Brooks rated several of the mechanics as 'not even fourth rate'. All the dealers gave the lie to Davies' claim of a well-run distributorship, complaining of constant price reductions, a low commission of 10%, which precluded the employment of salesmen, and the lack of, or

ABOVE Hubert C. French, Ford Australia Managing Director from 1925 to 1950

RIGHT Hudson Fysh (centre), founder of Qantas, and Paul McGuiness (right) prior to their departure from Longreach, Queensland on August 19, 1919.

inability, to obtain stock from Davies. None of the dealers held any inventory, claiming the constant price reductions precluded this. When quizzed on the frequency of visitation by Davies Regional Organisers, one dealer said he saw him 'approximately every six months'. French's summary was:

> *Dealers had developed as best they could with little or no assistance from Davies, no systematic sales system or a Ford owners list.* [6]

French, not known for his subtlety, bluntly concluded in his report to Campbell in Canada:

> *Mr. Lew Davies' thoughts are never made apparent by his facial expression and he is, frankly, a man I would not trust in any business matter.* [8]

Their reception in Brisbane was, if possible, worse than Sydney. Their accommodation again was a single room with twin beds, not a suite as requested. George Whatmore, the Managing Director of Queensland Motors, the Queensland Distributor, was not available, they were advised; 'Mr. Whatmore senior is on board his yacht and will not be returning for several days.' It transpired that with Whatmore on his yacht was a Mr. Carrington, a former employee of Queensland Motors and a current dealer for Hudson and Essex. French suspected that Whatmore, through Queensland Motors, also owned that dealership. While waiting for Whatmore to return, they visited several Ford dealers in Brisbane. They ascertained no Queensland dealers carried stock, the dealers placing orders on Queensland Motors, who built the vehicle and trans-shipped them to the sales point. They discovered also that Whatmore, on hearing of their impending visit, had hastily increased the number of sub-dealers in Brisbane from one to fifteen. These so-called dealers were given 10% off the list price

HUDSON FYSH, QANTAS & THE MODEL T

The legendary toughness of the Model T Ford made it the vehicle of choice for many intrepid outback explorers. One of these was Hudson Fysh when in 1919, he and wartime buddy and Qantas co-founder Paul McGuinness, were commissioned to survey the Darwin to Longreach leg of the England to Australia air route. They departed Longreach, their utility heavily loaded with fuel and supplies for the trip, and were the first vehicle to make the perilous trip. They trekked cross-country through outback Queensland defying bent axles, anthills and swamps, and arrived at Borroloola on the Gulf of Carpentaria twenty-four days later with only four gallons of fuel remaining. Two years later, in 1922, Qantas won the contract for the lucrative mail run from Charleville to Cloncurry, their first flight taking place that November.

for vehicles and 25% off for parts.

When French and Brooks finally met Whatmore, Whatmore refused to discuss Queensland Motors' finances and was very pessimistic of future sales, citing the effect of the current drought and the fact that banks were charging higher interest rates, between 1 and 1.5%. French also found that Queensland Motors actively undersold their own sub-dealers and seriously overstated their number of dealers, only three handling Ford exclusively. Whatmore was obstructive and evasive, raising irrelevant issues and often quoting Shakespeare. To a man as direct and blunt as French, this was too much, and he consequently lost his temper completely on several occasions in meetings with Whatmore. In his notes, French recorded that he detested Whatmore, feelings Whatmore reciprocated, which appeared not to concern French in the least. French believed the tentacles of Lew Davies extended into Queensland; French thought Whatmore was, at best, merely a district organiser, as Lew Davies had a controlling interest in Queensland Motors. French estimated they charged £45 too much for vehicles. In addition, Davies set the prices in Queensland for spare parts, and controlled the funding of dealer purchases and hire purchase of vehicles through his company, Australian Guarantee Company. French did not believe Whatmore when he said he was ignorant of the pricing structure of spare parts, as this was set by the Davies brothers in Sydney.

BELOW Hudson Fysh and Paul McGuiness beside a large termite mound, one of many obstacles encountered on their way to Borroloola

While in Brisbane, French and Brooks conducted a sales and service conference for the Queensland dealers. At the conference, all dealers welcomed Ford's visit, several confiding to French that Whatmore gave preferential treatment to service garages over his dealers in the sale of spare parts. The dealers also told French they wanted independence from Sydney. French was critical of Queensland Motors' handling of shipping crates, which damaged the products, and of the dealer letters that, while written regularly, twice a month, contained no useful information. Brooks' assessment was that Queensland Motors were more than ten years behind an equivalent dealer in Canada and that the New Zealand dealers were far superior to the Australian. Whatmore in turn complained that the commission on vehicles was too low and below that of Ford's competitors. French concluded the dealer set-up in Queensland was non-existent and that it was useless to continue his journey any further north. He and Brooks returned to Sydney to prepare for their journey to southern NSW and Melbourne.

BELOW Tarrant's Head Office and Melbourne Motor Body Company

On November 26, 1923, French and Brooks, accompanied by the Southern District organiser, a nephew of the Tasmanian distributor, Robert Nettlefold, set out to review the dealers in Southern NSW, before meeting Cornwell in Albury. They wound their way through southern NSW, stopping at any towns small or large, with a Ford 'Dealer', overnighting at Berrima and the small hamlet of Bookham, detouring off the Hume highway to visit larger dealers at Yass, Junee, Cootamundra and Wagga Wagga, before reaching Albury. Further damage to Davies' reputation as a distributor, if possible, was the knowledge that they did not supply their organisers with a company vehicle to visit dealers; they were required to travel by train from town to town, missing opportunities to display and demonstrate the company's products. They found the same depressing situation as in the northern region. One or two dealers, French believed, had potential, others were hopeless. None carried stock; all complained at Davies' pricing policies, who regularly reduced prices, deterring them from carrying inventory. Most were multi-franchise dealerships, but were prepared to change to become a single dealership, committed to Ford. District organiser visits were spasmodic and of little assistance.

Arriving at Albury, a region shared by Davies (NSW) and Tarrant (Victoria), they visited the local dealership of Blacklocks, finding the showroom dirty, poorly organised, with mixed stock of new and used vehicles, but well located and with plans to renovate. Well positioned in the town, holding stock and willing to shed their Oakland and Fiat franchises, French considered they had potential. Here they met Cornwell, the organiser for Tarrant, while Nettlefold returned to Sydney by train.

As French and Brooks visited the Victorian dealers, the positive influence of Cornwell was immediately apparent, although they considered the Bendigo dealer to be particularly poor. By contrast, those of Benalla, Ballarat and Geelong he considered well managed, had some idea of their region and held some inventory. French noted many of the premises were run down and in need of an injection of capital to improve.

French and Brooks spent some time in Melbourne and discovered a labyrinthine web of companies, with intertwining interests, all with the same company directors. Allied Motors Interests Ltd. was the holding company, with two wholly owned subsidiaries, Auto Car Industries and Tarrant Motors Pty Ltd. Auto Car Industries was the distributor in Victoria, Tasmania and the Riverina for four makes of passenger vehicles, and two trucks. Auto Car Industries also had two wholly owned subsidiary companies. The first, Olympia Motors Ltd., was the distributor of another three passenger vehicles with the same territory as its parent company, while the second, Melbourne Motor Body Company Ltd. (MMBCL) manufactured the bodies for all these makes, as well as some for Tarrant Motors, the Victorian distributor of Ford vehicles. French noted the transport of crates from the wharf and the uncrating and assembly operations were:

> *a disgrace…without a single mechanical device for the efficient handling of materials…confusion reigned supreme.* [9]

While Tarrant Motors obtained the Ford standard tourer and runabout bodies from MMBCL, they sourced the 'deluxe' bodies from the Holden Body Company of Adelaide, a company who also acted as a distributor for General Motors. French was appalled to find the deluxe chassis, assembled by MMBCL was then driven about a mile to Holden's Melbourne plant where the body was fitted, then driven back to Tarrant's new car department just across the road. He found the Tarrant Board of Directors, Ross, Lewis, Lew Davies, Wallace and Roach dysfunctional and uncommunicative, even amongst themselves. Arthur Davies, who travelled from Sydney to, in French's mind 'keep an eye on us', again declined to supply any financial data on the grounds of confidentiality, but in reality not without the approval of his brother, Lew Davies. French believed that Cornwell, initially employed by Davies, was a 'Ford' man, but one who was stymied in his efforts by his Board of Directors. Once again, French was highly critical of the stranglehold the Davies brothers had on the Australian automotive industry. He found there was an acute shortage of vehicles to supply, some dealers received preferential treatment over others, and the Davies brothers, through their web of companies, controlled the ordering of chassis from overseas. Brooks found that the price of spare parts, while set by Sydney was, 'charge what the market can bear.' Tarrant carried some of the dealer finance, while Australian Guarantee Company, controlled by the Davies brothers, handled the balance.

French and Brooks attended a Victorian Dealers Convention, on December 11 and 12, 1923, organised by Cornwell for his dealers and salesmen. French considered Cornwell had created the nucleus of a good dealership organisation. Interest of all attendees was high and when French announced at the end of the conference that Ford would immediately require all dealerships to be exclusively Ford and they would be required to hold stock, he was amazed his announcement met with a roar of applause and stamping of feet from all 200 attendees. I am not sure if the Davies brothers and their fellow directors shared in this enthusiasm.

French spent time talking to industry leaders and government department heads and was surprised at the disparity of views. He met and interviewed Sir George Knibbs, at the time the Director of Research and Industry, the forerunner of the CSIRO. While a statistician of some standing, he had less knowledge of business; for a senior government representative in a key role to support industry, he was most pessimistic. Sir George said he could not honestly

GETTING A CAR BY CRATE

Before 1925, distributors imported complete Ford vehicles in crates from Windsor, Canada. The cars were driven onto the crate base, four men then took an hour to disassemble and bolt down the wheels, windscreen, steering wheel, brakes and top, before closing the crate around the vehicle. Later, Ford imported the chassis in the same fashion.

(*Geelong Advertiser* July 29, 1995)

BELOW Tarrant factory

SECTION - FORD ASSEMBLING DEPT
No 2 BUILDING - Lt COLLINS St

advise anyone to consider the establishment of any industry in Australia that required the use of labour. He believed the unions had such a grasp on Australia that it required a revolution to either:

> *...clear the situation, or wipe Australia off the map as far as having a place amongst the important nations of the world.* [10]

Luckily, French ignored Knibbs' advice. Speaking to the Managing Directors of H.V. McKay and matchmakers Bryant and May, he felt he obtained a balanced view of labour relations in Australia, from the worst to best. McKay reported regular strikes that had little effect on their business, Bryant and May who reported no industrial action, and had a good relationship with their employees, were very positive.

From Melbourne, French travelled to Launceston, where he was met by the Tasmanian distributor, Robert Nettlefold. French was impressed by Hobart's harbour and availability of labour and briefly, but illogically, considered the island as a potential manufacturing site. He returned to Melbourne on December 19, where he met another manufacturer, Massey Harris, as well as having meetings with the Commonwealth Tariff Board, sounding them out on reduced duties for components, should Ford commence manufacture and assembling of chassis and bodies in Australia.

French's November report concluded that he was very disappointed with Davies and Davies, and that NSW would need immense efforts of reorganisation. Again, he was extremely savage in his criticism of the:

> *...useless titled folk of Davies and Davies who evidently feel it below them to actively travel their dealers' territories.* [11]

On the other hand, French noted:

> *...Victoria is different. Cornwell has shown willingness to work hard and cooperate. He is the only man I have seen in Australia who has anything like the comprehensive grasp of what is required of him as a distributor. He (Cornwell) admitted it was still a hit and miss affair, he has not been trained, nor trained his staff. (He) has had to constantly fight his board. If Cornwell is not blocked by the Davies' interests, sales in 1924 will be double 1923 in Victoria.* [12]

French and Brooks returned to Sydney in time for Christmas, and to prepare for their January trip to South Australia, which began well. French and Brooks travelled to Adelaide by train, and were met at the station by the Joint Managing Directors of Duncan and Duncan, Robert and James Duncan, Directors Archie and Richard Duncan and their sons—quite an entourage. Duncan and Duncan were, in addition to being the South Australia distributors, also a dealer for Adelaide.

The entourage toured the Mile End plant, French impressed with the new building, erected after an earlier fire had destroyed the previous one. Things changed very quickly when, like Davies, they refused to disclose their financial position and generally hindered French and Brooks as much as possible in understanding their business. Eventually French was able to ascertain that, while the sales company was Duncan & Duncan, another company, Duncan and Fraser, actually owned the entire inventory. Both companies had the same Directors and the two companies sold stock from one to the other, of course with a markup. French's opinion of Duncan and Duncan ended up being not much better than that of Davies and Davies.

While in Adelaide, on January 27 French met with Edward Holden of Holden's Motor Body Works.[13] At that meeting, Holden proposed that, with their expanded workshop, they could manufacture all bodies for Ford, not just the high series that they supplied to Tarrant's. French was not disposed to this as he felt that Holden had overcommitted themselves and were too close to General Motors, although it didn't stop him from using this approach by Holden to bait the distributors at their subsequent conference in February 1924. The Australian General Manager of General Motors, a Mr. Miles, having had problems dealing with the directors of Olympia Motors, particularly Ross and Davies, also approached French, seeking his support to exert influence over the Tarrant Motors subsidiary. Again, French was non-committal and his suspicions were later confirmed when on December 12, there was a press announcement that General Motors and the Holden Motor Company had signed an agreement for Holden to

OPPOSITE Tarrant's Ford assembly department. Note the static assembly stations

LEFT Model T, 1908

RIGHT Duncan and Fraser, Adelaide. The new post-fire factory in Franklin Street, Adelaide

manufacture bodies for all G.M. vehicles in Australia.

While staying in Adelaide, one morning a Mr. Wood approached French in his hotel lobby. He identified himself as having a majority financial interest in the Ford dealership at Grafton and told French that he was appearing constantly before the Australian Tariff Board, to prevent them from raising the duty on Ford parts that he imported direct. These constant applications for duty increases were, he said, made on behalf of Australian manufacturers' who claimed they could manufacture the components. These manufacturers were represented by a Mr. Hipsley, of the Ford Service Company, in partnership with a Mr. Lewis Davies.

On his return to Sydney French wrote again to Wallace Campbell, and was more direct:

> *...there is no part in my mind as to the urgent and almost immediate necessity for operating our own business in Australia, and entirely eliminating distributors. From all the information that I can get, the conditions in West Australia as to our distributors are even worse, and from my personal acquaintance with our people at Adelaide, I am expecting to find there only a repetition of the same story...Such as the Dealer organisation is, it not only will follow us, but will welcome us with open arms...At every turn I feel the Davies' influence...until we shake ourselves loose from Davies, both directly and indirectly, our business will suffer.* [14]

The final break came at the Distributors' Convention, held in Sydney on February 5–7, 1924. Not quite an ambush meeting, nevertheless French had corresponded with Campbell in Canada and established their position. Attending were:

Arthur & Lew Davies — Davies & Davies
Lock, and Carter — Davies & Davies staff
Ross and Cornwell — Tarrant Motors Victoria
George Whatmore — Queensland Motors
Archie & Robert Duncan — Duncan Motors SA
George Harris — Grave & Dwyer, WA
Robert Nettlefold — Tasmania

with French and Brooks representing Ford. The agenda was a full one. French opened by reviewing the sales for 1923, nationally 17,803 vehicles. All agreed the market could grow and expand further. They discussed a range of issues, a particularly sensitive one being that most dealers handled other vehicles, a point made by French that in future this would have to change, multi -model dealerships being seen as a weakness, particularly those with competing vehicle distributorships. This led to a discussion on overheads and their allocation, which the distributors feared would rise with the single dealer concept.

French raised the issue of General Motors announcing in December their sole business relationship with Holden Body Company, and the growth of Chevrolet due to the shortage of Ford vehicles. The aggressive marketing of GM vehicles had given them the advantage of higher volume, allowing them to make a series of price reductions, news of one they received that day, an announcement by GM and Overland of a reduction from £283 to £265. The distributors immediately blamed Ford's lack of support for them. French turned it back on them, for their failure to manage their territory, forecasting and obligations, merchandising necessarily being a local function.

Cartage was another issue. French criticised the usage of carts, horses and drays by the distributors in lieu of Fordson tractors.

LEFT Duncan and Fraser Company directors, 1924. Left to right: Archie Duncan, Richard Duncan, H. N. Perriam, John Burgess, James Newell Duncan and Robert Duncan

The distributors raised all manner of objections due to the capital expense and the tractors being idle between shipments. In the end, French's opinion prevailed, reluctantly accepted by those present. French also criticised the lack of automation in each assembly plant. Other issues were the vehicle storage charges and insurance.

Then the issue of spare parts arose. There was discussion regarding the definition and the determination of landed cost, at which French insisted that in future, list prices be set at the landed price plus 85%, instead of 100%. At this point Lew Davies refused point-blank to accept any reduction of costs. Heatedly, he said that all distributors had had cost reductions imposed on them and their last recourse to recoup these losses was with the sale of spare parts. He then stormed out of the meeting, loudly swearing at French, angrily telling his brother he would not sanction any reduction in price, nor permit his brother to agree; that he, Lew Davies, still owned the company and he intended to run it! After his brother had left, Arthur Davies then joined in, stating:

> *...he had come to the end of his rope and would not stand by and have their company ruined by so-called 'factory men'. With their company investing over £1 million pounds, the current pricing regime was going to make their return on investment not worthwhile.*

A heated discussion ensued, with Davies making unfavourable comparisons between Ford and General Motors regarding the prices paid for vehicles and the profit margin. French pointed out that he (French) had not been able to determine the financial position of any of the distributors because they had refused him access to their accounts. In addition, French added, he did not believe Davies, but should he supply the figures, he would examine them thoroughly. Cornered, Davies said he would have them at the end of the day. French closed the day by saying that it was obvious the business of being a distributor in Australia was not profitable, that it was therefore necessary for the factory to assume responsibility for the marketing of their products. He presumed all were of a like mind and that he would communicate this to Ford Canada.

A very long, stunned and painful silence followed. As French and Brooks gathered their papers and prepared to leave, Robert Nettlefold of Tasmania spoke. He said he did not agree with Davies, his company was profitable and he was satisfied with his contract. Davies turned on Nettlefold, but Nettlefold stood his ground. One by one, first Duncan of South Australia, then Ross of Victoria disassociated themselves from the Davies. It was a crucial moment. In one masterstroke, the Davies brothers and Whatmore of Queensland had been isolated. French this time did

SPORTS ROADSTER

(illustrated at left)

with body in Tanuara and with mouldings and centre of rear deck in Virginia Cream. Fenders are black: wheels Virginia Cream. This colour combination is available also on Sports Phaetons.

SPORTS ROADSTER

(illustrated at right)

with body in Glacier Green with mouldings in Robin Hood Green, lined with Glacier Green. The fenders are Robin Hood Green and wheels black.

SPORTS PHAETON

(illustrated at left)

with body in Mariners Green and mouldings in Cascade Green, lined with Orinoco Vermilion. Fenders are Cascade Green and wheels black. This colour combination is available also on Sports Roadsters.

Standard Roadsters and Standard Phaetons may be had with bodies of Mariners Green, but with black fenders and black wheels.

SPORTS PHAETON

(illustrated at right)

with body in Santa Barbara Sand and mouldings in Fallow Field Brown, striped with Virginia Cream. Fenders are Fallow Field Brown and wheels Orinoco Vermilion.

Standard Roadsters and Standard Phaetons may be had with bodies in Santa Barbara Sand, but with fenders and wheels in black.

FORDOR SEDAN

(illustrated at left)

with body in Argonaut Brown with Fallow Field Brown mouldings, lined with Virginia Cream. Fenders are of Fallow Field Brown and wheels black. This colour combination also available on Sports Phaetons.

FORDOR SEDAN

(illustrated at right)

with body in Mist Gray and with mouldings in Ivanhoe Green, lined with Virginia Cream. Fenders and wheels are black. This colour combination is available also on Tudor Sedans.

SPORTS ROADSTER

with body in Prairie Vale Green and with Liberty Blue Mouldings, having double stripes of Orinoco Vermilion. Fenders are black and wheels Orinoco Vermilion.

SPORTS ROADSTER

(illustrated at right)

with body of Corinthian Purple and with mouldings in Virginia Cream, striped with Corinthian Purple. Fenders are black; louvres have a stripe of Virginia Cream. The wheels are Virginia Cream.

SPORTS PHAETON

(illustrated at left)

with body in Abyss Green, and with mouldings in Ivanhoe Green, lined with Abyss Green. Fenders are of Ivanhoe Green and wheels black.

Standard Roadsters and Standard Phaetons may be had with bodies in Abyss Green, but with fenders and wheels in black.

SPORTS ROADSTER

(illustrated at right)

with body in Empress Yellow and with black mouldings, striped with Virginia Cream. Fenders are black, louvres on the bonnet have a black line and wheels are Orinoco Vermilion.

SPORTS ROADSTER

(illustrated at left)

with body of Liberty Blue with black mouldings, striped with Virginia Cream. Fenders are black and wheels Orinoco Vermilion. This colour combination is available also on Sports Phaetons.

Standard Roadsters and Standard Phaetons may be had with bodies of Liberty Blue, but with black fenders and black wheels.

SPORTS COUPE

(illustrated at right)

with body in Abyss Green, with mouldings in Mist Grey. Fenders and Wheels are black.

1929 Ford Model A

MAURICE SHMITH

Maurice Shmith will always remember St. Patrick's Day in 1905. He put on his Sunday suit, got a haircut and walked to Tarrant Motors and asked for a job in the workshop. Engines and carburettors fascinated the eighteen-year-old more than the work he was doing in Blogg Bros., city chemists.

Colonel Tarrant put him on the payroll at ten shillings a week, oiling, greasing and washing cars. Maurice remembers the early days in Tarrants, when they took five to six months to hand-make every car—the only two parts imported were the magneto and the radiator. At the time, Tarrants assembled three makes: the Tarrant, De Dion and the Argyll, from Glasgow. 'Then the firm was talked into having a look at a new car built by a chap named Henry Ford. We worked late one night assembling a Model S when it arrived.

Colonel Tarrant arrived at 1am to take it for a test drive.

When it zoomed up Russell St in top gear, we knew we had a winner. Tarrants sold a record fifty-two model Ts in the first year. 'The boss was worried we'd reached saturation point,' recalled Maurice. In 1924, he imported the first Yellow Cabs and in 1932, moved to Sydney where he founded York Motors, Brooklands Motor Accessories and finance company Industrial Acceptance Corporation.

(*The Herald* March 30, 1966)

RIGHT 1920s Ford Runabout advertisement

adjourn the meeting stating bluntly that Ford Canada knew all the distributors had made huge profits with no benefit to Ford.

The next morning before the meeting began, Arthur Davies addressed the meeting and completely backed down, apologised to French and withdrew completely his remarks about their profits. He was concerned, he said, that Ford Canada was beginning to exercise unwarranted control over them. The meeting continued that day in a far more congenial atmosphere. While the distributers feared strikes could disrupt deliveries from a single, central assembly plant, they agreed that the higher volume would lower costs, but all declined to participate in creating a consortium.

That night at a private meeting requested by Arthur Davies, he (Davies) revealed he had heard that French had had discussions with Christian (Harry) Kloster, a Sydney Dodge distributor, who had purportedly visited Canada and held discussions regarding taking over the NSW distributorship. He apologised again at his lack of tact or diplomacy towards French, and spoke at length of his company's growth as a Ford distributor and what Ford meant to him personally. Denying he held discussions with Kloster or knowing Kloster had visited the Canadian factory, French did nothing to allay Arthur Davies' fears of losing the Ford distributorship.

The seminar closed with a dinner, hosted by French and Brooks. The seminar had been a success, expressing a desire for the factory to keep in close contact with them. French concluded:

> *...I feel the distributors were left in a far better frame of mind than was the case when the conference opened.* [15]

In April 1924, French travelled to Perth in Western Australia, expecting and finding his fears realised. Of the distributorship principals, Grave had been declared mentally incompetent and bankrupt, while Dwyer was in poor health. Harris, the person

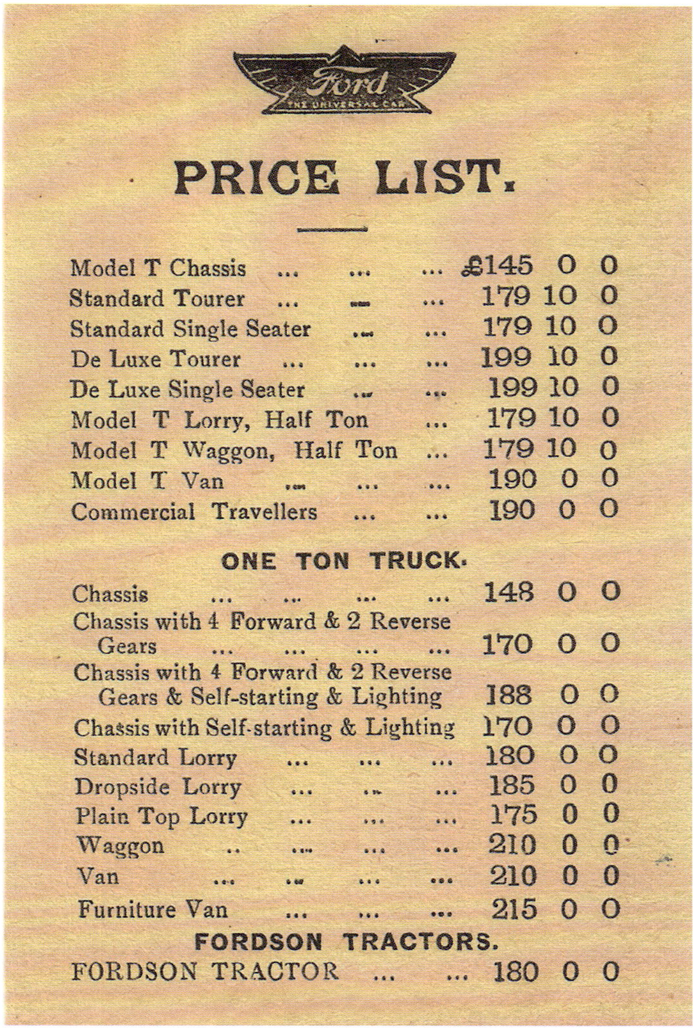

Ford
THE UNIVERSAL CAR

PRICE LIST.

Item	£	s	d
Model T Chassis	£145	0	0
Standard Tourer	179	10	0
Standard Single Seater	179	10	0
De Luxe Tourer	199	10	0
De Luxe Single Seater	199	10	0
Model T Lorry, Half Ton ...	179	10	0
Model T Waggon, Half Ton ...	179	10	0
Model T Van	190	0	0
Commercial Travellers	190	0	0
ONE TON TRUCK.			
Chassis	148	0	0
Chassis with 4 Forward & 2 Reverse Gears	170	0	0
Chassis with 4 Forward & 2 Reverse Gears & Self-starting & Lighting	188	0	0
Chassis with Self-starting & Lighting	170	0	0
Standard Lorry	180	0	0
Dropside Lorry	185	0	0
Plain Top Lorry	175	0	0
Waggon	210	0	0
Van	210	0	0
Furniture Van	215	0	0
FORDSON TRACTORS.			
FORDSON TRACTOR	180	0	0

LEFT 1925 Bayford Motors price list

who had been appointed to manage the business, had virtually abandoned the rural dealers entirely. French wrote :

> *...We cannot long continue with this representation in Western Australia.* [16]

French had already made up his mind. In his December 24, 1923 memo to Campbell, he had predicted potential sales of 25,000–30,000 vehicles per year, with Ford controlling the distribution through five or six sales outlets. He had also written:

> *...to attempt to educate our present distributors is both hopeless and useless...both Brooks and myself are devoting our entire time and effort to the Dealer organisation, in order that we may have them thoroughly in hand when the right time comes...* [17]

French wrote his final report on his way back to Canada. In it, he addressed a range of issues, all which supported his December 24 memo. He had no doubt that Ford must establish plants in Australia.

On his return to Canada, over a series of meetings French convinced Ford Canada Vice-President Wallace Campbell of the viability of the project. Campbell's memo to Edsel, written on September 10, 1924, made in summary, the following proposal:

> *Eliminate the current six Distributors and promote all sub-dealers to dealers. This would allow Ford to reduce their retail price by 10% while increasing the commission to dealers by 33⅓%. The erection of a Ford manufacturing plant, and five assembly plants would improve efficiencies further and lower costs, creating the environment for dealers to carry stocks, financed by a new financing organisation supporting dealers and offering finance to customers.*

Not stated was the fact that this would break the Davies and Davies stranglehold on the current financing arrangements to dealers and the other distributors, through their company, Australian Guarantee Company. Staff from Canada would provide initial management and technical expertise.

Campbell also warned Edsel that General Motors had a relationship with a South Australian body builder (Holden Motor Body Builders) who had recently expanded and were now manufacturing quality bodies on modern facilities, allowing them to reduce costs and prices approaching Ford's, potentially making Ford vehicles non-competitive. This was unacceptable.

Based on a realistic volume of 30,000 vehicles per year, an investment of US$3.5 million would give a return on investment (ROI) after tax of between 28–43%, a payback of between two and four years. Campbell referred to Ford Canada's similar successful operation in South Africa and his plans to repeat them, after Australia, in New Zealand and India. [18]

The decision to proceed was predictable. After correspondence between Ontario and Detroit over the next three weeks, B.J. Craig, Secretary of Ford U.S wrote to Campbell on October 1, 1924:

> *The Ford Motor Company agrees to extend your company a line of credit of (US)$3,000,000...beginning January 1, 1925... These notes shall carry an interest charge of 4% until paid, with prepayment allowed at any time...Advances made will be in United States gold coin, with repayment by your company in like currency.* [19]

Ford US liked the potential return on investment but was never going to be charitable! The adventure was about to begin.

CHAPTER 2

DEPRESSION & RECOVERY

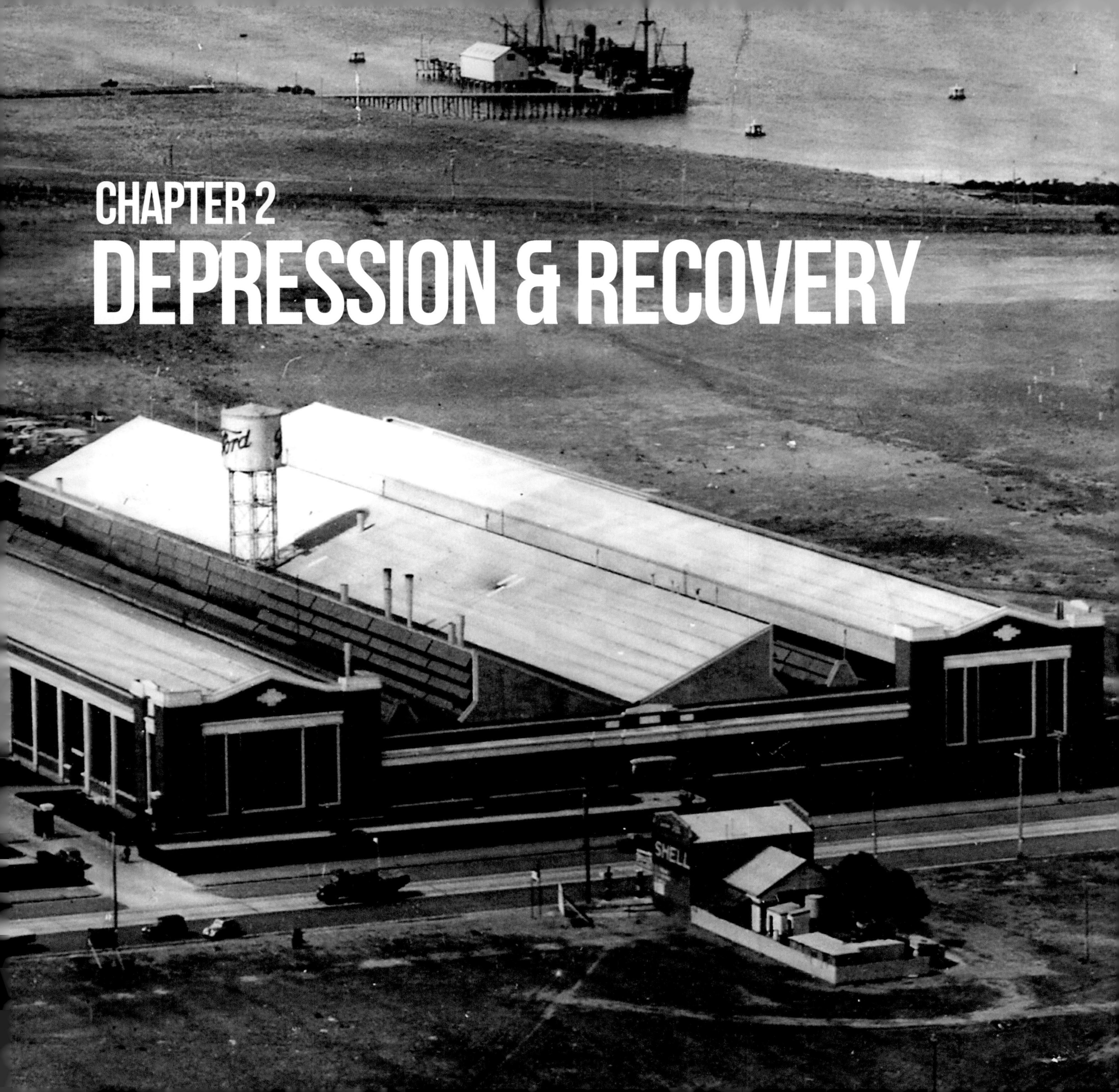

THE FORD YEARS 1930—1939

1930: Assembly plant opened at Leighton Beach in Fremantle, Western Australia.

1932: Introduction of the Model B (4-cylinder) and B18 (V8) Series, the first successful casting of a V8 engine block in one piece, the advent of the V8 causing an even greater sensation than that of the Model A.

1933: Model 40 Series released.

1934: First extension to Geelong Manufacturing Plant. First English vehicle, the Model Y Series introduced. World's first Coupe Utility designed by Lew Bandt, built in Australia.

1935: Geelong Manufacturing Plant second extension. Model 48 Series released. First all-steel body, fabric-roofed sedan. English Y20 range released.

1936: Homebush Assembly Plant in Sydney opened March 17. Eagle Farm Assembly Plant in Brisbane extended. Model 68 released, the first Australian turret top all-steel car body produced. English CX20 range introduced.

1937: Extensions to Geelong Assembly Plant and Manufacturing Plants. Model 78 introduced. English 7W range released. Model 93 series introduced.

1938: Homebush Assembly Plant in Sydney extended. Model 81 Series introduced.

1939: Ford 91 and Mercury 99 Series released. Eagle Farm Assembly Plant in Brisbane extended to commence Fordson tractor production. World War II declared. All plants begin converting to wartime production.

In October 1924, the first of two groups arrived in Sydney to establish a Ford Sales and Manufacturing facility. The brightest and best of the staff of Ford Canada, this group was to play an enormous role in the future growth of Ford Worldwide. These groups, known in later years as Program Groups, were brought together for a specific task, or program. Each member of the group was ambitious, forceful and assertive, skilled at their job and knowing their next position on the corporate ladder was dependent on their performance *today*. Senior amongst them was Phillip Grandjean, secretary and treasurer of Ford Canada. Accompanying him was Hubert French, Thomas Lamb, M. Brooks, L.W. Lee, C.C. ('Slim') Westman, R.A. McFarlane, Ewart Hughes, Rhys Sale, J.B. Caraghan, and B.O. Stevenson.

Of this elite group, French was to become General Manager, later Managing Director of Ford Australia, Rhys Sale, President of Ford Canada, and B.O. Stevenson, Managing Director of Ford India, then Ford South Africa. J.B. Caraghan would go on to become Director of Finance for Ford New Zealand, while Tom Lamb, L.W. Lee and Ewart Hughes would all become directors of Ford Australia; R.A. McFarlane was to be Ford Australia's first Sales Manager.

Tom Lamb studied engineering at the University of Toronto, graduating as a civil engineer. He served with distinction in the Canadian Expeditionary Forces in WWI, rising to the rank of Captain and awarded the D.S.O., M.C., M. M., and Croix de Guerre. He was to become the first New South Wales branch manager, responsible for establishing the branch, before becoming Sales Manager in 1926 and member of the Board of Directors in 1934. Ewart Hughes was to become Finance Director, while 'Slim' Westman was later to become the Superintendent of Manufacturing at Geelong. Another group followed shortly after, in all, eighteen Canadians would comprise the Program Group.

Their first task was to determine the sites for assembly plants and most importantly, the location of the manufacturing plant. While French had waxed lyrical over a site in Tasmania, the group rejected his proposal, because of its remoteness from its markets, despite the promise of subsidised shipping costs. Also abandoned was the plan to have one central assembly plant supplying all states, due to problems of shipping vehicles over the various railway gauges in each state. Over the next few months, the group crossed the continent evaluating sites and premises, while in the background work proceeded rapidly to establish Ford in Australia.

While Grandjean proceeded with the selection of sites, French began negotiations with the distributors. Ford's assumption was for assembly and manufacture to take place in a series of stages, the timing dependent on availability of components from Canada and the inventory held at each state distributor. The plan was complex but vital in maintaining sales.

PAGES 26–27 Ford Motor Company of Australia Head Office with assembly and manufacturing operations at Norlane in Geelong

LEFT Rhys Sale, Hubert French and Ewart Hughes

Phase one was for Ford, in each state, to assume the importation from Canada and the assembly of the chassis. Ford would then ship the completed chassis to that state's distributor, who would continue to manufacture and assemble their bodies. The second phase was for Ford to purchase the distributors' stock of chassis and Ford body components they had imported, balancing the components with stock imported by Ford. The distributors would return their stock to Geelong where, at some point, Ford would begin manufacturing bodies, from this and imported components, shipping the primed bodies to each Ford plant for final assembly, painting and marriage to the chassis. To determine the inventory at the now disgruntled distributors, negotiate the purchase of this inventory, leave them with sufficient stock to continue to supply their customers, and match this with stock procured from Canada to attain complete vehicle sets, was a nightmare. Ultimately, it cost Ford Australia £553,000.[20] Worse, the volume of inventory substantially delayed the introduction of the Model A until May 1927. Their competitors, relishing the opportunity, continually lowered prices, and produced vehicles as fast as they could to build market share at Ford's expense. As soon as they could obtain body components from Canada, Ford planned to begin assembly of their own vehicles.

March 31, 1925 was a momentous day. Ford Motor Company of Australia Ltd. and Ford Manufacturing Company of Australia Ltd. became legal entities, each with an authorised capital of £1,500,000. Grandjean and French announced the appointment of a board of Directors comprising Sir Arthur Robinson of Arthur Robinsons, W.R. Campbell, Grandjean and L.W. Lee. Grandjean also announced the purchase of 100 acres (40 hectare) of land at North Geelong, from the Geelong Harbour Trust. Reported in *The Melbourne Herald* on March 30, the *Geelong Advertiser* made the announcement with banner headlines and front-page news, quoting Grandjean:

> *This (location) has been selected principally by reason of its splendid harbour facilities, together with its advantages as a railroad distribution centre. Other features have of course entered into consideration, such as the advantages obtained by stable labour conditions that exist in a community the size of Geelong. It also has a frontage extending to wharves situated at Corio Bay. Crossing the property at the south-west corner is the Geelong–Melbourne railway line which, together with other branch lines radiating from Geelong should give us ample railroad services.*

Grandjean went on to announce the commencement of building immediately on the new site, describing the building, the initial employment of men (500), with more as the business grew. He warned of the substantial investment and the time taken to achieve efficient production, to 'correct certain rumours' that the establishment of Ford in Australia would lead to an immediate reduction in price. The *Geelong Advertiser* in its editorial noted the announcement was the biggest ever industrial coup for Geelong and caused 'the utmost gratification to all classes of the community', ushering in a new era of employment opportunities.[21] April 9 saw the completion of the purchase of 26 acres of land at Eagle Farm, Brisbane.

Two days later, on April 11, the entire management group visited Geelong, to attend a civic reception given by the mayor, Cr. Ritchie. Included in that group were the Branch Managers-elect of South Australia, Victoria, New South Wales and Queensland. Of note, the Branch Manager of Queensland was G.V. Cornwell, late of Tarrant Motors, Melbourne. The management group, previously headquartered in Sydney, announced their immediate relocation to premises in Market Square, Geelong. Another to attend was Scott Inglis. A WWI veteran who served with the Australian Flying Corps, he had joined Duncan and Fraser in 1919 as a salesman. He married Grace Duncan, the granddaughter of Duncan and Fraser founder, James Duncan in 1921. Along with Cornwell, Ford cherry-picked the best around the country, recruiting Inglis initially as service manager for South Australia. However before he took office, he was transferred to Geelong as Ford's National Service Manager. The Inglis family would be prominent in Ford Australia for nearly fifty years.

At the inaugural Directors meeting held three days later in Geelong, the Directors were acquainted with negotiations for rented premises offered by Dalgety & Co. in Geelong. Grandjean announced the purchase of 165 acres of land at Granville, Sydney

W. J. (BILL) HUSSEY

Bill began his working life at Geelong in December 1925, assembling the first of the Duncan and Fraser Model T bodies. Eager to make a good impression, he arrived at work the first day with a full kit of tools, which were admired by all.

However, he was quickly told by his foreman to take them all home again, except for the heavy hammer. 'That's the only tool you'll need for assembling these bodies,' he was told.

GEELONG ADVERTISER

NO. 24,278 85th YEAR. TUESDAY, MARCH 31, 1925.

GEELONG TO BE FORD'S AUSTRALIAN HEADQUARTERS

WITH BRANCHES IN SYDNEY, BRISBANE, ADELAIDE AND PERTH

SITE OF ONE HUNDRED ACRES SECURED AT NORTH GEELONG

TWO COMPANIES TO BE FORMED, WITH CAPITAL TOTALLING £3,000,000

DECISION RECEIVED WITH PLEASURE BY WHOLE COMMUNITY

THE CHOSEN SITE.

OFFICIAL STATEMENT

RIGHT Front page headlines on March 31, 1925 announce 'Perhaps the most important statement that has ever been issued in connection with industrial undertakings at Geelong...'.

THE 'LIGHT HOUSE'

In 1925, Ford's temporary office was located in Ryrie Street, and as usual at Ford, long hours were worked. One employee related he was in a billiard saloon after work one evening playing snooker. During the course of the game, one of the other players said, 'You work at the light house don't you?' He denied it, but for the remainder of the game racked his brains to remember if he had even seen a light house, but not recalling seeing one, concluded the player was crazy. At the end of the game however he was embarrassed to be told that the Ford office was called the 'Light House' due to the fact there was always a light burning day and night.

(*Geelong Advertiser* July 29, 1995)

for £20,000. The board also ratified all of Grandjean's decisions prior to incorporation, including the purchase of the Geelong property and appointed E. Hughes Secretary, Treasurer and Public Officer.

Ford began survey work immediately after the March 30 announcement. The architects adapted the U.S. 'Ford Standard Plant' design of the day to Australian conditions, a major one being lightening the design of the roof trusses, there being no need to allow for 4 feet of snow on the roof in winter. Used for all plants in Australia, these designs shortened build time and made Ford plants readily recognisable, even today. One of the first requirements for Ford at Geelong was the railway spur line into the plant. During the land purchase negotiations between Ford, the Geelong Harbour Trust and the Victorian government, the government estimated it could take them up to five years to build the spur line. Ford began earthworks in May. By the end of June, less than three months later, one spur line was complete and connected to the main Melbourne–Geelong railway line at North Shore Road. Foundations for the first building, the Assembly Plant, nearest North Shore Road were complete and trains had begun delivering steelwork and roof trusses directly to the site.

As work steamed along at the Melbourne Road site, other engineers were busy laying out the Dalgety building in Gheringhap Street in Geelong to begin the assembly and painting of the Model T chassis. Already components had started to arrive from Canada, along with essential equipment to carry out the assembly work, including the rudimentary conveyor lines, installed on the ground floor alongside the paint shop.

BELOW The Government estimated this spur line to the assembly building would take five years to build. Ford built it in less than three months.

CHARLIE SHERSON

Charlie Sherson had served his apprenticeship as a motor trimmer at Tarrant Motors, Victoria's Ford distributor, then its subsidiary Melbourne Motor Body Company:

> *After the Ford announcement, I was retrenched. I saw an advertisement on May 4 1925, calling for tradesmen at Ford so I took the train down to Geelong to apply for a job and they asked me to start immediately! I had no tools and no accommodation, so I came back and started the next day. We trimmed the car bodies on the first floor, above the assembly line at the Dalgety plant before we moved to the new factory in 1925. It was tough at first, we were working in sheds made from car boxes.*

Charlie also trained employees at Hobart, in the old Cascade Brewery Ford assembly plant, and at the new Homebush plant in Sydney.

(*Geelong Advertiser* July 29, 1995)

RIGHT A line-up of early Model Ts ready for delivery outside temporary assembly plant located in Dalgety's old wool store. Right to Left: Joe Knight, Les Icke, C.Simpson, Les Lupton, George Freeman, unknown, Tich Powell, unknown, Ossie Prowse, unknown, Tom Finnigan, unknown, unknown, Tom Semen. Ford Australia produced 30,528 passenger and commercial Model Ts between July 1925 and April 1928.

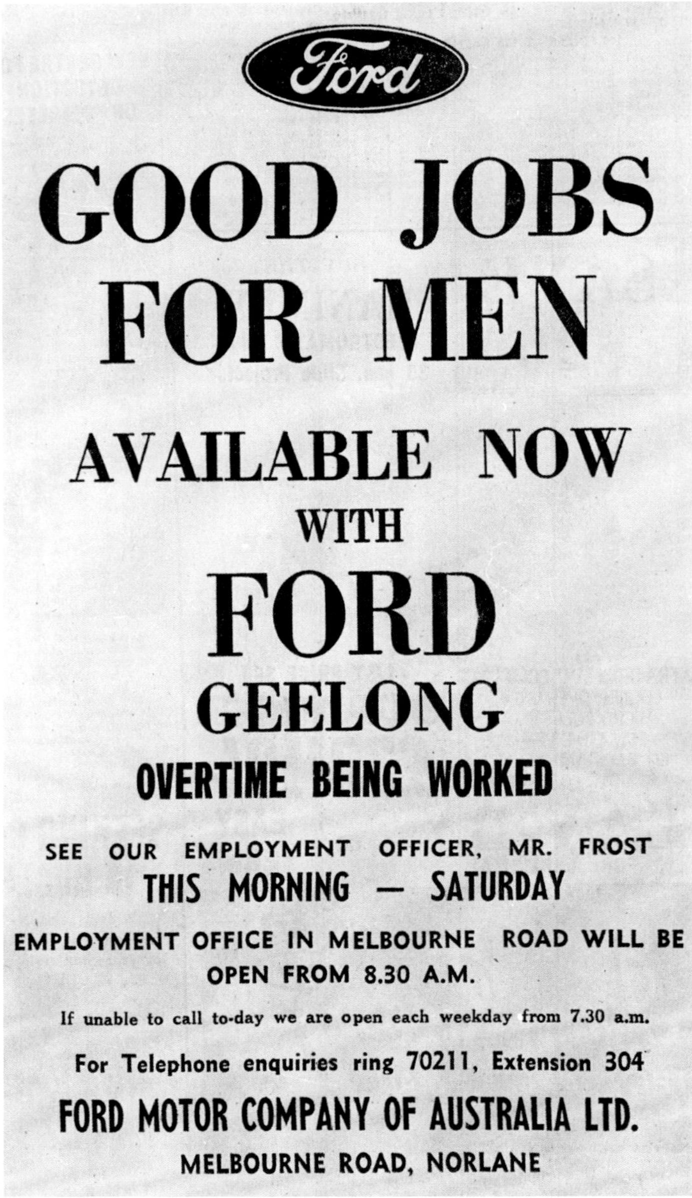

FAR RIGHT Job adverts for Ford in the 1920s

Advertisements for skilled and unskilled labour began appearing in the local newspaper and a steady stream of new starts began training. One of the new employees to join in May 1925 was Charlie Sherson. Charlie had served his apprenticeship as a motor trimmer at Tarrant Motors, then with its subsidiary Melbourne Motor Body Company. Another employee to start that month was Les Angus. On a warm clear day in 1925, sixteen-year-old Les Angus was pedalling up Gheringhap Street in Geelong. Outside Dalgety's wool store, he noticed a couple of men painting a car chassis on the footpath. As Les watched, leaning over his handlebars, a man suddenly emerged from the dark doorway of the wool store. 'He offered me a job and I accepted,' said Les. He recalled that after his first job of painting chassis, he transferred to the assembly line:

> *It was a pretty rough show in those days, everything was done by hand. We built the chassis and sent them to body builders in Melbourne. They painted, trimmed and wired the cars. There*

LEFT Tarrant factory trimming department

wasn't enough room in the store, so we worked in the street. When we transferred to the new Geelong Plant, conditions improved and production rose as we became more skilled with mechanical assembling tools.

The May 1925 Directors meeting appointed Hubert French as General Manager, approved the lease of the Dalgety premises in Geelong, at £28 per month, and the rental of Adelaide premises from June 15 and Brisbane premises from July 1. Also approved was the tender from Concrete Constructions Limited for construction of plants in Geelong, Brisbane and Adelaide, as well as the refurbishment of a building on the site at Granville in Sydney. The Board ratified contracts to Fyvie and Stewart of Geelong to act as architects in all states, as well as those for the supply of steel and concrete to the Geelong site. Also accepted was Arthur Davies' offer to form a finance sales company for all states except for South Australia, where Duncan Motors Limited had made a similar offer. Considered the best of the manufacturing plants, Duncan Motors were awarded a contract to supply 5,000 bodies over a period of six months, commencing June 21, 1925, for £36/5/0 each.

Members of the program group immediately left for Brisbane, Adelaide and Sydney to commence the installation of equipment and assembly lines for chassis and bodies in temporary accommodation, while others, working with the architects, began work on construction of the new plants.

It was a chilly overcast midwinter morning on July 1, 1925, that history was made when the first model T manufactured by Ford rolled off the makeshift assembly line in the Dalgety wool store factory, the first of about twelve vehicles a day to be built that month. At the Directors meeting held in Market Square on July 20, French advised the board he had reached agreement with all the distributors for the termination of their contracts, and the assumption of their stock of components as of July 1. He also announced the rental of premises in Perth, at Fremantle, at a rental of £168 per annum, plus the cost of a rail siding. Work now began converting the Westralian Farmers Society warehouse into an assembly plant.

The Program Group, spread thin on the ground with the construction or modification of six plants around the Commonwealth, were hiring locals as rapidly as possible and training them up to spread the workload. Not long after the first

RIGHT Water tower, Geelong

RIGHT An early photo of staff in front of the Geelong Assembly Plant

FORD AND GEELONG FOOTBALL CLUB – JACK JENNINGS

In 1925 Hubert French, living at Barwon Heads, became friends with a neighbour, Jack Jennings. A keen supporter of the Geelong Football Club, Jennings often discussed football with French, who was keen to learn the game. The friendship resulted in Ford sponsoring the club, one that continues today and is the longest period of sponsorship in the sport. Jennings went on to be the club's longest serving president, for twenty-six years, during which time the club won premierships in 1951, 1952 and 1963.

chassis were rolling out the door at Gheringhap Street, they started building bodies, and set up trim operations on the first floor. To simplify matters, trucks built at Gheringhap Street were sent to William Egan's Coach-building workshop just around the corner in James Street Geelong. Egan's built the trays and assembled them to the chassis, delivered from Ford.

Andrew Reid began his apprenticeship enameling bicycles before transferring in his third year to Egan's, to be with his brother, Allan, a motor body trimmer. Andrew's skill in bicycle enameling enabled him to freehand paint the decorative stripes on the T Model truck trays Egan's built and assembled to the Ford chassis: the same ones Andrew recalled he and his brother would drive up and down the laneways of Geelong at breakneck speed when things were quiet. Later, in 1928, after finishing his apprenticeship, Andrew and his brother Allen applied for work at the new Ford plant, Andrew as a spray painter, cycling to work from North Geelong with his brother. Another long-term employee to join Ford, in Brisbane, was Gertrude Jack. Gertrude had joined Queensland Motors in 1915, working for George Whatmore as an office clerk, later as stenographer. When the Eagle Farm plant opened in 1925, Gertrude transferred to Ford. Her long career included mentoring other 'girls', particularly during World War II, until her retirement in 1961, after forty-six years' service.

Building continued, and as soon as the roof trusses were covered, concreting of the floor began underneath. By September, the roof of the assembly plant was almost complete and concreting well under way, the exterior walls progressively filled in with brick and glass and work had begun on the front offices. Construction of the manufacturing plant was about two months behind that of the assembly plant, but by January 1926, it too was having equipment installed as soon as it arrived from America, even before completion of the exterior walls. By March 1927, just ten months after work began on the site, the buildings were complete, the offices were almost ready for occupation, final

Geelong plant construction, October, 1925

Construction of the iconic front facade of the Geelong Assembly Plant, 1925

Office fitout at front of Geelong Assembly Plant, 1926

Melbourne Road looking north across Cowies Creek to Ford Manufacturing Plant, January 1926

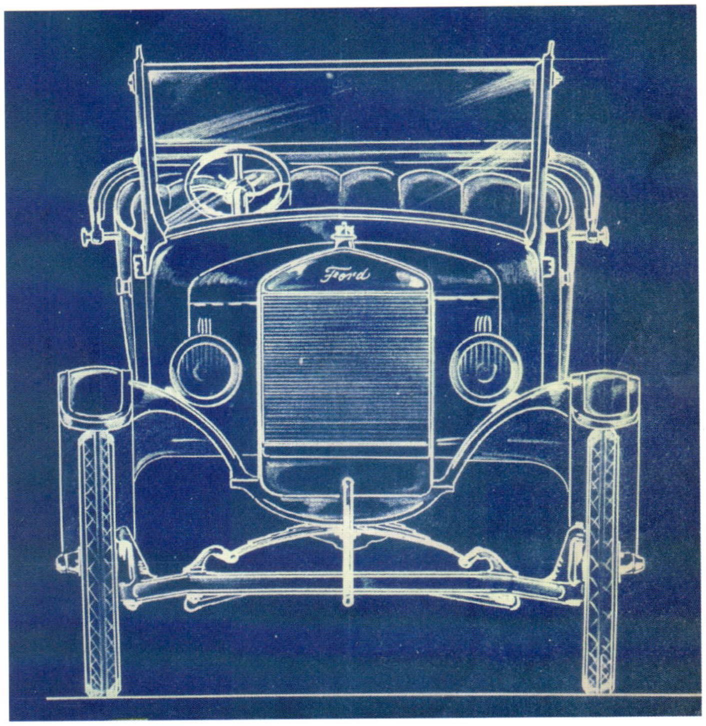

RIGHT Model T drawing by Lewis T. Bandt

FIRST MOTORING REVIEW

A journalist wrote the following review of a Model T in 1926:

> *The new Ford Touring Car is much improved over its predecessors. The body has better lines, is more comfortable and more convenient in every way. The scuttle merges into the bonnet in a much more graceful manner than did the old model, whilst a better type of windscreen and hood are fitted. The body is fitted with four doors so that the driver does not have to squeeze past his front seat passengers, when entering, or leaving the car. The seats are set low down, so that one actually sits in the car not on it. The upholstery is of very good quality, Grey Antique Fabrikoid, whilst the coil springs used in the construction of the seats and squabs are of 'Premier' wire, said to be the best spring wire produced. The hood and side curtains are made of Biekmyre Canvas, a material which has a very good reputation amongst body builders and tent makers. A rectangular glass light is fitted to the rear curtain. Purchasers have the choice of three body colours, namely Empire Grey, Cobalt Blue and Imperial Buff. The appearance of the car is further enhanced by the nickelplated radiator shell, headlamp rims, windscreen standard and rim of the rear curtain light.*

(*Geelong Advertiser* July 29, 1995)

landscaping and paving being completed, and the water tank and stand, a feature of all assembly plants, complete with the signature Ford logo was standing proudly above the site. Personnel began the move from Dalgety's as equipment was installed and ready for production. Charlie Sherson remembers the move: 'It was tough at first, we were working in sheds made from car boxes.'

The commencement of production at Brisbane Eagle Farm, Sydney's Granville plant, and Adelaide's Port Adelaide plant were a copybook of that of Geelong. Before the buildings were completed, equipment began to arrive, was installed and production started immediately stock became available. The frenetic pace continued. The September Directors meeting approved the purchase of land at Jetty Road, Port Adelaide for £2,720/17/10. French was able to turn his attention to Tasmania, which with lowest volume of sales, he could afford to attend to last. At the December 14 Directors meeting, French reported that negotiations had been completed for the termination of Robert Nettlefold's Tasmanian distributorship on December 1. Also negotiated was for Ford to lease Nettlefold's premises in Collins Street, Hobart, for three years at an annual rental of £600 p.a., to begin assembly and supply to the Tasmanian market. As part of the launch in Hobart, Charlie Sherson was sent there from Geelong to train the Tasmanian staff in trimming and assembly.

Production started in all states in 1925, and assembly operations transferred from the leased to the new plants as each was completed. By the end of 1925, the fledgling Ford Australia had produced 6,104 vehicles, 2,976 passenger vehicles and 3,128 trucks, much less than the 17,803 vehicles sold by the distributors in 1923. French was able to declare a small profit by December 1925 of £8,171. By the end of the 1925–26 financial year ending March 31, profit had increased to £33,263.

The next year was one of consolidation and growth. Regular dealer conventions and ready access to stock enabled French to report to his board that the dealers were enthusiastic and the state branches actively engaged with the sales force.

That year, 1926, Ford Australia more than doubled sales, making and shipping 13,326 Model Ts, 7,076 passenger, and 6,250 trucks, still nowhere near French's prediction to W.C. Campbell of 25,000–30,000 vehicles per year, while profit to 31/3/1927 slipped to £7,087.

An early employee benefit was the supply of the 'Ford Bus',

SIX IN A COUPE

Perhaps you have heard some Ford stories. Yes? Well, here's another one. The Ford sports coupe is built for six passengers. I proved that by packing three full grown persons in the driving seat, three children ranging from small to not too small in the dickey seat. I secreted an average sized suitcase under their feet, and decorated the handy shelf at the rear of the driving seat with a two-gallon can of water, a couple of billycans, an odd box of cakes or so, and some fruit. Neat packing to get a whole picnic, complete with picnickers into a coupe you'll say. But it wasn't any effort, and the running boards were not touched, so there was still lots of room.

LEFT US Model A which differs slightly from the Australian version. Ford Australia produced 20,561 passenger and commercial Model A Fords.

used to transport employees to and from main stops in Geelong to the plant before and after each shift. Unlike in later times, when residential housing surrounded the plant, in 1927 Ford was on the outskirts of Geelong and transport an issue, with bicycles and motorbikes being the order of the day for many workers. The 'Ford Bus' system was a feature of working in the Geelong plant, particularly later during WWII with petrol rationing, and provided secure transport for the many women working shift work.

As in many small towns of the time, sport was the glue that held a town together, and often carried over into the workforce. It did not take long in Geelong for rivalry between the office and the two plants to result in regular football grudge matches, where rank had no privilege: the 1926 manufacturing plant team included Superintendent 'Slim' Westman and Charlie Sherson, while the office team included Vern Rowley, Jack Howell and George Johnson, later the South Australian Branch Manager. The records show the plant team won, at least that year.

There were many warning signs as the year of 1927 progressed. In the United States, Ford was facing increasingly stiff competition, in particular General Motors who had begun annual model upgrades, regularly updating features and colours. One particularly beneficial improvement was the introduction of the sliding shift transmission, instead of the older, more difficult to operate planetary gear crash-gate transmission used by Ford. In addition, his competitors had begun offering time payment plans for customers purchasing their vehicles. Henry refused to change the Model T, nor contemplate any form of a customer credit plan. The perception of the motoring public grew that the Model T was out of date, and sales suffered accordingly. Eventually the dropping sales convinced Henry he had to introduce a new model.

Beginning with a clean sheet, Henry focused on the mechanical aspects of the vehicle, leaving the styling to Edsel. Then, in May 1925, Henry announced the closure of his United States assembly plants for nearly six months, while Henry, Edsel and his engineers redesigned and retooled for the new vehicle, the Model A. The closure threw thousands out of work in the US, sent many suppliers to the wall and forced many dealers to either close or switch to other manufacturers. The damage done to the Ford reputation and image was incalculable.

Australia's place in the world was as a primary producer, supplying the British Commonwealth, by far the greater amount to the United Kingdom. In 1925, Great Britain, still suffering from the Great War, with high unemployment and a recession, decided to put the pound sterling back onto the Gold Standard, effectively devaluing the pound. As Australia's gold reserves were held in Great Britain and the Australian currency pegged to the British pound, Australia also effectively devalued. However, in 1927 with Great Britain still struggling, trade with Australia's largest customer fell by 11%, while imports fell only by 4%. Overall, Australia's trade balance sank in the first nine months of 1927 from a £6.1 million surplus to £21.3 million debit.[23] The primary producers felt the pressure on prices first, then the general population with pressure on wages. Trade Unions, agitating for wage increases, formed the Australian Council of Trade Unions in

ABOVE Model A Instruction Book

1933 Model Y Delivery Van drawing

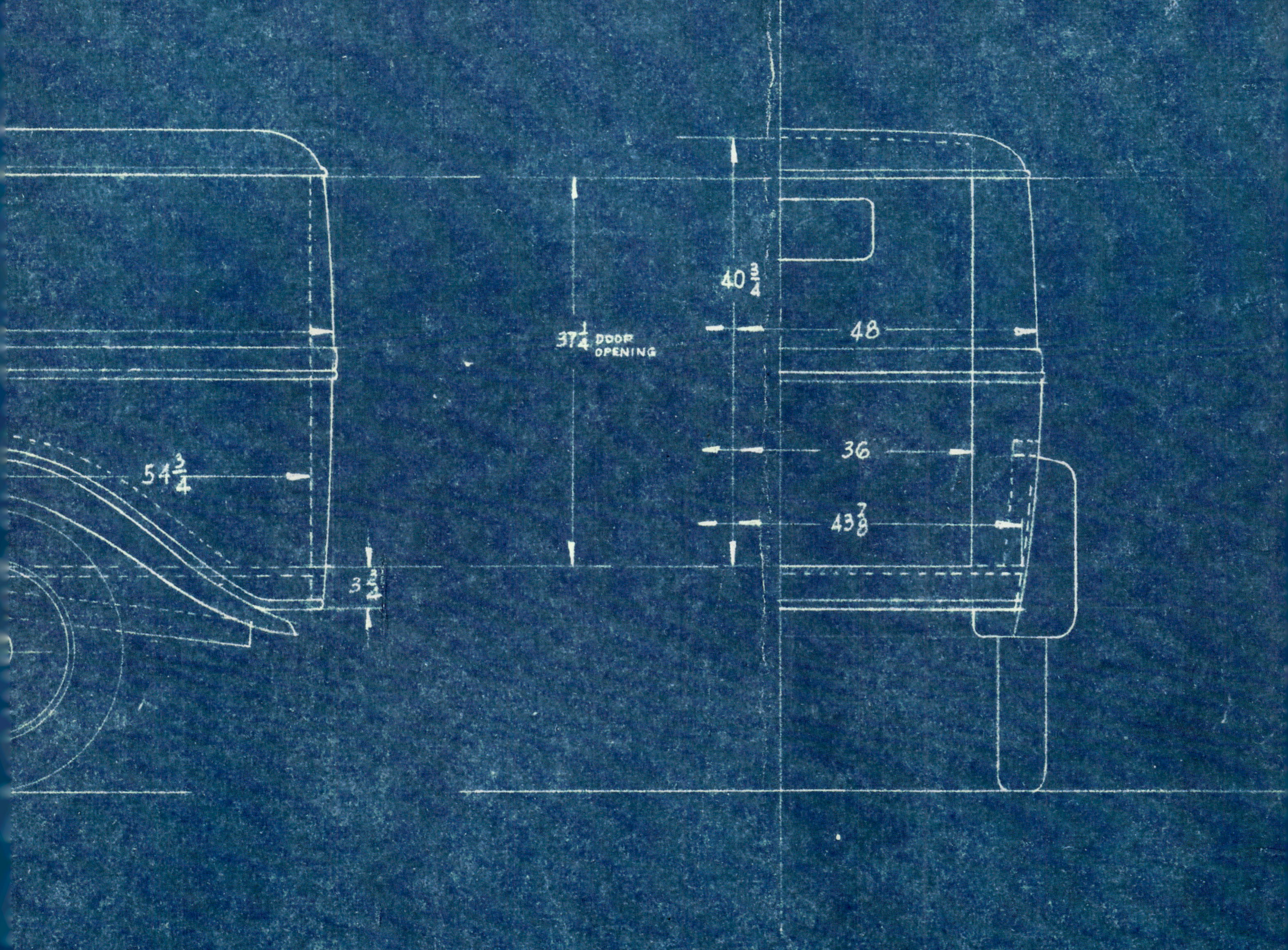

54 3/4
37 1/4 DOOR OPENING
40 3/4
48
36
43 7/8
3 3/4

RON PHILLIPS

When I joined the company, I went to work in the Pattern Shop. At the start, there were less than 100 of us. By the time we were into the Model A, we had progressed to making the dies for the four-door sedan body, the first time that had been done in Australia.

RIGHT Ford Managers at Perth Railway Station, 1928

May that year, the objective 'the socialisation of industry'. But the labour movement was in turmoil in New South Wales, under the leadership of Jack Lang and it appeared that the dire prediction of revolution by Sir George Knibbs would be realised. Meanwhile both the Commonwealth and State governments had committed to major public works, railways, highways and soldier settlement schemes, all funded by loans raised in the City of London.

The difficulties faced by French and his board were immense. Not only did they face competition from General Motors through Holden Motor Body Works who, in two years had increased their output from more than 22,000 bodies in 1924 to nearly 36,000 bodies in 1926, they had to use up the stock of the Model T purchased from the distributors. Now when competition was greatest, and demands and expectations of a better vehicle increased, sales were dropping. Again, the Model T suffered in comparison with other vehicles; the public perception was it lacked glamour, was noisier than more modern competitors, difficult to drive and with the transverse cart springs, uncomfortable. Similar to the United States, where Ford's market share of more than 50% almost halved in the two years to 1926, the good result in 1926 for Ford Australia was unsustainable. In 1927, Ford Australia sold only 4,887 passenger vehicles and 5,103 trucks, a total of 9,990 vehicles, but still managed to achieved a profit increase to £21,388 and declare a maiden dividend of 3.5%. Model T production by Ford Australia by now had totaled 15,280 passenger and 15,248 commercial vehicles.

Hopes were high for a better year in 1928. The release of the Model A in the United States had been met with great acclaim, and thankfully, high volume sales. With a strong gearbox, hydraulic shock absorbers better insulation and balloon tyres, even a safety glass windscreen, the Model A was a vast improvement. Ford imported components as soon as they were available from Windsor, Canada, and in great secrecy imported several vehicles. Making good use of the publicity the Model A had received in the US, French and his National Sales Manager, R.A. McFarlane created an air of anticipation. They revealed the first vehicles to employees and local citizens at Geelong on May 14, 1928, then transported them to the Melbourne Town Hall at 2am the next morning to place them on display. It was a stunning success. Over the next four days, more than 100,000 people queued to inspect the new model. The display in Sydney a few days later was even greater. When the vehicles went on display at the Wentworth Parking Station, traffic jams in Jamieson Street created havoc as people pushed and shoved to get a view of the new model. The launch was a marketing coup and could not have had a better result. The first Model A vehicles came off the Geelong production line in June 1928, all plants coming on stream the same month.

Ron Phillips was there at the beginning. He rode his bike out to the Melbourne Road site and got a job on the building site. With the buildings completed, Ron then joined Ford as a patternmaker, in the Pattern Shop:

> *We had to learn something new—the mass production of motor bodies. At first, our press shop used dies sent from overseas to stamp out the body panels for Tourers and Roadsters, but soon we were making our own dies.* [24]

However, 1928 had not started well in Australia. The first four months had only seen 341 Model Ts produced. Ford Australia desperately needed the Model A, and it delivered. The June build was thirty-five, July 477, more than the previous five months production of the Model T, but the recovery was patchy. While the popularity of passenger vehicles in 1928 continued, actually increasing to 6,189, of which 5,848 were Model A, commercial vehicle production crashed to a low of just 1,538 vehicles as

ABOVE Row of Ford Model A vehicles

businesses reduced their expenditure. Only 771 commercial Model AA were produced, in a total vehicle production for the year of 7,727 vehicles. However, the Model A allowed Ford to record a profit for 1928 of £108,770 and declare another 3.5% dividend.

In November 1928, the Board of Directors extended the lease of the Fremantle plant to December 1929, then visited Perth to finalise the purchase of land at Fremantle, across the road from their rented premises, and approved the start of earthworks for a new plant, to begin in August 1929. The November Board meeting also decided to close the unprofitable Hobart assembly plant at the end of the lease, effective March 31, 1929.

An excellent wheat harvest in the United States in 1928 was followed by bumper crops in France and Italy, then six months later by Australia. The oversupply resulted in the price collapsing. This was shortly followed by a collapse in the price of wool, although increased volumes sold by Australia compensated somewhat. The general malaise in overseas trade continued however, and imports and exports both declined, total Australian overseas trade sank by 6% in financial year 1927–28, and another 1% in 1929–30. Businesses responded by reducing costs, employee numbers and attempts to reduce wages; one immediate consequence was increasing militancy in the work force. In an attempt to allow businesses to rapidly reduce wages, the then conservative Prime Minister, Stanley Bruce, made moves to dismantle the conciliation and arbitration system of wage fixing, a move bitterly opposed by the Labor Party and the union movement. Opposition Leader James Scullin branded Bruce as the destroyer of Australia's good wages and working conditions and the public agreed.

Amongst the worst of the many strikes in this period, was the waterside workers strike in September, 1928 called by unions in protest against a new award. Violence between union and non-union volunteers was common. The government called out troops to quell rioting waterside workers in Adelaide and the coal miner's strike in the winter of 1929 crippled the country. Violence broke out at several New South Wales Collieries, when the government sent in strikebreakers to break the ten month long strike. The union movement led the stoppages, with the 'Wobblies', communist agitators from the World Wide Workers movement active on the fringes of the union movement. The October 17, 1929 federal election saw the Bruce government replaced by James Scullin's Labor government. They were sworn into office on October 29, the very day the Wall Street share market crashed.

In a depressed 1929, sales of the Model A improved year over year to 6,817. However, sales of the AA commercial vehicles sank further to only 1,387 units. Profit more than halved to £43,542 and, with the closure of the Hobart plant, Victoria assumed responsibility for Tasmania. Then in mid-1929, Ford were approached by the Shell Oil Company, wanting to buy 150 of the 175 acres of land at the Granville Sydney site. The transaction allowed the company to record an additional profit of £26,853.

Nationally, affairs worsened. The Scullin government invited

TED FROST

Ted started with Ford in the Dalgety building in 1926 assembling doors. When asked about the Model T, he said:

> *...they were tough, 21 hp, only weighed about 1,500 lbs (682 kg) I remember one I owned, I drove it down to Torquay for the weekend. Coming back, just as we got to the railway crossing, there was an awful crash in the gearbox. Every time we went to drive forward, it would go into reverse. So I took off the top of the gearbox, took out all the broken bits and drove it home!*

RIGHT Ford Sports Coupe advertisement, 1931

Sir Otto Niemeyer of the Bank of England to come to Australia and advise it on economic policy. While the New South Wales Lang Labor government wanted to renege on interest payments to Great Britain, Niemeyer insisted that Australia continue to meet its commitments, balance the budget with expenditure and wage cuts, reductions in welfare, and defence expenditure. The government announced a range of programs that April, one being a significant increase in import duty, aimed to reduce imports by £10 million per year. Another was a range of currency controls prohibiting remitting money overseas, then in September 1930, devaluing the Australian dollar in relation to the British pound, ultimately by 30%. It was not enough. The Federal government defaulted on interest payments on its bonds in 1931 and Scullin travelled to London to re-negotiate Australia's interest repayment scheme. The Australian economy stagnated as commodity prices continued to fall and unemployment rose as business after business collapsed. Imports halved in 1929–30, while exports reduced less due to the devaluation, resulting in a surplus in trade for the year.[25] Unemployment rose from 6% in 1927 to nearly 30% in 1931–32, while average weekly wages dropped more than 15%, to £4/6/10 per week.[26]

As sales reduced to a trickle, auto-workers were retrenched en masse. The currency export controls severely restricted the automotive companies, preventing them remitting funds overseas to pay for the importation of tools, machinery or components, the import duty increases raised prices of the goods they could obtain, affecting profitability and reduced employment further. Not only factory workers suffered. A memo from French to all Branch Managers advised that from May 1, all 'A' class salaries would be reduced by 10% and all 'B' class employees would have to take one week in nine off work without pay. Nationally, by March 1, 1930, staff numbers at Ford, already reduced, were 214. By August 1, 1931, it was down to 117, three weeks later a mere ninety-five. French assumed the position of General Manager of both Ford companies, Manufacturing and Sales, while Lee returned to Ford Canada. The board also considered an almost unthinkable, drastic option: abandoning manufacturing in Australia altogether.

Late in 1930, French met with Edward Holden and requested prices from Holden Motor Body Works to supply all bodies to Ford, complete ex Adelaide.

The Holden Motor Body Works had expanded exponentially in the 1920s. In 1924, Edward Holden signed an exclusive agreement to build bodies for General Motors, volume increased from 12,700 to 22,150. By 1926, Holden was producing in excess of 36,900 bodies, devoted the Woodville plant exclusively to General Motors products and was the largest body builder in the Commonwealth. Volumes dropped in 1929 and rapidly grew worse when both General Motors and Ford cancelled forward orders. Meanwhile,

General Motors were reviewing their Australian business model. A.N. Lawrence, an American from New York, arrived in Sydney on March 24, 1930 with H. Tipper, GM's export manager, and travelled to Melbourne for the February 1 directors' meeting of General Motors Australia. This was a crucial meeting: the incumbent Managing Director of three years, Innes Randolph, resigned, replaced by Lawrence. Two other directors also resigned, pushed out and replaced with new blood. Lawrence supported the government's financial strategy publicly, but other plans were in play. Holden's volume from 1929 to 1931 dropped by 95%. In 1931, they only produced 1,651 bodies and despite closing the plant regularly and diversifying into other metal and wood products, including golf club heads and filing cabinets, the writing was on the wall. Unable to remit funds to the United States due to currency restrictions, and General Motors with surplus funds in Australia, Holden Motor Body Works finally fell to General Motors with a debt for equity exchange, at less than half the value of the organisation. Edward Holden became Chairman, in French's opinion a nominal one, the Australian Directors remained, joined by Lawrence and GM director John Butters, the creation of General Motors-Holden the result.[27] French got on well with Edward Holden, considered him a fine body builder, but not 'experienced in the automotive industry' and considered Holden had 'fallen into a den of thieves'. Returning from a trip to Sydney in April 1931, French met Edward Holden again on the train. Holden pressed French again for a deal on making bodies for Ford, saying his job was to improve GM-H's tarnished reputation in Australia and would clear up any misunderstandings. French prevaricated, telling him 'certain moves' made by Lawrence made him inclined not to proceed. Holden persisted, visiting French in Geelong in August the same year. Again, he wanted French to raise prices in concert with GM-H, surely illegal in later years, and wanting French to cooperate with him, telling him Holden had lost £550,000 to June 1930. Suspicious of Lawrence and believing Holden was 'not the key man in Australia', French again declined.

In an attempt to improve sales, in 1930, Ford Australia introduced the 'improved' Model A sedan, 7.5 cm longer than the U.S model, to increase the rear seat leg room,[28] with little effect on sales. Ford sales for 1930 totaled 3,976 vehicles, 3,611 passenger and 137 trucks. It was worse in 1931; Ford sold a mere 972 vehicles, 835 passenger and 137 trucks, less than four vehicles per day. The financial losses were huge for the time: Ford lost £32,745 in 1930, £61,673 in 1931. Unlike GM-H, Ford had excess stocks due to the rapid downturn in business. W.C. Campbell sent an advisor, a Mr. Kew, from Canada in mid-1931 to review the Ford business model with French. His report concurred with French's actions in closing the Victorian, New South Wales and Tasmanian branches, operating them from Head Office. He also arranged the movement of excess stock to Canada, Singapore, Malaya and South Africa, the only profitable Ford entity in the region, and (eventually) getting duty rebates from the government. Ford sold the 700 excess tractors with one years' fuel as an incentive and ceased assembly at the South Australian plant, which became a depot for storing vehicles for delivery to dealers. There was no market for the sale of the Adelaide or Sydney land and French resisted more wage cuts than the 10% reduction in December 1930, in line with the Federal government guidelines. French even went so far to suggest in a letter to Campbell in November 1931, that they take advantage of the funds frozen in Australia and invest in building plants for the future.

Andy Reid was lucky to survive this time. Two years after he joined, in 1930, retrenchments resulted in him transferring to the pre-delivery area, one of only two people in the area. Needing to move one of the A models to a workstation, and not able to drive, Andy thought, 'It's time I learnt to drive, I can do this'. Unfortunately, it wasn't and he couldn't. Out of control, he drove into rows of A model two-door bodies, knocking them over:

> *...like a pack of cards and caused £400 damage. I didn't tell my supervisor until the next day. I was laid off, as were the others who saw me but didn't report it. They were back a day later; three days later, I was reinstated and carpeted. That's how I got the nickname 'Knocker'.*

Adversity brought people together. The homeless moved in with those who had homes. Landlords often forwent rents, or reduced them to a peppercorn, preferring to have a house occupied by tenants than leave the house vacant to be vandalised or occupied by squatters. Those with jobs supported those without. The philosophy of mateship and making do, long a feature of Australian society, supported by government 'susso' and social welfare organisations, supported many. Many suffered, many were worse off, but people helped one another.

Jess Pittman recalls a WWI serviceman with an artificial leg, re-employed on his return from the war, was having difficulty working in the plant, and losing time on the line. She talked to 'Slim' Westman, the then Manufacturing Manager of the Geelong site. 'Slim' was technically brilliant but feared in the plant, erratic at times, known to shout and scream, and with a housekeeping fetish. Westman quietly arranged for the company to supply the ex-serviceman a new artificial leg.

The same 'Slim' Westman actively discouraged the taking up of collections around the plant as they disrupted the work schedule. When Roy Bragg, a popular employee became very ill and unable to work, his mates began a collection of one shilling a week from all the employees in the area—about sixty people. Westman never

RIGHT 1932 US Model B chassis

TED FROST

Things were tough during the depression. As part of a job interview, we would ask a new employee for their name and address. One rough looking man, obviously down on his luck, gave his address as 'under the third hedge on the left just down from the gate.'

admitted it, but he was also a quiet, regular, one shilling a week contributor.

The industrial relations of the time were very much of master and servant, and to an extent followed the practice of Ford US. Henry Ford was antagonistically anti-union. Following the concepts espoused by Frederick Taylor's 1911 book, *Principles of Scientific Management*, he perfected the moving assembly line in 1913. Then in 1914, Ford made headlines when the company offered the ordinary line worker the opportunity to double his take home pay, to $5 a day. There were strings attached of course, continuity of attendance, length of service and other provisions, but the publicity meant that Ford attracted workers to his Highland Park plant. The unions resisted what they believed to be 'slavery to the assembly line', even calling it 'Fordism'. Finally the unions combined to form the UAW, the Union of Automobile Workers and began to unionise the industry. The UAW targeted General Motors, then Chrysler before tackling Ford. A tough, sometimes dirty campaign by both sides came to a head on May 26, 1937, the day of 'The Battle of the Overpass'. Henry Ford's tame thug Harry Bennett, Ford's 'Head of Service Department' and his bullies hospitalised several union leaders handing out recruiting pamphlets, in a bloody battle on the walkway overpass between the Rouge Plant gates and the carpark. The struggle continued until Henry Ford finally accepted the inevitable and agreed to a closed shop in June 1941.

By comparison, Ford Australia's industrial relations were relatively benign. But right from 1925, the industrial relations atmosphere was tough, some would even say brutal, but then the 1920s and 1930s were tough times. 'Tunner' Kenworthy, in his reminiscences recalled that the depression of the 1930s hit Geelong particularly hard. After most of his family had lost their jobs, 'Tunner' found work where he could, even becoming a professional boxer. He attended the Ford employment office each day for a week, along with 400–500 hundred others, looking for work. Eventually accepted, he began work in the spring department in June 1935, earning £3/19/11 per week. For that he worked a forty-eight-hour week with no sick pay or holiday pay and was liable, at any time, to the 5pm layoffs where a foreman would walk down the line picking out those who were to be laid off, no reasons given.[29] Even though Ford was anti-union, 'Tunner' and five workmates were determined to improve conditions. They contacted the then Coach-maker's Union, wishing to form a sub-branch of the union. The Union told them they had to recruit 300 members before a sub-branch could be formed. 'Tunner' recalled later:

LEFT 1932 US Model B Deluxe Roadster

> *We had a heck of a job recruiting members. Most people were scared of being laid off by the company if they joined.*

Eventually after six months, in 1938, at a meeting at the Geelong Trades hall, a Ford sub-branch of the Coach-builders Union was formed, subsequently re-named the Vehicle Builders Employees Federation (VBEF), the same year. Probably after Ford US had agreed to a closed, unionised shop in 1941, Ford Australia followed.

LEFT 1932 US Model B Fordor Sedan

The Great Depression was to continue for a number of years, but for Ford, 1931–32 was the low point. By maintaining tariffs on imported goods, persisting in a balanced budget and lower costs to business, the country slowly began to recover, and more rapidly than the United States. Losses for Ford continued in 1932, with sales of just 2,250 vehicles, of which 1,943 were passenger vehicles, an increase to nine per day. Overall, Ford Australia's total production of the Model A was 17,670 passenger, 2,891 commercial vehicles.

The reduction in sales in the United States forced Henry Ford into action: price reductions no longer worked. Typically, he approached the next model from an engineering standpoint, although he allowed Edsel some greater freedom in the styling of the Model B.

At the time, V8 engines were limited to luxury vehicles, straight sixes on the basic models. Henry was determined to manufacture a V8 using a single casting engine block, many rival V8 engine blocks were an expensive two or even a three piece casting. Over twelve months and thirty different engines later and with an investment rumoured to exceed US$50 million, he succeeded. Ford released the Model B with two optional engines, a four cylinder or a V8. Both would fit into the same engine bay with no change to the body or chassis. Even though French couldn't wait for the new model, he urged caution. He didn't want the same post-launch quality problems that Ford Australia had had with the Model A. In a letter to Campbell on October 1, 1931, he wrote:

LEFT 1932 US Model B Deluxe Coupe

> *...better to delay (introduction) as mechanical difficulties in*

SLIM WESTMAN & THE UNION

In the early days, Ford's apathy to unions and unionism, particularly in the United States, was well known. When the Coach Builders Union (the predecessor of the Vehicle Builders Union) first met to form a union at Ford in Geelong, they called for a meeting to be held on the lawn outside the gates, near Melbourne Road. Legend has it that the automatic lawn sprinklers suddenly developed a fault and mysteriously turned full on, causing the meeting to be abruptly abandoned. Slim Westman was believed to be the primary, unproven culprit.

Australia are far more greatly emphasised here than in Canada!

After some delays, Ford Australia released the Model B, with much fanfare in early 1932, the same as Canada.

George Wilden was another employee who joined Ford in 1932:

> *Motor vehicle design was really beginning to develop and I first heard of the V8 engine. (Later) it wasn't just a matter of changing one engine for another, it called for all new bodies to build, and a new type of chassis to assemble.*

The Model B passenger vehicle range was as before, Phaeton, Roadster, Sport Coupe, Fordor, (Ford terminology for four door), and Town Sedan, while the commercial range was reduced to the Light Delivery Van (VL) and the Cab Truck (BB), all of course with either four or V8 cylinder engines. However, even the terminations, mothballing the Sydney plant at the end of February 1933, introducing a sliding scale of salary reductions for middle and senior management and reducing tradesmen wages back to the award, could not prevent the company recording an even greater loss for 1931–32 of £74,397. Henry had learnt his lesson.

New models now became a regular feature of Ford operations. The Model B and B18, (4 and 8 cylinders) only remained in production from early 1932 to September 1933. Already the next model was well underway, the Model 40 Series, introduced July, 1933. By raking back the angle of the radiator grille and the bonnet side louvres, Edsel cleverly transformed the rather

RIGHT 1930 Sports Roadster advertisement

dumpy-looking B Series into a quite attractive vehicle and the public agreed. Introduced in July 1933, the Model 40 sold 1,879 passenger vehicles in the second half of the year, three times more than the Model B in the first half. More importantly, truck sales tripled in the same period, from 285 Model B to 830 Model 40. The turnaround was complete. Total vehicle sales rose to 3,563, the higher truck sales contributing to the first profit in three years, £94,973. Ford celebrated the return to profit by immediately resurrecting previously shelved expansion plans.

Late in 1932, the wife of a Gippsland pig farmer wrote to Ford asking them to make 'a vehicle comfortable enough to take her to church on Sunday and her husband to take the pigs to market on Monday'. Banks rarely lent money for a vehicle to farmers during depression, other than a truck for farm purposes, and few could afford two vehicles. No copy of the letter has been found but, according to legend, it was passed to the head of the then fledgling design centre, Lew Bandt.

Along with French, Lewis Bandt was one of the six most

LEW BANDT

In 1928, Lew joined Ford as a body engineer and draftsman. He quickly demonstrated his flair for drawing and vehicle design as Ford worked on the Australian body designs for the Model A and Model B. Promoted to head up what would become the Ford Design Department. Lew is best known for his design of the first utility. After heading the design centre, Lew worked in the body engineering section of what was to become the Product Engineering Office until his retirement in 1972, after forty-four years. Some of Lew's creations were the steel-roofed convertibles for the 1962 Miss Australia quest and the first Australian Fairlane, released in 1967. Possibly his most undervalued contribution to the nation was his work during the WWII, when he was the go-to man, resolving design problems in supplying products to the Australian army, navy and air force. After Lew retired, he restored his original utility and was often seen driving it around Geelong. Tragically, he was killed in 1987, in an accident while driving the utility.

(*Geelong Advertiser* July 29, 1995)

LEFT John and James Morrisey head for Perth

FAR LEFT 1934 ute designed by Lew Bandt

influential persons in Ford Australia's history. Born in South Australia, Lew had worked for Duncan and Fraser in Adelaide, before joining Ford in 1928, as a body engineer and draftsman. He quickly demonstrated his flair for drawing and vehicle design. As Ford Australia worked on the Australian body designs for the Model A and the Model B, his talents were recognised and he was selected to head up what would become the Ford Design Department. Bandt took the front half of a Model 40 sedan, married the cab to a steel-sided truck body and added a drop-down tailgate at the rear. He rounded the cab off behind the front seat and added rear-side quarter windows for visibility; creating the world's first coupe utility. Hubert French approved the first model built in the pattern shop in early 1933, and tooling commenced with production offline in early 1934.[30] GM-H brought out their own Chevrolet version twelve months later and after Ford sent a vehicle to Detroit in 1935, Henry Ford himself invited Bandt to Detroit to show the Americans how to build the Coupe Utility, a vehicle now built worldwide.

Meanwhile the Model T had managed to work its way into everyday life in Australia. John Morrisey was twenty in 1933 when he, his brother James and Gibson Stupart decided to leave their Dalby, Queensland home and try to find work in Western Australia. Their vehicle, a Model T coupe, was a squeeze for three strapping lads and all their gear, but the Ford took it all. They headed east to the coast and turned right, heading south for Sydney. Camping for all except one night, they continued south to Batemen's Bay where they turned right again and passed through Canberra, Wagga and Hay, where they camped by the river. Outside the butcher's shop the next morning, the strangers in town were arrested by the police as suspects for an attempted bank robbery the night before! Managing to convince the police of their innocence, they hurriedly headed for Mildura and Adelaide, where they saw their first, recently released Ford V8, and were so impressed they scratched V8 signs on the side of their coupe. They continued their journey through Port Augusta and across the Nullabor where the roads, generally bad in populated areas, deteriorated badly, resulting in several broken springs; luckily spares were readily available in the towns along the way. Progress

RIGHT 1932 US Ford DeLuxe Phaeton

slowed to a mere 150 miles a day as the road got progressively worse, with limestone outcrops every few hundred metres. Finally they reached Eucla, to find petrol there was four times the price of city prices, four shillings a gallon. If possible, the road was even worse as they tackled the Madura Pass, so steep on the return journey, they dragged an enormous tree trunk behind the Ford as an extra brake. The road was easier past Coolgardie and they had the benefit of taps in the huge pipeline bringing water to the goldfields for luxurious open-air baths. They returned home some weeks later, detouring via Melbourne and the Princes Highway. The climb up the Bulli Pass near Wollongong was so steep, the two passengers had to get out and run alongside to reduce weight. Who said you needed a 4WD?

By 1934, the Manufacturing Plant had to expand. The increased cost of importing panels had made it more economical to produce them in Australia, which in turn required more and larger presses capable of stamping out the ever increasingly large panels. As the expertise in patternmaking and toolmaking in Australia grew, so did the demand for larger and larger machine tools to manufacture the dies. Ron Phillips recalled:

> *By the time we were into the Model A, we had progressed to making the dies for the four-door sedan body, the first time that had been done in Australia.* [31]

As more and more components were stamped or cast from steel, so the use of wood as structural components in the body waned, eventually resulting in the elimination of the many wood curing kilns at the Geelong plant. With the launch of the Model A, the tool room could foresee the need for larger machine tools, including the large Keller Mills, used for copying the forms from the patterns into the steel tools. Even during the recession period of 1931–1933, the toolroom was manufacturing tooling for the new models, the B, the 40 and the English designed smaller, Model Y. By now French was worrying whether staff cuts had been too severe, and in his December 13, 1933 memo to Campbell,[32] even suggested employing young men on what could be the first graduate program for Ford.

Now the national economy had begun to recover, sales were picking up, investment in plant and equipment became an ever-increasing demand. The Manufacturing Plant was extended in 1934, and again in 1935, to cope with the increasingly larger tools and press lines for the larger panels compared with those of the Model T. Now for the first time, the technology and equipment was available for steel to replace the fabric turret roof of the 68 Series sedan. The smaller roof panels of the trucks, and the new coupe utility used steel, but now, for the first time an all-steel sedan body became a reality when the Model 68 commenced manufacture in January 1936. The blanking and piercing tools used for the sedan roof were the largest stamping tools manufactured to date.

THE ALL-STEEL BODY

The all-steel bodied 68 Series Ford was a breakthrough in automotive design and assembly but the process to make the roof was not so high-tech. Lindsay Sheppard tells how the roof panels were made back in 1935, before the large presses of the 1950s arrived.

> *The first (largest) press was used to form the roof shape. Then, using a template, the perimeter of each roof was then individually marked out, and then cut out of the sheet of steel by an operator using a bandsaw. Some of those guys were pretty good! Then the roof went back to the press line for re-strike (reforming) before metal finishing. It wasn't until after the war when we got the presses set up inline, that we could do the now common blank-pierce-trim process.*

LEFT Stamping roof panels at Geelong, circa 1940s

The growth and expansion continued in 1935 and both Manufacturing and Assembly plants at Geelong were constantly changing. George Wilden who had started work on the truck assembly line remembered:

> *In 1934 big changes were looming, bodies built of steel and wood were to give way to all steel. We had to enlarge our Geelong and Queensland plants and build a new factory in Sydney. They were busy times, assembly lines were mechanised and gear installed for the new type of welding to be done. Then the new equipment started to arrive—our eyes popped when we saw one of the presses—a thousand tonner!* [33]

LEFT Hec Murray, Lew Bandt and Jack Taylor with life-size wooden model, Oscar

The changeover from using wood to an all-steel body was complete, and now totally Australian made. George also spoke of the need for tighter quality control:

> *There was little room for error in making the all-steel body, so we set up an inspection department with precision gauges and other testing equipment. We were learning our jobs all over again.* [34]

Not forgotten with the recovery of the company, were its employees. The 10% wage and salary reductions of 1930 were cancelled by the board at its January 1934 meeting, after its 1933 profit of £94,973. Salaries increased again in March 1935, this time by 15%, and shortly after, Ford began advertising for skilled tradesmen, following the surge in 1934 sales to 7,884 vehicles. Passenger vehicle sales more than doubled to 5,110, commercial vehicle sales also doubled to 2,395, while for the first time, manufacture and assembly of the smaller, English designed 8hp Anglia commenced, with sales of 379. Recognising the closure of the New South Wales plant had badly affected sales in that state, the company rented a property in Ultimo, Sydney, and in April 1934, employed a new Branch Manager, A.F. France, at an annual salary of £83/6/8.

OPPOSITE PAGE Vintage Ford advertisments. Clockwise from top left: 1936 V8 Sedan, 1937 V8 Sedan, 1937 V8 Sedan, 1939 Prefect.

Production almost doubled again in 1935, to an annual total of 12,469, only 500 short of the highest production year, 1926. Passenger vehicles were a record 7,016, trucks doubled again to 4,383, while English-sourced vehicles tripled to 1,079. Model changeovers now came thick and fast. The 40 Series Canadian vehicles ceased in March, 1935, to be followed by the 48 Series in May, only to be replaced in January 1936, by the 68 Series. The English Y19 series vehicles followed the same timetable, replaced by the Y20 and, in turn, by the CX20 series. The month of April 1935 was wholly committed to the production of the larger, 51 Series trucks. The year closed with a profit of £169,401, a dividend of 12.5%, the purchase of land and the commencement in July, of the new assembly plant at Lidcombe, later known as Homebush.

The next year, 1936, was just as busy. Large extensions were made to the Brisbane plant and the new Homebush plant opened to great fanfare as the first vehicles rolled off the new assembly line on March 17, Saint Patrick's Day. There was no employee car park; only ten employees had cars, although there were several rows of bike racks. Gordon Symsey was one of the 286 workers, six of whom were women, who started at the plant, building fifteen vehicles a day. Gordon recalls:

> *I worked on what we called 'The Dead Line'...because the chassis was upside down while we assembled both front and rear axles, springs, the mechanical brakes, the running boards and the front and rear bumpers.*

Gordon also recalled the primitive employee conditions:

> *We didn't have lockers in those days! We had clothes racks, suspended over the aisles where we worked. When the whistle blew, they were wound up out of the way until lunch or knock-off. Although...we did have a lunch room and the tea was free!*

Superintendent Jack McLaughlin ran the plant, with one foreman in charge of production. A Leading Hand looked after each section and earned five shillings a week (50¢). Another to work at Homebush was Charlie Sherson. After starting at Geelong, Charlie's skills as a motor body trimmer had taken him to Hobart in 1925 to train employees in the trade. Moving back to Geelong for the next few years, he then moved to Sydney where he trained new employees there before the plant opened.

By now, the introduction of new models was a regular occurrence. Some were only facelifts, but this was a radical change from Henry's original stance of not changing his product:

> *...we want the man who buys one of our products never to have to buy another.* [35]

Ford had upgraded features before in defiance of his original stance but now, with severe competition from General Motors and other manufacturers, he was obliged to embrace the regular new model concept. The Homebush plant commenced production with the Model 68, V8 Deluxe sedan and the smaller CX20 from England. From the start of Sydney production to 1939–40 and the commencement of World War II, the plant built the 78, 81, 91 models and the Mercury model 99 as well as the English 7W and 93 models, each with an average model life cycle of just twelve months. The hectic series of model changes also occurred in Brisbane and Geelong. With the frequent model changes, the toolroom was kept busy with new model tooling, or tooling to replace imported components, as import duty on many components was still high. As a result, volumes grew, as did profitability. In fact, the period 1935 to 1940 could be termed the first Golden Era for Ford Australia.

The power and legendary toughness of Ford trucks allowed them to permeate into all areas of the Australian fabric of life. Ford still supplied chassis through their dealers to independent motor body builders and soon specialised vehicles were providing bus services between towns, the logging industry, delivery vans for businesses as well as ambulances, even hauling the Sole Bros. 4-tonne elephant 'Topsy', around the country, as gleefully reported in a 1935 issue of *The Austraford Newsletter*. As cars and trucks became the norm on roads increasingly bituminised around the country, the Victorian Country Roads Board used Ford V8 trucks.

Meanwhile the Commonwealth government, embarked on a project to develop mechanised transport for the Defence Forces. Defence Department engineers worked closely with Ford engineers, developing armoured cars and specialised trucks for the army. A 1936 issue of *The Austraford Newsletter* featured a V8 forward-control truck built on an English chassis, designed for towing a field gun, with accommodation for the seven crew, and ammunition. The special purpose-built body was designed and built at Geelong. Strangely, the trucks used for towing artillery were termed *tractors*, an American term, which initially caused confusion, as *agricultural tractors* were also built in the same plant.

The period 1937 to 1940 saw the greatest sales for the company to date. The peak was 1938, the year the Board of Directors approved a large extension to the Homebush plant in Sydney, the last before the war, but an important one considering the later involvement and contribution of Sydney to the Australian war effort. Ford plants produced twenty-four unique, different models in 1937, eighteen in 1938 and twenty-five in 1939, as well as tractors on their own assembly lines. The same number of chassis were also supplied to independent body builders. The peak volume year was 1938, with 15,773 vehicles. However, things were just about to get a lot more complex.

An Exclusive Array of Fine Car Features

FORD V-8 for 1936 has been designed and built with one objective: To give the finest motoring at the most reasonable cost. It has an exclusive array of fine car features, each of which is an essential part of the basic design of the car. This 1936 V-8 is the product of the best in modern scientific and engineering knowledge. It is safe because it has Safety Glass all round, All-steel closed body, Super Safety mechanical brakes and easier control of steering and gear changing. It has unrivalled performance with economy because it is powered with the highly efficient V-8 engine. It is comfortable because it has Ford Centre-poise riding, and it is beautiful and satisfying because of its modern style and luxurious fittings. There is a reason for the world-wide popularity of Ford V-8—and that reason can be expressed in the one word, value. Your Ford dealer will gladly arrange for you to drive this splendid V-8. Easy purchase terms may be arranged.

Ford V-8 FOR 1936

A BRITISH EMPIRE PRODUCT

Setting A NEW MOTORING FASHION

Illustrating the De Luxe Club Coupe

THE Club Coupe and the Club Roadster, introduced with the brilliant Ford V-8 series for 1937, are the latest and smartest ideas in motor car design . . . Their advanced style sets a new fashion in motoring. The Club Coupe has the appearance of an ultra-smart coupe and yet seats all six passengers inside the body. It has All-Steel body with one-piece steel roof and Safety Glass all round. The interior is a triumph of modern design, both as to comfort and convenience. The rear seat may be removed providing exceptionally large carrying space right through to the boot. With new easy-action brakes and finger-tip steering, driving is effortless. And this exclusive Club Coupe has all the features of design and equipment that have made the 1937 models the greatest of all Ford V-8's. The Club Roadster is the open car version of the Coupe—a distinctively smart model which, at the same time, is particularly utilitarian in design. See these models and others in the fine Ford V-8 range for 1937. They are now on display at your Ford dealer's and he will gladly arrange to place a car at your disposal for your own test on the road. Easy terms.

FORD V-8 *for* 1937

BUY FROM YOUR LOCAL FORD DEALER

PACE— GRACE and SPACE

A FLATTERING CAR OF GREAT PERFORMANCE . . .
NEW LOW PRICES AND 35 TO 40 MILES PER GALLON

At the new low prices the "Prefect" offers unrivalled value among 10 H.P. cars! Big in size with plenty of leg and headroom for adults, it offers every feature for really comfortable and safe motoring, including all-steel closed bodies with safety glass in windscreen and all windows; automatically compensating brakes; exceptionally large luggage accommodation; adjustable front seat; many de luxe refinements—enclosed glove compartment, clock, ashtrays, choice of interior colour ensembles and body colours. Fordor Saloon, Tudor Coupe Saloon, Sport Tourer and Sport Tourer de Luxe available. Prices commence at £262 (F.O.B. Ford Plant, plus Sales Tax).

Why not test the "Prefect" for yourself? Visit your nearby Ford Dealer — now! Exceptionally easy purchase terms available.

***The* "PREFECT"**

BUY FROM YOUR LOCAL FORD DEALER

FORD MOTOR COMPANY OF AUSTRALIA PTY. LTD. (INCORPORATED IN VICTORIA)
Ford 8 H.P. . . . "Prefect" . . . Ford V-8's . . . Mercury . . . Lincoln-Zephyr . . . Lincoln V-12

F69.ME

Style WITH COMFORT . . .

The Modern Note in Car Design < < <

Ford V-8 design has a distinction and individuality of style that is reminiscent of the smartest Continental cars. This modern note is expressed externally in the gracefully contoured body lines and it is matched by the luxury and complete comfort of the splendidly appointed interiors. V-8 comfort is complete comfort because you sit in the relaxed but semi-erect position you would assume in your favourite armchair. That is why a long drive in a Ford V-8 is so much less fatiguing. These advanced ideas of style and comfort, its outstanding performance with economy, its famous all-steel body with safety glass all round and its many other value features are the reasons for the world-wide popularity of the Ford V-8. See and drive this really modern car — you will not be satisfied with anything less than its exclusive style and comfort. Easy purchase terms may be arranged.

FORD V-8 *The Style Leader*

Buy From Your Local Ford Dealer

FORD MOTOR COMPANY OF AUSTRALIA PTY. LTD. (INCORPORATED IN VICTORIA) F214.MV

Z2
37665

CHAPTER 3
WAR & PEACE

THE FORD YEARS 1940—1949

1940–1945:

Ford donates land, the government builds 'The Annexe', for Ford to produce Naval mines. Extensions to Geelong Stamping plant in 1941 and 1942. Ford builds airplane auxiliary fuel tanks, airplane high altitude oxygen cylinders, Bren Gun Carriers, machine tools, equipment, assembles trucks, jeeps, other vehicles for the armed forces. Geelong, Brisbane and Sydney plants build wood and steel vessels, barges and pontoons. Ford begins reconditioning airplane engines, initially at Geelong before transferring to a new site, Brisbane's Rocklea engine reconditioning plant in 1943. Brisbane Parts & Service depot built. Sydney Part & Accessories building erected in 1944.

1945:

Resumption of peace time civilian vehicle production. The Ford submission to government to build 'Australia's Own Car' included a request for subsidies, and was rejected in favour of GM-H, which did not. Government subsequently had to loan funds to GM-H to complete the project. Ford re-purchases vehicles back from government, reconditions them and sells to civilian population. Ford V8 sedan launched by Prime Minister Ben Chifley. Fordson E27N Model Tractor introduced. Henry Ford II appointed Chairman of Ford Motor Company.

1946:

Ford Freighter utility introduced—the forerunner of the F-Series. Ford leases a potato dehydration plant in Ballarat from Commonwealth government for forty-two years, for door and spring assembly. Ballarat Plant begins making seat springs, panels, all doors for the cars produced in Geelong, and utility bodies.

1947:

Central Parts Depot on other side of Geelong Road extended.

1948:

Brisbane and Fremantle plants extended.

1949:

All-new Ford V8, the Single Spinner with independent front suspension introduced. Ford Pilot V8 imported from England. Thames range of trucks introduced.

As the Great Depression slowly receded, the Australian government watched the growing militarism overseas with mounting concern and began preparations for war. In 1935, the Commonwealth government had begun a project to mechanise the armed services.

Ford, with the Australian Tank Corps and the Munitions Supply Board, had begun developing specialised vehicles for the Army, using standard Ford bodies and chassis. In addition to the Field Gun Tractor, Ford built the first Australian Armoured Car based on their 30 cwt, 4-cylinder truck chassis. Copied from the British armoured cars designed and built by Rolls Royce in the 1920s, it was designated LP1 (Local Pattern 1). Considered too slow and flimsy, Ford developed the LP2 in 1938, based on a shortened three-tonne chassis and fitted with a V8 engine. Later designs also had the ability to incorporate the Marmon-Herrington 4WD system. Eventually Ford supplied two major design styles of truck to the Army and the Air Force, the first with an English chassis, the snub-nosed forward control version, which looked like it had run into a brick wall, the second a normal control truck based on the American design 3-tonne chassis.

So concerned was the Joseph Lyons' government with Australia's ability to defend itself, that in 1938 the government began a recruitment drive for the armed forces and introduced a bill into parliament to increase the duty on vehicle chassis and body components. The intention was to create funds for a bounty to encourage local manufacture of engines of greater than 15hp. There was a sliding scale for the bounty, £30 for the first 20,000, £25 for the next 20,000 and £20 for the third and final 20,000 engines. There were other limitations, among them that any company producing engines must be Australian owned and controlled. The bill met resistance. On the one hand, Ford and GM-H, as foreign controlled companies under the definition of the act were excluded, and as major importers of chassis and other components, actually faced increasing prices. On the other hand, J.S. Strong of the Society of Motor Manufacturers and Traders, (SMM&T) the Australian representative for the British manufacturers, Austin, Morris, Standard and Triumph also opposed it, claiming that the British Empire had sufficient capacity, and Australia should source motors, indeed vehicles from Great Britain, instead of manufacturing in Australia.

PAGES 52–53 Street Parade, Melbourne, 1941

LEFT Armoured vehicle assembly, Geelong 1941

Politically, other forces were in play. The Commonwealth government was a coalition of the United Australia Party and the Country Party. The coalition was fragile, rendered ineffectual by personal enmities and ambition. After Prime Minister Joseph Lyons died in 1939, the country had three prime ministers in three years.

Following Great Britain, Australia declared war on Germany and Japan on September 3, 1939. Despite the recruitment program and military spending, Australia was still unprepared for war. Amongst the many acts of parliament passed in the last quarter of 1939, was the *National Security Act*. This bill transferred the States right to levy income tax to the Commonwealth, allowed the government to control businesses, the labour force and to conscript men for the defence of Australia. Another Act passed in December was the *Motor Vehicle Engine Bounty Act*.

As part of the negotiations between the government and business over the increased import tax and the engine bounty, the government had heavily promoted the concept of a 'National Automotive Company' involving a coalition of automotive companies. As part of this concept, the government then controversially granted a five-year monopoly on engine manufacture to Australian Consolidated Industries, (ACI).

The Managing Director was William Smith. Smith, born in 1882, had a background of glassblowing and over the years had built an empire based on glass manufacturing, and had diversified into machine tools, structural steel and cast iron products, becoming a diverse industrial empire with close contacts with the government.

'Knockabout' Smith and John Lawson, the minister who granted the monopoly, were friends, jointly owning a racehorse (Lawson later resigned over the relationship). The granting of the monopoly enraged the business community, automotive and otherwise, doing little for the minority government's reputation. When the Curtin government later repealed the legislation in 1946, ACI sued and was granted £56,000 compensation after arbitration. After the war, ACI expanded into manufacturing fibreglass.

RIGHT Armoured vehicle assembly, Geelong 1941

Meanwhile, E.W. Holden, the tough but gentlemanly chairman of GM-H, with a family history of seventy-five years in the business, had clashed often with the equally tough, brash American Managing Director, A.N. Lawrence.

General Motors Vauxhall division in England had sent Lawrence Hartnett to Australia as General Motors-Holden's Managing Director in 1934, with orders to either 'fix GM-H or close it'. Hartnett found GM-H to be, 'an organisation rent by internal bickering, impeded by a cumbersome administrative structure and widely resented as a rapacious foreign profiteer'.[36]

Hartnett restored harmony, overhauled the management practices and, like Ford, embarked on major expansions, reopening assembly plants, building new ones, and in the process transferring the GM-H headquarters from Adelaide to Fishermen's Bend in Melbourne. He established a close working relationship with Essington Lewis.

Lewis, born at Burra, South Australia in 1881, had dreamt of becoming a solicitor but was prevented by his father, ('You haven't got the brains, and I'm damned if I'll give you the money!'). He enrolled instead at the South Australian School of Mines and Industries in 1901 and on graduating, joined BHP Pty. Ltd. at Broken Hill. Tall, (178 cm), broad shouldered and with fair hair, Lewis's attention to detail and obsession for punctuality, order and efficiency impressed the then Managing Director of BHP, Guillaume Delpratt, who sent him to Newcastle even though at the time, he knew nothing of steelmaking.

Appointed General Manager of BHP in 1921, Lewis was responsible for the upgrading of the steel industry in Australia, and the development of down-stream companies for the steel products BHP produced. On one of his overseas trips, in 1934, he was so concerned about the increasing industrialisation and militancy of Japan that on his return to Australia, he set about increasing stockpiles of raw materials.

A formidable pair, Hartnett and Lewis had the ear of government. With three other companies, in 1936 they formed the Commonwealth Aircraft Corporation, also located at Fishermen's Bend and were soon building the Wirraway, then the Beaufort bomber aircraft, importing the engines from England. When, after the disaster of Dunkirk, the British banned the export of war material, including the Beaufort engines, Essington and Hartnett, with John (later Sir John) Storey began building engines at Fisherman's Bend. In 1940, appointed by Menzies, Essington

LEFT (TOP AND BOTTOM) Parade through Melbourne of war munitions and equipment manufactured in Australia

Lewis became the Head of the Ministry of Munitions, the most powerful industrial position in the country. He could compulsorily acquire any material or building he wanted, issue contracts without tenders and spend up to £250,000 on any project without approval, an enormous sum at the time.[37]

Not far from Ford in Geelong, on the other side of the railway line, on North Quay road was the new plant of International Harvester. The same tariff restrictions as the automotive companies saw IH build the plant in Geelong to manufacture locally. An important part of I.H.'s operation was the construction of a foundry, casting much of their agricultural machinery components, as well as assembly lines for the equipment. Thompson Engineering and Pipe Co. Ltd., complemented the Geelong group of companies. Established in Castlemaine in 1875 to service the gold mining industry, they had soon began manufacturing a wide range of foundry-based products for the Victorian and Commonwealth Governments. So began the great Australian industrial triumvirate: BHP, manufacturing steel and armaments at Newcastle and other sites, the GM-H/ Commonwealth Aircraft Corporation group located at Fisherman's Bend and the Ford/International Harvester/Thompson group, located at Geelong and Castlemaine.

Initially there were murmurs in manufacturing circles that the government war effort was becoming 'too General Motorised', with Essington appointed Director of the Ministry of Munitions and Hartnett, seconded from GM-H for the duration of the war

RIGHT Lew Bandt and Ford engineers review a boat model

as Director of Ordnance Production, but in a letter to French, Harnett went to great lengths to reassure him that:

> *I will be meticulously impartial as to makes, varieties of equipment and the like. If anything, I expect I will lean towards your product for fear of it being thought I might be favouring General Motors…I am putting (only) one thing in your mind just now and that is getting the job done and contributing whatever is possible to this war effort, which I know is the case with you.*[38]

The contribution of Australian manufacturing to the war effort could only have been possible with the close working relationship between these three men.

That is not to say that there was no suspicion of motives and competition between the men and their companies. Even then, and throughout the war, Hartnett was making plans to manufacture an all-Australian vehicle as notes from a meeting at the Ministry of Munitions in 1941 show.[39] The Secretary of the Ministry of Munitions, Professor James Brigden called a meeting after Harnett had made a statement to the War cabinet that it was time for local manufacture of War department trucks. The government believed a shortage of trucks was imminent; the English source was closed and the US and Canadian situation was rapidly deteriorating as the Japanese advanced. At this meeting, chaired by Professor Brigden, and attended by French, Hartnett, Lewis, Smith of ACL, and others, the Minister for supply and Development, Senator McBride said the government wanted an Australian truck, despite the lack of skilled labour and machine tools. However there was disagreement right from the start. Essington Lewis said he believed any decision should be based on the needs of the war effort, not economics. Hartnett, representing both the government and GM-H did not reveal his hand, but hedged, stating he believed the meeting should follow the government's wishes. William Smith objected, declaring he 'had a contract with the Prime Minister and did not intend to be shut out'. When Hartnett announced an impending shortage of GM trucks, French advised Ford of Canada had offered four to five thousand trucks while Strong of the SMM&T said British interests should be taken into account. The meeting ended with no resolution.

The next meeting, on June 30, was no better except Hartnett was more bullish than before. Strong of the SMM&T said the British were now in no position to supply, nor would be in the future. McHenry of International Harvester was noncommittal, Fergusson, of Chrysler committed the Adelaide plant to support the government but said his US principals needed specifications before they would consider any action.

French opposed the Hartnett plan, doubting the ability of the Australian industry to supply the best vehicle available to the armed forces using second-hand equipment from the USA. Besides, he added, everyone was sidestepping the issue of postwar advantage, each nervous that one manufacturer could have an advantage in control of the post-war civilian market. When Professor Brigden asked if anyone had thought of forming a company involving all those companies present, French said he had, but knew there was no way this could be achieved. He knew their respective Head Offices would never have agreed to such a position. Again no outcomes. All Brigden could do was to close the meeting. The meeting ended with no resolution.

The government persisted, issuing a letter requesting proposals for an Australian designed and manufactured truck. After long conversations and cables back and forth to Canada, French, Westman and Hughes completed the Ford proposal and presented it to Professor Brigden at the Ministry of Munitions on July 21, 1941. The proposal totaled more than US$5 million and over 1,005 pieces of equipment or tooling. Professor Brigden indicated that no decision would be made for several weeks. The Ford proposal apparently took the Department and General Motors by surprise. French reported in his August 22 memo to Campbell that:

> *…our chief competitor was informed of our proposal immediately…he advised his New York office by telephone and there were signs in his camp akin to panic.*

A little later, obviously alarmed by the developing situation in Canberra, Harnett urgently called for a meeting with French and McHenry of International Harvester at the I.H. offices. Concerned the government would socialise the industry, he

LEFT Drawing office, Geelong, 1943

wanted to enlist their support for his program. They refused. On August 14, Professor Brigden wrote to both GM-H and French, advising them that due to cost, the project would not proceed. Hartnett, in a memo to French on August 18, was absolutely livid that his plans had been shelved.

Coincidently, within days Menzies had resigned as Prime Minister and leader of the UAP, to be replaced by Arthur Fadden and Billy Hughes respectively. Without support of the independents, the Fadden government lasted only a month. The Labor Party formed a government with John Curtin as Prime Minister on October 7, 1941, just eight weeks before Pearl Harbour.

It took a little while for Australia's industry to gather impetus in supplying material to the war effort. Ford reorganised the management team and delegated a specific group, headed by Lyn Hamilton, to become the interface between the various armed forces, Army, Navy, Air Force and later, the American armed forces. This group disseminated government equipment orders, known as Department of Defence Demand Notices, to the organisation in each state. The first of the Ford Defence Memoranda, issued on April 4, 1940 informed the organisation of the varied designs and inventory levels. Over the next six years, these memoranda tracked the many design changes and products supplied to the armed forces, after the government legislatively assumed control of manufacturing in 1939 which prohibited manufacture of products not directly supporting the war effort.

Many employees joined the armed forces, Ford guaranteeing their jobs on their return from active service, while managers were seconded to the government to provide expertise. One such employee was Les Neilson, who joined Ford in 1935 as the head of the Victorian commercial vehicles branch. He considered enlisting in the Air Force, but was instead offered a job with the Directorate of Ordnance, one element being responsibility for the production of military bridges, another the development and production of assault and tank landing craft. At one stage, Les was in charge of the production of all internal combustion engines in Australia. Les rejoined Ford in 1945 to become the Commercial Division Manager for Ford Australia.

Noel Pritchard remembers his father and uncle worked for Ford during the war. His uncle, Alexander worked the trim line in the Assembly Plant, while his father was a truck driver. Each day Albert drove his semitrailer to the Melbourne, North and South Wharves and Victoria Dock to pick up freight. Due to fuel rationing, charcoal burners powered each semitrailer. Returning to Geelong at night with a fully laden semitrailer was an adventure. The (then) two-lane highway was barely visible, lit by shielded headlights, reduced by law to three-inch slits of light.

Lyn Hamilton began his career at Ford as a sales clerk in the then Home Office (Head Office). Transferred to the Geelong Branch two years later, Lyn became the sole clerk, attending to dealer orders, and vehicle deliveries. Appointed Sales Manager in

RIGHT Rocklea Assembly Plant, Wright aircraft engine rear section assembly, 1944

JESSIE PITMAN

Jessie Pitman was operating a post office and general store when she first heard that Ford planned to employ women:

> *I had lost my husband, and business wasn't so good, so I wrote to Ford and applied for a job, any job. I had two interviews. They must have thought I had ability to interview people, as I didn't do any other work...All sorts of women applied for jobs. Even if their only work with machinery in the past had been with an eggbeater at home, they would find a job at Ford. That appealed to many women. Some had never had the chance to go out and get a job previously.*

(*Geelong Advertiser* July 29, 1995)

1930, he was one of only two District Sales Managers (DSMs) handling Victoria, the Riverina, south-east South Australia and Tasmania. After a stint in Brisbane, Lyn returned to Geelong as Home Office Assistant Sales Manager. A longtime supporter of military training, from his interest in school cadet days, Lyn had progressed through the ranks to become a Major in the Army Reserve. At the outbreak of the war, he was forcibly retired from the army, deemed more valuable in his role as liaison between the armed forces and Ford.

Lew Bandt was another employee prevented from joining up. As design engineer, Lew was involved in resolving many of the design problems, with innovative solutions to concepts developed by the armed forces. With so many men joining the armed services, women flooded to Ford to replace them. Prior to the war, in 1939 the headcount at Ford was approximately 2,000, the only women being office workers. One estimate in 1944 had the work force totaling more than 5,275, of which 40% were women. New starts received intensive training, and work design was analysed repeatedly to allow women to perform all except the most arduous tasks at Ford, many highly skilled. Lew Bandt recalled one night returning to Geelong on the Ford bus, complimenting one woman on her welding skill. Her reply summed up the feelings of many:

> *'I have three brothers on Crete', she said, 'and what I do here might help to keep them safe.' Throughout the war, Bandt said, I never forgot that simple statement.*[40]

The 'Ford bus', introduced when fuel rationing removed most private bus lines from service, were semitrailers powered by charcoal burners. On the trays, constructed from the plywood crates used to import vehicles, were seats. One configuration was like the old 'Red Rattler' train compartments, entered from the side of the truck tray. Others later had a central aisle.

The Ford contribution to the war effort was significant, extensive and total. Even Ford Canada was not aware of some of the activity in Australia. One such decision made by French, was to supply the land over the road from the main plant to the Commonwealth government to build the 'Annexe' in 1941, without Ford Canada's knowledge. The Annexe, a separate building over the road from the assembly and stamping plants, and the installed equipment cost more than £100,000. French believed they were vital to the war effort, saying, 'I'll deal with Canada at the end of the war.' In 1946, when informed of the expenditure, there were no recriminations from Ford Canada.

Ford used the Annexe mainly for the manufacture of sea mines, the only complete mine production site in the Southern Hemisphere. The Navy provided the product drawings, leaving the production implementation to Ford. Made up of seven main assemblies, each mine comprised 1,688 components. The Australian manufacturing system, using local equipment and systems of manufacture differed from the English system, fabricating the hemispheres by cold-pressing flat, circular 4.5 mm thick steel plates, the assembly of sinkers on a production line basis and malleable castings instead of forgings. Perhaps the greatest innovation was the use of an automatic welding jig to weld the two 900 mm hemispheres together on a rotating jig. Original production was set at ten mines per day, but peak production was more than double this: 390 per month. The sinker box, the system controlling the depth the mines were laid, was also manufactured in the Annexe. Alick Smith joined Ford in 1934:

> *I was one of the lucky ones chosen from the regular fifty or so outside the gates every morning...When the war started a couple of mates and I volunteered to transfer to the Annexe assembling sea-mines. I ended up knowing more about mines than I did motor cars by the end of the war!*

Ford produced 12,987 mines and sinker sets in the last four years of the war. An interesting highlight was many of the mines were laid by a vessel requisitioned by the government from the Adelaide Steamship Company and fitted out as a minelayer. With a displacement of 3,043 tonne and 109 metres in length, HMAS Bungaree was commissioned in 1941, with a carrying capacity of 423 mines. She laid mines off Port Moresby, in the Torres Straits and passages in the Barrier Reef. Decommissioned in 1947, she was returned to the Adelaide Steamship Company before being sold in 1960. Renamed the Eastern Mariner, it is ironic that while operating in South Vietnamese waters in 1966, she struck a mine in the Saigon River and sank. [41]

Another initiative by Ford during the war was building auxiliary fuel tanks for aircraft to extend their flying range. In 1943, the Japanese were a very real invasion threat to Australia, to the point the military had drawn up a defence plan, known as 'The Brisbane Line; to evacuate Australians north of an east-west line running through Brisbane, abandoning the north of the country to the Japanese and leaving guerillas to fight them. The Japanese advance seemed unstoppable: the battle for the Huon Peninsula in New Guinea was raging, and the allied ground forces were being battered by attacks by Japanese warplanes flying out of Wewak, which was outside the range of Allied aircraft. Early in August 1943, a P47 Thunderbolt fighter from the US Army Air Corps flew to Geelong, landing on an airstrip at the rear of the plant, over the railway line on North Shore. The assignment was to design and build 100 auxiliary fuel tanks in ten days, to give the Thunderbolts extra range. Lew Bandt had had some experience designing belly tanks for Spitfire fighters for the Middle East. Working twelve-hour shifts, twenty-four hours a day, the designers and engineers worked to produce a prototype, test it, then fabricate the tanks by hand: there were no working drawings, no time for tooling. The tanks were built and quickly loaded onto waiting transport planes and flown north. One of those working on the tanks was Chrissie Woods. Diminutive in stature, her task was to squeeze inside each

LEFT Naval mines produced at Geelong

LEFT A Hamilton Press, pressing hemispheres for naval mines, Geelong, 1941

▶ **RIGHT** Ship hull manufactured at Geelong

tank and weld together the tank halves, sealing them from the inside, a dark, cramped and claustrophobic job. French later wrote in *Strong Grows the Future,* the book produced to celebrate twenty-five years of Ford in Australia:

> *Some days later, around the 17th or 18th of the month, I received the following telegram, 'Thanks for delivering the goods—listen to the news tonight'. It was signed by the Commanding General, Air Services, South-West Pacific Area.*

Days earlier, the P47s had staged a series of attacks on Wewak, catching the Japanese fighter planes on the ground and destroying more than 200. It was a major setback for the Japanese advance and significant relief to the ground forces. French concluded:

> *That was one of a number of occasions I felt proud of Ford Australia. Thankful too, that the engineering resources we had built were of value to the nation in time of crisis.*

Working with the RAAF, the US Army Air Force and the Commonwealth Aircraft Corporation, Ford ultimately manufactured 68,499 wing or belly auxiliary fuel tanks for the P38 (Lightning), P39 (Air Cobra), P40 (Kittyhawk), P47 (Thunderbolt) Spitfire and Mosquito aircraft, ranging from thirty to 200 gallon capacities. While the major production site was Geelong, Sydney and Brisbane plants also produced auxiliary tanks.

Ford continued the core business of manufacturing vehicles during the war period, although now with only one customer, the government. An array of vehicle body styles originated from the standard range of passenger and commercial vehicles, as well as a wide range of specialty vehicles. Trucks varied from the 1-tonne and 15-cwt utility and panel vans, to 2, 2.5, 3, 4 and 5-tonne trucks, to semitrailer prime movers (confusingly using the American term 'tractors') and 20-tonne trailers. Specialty vehicles ranged from Amphibian vehicles, Machine Gun Carriers, known as Bren Gun Carriers (in Army terminology, *'Carrier, M.G., L.P. No 2,*

▼ **BELOW** Geelong link-up extension building—note vessels in foreground

PAT YENIK

Pat joined Ford in 1948 and for nearly three years has been driving an overhead crane. She was born in Hamilton, Victoria and was a hairdresser in Warrnambool for fourteen years. During the War, she drove a Royal Mail service bus between Warrnambool and Ararat, then managed a hairdressing salon for two years in Geelong before joining Ford. Pat is regarded by Department Heads as one of the best crane drivers in the plant and has never had an accident. 'I would never go back to hairdressing again,' said Pat, 'In the cab of my crane I'm on my own and I'm my own boss'. She likes crane driving better than driving the hi-lift fork trucks that she first drove. Pat's crane, one of the first installed at Geelong, lifts all sorts of objects, from car bodies to crates of spare parts. Two other women have recently started driving overhead cranes in the Central Parts depot at Geelong, Laura Smith and Roma Walters.

LEFT Ford Universal Carrier

134" W.B.'), trucks mounted with 40 mm Bofors guns, to semi-trailer prime movers and trailers for towing aircraft, or in army terminology, 'Trailer, S.B.G.' (Standard Box Girder).

Notes from a meeting in French's office on December 12, 1940 discussed the terms of a contract and agreed to the assembly, in Sydney, of 150 Carriers, M.G. L.P. No. 2, at rate of ten per week, with engines and transmissions supplied ex Ford Canada. Terms of the contract were cost plus 2.5% on production costs, with labour and overhead at cost plus 7.5%. There were to be separate orders for tools and designs, payments to be monthly.

Ford supplied bodies to International Harvester, components to General Motors, assembled General Motors bodies to Ford Chassis, assembled Studebaker and Mack trucks, fitted Marmion-Herrington four wheel drives and assembled Ford and Willys Jeeps. By far the most popular truck was the 3-tonner truck of which Ford produced more than 16,500, with wheelbases of 134 inches, 158 inches and 176 inches and twenty-nine different body styles, from ambulances to water tankers. Analysis of production records and Defence Force memoranda shows Ford produced more than 63,701 vehicles of various types and models between 1940 and 1945, volumes equal to the prior year's civilian quantities and certainly with a far greater complexity than ever seen before.[42] Geelong produced the greater quantity, 40,424 vehicles, but the production records show all plants contributed, Brisbane 5,831, Fremantle 2,133, Sydney 15,268 and Adelaide forty-five vehicles. With such a complex operation, more space was soon required for assembly operations. Following the government's directive to decentralise wherever possible, Ford found a new building in Ballarat, one the government had appropriated: a potato processing plant previously used for the production of dehydrated potatoes. The plant soon rang with the sounds of metal finishing of doors, centre pillars and even seat spring assemblies, using specialised equipment.

Ford not only produced products for land, air and under the sea, but also naval vessels and equipment. Geelong, with the greater area and heavier industrial manufacturing equipment produced larger vessels, in wood and steel. The demands of amphibious operations in the tropics made the Brisbane plant a logical choice for the manufacture of various vessels, including landing craft and barges to carry fresh water. Brisbane plant created an open-air workshop, operating on three shifts, employing both men and women, the production jigs on bogies running on railway lines. With the bottom plates first welded into place, the incomplete skeleton was transferred to a wooden bogy and the vessel built down the outdoor assembly line.

Once completed, a special-built transporter moved the vessel and bogy to Boggy Creek, near the mouth of the Brisbane River. The ramp to launch the vessels was quite long and fifteen metre wooden poles were used as skids. The only location for timber of this length at the time was on Frazer Island.

Landing craft built at Brisbane saw action in battles for New Guinea beaches at Cona, Buna and Sananand‍a. Sydney Plant used a similar assembly system, albeit indoors. The launch site for their vessels was on the Parramatta River near Homebush. Geelong, with the larger area and heavier equipment was able to both build completed vessels in-plant as well as fabricating sections.

RIGHT The 106 foot cargo ship AV2082 Dora. All Ford-built ships were given names starting with D: *Daphne*, *Dulcie* and *Delilah*, to name a few

RIGHT *Dolores* launched off Western Beach, Geelong

One, a 44-foot landing craft, was modified to become a special purpose tug, then transported by road to Melbourne for launching and fitting out. Similar to the Sydney plant layout, Geelong built workboats and steel cargo lighters, transporting them to Corio Quay for launching. Larger vessels, the 100 foot, A.L.C. 120 tank landing ships and the 106 foot D class series vessels were fabricated in sections, and transported to Geelong's Western Beach. There they were assembled, welded together and launched, sideways, off the beach. One iconic photograph shows the launch of 'Dolores', while in the background stands the Dalgety Wool Stores building where Ford first began operations.[43]

Eleven D class vessels were built, 106 foot long, with a displacement of 228 tonne, two masts, all welded steel, powered by three, 50HP, 4-cylinder diesel engines. Armament consisted of one Bofors gun mounted on the stern behind the wheelhouse and a 20 mm quick firing gun mounted on the bow. Each was named with a female name commencing with the letter 'D', i.e. Daphne, Dora, Dulcie, Doreen, Dorothy, etc. A joke at the time was that Ford only built eleven because they ran out of names.

One epic trip recorded by the 'Ford fleet' was when two A.L.C. 20s departed Geelong in 1943, carrying supplies for Jacquinot Bay in New Britain a distance of over 4,600 km. They left Geelong and sailed via Brisbane. After refueling, they were joined by a flotilla of eighteen A.L.C.40 craft and two 40-foot workboats. The whole journey passed without incident.

Ford produced 467, 35-foot steel lighters (unpowered vessels) with a beam of 15-feet for the US forces, and eleven, 55-foot, 50-tonne lighters with a beam of 16 foot for the Royal Navy. In all, Ford produced over 500 vessels, lighters, pontoons and floating docks, and many of production welders and crane drivers involved were women.[44]

Soon after the American Forces arrived in Australia, the Department of Aircraft Production assigned Ford to set up facilities to recondition aircraft engines, which required the substantial expansion of the Geelong department used for reconditioning vehicle engines. Ford planned the expansion to accommodate post-war reconditioning of passenger and commercial vehicle V8 engines. Two hundred new recruits were trained, mainly women and girls, few of whom had any mechanical experience. A production line was set up to recondition Wright Cyclone 9-cylinder single row engines and, as training progressed and the women became more familiar with the process, the reconditioning time for an engine halved.

Late in 1943, as the threat of invasion faded and the Allied bases secure in New Guinea, the government decided to relocate the reconditioning plant closer to the field of operations and expand its operation to include Wright Cyclone 14-cylinder, Pratt and Whitney 14, and 18-cylinder engines. The Commonwealth made available a former ammunition factory at Rocklea, southwest of Brisbane and near the Archerfield air field. While the government renovated the 37,550 sq. metre plant, Ford shipped the Geelong equipment north and temporarily relocated experienced personnel to train the new operators. Again, the majority of workers were female.

Engine bay testing initially used mobile test cells, but was later made more permanent by excavating a nearby hill and building twelve test cells into it, each with a 16-metre exhaust stack. The complex was extensive and contained degreasing facilities and chromium, nickel, cadmium and lead plating facilities, as well as its own maintenance shop. The production line concept from Geelong proved successful. From an initial output of eight engines per day, 7,230 engines were reconditioned at Rocklea, with a workforce which peaked at 1,100 employees.[45]

Rocklea operated independent of the Brisbane Plant but after the war when it closed, some of the personnel transferred to Brisbane. Geoff Chinchin, manager of Rocklea replaced G. V. Cornwell, who retired after many years' service in Queensland and Victoria. Others returned to the plant after war service; Jack Stratigos as Sales Manager was one, Duncan Norris another after his stint in the navy, later to become the longest serving Plant Manager of Brisbane Plant.

Among the many other miscellaneous products produced by Ford, were aircraft oxygen cylinders to provide high altitude breathing to aviators. Made from stainless steel, the deep drawing process was technically a difficult one, requiring three stages to reach the depth, the semi drawn blanks annealed between each operation. Other miscellaneous products were benches and cupboards for fitting out various truck bodies and more than 235,000 ammunition boxes for P58 and C206 shells, produced on a mini assembly line. Also produced were vehicle toolboxes, covers and tarpaulins, kits to modify vehicles, 250-gallon water tanks, tyre chains and wheels. Many local industries supported Ford, as the major contractor. In a letter from Westman to Hartnett, it is evident that Ford was involved in machining shell cartridge cases in 1940, and drawing on the services and experience of Thompsons in Castlemaine, Australian Cement Company and International Harvester in Geelong for casting and machining.[46]

When the army were no longer able to source split steel rim wheels from Britain for army vehicles, the army turned to Ford, asking 'Slim' Westman if Ford could produce them. The largest press at the time was a triple action Southwark press. It had two stages for downward stamping, of 600 tonne and 230 tonne, a total of 830 tonne, and an upward press capacity of 480 tonne. The split rim wheels required a total force of 1,300 tonne. Westman designed an ingenious device, known in plant as 'The Nutcracker' which, using toggles was able to utilise the upward force, couple it with the downwards force to produce a total of 1,310 tonne force—just enough to draw the 5/16" thick steel. Together with makeshift tooling, designed in the toolroom, the army got its wheels. After the war was over, Ford Canada was told of the manufacture of split rim wheels. They cabled back that on the best advice from Canada and the US, that the Westman process would not work, 'We doubt if it could be done, and even if it could, it would be no good.' Westman took great delight in cabling back, 'Cannot accept statement that method is impractical. Suggest submit proposal to competent jobbing houses'.[47] So there!

TOM CLANCY, SYDNEY PLANT

During the war, there were about 1,700 people working here at peak times, although numbers fluctuated quite a lot. Many women worked here—either on the Trim Line or as welders on the barges. It was nice to have them around! Production was semi-KD. We made Jeeps, Bren gun carriers, wheels, barges, 35-foot lighters and even Diamond T trucks. All in all, the war was a busy time in Sydney.

There were very real concerns from the government that there were insufficient machine tools in the country to sustain the war effort, as most equipment was imported from England and the USA. While Hartnett had advocated the importation of second hand machine tools from the United States, French demurred. The Ministry of Munitions then called on Ford to contribute. One particular problem solved was to design and build 100-tonne presses with an 18 inch (457 mm) crankshaft throw to achieve the 36 inch (914 mm) stroke required to produce brass cartridge cases. Also designed and built were 400-tonne presses for heading the brass cartridge cases. Various types of lathes were manufactured: eighty-six lathes, type '26', with a 13-foot bed were built for the 250 lb armour piercing bomb shop, while other automatic lathes with a 9-inch collet were built to produce 500 lb bombs. Also manufactured were several unique lathes with a 48 foot (22.5 metre) long bed to produce the 3.7 inch ack-ack gun barrels. Ford also built Australian copies of 'Wirth' semi-automatic lathes for turning and parting 6 inch shells. The largest machine tools ever produced in the country at the time were the two horizontal boring machines made by Ford. The largest stood 9.3 metres high, weighed more than 90 tonnes and took up more than 14.5 x 11 metres in area. When Ford advised the Ministry of Munitions of difficulty finding equipment to carry out a particular machining operation, the Ministry found an old 1890 vintage 'Lang' lathe in the Geelong Harbour Trust workshops, had it shipped to Ford, who renovated it and adapted it for the job.[48]

➋ **RIGHT** Launching a Ford truck off an ALC at Toko, Bougainville in the Solomon Islands in 1945 (AWM 079810)

➋ **RIGHT** Prior to proceeding to Jacquinot Bay, barges called at Milne Bay in the Territory of Papua (now part of Papua New Guinea) to take on further supplies of rations for the remainder of their journey. Note the 44-gallon fuel drums on the beach. Nineteen ALC 40s and one ALC 120 of 41st Landing Craft Company, Royal Australian Engineers crossed the Coral Sea during the epic voyage from Cairns, Qld, to Jacquinot Bay on the southern coast of New Britain, 27 May, 1945. (AWM 018164)

These are only some examples of what was a demanding and extensive war effort. A multitude of other components and products were produced, many with complex and difficult design issues. Significantly, most of the work conducted for the government was on a cost plus a low percentage of approximately 3%; Ford certainly did not profit excessively from the war.

Early in 1945, with attention turning to post-war production, Ford faced the issue that many workers, including skilled women, may have to be retrenched, either as there was no work, or to take back into employment the many servicemen returning home.

Ford contracted with the government to re-purchase many of the surplus trucks and equipment that could be modified for civilian use, refurbish them and sell them to the public, starved of new vehicles of any kind. It was jokingly referred at the time, that Lyn Hamilton had the unique distinction of selling many vehicles twice, once to the Ministry of Munitions, then later to the public.

As an aside, one interesting use of redundant Bren Gun Carriers was observed by the author in the 1950s. With no bulldozers available, four gun barrels welded end-to-end and attached to a Bren Gun Carrier were an ideal method for clearing Mallee Scrub in rural Victoria.

Even in those dark days of 1942, the government established a planning authority, whose job it was to develop the country after the war: the Department of Post-War Reconstruction. One of the committees reporting to it was the Secondary Industries Commission. Established in 1943 and headed by John Jensen, it was charged with the development of secondary industry after the war. He and another public servant on the commission, John Storey were close friends of Hartnett. With the automotive companies deeply involved in armaments and heavy industry, and the need to employ returning servicemen, the government once again raised the concept of an Australian motor car, no doubt sponsored and supported by Hartnett, Jensen and Storey.

The FCAI (Federal Chamber of Automotive Industries) made a detailed submission to the 1942 Tariff Board enquiry into the automotive industry. The FCAI submission was that import quotas, or prohibitive barriers were not needed and also pressed for the repeal of two pieces of legislation, the *Motor Vehicle Agreement* and *Engine Bounty Acts*. When asked by the Secretary of the Tariff Board of employment opportunities with local manufacture, French responded he felt 20,000 extra employees would be needed.[49]

Nothing happened for several months; meanwhile French was not just concerned about local manufacture. At a meeting with John Dedman, on December 31, 1943, French told him he was far more concerned with declining orders, and told Dedman that Ford would run out of orders in three months, and all stock by October, while GM-H and I.H had stocks of twelve months or more. Dedman told French that truck orders were declining and the government would not order more in 1944. No doubt aware of the implications for many of his constituents, after a pause, Dedman expressed an opinion that Ford 'had not been well served by DIVIMPRO (Division of Import Procurement) or the BPC (British Purchasing Commission) in Washington.' French agreed, saying that he knew 'our greatest competitor' knew of any Ford orders as soon as they were placed, obviously referring to Hartnett. Dedman also revealed tensions within the War cabinet, telling French of an ongoing argument between he, Jack Beasley, (Minister for Supply and Development) and Norman Makin, (Minister for Mines and Munitions) as to who would head up the

LEFT Cover of Ford magazine *US*, December, 1944. During WWII this magazine was published monthly by Ford Motor Company of Australia in collaboration with the Ford Employees' Shop Committee

portfolio of Post-War Development. Curtin solved the argument by passing the portfolio instead to Chifley, and establishing an advisory committee under John Jensen to look at the possibility of local motorcar manufacture.[50]

Nothing came out of Canberra for another nine months, until an excited Dedman rang French to tell him the subcommittee, comprising himself, Senator Jack Keane, Chifley and Norman Makin had decided to make a recommendation to Cabinet, to call for expressions of interest from the industry to make a local motorcar. No doubt, Dedman saw a great potential and future for his electorate. Dedman added one of the conditions was, 'If no ideas are forthcoming, we'll build it ourselves.' He also advised French that the time factor was critical and that French should arrange to travel to Canada immediately. French did so, leaving Australia in early October 1944. On October 10, 1944, the government issued the call for Expressions of Interest, which read in part:

1. *The repeal of the* Motor Vehicle Agreement Act.
2. *The repeal of the* Motor Engine Bounty Act.
3. *All interested parties be invited to submit proposals to the government.*
4. *When considering proposals, the utilization of government facilities for components should be considered as efficient units for future defence production.*
5. *If no satisfactory proposals received, the government would set up a Corporation to manufacture a complete car.*
6. *With a view to decentralisation, financial consideration be given to freight equalisation.*

Significantly, days after French left, Jensen, also on October 10, wrote to French, virtually spelling out what the government required, although couching it in terms of offering advice:

> *...as chair of the Secondary Industry Commission, I believe motor car manufacture will expand industry. (I am) not offering advice, merely expressing an opinion for Ford to note when making a submission.*
>
> *There is post war demand for vehicles.*
>
> *I believe a lower priced car will be most popular & economic proposition for the typical purchaser.*
>
> *Personally, I do not think the large American car, the typical prewar type, will meet the bulk of the market. A small car, economical to run and with light fuel consumption is the type people will prefer.*

He went on, saying he was impressed with small English cars, but not their engine, feeling a car in between the two would be preferable. He also expressed the confidence that Ford, with its heavy industrial investment and wartime experience had the ability to produce such a car. He added there would be no discrimination against foreign capital, and concluded, 'Do not hesitate to contact me if needed.'Pity French only read the memo on his return.

On January 5, barely three months after the government call for Expressions of Interest, Hartnett and GM-H made their submission to the government, detailing plans for a five-seater sedan and related utility, unique to, and of, Australian design and specification. GM-H would draw on GM sources from overseas for technical assistance, and use existing facilities to ensure low cost. Body manufacture would be at the South Australian Woodville plant, meeting the government's desire for decentralization, while Melbourne would manufacture the engines and transmissions. GM-H would invest £2,500,000 but sought assurance of no government competition, that GM be allowed to build other vehicles and that the undistributed profits tax would be removed.

In content and structure, it was almost identical to the government memo and Jensen's letter to French. A three-month time frame to pull together a proposal of such size and detail smacks of foreknowledge by Hartnett, and cynicism in approach on the part of Jensen, almost certainly of collusion between the two, although probably not for personal gain. Perhaps the following comment in Jensen's biography in the *Australian Dictionary of Biography* says it all:

> *...from 1943 he had been foundation chairman of the Secondary Industries Planning Commission in the Department of Post-War Reconstruction: the dubious procedures by which he encouraged General Motors-Holden to begin manufacturing motor vehicles in Australia have been criticised...*[51]

However, French and Ford of Canada blew it. They completely missed the pent up demand following the austerity of the war years. They misread the market as to the type of passenger vehicle the population would want, and as envisaged by the Government. Or perhaps they dreamed of the days of Henry Ford, with market domination and shares of 30% or more. In any case, French and Ford of Canada focused on the necessity of achieving a volume of 25,000 vehicles, a third of a projected total market. They believed this could only be met with a combination of passenger vehicles and trucks, thus completely ignoring the point of the Governments' invitation and the (tardy) Jensen memo.

The Ford submission, in brief called for the manufacture of:

- Two sedans, both of 118 inch wheelbases, one based on the Ford vehicle, the other based on the more luxurious Mercury
- Two coupe utilities and two station wagons, one each on 114 inch and 118 inch wheelbase
- A Panel Van with 114 inch wheelbase
- Complete range of trucks with wheelbases of 134 inch, 158 inch, 174 inch & 194 inch, plus a bus chassis

RIGHT 1946 Mercury Sedan Brochure

The project required an investment of £4,000,000. Ford requested twelve 'undertakings by Government' including a favorable exchange rate with the Canadian dollar, and a subsidy of £850,000. Ford requested increased tariffs and import controls on rival companies' chassis, and relief from the existing price controls. Ford also suggested a public share offering, with the Government to take up shares in the new structure.

Even within Ford, there were doubts as to the wisdom of such a restrictive and exclusive proposal that relied on significant government support. Sir Arthur Robinson wrote to French on March 8, 1945, expressing his concerns that the Ford submission, in asking for capital support would be financially and politically unacceptable to the Government. On the other hand, Ford Canada was adamant in asking for government assistance. On March 22, the export manager of Ford of Canada, Milliken, wrote:

> *...agree with your presentation provided it is made quite clear that assistance will be necessary and that agreement as to the nature of such assistance will also be necessary before you can proceed to complement your proposal.*[52]

French made the Ford submission to Jensen in Canberra on April 4, 1945 and on April 28, John Dedman advised French he had received the proposal and that a subcommittee, chaired by W. Scott of the Secondary Industry Commission (SIC), would review the proposal.

The negotiations were rather public. Both GM-H and Ford wrote to their respective dealerships advising them of the details of each submission, optimistically requesting they remain confidential. There was an article written in the London Financial Times on March 15 1945, announcing the Australian government was negotiating with American and British manufacturers with a view to local manufacture. It informed readers that two were most likely to materialise, one from GM-H, the other from the English Nuffield group (British Motor Corporation). There was no mention of a Ford or a Canadian submission.

Through May and June 1945, the subcommittee met with Ford. While much time was spent analysing the project, little progress was made, as French noted when reporting back to Canada, that he felt the committee was obviously having a great deal of difficulty in grasping the detail of the submission and getting cooperation from all of the many government departments involved.

LEFT 1946 Mercury Club Coupe Utility Flyer

Meanwhile, with peace in Europe and imminent in Asia, the government was facing its own problems. Prime Minister Curtin, incapacitated from April, died in July 1945, and was replaced by his deputy, Ben Chifley. As treasurer during the war years Chifley, with memories of the problems caused by the WWI debt and the 1930s depression, had managed the wartime economy with a mixture of increased taxation, war savings loans from the public, central bank credit and repeated calls for austerity and sacrifice. However, in the aftermath of the war, Australia still had significant problems with debt and the government simply did not have the ability to lend money, let alone allow overseas debt to balloon. The government and the country now faced several years of stringent currency and import controls. Moreover, in 1945–46, the situation was getting worse.

On September 8, subcommittee chairman Scott met French at his hotel in Sydney. The news was not good. The dollar exchange situation was now critical, Scott said, and had worsened since the Ford proposal in April. He told French the government could not agree with the Ford proposal:

- It was impossible for government to undertake to provide dollar exchange.
- The government would not provide funds, although the government might be willing to subscribe to some Capital shares.
- The government was unable to make any special provision for Ford, nor be able to increase tariffs, exercise import control, or extend any assistance. Nor would there be any relief regarding price control.

As a last throw of the dice, French requested a meeting with Prime Minister Chifley on September 12. At that meeting, French explained to Chifley that while local manufacture was the

RIGHT *Women's Weekly* advertisement, September 1945

FAR RIGHT *Women's Weekly* advertisement, May 1946

primary reason for his visit, it was of secondary importance to employment. Even though Ford of Canada had allotted early production of chassis for Australia to help, Ford had 900 men returning from service and their employment was a serious concern. On discussing the currency crisis, French asked whether Ford could purchase goods in Canadian dollars. Chifley reiterated the dollar exchange situation generally was serious, import restrictions could not be lifted, and the best Chifley could hope was for only one-third of Australia's currency requirement to be met from the London dollar pool. Australia's expenditure in dollars had to be carefully screened and confined to essential requirements. When French asked Chifley did he not consider the auto industry a vital industry, Chifley responded that while commercial vehicles were highly essential, he had reservations about passenger vehicles, although no doubt, some could be considered essential. French pushed harder, asking Chifley about purchasing goods in pound sterling. Chifley responded that the pound sterling was quite buoyant but if imports from UK were in any large volume, this would also be under pressure in a few months, and would continue. The discussion turned to local manufacture and the Ford proposal. Chifley said that, as the dollar import problems would persist for some years the government was not prepared to offer Ford the assistance they requested. He suggested he would like to see the Ford proposal implemented, as it had a genuineness lacking in others.

Further meetings with the subcommittee took place over the next two months but made little progress, French and Ford were on the back foot and time was against them. At one meeting when French, wanting assurances of achieving the 25,000 sales, asked the committee whether the government would limit currency to GM-H to reduce imports of other vehicles, the committee prevaricated. French recorded later it was obvious no progress was made. The meeting concluded with Scott arranging to advise officially the Ford proposal could not be accepted in total and they would offer alternatives.[53]

Finally, on November 28, 1945, Prime Minister Chifley wrote to French, acknowledging the Ford submission. He noted that while the Parliament had repealed the *Engine Bounty and Motor Vehicle Agreement Acts,* and passed the *Sales Tax Exemption Act,* it was unable to accept the Ford proposal. He wrote the government had now determined its policy and hoped Ford could proceed with the new local content rules, which he detailed.

This was clearly a setback, but French replied to the Prime Minister on November 29, 1945, advising he was reviewing how he could achieve the government's objectives while satisfying his overseas shareholders. He presumed he would have to make any further submissions through the Secondary Industry Commission. He wrote to Milliken in Canada the same day, anxious to get a response. By February, however, things were clearly going badly for Ford. French wrote to Milliken:

> *We are being pressed to submit new proposals for substantial manufacture based on the Prime Ministers letter of November 29. We are told by an official of chief competitor that they expect to produce a local car in 1948 and are planning on 8,000 first year, 12,000 the second year and 20,000 the third year, with design and prototypes being developed in Detroit. In an interview with Minister for Post-War Reconstruction, our attention was sharply drawn to the probable drastic curtailment and strict control of both Dollar and Sterling exchange for several years and he indicated that the automotive industry should take prompt action in its own interests. In view of the wide divergence between the facts stated in your cable and the views of the Commonwealth government as expressed herein, the position is more than ever confused and we would welcome your thoughts as to the type of approach we should next make.*

Ford of Canada meanwhile had its own problems. A major strike had closed the plant for more than two months, pickets had even prevented the offices in Windsor operating. French wrote again to Milliken on March 7, 1946:

> *I recognise the difficulties with which you are confronted…We have thus far staved off any further conference with the SIC, but I think it will be unwise to postpone it much longer. We will probably have a further preliminary skirmish with them in the next couple of weeks, but the conference will be purely exploratory as far as we are concerned and we will naturally make no commitments.*

TOM CLANCY

Things have changed quite a bit from when I first started, he said. *There were paddocks all around the plant—real countryside! And most people used to come to work on pushbikes. Instead of a car park full of cars, there were racks and racks of bikes. There was no canteen. There were stools along the back of the building, and we sat wherever we could find room. The nearest shop was one on Parramatta Road owned by a lady called Mrs. Stevens. We ordered our lunch—you could only get sandwiches—and the shop brought it up to the plant. Trucks could only enter and leave via Parramatta Road, where the Medical centre is now. There were railway lines too, although they've been concreted over. They went right through the plant and big buffers full of stock, came all the way from Geelong. After the war there was a recession,* Tom recalls. *We were down to only producing about six units a day between 1946 and 1948. They were hard times for many people. My office in the plant was a desk and a chair surrounded by a wire fence. It was a bit draughty!*

Clearly, French knew the battle was lost. Neither the government nor Ford of Canada would budge on the position of government assistance. As long as Ford persisted in achieving the volume with a complete range instead of just the sedan and a utility, the Ford investment would be too high, driving the need for government investment. All the dire predictions of currency controls and import restrictions by the government came true, and to Ford's clear and distinct disadvantage. The failure would haunt Ford for the next fifteen years.

French turned to other avenues in order to keep his workforce. The program to purchase and refurbish obsolete military vehicles was already well underway. French lobbied hard for Canada to approve funds for equipment to recondition engines, and as the government was vacating the Annexe, funds to purchase both the building and the equipment, before it was removed by the government as war contracts ended. Attempts to find work for the company and to circumvent the currency crisis varied. Lamb wrote to French on August 17, 1945 suggesting that, as Dagenham prices for Anglia and Prefect components had risen by 68% and 64% respectively compared to Australia's manufacturing costs increase of 30%, previously imported components should therefore be manufactured in Australia. He also suggested introducing a four-door saloon, as 'the English two-door does not sell here'.

ABOVE 1949 Anglia 10 brochure

One of the surprise successes for Ford in 1949 was the importation of the English V8 Pilot sedan. Not known for its reliability, the Pilot was a vehicle cobbled together from old components dating back from before the war and newer body components. They sold like hotcakes.

Lyn Hamilton recalled that Ford charted ships to get them to Australia as fast as they could. Many were fully assembled, some semi built up, but every single one sold as soon as they hit the showroom floor. On smooth roads the Pilot rode well but did not perform well on corrugated roads; the grille alone had a tendency to rattle and fall apart. You either put up with it, or kept replacing the grille. With the Pilots, Ford also began importing the Anglia and the cheaper, Prefect. Ford imported more vehicles from Canada, notably the single spinner and twin spinner Customline

LEFT 1949 Ford Single Spinner advertisement

FAR LEFT 1948 Ford Prefect 10 advertisement

sedans. The tipping point was 1948 as the Ford product range source swung from Canada to England.

The anniversary celebrations of twenty-one years in Australia were relief as much as celebration. Ford had survived a tough decade, capping it off with the historically highest production on record. However, the stress had taken its toll on French. In 1949, he announced a program of expansion to increase local content of Ford cars and trucks in line with government legislation, integrating chassis components which, in typical Ford fashion, returned a greatest percentage return for the investment. It was a compromise but a huge defeat for the company and French personally. After announcing the expansion program, Hubert French aged sixty-eight, announced his stepping down as Managing Director. He remained a director of the company for another two years before retiring permanently to Barwon Heads. Ford of Canada appointed a new Managing Director, Charles (Charlie) Smith, and a new chapter of Ford in Australia began.

After the war and while the tooling for the FX Holden was being built, GM-H imported chassis from the USA, building Buick, Chevrolet, and Pontiac vehicles, and from England to build Vauxhall vehicles. To further rub salt into Ford's open wounds, although only a couple of hundred Holden were built in 1948, 18,000 people signed up to buy one, sight unseen. By 1950 GM-H were building eighty vehicles per day. The Dandenong plant was built in 1951 and by 1952, were selling 32,000 a year, far in excess of French's desire to build 25,000 vehicles. It is ironic however, that Laurence Hartnett, the man who had driven so hard to make 'Australia's Own Car' was not at its launch in November 1948. A maverick to the end, he had pushed General Motors too far, was sidelined in December 1946, and resigned in April, 1947. His successor, H.E. Bettle, had the honour of driving the first FX Holden.

CHAPTER 4

1950 – 1959

THE FORD YEARS 1950–1959

1951:

Consul Mark I and Zephyr models introduced. £6 million expansions announced for Geelong, Brisbane, and Fremantle.

1952:

Fordson Major tractors introduced. Customline and Australian designed Mainline utility introduced. Zephyr Six introduced.

1954:

New model Prefect and Familiar introduced. $540,000 expansion announced for Geelong, new stamping press lines installed. New engine assembly lines installed. Nationwide, The Ford Radio show launched reaching one million people.

1955:

Australian-built Customline and Mainline vehicles assembled with new locally assembled V8 engines. New Anglia and Prefect range released and the English commercial range extended. Utility version of Zephyr and Consul designed and produced in Australia.

1956:

Melbourne Olympic games. Mark II Consuls and Zephyrs released. Brian Inglis completes overseas Graduate Training program. Four hundred acres of land purchased for new assembly plant at Campbellfield.

1957:

New model plans for Mark III Zephyr cancelled. Falcon selected. Foundations commence at Broadmeadows site. Two new Zephyr and Consul utilities launched, designed, tested and built in Australia, developed by Ford designers at Geelong for the Australian market.

1958:

Modernisation program commences at Geelong, new engine plant, office building, Sydney P & A building extended. Fordson Dexta light tractor range released. A new vehicle range which has never been marketed by the company—the Thames Series 800—is introduced to the Australian market.

1959:

Ballarat plant converted to engine reconditioning. Broadmeadows plant commissioned, first vehicle offline on August 20, 1959—a Fairlane 500. Charles Smith retires, replaced by John McIntyre. Ford Australia release 1959 range of Consul and Zephyr sedans and utilities. Station wagons, the first Ford has designed and manufactured in Australia, are also released.

Charlie Smith was like French, of solid build although shorter in stature by some 10 cm. Baby-faced, balding, what little hair remaining swept straight back, Smith was born in Birmingham, England and migrated to Canada in 1911. Joining the Canadian Second Division, he saw five years active service in France and Belgium. He joined Ford in 1926 as a sales clerk in the Regina branch, Saskatchewan, was a branch auditor from 1930 to 1941, then branch manager in Regina and Winnipeg. During World War II he was the company's technical liaison with the British Army, with the nominal rank of Major, before returning to Winnipeg after the war.

With Ford of Canada responsible for the operations of countries within the Commonwealth, it sent rising stars overseas. Appointed Managing Director of Ford South Africa in 1946, Canada asked Charlie to move again in 1950, this time to become, at fifty-six, Managing Director of Ford Australia. His round softer looks belied his manner; Charlie Smith was a good operator, easy to talk to, a keen judge of character, but demanding and tough. One of his first official functions on assuming his Australian role was, as part of the Silver Anniversary celebrations, to address employees in Geelong and Ballarat and present gold watches to pioneer employees who had been with Ford from 1925. Smith's message was unequivocal:

> *Leadership in sales, in the standard of service to owners and in the quality of our products. We should be satisfied with nothing less than this in Australia.*

There were difficult times ahead however: overseas, Ford US was struggling with outdated vehicles and technology, slipping to third place in the market, behind G.M. and Chrysler Corporation. The malaise had filtered through the entire organisation, with Ford of Canada complacent with Ford Australia remaining an importer and assembler. Profitable, but hampered by currency restrictions, import controls and the onerous burden of the local content rules which drove investment by demanding 85% local content. Smith had to re-energise the company, changing its attitudes and beliefs. As French had said, the government seemed focused on engine manufacturing as a priority. It seemed appropriate that Smith should begin lobbying hard for Ford Australia to commence an expansion program, which included building V8 engines.

In a publicity release in September 1951, announcing the £6 million expansion over the next four years, Smith made much of aligning Ford with the government's philosophy:

> *We have tailored our expansion project to fit the national expansion plans of the Australian Government and throughout the intricate planning involved have been given strong and valuable support by (local member) Mr. R.G. Casey and the present Minister for National Development, Senator Spooner.*

The release went on to say that in the event of a national emergency, Australia would be able to produce power units for heavy military vehicles and other defence needs—removing what in the past had been one of the most serious handicaps facing

PAGES 74–75 First Fairlanes complete final inspection, August, 1959

BELOW Homebush Assembly Plant in Sydney, 1950

ABOVE *Austra-Ford Gazette* reports snow in Geelong, September 1951

those planning Australia's defence. The release itemised the expenditure for Geelong (£4.75 million), Sydney (£780,000), Brisbane (£325,000) and Perth (£150,000) and also spoke of Australia's transport needs, the technical details of the investment and the local content of the Ford V8, (approximately 60%). The article also predicted Ford local content would be 90% by 1955.

While the release spoke of doubling Ford's capacity, there was nothing from his previous address to employees and the main reason for the investment—leadership in sales, service and quality. Later, the October issue of Ford's in-house magazine *The Ford Gazette* detailed the expansion. Capacity of the West Australian plant would rise by two-thirds, 'huge sand hills will be moved to make way'. Homebush would have a new three-acre building erected to supply the New South Wales market as well as producing V8s, Consul and Zephyr bodies for Queensland. The Queensland plant capacity would expand by 50%, with a new paint shop to allow bodies to be finished with a special tropics-resistant 'high bake' enamel. The recently expanded South Australia plant would produce Consul and Zephyr bodies for Western Australia.

The news of the expansion revitalised both the company and its dealers, who spoke enthusiastically of the program when interviewed by their local papers. The publicity alone boosted confidence in the company.

Buried in the same issue of *The Ford Gazette* was a small article reporting that a young Engineer, Brian Inglis, had recently returned from Canada after more than two years overseas, participating in Ford Canada's executive training scheme, to establish an Industrial Engineering department, later to become Manufacturing Engineering. Mentioned elsewhere at the same time, was news of the establishment of a 'Methods and Coordination' department headed by a young man from the Finance department, William (Bill) Dix.

Smith initiated the graduate training program, styled on that of Ford Canada. The initial intake was ten per year, eight recruited

RIGHT Prefect assembly line Fremantle, 1953

LEFT 1956 Consul Mark I

from universities around Australia, two places reserved for internal candidates already employed by the company. This program provided the nucleus of future management with spectacular and far-reaching results. Many were to become directors of the company and influence Ford in the future, to mention only a few: John Marshall, later Director of Manufacturing, Ken McDonald, later Director of Human Resources, Ian Vaughan, Vice President of Product Development and his brother Roger, a manager in the Supply Office.

Another program, if not initiated by Smith, certainly fostered by him, was the apprenticeship program. With the expansions planned, the tool room would be a three-shift operation and initially, there were not enough tradesmen in the Geelong area. The Ford Geelong apprenticeship program was extensive and highly sought after. The prestige of being selected to become a Ford apprentice had some standing within the community and the competition resulted in selection of only the best and brightest. Ford established the apprentice school under an apprentice master in the Annexe across the road for a time before transferring it to its own complex, when the building was taken over by Parts and Accessories. The fifty or sixty apprentices of all trades selected each year also provided a future management resource that paid dividends for years to come.

Ford introduced the 1951 Consul and Zephyr models with much fanfare, but import and currency restrictions limited the market penetration of both—the Zephyr handicapped by a volume and price disadvantage to the all-conquering Holden. While not manufacturing any individual vehicle anywhere near the scale of the Holden, volumes continued to grow and Ford, with its full range of vehicles, managed to achieve its highest sales ever that year, with a total of 25,567 vehicles, comprising 10,296 English passenger, 4,695 Canadian passenger and a total of 10,576 English and Canadian commercials.

RIGHT 1954 Zephyr-Six advertisement

RIGHT Cortina Utility, Tip Top bakeries

'TICH' MCGLEISH & JOHN MCCABE

Slim of build and short in stature, 'Tich' McGleish had been involved with a circus before he joined Ford Geelong. 'Tich' was quite a climber and thought nothing of scaling the plant columns and walking along the roof trusses for fun, even changing the bulbs of the large arc lights above the trusses. Plant Manager John McCabe, ever concerned about safety, issued an edict that before climbing a ladder, one must ensure the ladder was secured at the top by tying it in place with a rope. Unworkable? Not at all. 'Tich' scaled one of the columns, walked through the trusses until he got to the ladder, tied it in place, returned along the trusses and climbed down again, then proceeded to climb the ladder. That edict didn't last long.

Sales dropped somewhat in 1952, then with the increasing availability of vehicles from England and overseas currency to pay for them, over the next three years Ford broke all previous production records with totals of 32,987 vehicles in 1953, and 37,208 in 1954. With the Korean conflict dragging on, Ford continued the relationship with the army with substantial sales of trucks to the army as well as, for the first time, a common Defence Force ambulance.

Charlie Smith gave Lew Bandt the go-ahead to develop a Consul utility during 1953 and two prototypes were made, one to be sent to the U.K. for evaluation and approval. However, FOB took so long with the evaluation that it became impractical to introduce the model before the introduction of the Mark II series in 1956. Another series of prototypes were built, six in all, this time using the Zephyr as the base.

Without approval from FOB, Lew, Ken Williams and Fred Arkley set off on what was probably the first Ford Australia durability run, to Perth and back across the Nullarbor. For safety, a Canadian Mainline utility was used as backup, carrying fuel and spares, there being little of either between Port Augusta and Coolgardie. The road between Penong and Coolgardie was deeply rutted and corrugated, worse than the previous sectors. Lew, driving one of the Zephyrs, set such a cracking pace the others had difficulty keeping up with him.

LEFT 1952 Ford Mainline Coupe Utility brochure

The durability run was a disaster, but not for the Zephyrs. The Mainline suffered terribly during the run, unable to match them. Finally, after changing twenty-two front shock absorbers and breaking the left-hand steering idler arm on the Mainline, they ran out of spares. Lew camped for several days by the side of the road with the stricken Mainline while the others drove the Zephyrs back several hundred miles to Penong, where the Ford dealer rang Dalgety's in Adelaide. When the parts arrived from Geelong, Dalgety's flew the parts to Ceduna, another 45 miles further back. Luckily, no further incidents occurred during the rest of the trip. Production of the Mark II Consul and Zephyr Utes began August 1957 in Geelong, September in the other four plants.

Even in this record-breaking period, Ford could not compete with GM-Hs Holden, which now controlled 50% of the market. Sir Brian best expressed the mood of the time in a 1988 interview with Professor David Lewis:

> *...Charlie Smith had visited the GM-H plant in Melbourne in 1952 and been shown around by the Directors. He reciprocated, inviting them to Geelong. Shortly after, Charlie called me to his office and asked me to show the GM-H Director of Purchasing around the plant. I took him through the stamping plant, which in those days were mostly second-hand presses sent out from Canada in 1924. The presses*

RIGHT 1951 Ford Thames Truck brochure

weren't set out in press lines then, (they were) laid out in what we called the oasis system, with a major draw press almost surrounded by a circle of single action presses, which were used as appropriate for the job being run. It was fairly crude, looking back. Anyway, after the tour, I took him back to the Managing Director's office where we had to wait a few minutes. As we waited he said, 'I want to thank you for taking me around, I'd like to summarise what I've seen. I've looked at your facilities and honestly, you are twenty years behind us. We have new facilities installed, modern presses set up in production lines, its productivity is substantially greater than yours and the volume that goes with it has allowed us to greatly reduce our costs. Your work tempo is hampered by the way it is organised, it's very old-fashioned and labour-intensive compared to what we have in GM. Not only is our volume three to four times yours, yours is also fragmented. Our costs are much less than yours will ever be at your volumes. We have our own product development, a large product-engineering centre, test tracks and the supporting infrastructure of which you have none. Our dealers are in prime positions; they are wealthy and with facilities you can't match. I can't see how you will ever catch us'.[54]

The peak for Ford came in 1955, with the release of the new Anglia and Prefect models and the Mark I Consul and Zephyr range. The release of the 5A Customline sedan and the 51AU Mainline range of utilities from Canada the same year complimented the range. In that year, Ford built 40,087 vehicles, of which 24,056 were English passenger vehicles, 10,847 Canadian passenger and 5,184 trucks, a volume which Ford would

LES POWELL

If you want to know anything about the Ford at Geelong, ask Les Powell. Les is the Guest Relations Officer on the Public Relations staff. His task is to conduct visitors around the huge manufacturing plant at Geelong—a job that takes on a seven miles trek each day, explaining the working of each of the machines that turn out 100 cars daily. Les conducts 700 people over the plant each month. About half are visitors to Victoria—from all states and New Zealand. They shoot all sorts of questions at him as he goes along and he's never been known to be stuck for an answer. Les estimates he's asked about 1,500 questions a day. That's getting on for half a million questions, and answers, a year! Surveying the mountain of tyres, one visitor asked, 'How many tyres a year are needed?' Les promptly replied, 'The figure last year was 145,781'. A woman, fascinated by the sewing in the upholstery department will enquire about the amount of cotton thread used and be told it spins out to 12,000 miles per year. A party of pressmen recently visited the plant as part of the launch of the 1951 models and were staggered with his familiarity with every detail of the thousand and one operations. That and his knowledge of the Christian name of more than half of the 3,000 employees at Geelong, which he says is a result of a long association with Ford and a cheery good nature that makes friends easily.

LEFT 1956 F500 V8 truck

only exceed with the introduction of the Falcon in 1960. The expansion plans put in by Charlie Smith were paying off and the profits continued.

Both the Consul and Zephyr, designed with McPherson Strut front suspensions, meant they handled well and gave a superior ride to the Holden. The Zephyr, with its light body and 6-cylinder engine was quick off the mark and competed well with the Holden, although at a price disadvantage. However, Ford like any importer, then and now, were supplying vehicles designed for other markets. There was no test and development, or durability trials. The vehicles came in CKD (completely knocked down) cases, assembled on the assembly line and shipped to the dealers. Local components were the same as their overseas counterparts, made from the same product drawings. Any build problems or quality issues were fed straight back to the manufacturing or shipping source.

The good times were not to last. Max Gransden recalled the Mark I Consul suffered from two major problems, one directly related to the different road conditions encountered in Australia. Differentials on country vehicles often lasted only 1,500–2,000 miles and a savage clutch, with its sudden take up often resulted in 'kangaroo hop' starts. In an interview with *Ford News* on his retirement in 1989, Max Gransden quipped:

> *Where other companies had change-over starter motors, Ford had changeover diffs for the Consul!* [55]

City vehicles lasted longer, but fleet owners soon noticed the problems and stopped buying the Consul. The public followed suit; quality issues and price penalties are death in the automotive industry, and over the next two years, Ford total vehicle production declined by 30%. While registering a small increase in 1956 over 1955 with the launch of the Mark II Consul in 1956, volumes dropped 42% in 1957 and never recovered. Complaints to FOB came back with the same answer: 'We don't recognise that issue as a problem here', and no corrective action resulted.

Adding to Ford's problems, the Federal government raised personal income tax in January 1956 from 35% to 40%, followed in March by an increase in sales tax on passenger vehicles. Then in April the same year, the government cut import quotas from non-dollar sources by 5%, followed by a further 30% from July 1, 1956. Total sales collapsed from the record 40,087 in 1955 to 29,258 in 1957.

The quality concerns only marginally affected the Zephyr, which dropped by 3,327 units in the 1956 launch year, recovered completely in 1957 before increasing to 19,792 vehicles in 1958, remaining at that level for the remainder of the model life. However, with the popularity and fuel economy of the Holden,

RIGHT 1958 8A Customline

Canadian vehicles also declined in volume. The 5A Customline sedan production in 1955 was 7,699 vehicles. By the time the 8A Customline was released in 1958, volumes had halved to 3,386. Similarly with the Mainline 51AU utility; from production in 1955 of 3,148, by 1958, with the release of the 59AU, production was a mere 1,057 vehicles.

The quality and cost differentials, followed by the imposition of import controls only spurred Smith further to agitate for an Australian manufactured vehicle. The Ford US product was not what Australians wanted, while the Zephyr, closest to the Holden in size and performance could not compete with it on price. Smith began pressuring Ford Canada and lobbied Ford US for funds and approval to build the Zephyr in Australia. Smith knew that if Ford was ever to become more than just another high-cost, low-volume assembler, Ford had to meet the government's 85% local content rules and manufacture a vehicle that matched or beat the Holden in every respect.

As well as the Consul quality issues and the import quotas, Smith flagged the ongoing investment by GM-H, the increasing competiveness of Chrysler, the Rootes group and Volkswagen as potential threats. All were investing in assembly plants to meet the local content requirements of the government. All his business plans projected, and were verified by forecast and actual sales, that Ford was increasingly dominant in a declining 'large car' V8 market, while GM-H was growing more dominant in the 'medium car' 6-cylinder market.

Ford Canada finally conceded in 1955 that the local content requirements and changes in market dictated that stage four of the side-valve V8 engine plant, launched in 1951, should be deferred pending a review. Stage four was the local casting of the

JESS PITTMAN

After the war, many migrants came down from Bonegilla looking for work. Late one Friday a well-spoken man came into the office to apply for a job. When he filled out his application form, his handwriting was just beautiful. 'You must be a poet,' Jess joked. Seriously, he replied, 'Yes I do write poetry.' The office had closed by then and any new employees would not start until the following Monday, but he was desperate for any work. Mr. Westman had told Jess there were no jobs left, but when she looked at his application form, she saw he was a doctor and spoke seven languages. She went back to Mr. Westman again to see if there was one position available. There was; sweeping floors, and he could start the next day (Saturday). Jess recalled, 'He was so grateful. He would bow to me every time I walked past him in the plant. Shortly after, there was a vacancy in the first aid office, so I recommended him. Mr. Westman rang me and told me to go to the first-aid office later that morning. There he was, decked out in a white coat, stethoscope and all, proud as anything, really looking the part. He was the best first aider we ever had.'

FORD AIDS BARWON RIVER FLOOD VICTIMS

Many employees living at Geelong and Barwon Heads were rendered homeless by Victoria's worst floods in twenty years when the Barwon River burst its banks in 1952. The floods first affected the migrant hostel at Belmont. Ford sent home all affected employees, followed by fellow employees and Company equipment. All residents of the hostel were evacuated safely, which was soon 4 feet under water. Guest Relations Officer Les Powell worked long hours helping others, but soon found his own Barwon Heads home also under threat. A tractor school for dealers was being held at Geelong and soon a semitrailer carrying Fordson tractors was on its way to Barwon Heads. While many employees were filling sandbags, Ford tractors equipped with bulldozer blades and rabbit rippers set about digging channels and building banks to divert the floodwaters, banked up by high tides and rough seas, which flooded the town. Three weeks later, the town was again threatened with flooding after more heavy rain. Ford employees and equipment responded a second time to avert a second flood, which luckily was not as severe as the first.

engine block, cylinder head, crankshaft and camshaft. The review determined it was better to delay the introduction of stage four and wait for the newer OHC-V8 engine being introduced in the US. Canada also agreed with the need for a new assembly plant, somewhere in Melbourne, extensions to existing assembly plants, and new presses and dies.

Projects totaling £21.6 million were approved, but Smith was not satisfied, he wanted market leadership. The expansion was only to produce 170 vehicles per day nationally, 40,000 per year, while GM-H already had capacity to build 100,000. Smith went for broke. The 1955 business plan included a complete review of the company and its products. Plan 1956 contained four options, which examined each of the existing product groups. North American (NA) sourced passenger and trucks were approximately 80% local content and set to increase with completion of stage four of the V8 engine project. The Consul and Zephyr ranges were only about 60% while the other UK sourced products were assembled from CKD packs.

Broadly, plan 1956 considered a locally built Zephyr, extensions to the existing V8 engine plant to include manufacture of 6-cylinder engines, chassis plant extensions, a new assembly plant and extensions to the other four. The plan also considered four options involving the other UK and North American sourced vehicles, all options being a variation of the theme. The review presented advantages and disadvantages of each plan, but plan 1956/1 was always preferred, despite forecasting no dividends for five years. The other three options contained no real long-term benefits.

The key advantages of plan 1956/1 were market leadership, containment of GM-H and relief from import quotas.

And, with typical Smith enthusiasm, 'Oh and by the way, we'll need a total of £76.8 million (an increase of £36.9 million), but look at the return on investment (before tax) of 19.7%'! Who could say no?

Ford US, in the process of subsuming Ford Canada, agreed with some of the proposals and rejected others. It made sense to defer the completion of the V8 engine plant project until the new OHC-V8 engine from Ford US became available. Ford would continue to import the major components and machine them locally, while building a new local, US designed 6-cylinder engine. They approved the new assembly plant and the retention of the other plants, expanded or modified. KD import of some US V8 vehicles would continue on a reduced scale with some UK models dropped. As usual, Ford US told Smith to thrift the project by 10% before approving the now-reduced, £20 million project. Smith complied gladly; he'd padded it that much anyway.

Local manufacture of the Mark III Zephyr range was approved. Now all Ford Australia had to do was double the (national) vehicle assembly rate from 170–320 vehicles a day, build a new 715,000 square foot assembly plant from scratch, change a vehicle assembly plant into an engine plant, modify four other assembly plants, expand the tool room by nearly 50%, expand the stamping plant by 30%, and double the number of employees. Simple.

In 1956, spurred on by his workmates, 'Tunner' Kenworthy applied for a job advertised on the plant notice board for an Industrial Officer. After an interview with Personnel Manager Maurie Williams, 'Tunner' was offered the job. It was an inspired move. 'Tunner' was fair, pulled no punches and did much to resolve, not only industrial issues, but many personal issues with employees, particularly migrants, many of whom had moved into the suburb of Bell Park. The union, under 'Tunner' did much for the employees, initiating the Children's Day that, when it became too large to hold in local halls, was transferred to the plant, with Ford subsidising the cost. The annual Christmas party was another initiative with 'Tunner' as a prime mover.

The core elements slowly came together. On Brian Inglis' completion of a Graduate Training program in Canada and a stint with Overseas Operations in Canada and the United States, Charlie Smith asked him to return to Australia in 1956 to head up an Industrial Engineering Group, later known as Manufacturing Engineering. This group absorbed one earlier formed by Harry Hickman and reported initially to Slim Westman. Brian later recalled Westman built them a new office in the assembly plant (none of this front office stuff), above a bank of air compressors:

> *The compressors shook the office, you could say we were in a constant state of agitation, pencils would be vibrating all over the desks. But we were very enthusiastic about bringing change (to a static organisation). We brought in a group for material handling and a group for work standards. Our work was not really understood and it was said there would be terrible union opposition. We were really starting from behind scratch, both technically and psychologically.*[56]

Smith recruited another Canadian, from South Africa, Gene Chorolsky to head up the Plant Engineering function of the Program Group. Their task was to provide modern facilities, install equipment with the latest technology to produce the required volume at the projected cost.

One of the first decisions made was the site of the new assembly plant. While not far from Melbourne, nevertheless, the size of the project and the proposed workforce mitigated against Geelong. Ford evaluated twenty-three sites nationally, but rejected most early in the process. The new plant had to be closer to one of its major markets; Sydney was too distant from Geelong.

Coincident with the Ford plans, the political landscape in Victoria had changed. Up to 1955, there had been five turbulent years with Liberal and Labor governments, minority governments and changes in leadership. Then in 1953 after the loss of three leaders in eighteen months, Henry Bolte became leader of the Liberal-Country party. The 1955 split in the Labor party and the creation of what would become the Democratic Labor Party (DLP) allowed Bolte to get an act of no confidence in the Labor government passed and on May 28, Bolte and the Liberal Country

KEN 'TUNNER' KENWORTHY

'Tunner' Kenworthy was born in Ballarat and was two when he and his family moved to Geelong. He began his career at Ford in 1935, working in the spring department. With his father the Secretary of the Geelong Trades Hall, Tunner was always interested in unionism. In 1936, he and several others attempted to form a sub-branch of the Coachbuilders union. Tunner recalls it was hard getting employees to sign up, but eventually after several months, enough had signed to form a sub-branch. Tunner recalls they were never there to create trouble, but to work for the benefit of the employees and Ford. Sometime during the war, Ford agreed to the company being a closed shop, i.e. mandatory unionism. After the war Tunner, having worked as a welder on gun carriers, tanks, and barges, returned to the spring department, even moving to Ballarat for three months to help establish the Ballarat door and spring plant there. Eventually becoming President of the Vehicle Builders Union in Geelong, he applied for the position of Industrial Officer in the Industrial Relations department. 'Some people were upset when I resigned from the union to join 'The Other Side', he said, 'but I think it worked well for both the employees and the Company. That's what it was all about.'

THE FORD RETIREMENT FUND

'Tunner' Kenworthy said one thing that gave him a great sense of satisfaction was, with Alan Tyrer, Head of Industrial relations, to introduce the employee retirement benefit. 'We interviewed two or three people at a time to get them to sign up, explaining the retirement and death benefits for only 'a glass of beer a week', 1/3d.' One little guy, who worked in the yard breaking down crates, refused, he said. The next day he approached Tunner and apologised for not signing up, explaining he couldn't read or write, so Tunner filled out the forms for him. 'He rented a commission house, had a wife and two or three kids. Anyway, a month or so later, he went home after work, hopped into his old ute to go and pick up some paint, backed out of the driveway, was hit by a truck and killed. I visited his wife to give her his wages, we arranged his birth certificate for her and she and the kids got £1,000, enough to ensure they were not destitute. Sad but it demonstrated the benefit,' he said.

LEFT Premier Henry Bolte reviewing plans of Broadmeadows Assembly plant

party were elected to office. Bolte promised a government of action, but with a burgeoning population and consequent demand for services, could not afford to be generous. When Ford approached the government, looking for land on which to build the new assembly plant, Bolte was happy to negotiate the sale of 600 acres of Housing Commission land at what would become Broadmeadows for as little (then) as £500 per acre. Bolte was determined to keep Ford in Victoria. The only proviso was that in order to develop the site, Ford would have to lend £900,000 to the Victorian government, interest-free. In return the government would build Barry Road through to Pascoe Vale road, including a bridge over the main north–south Melbourne–Sydney rail line, and the Somerton Reservoir to extend water and sewerage services to the area. The government would also construct the Upfield railway station and a spur line into the plant.

Ford Canada considered the size too large and rejected the proposal but accepted an alternative proposal, the purchase of the southernmost 400 acres. Clyde Industries took up the remainder. Architect Stan McConnell visited the site, in great secrecy, in 1956 and wrote in 2002:

> *Barry Road was just a narrow dirt road across the uninhabited land between what would become the Hume Highway, and the very old single rail track where the Upfield railway station is now located. I remember driving very carefully up the unmade road to nowhere only to find a large boxthorn bush, a railway sign, and a couple making love in the backseat of a car behind the bush. There was nothing else for miles around, no buildings on Sydney Road which was a one-lane up, one-lane down rough edged bitumen road. Horses and cattle roamed freely across the paddocks which were flooded from the previous day's rain.*[57]

Bolte and Ford Canada signed the contracts in Canada, the deal announced in *The Sun* in Melbourne on October 24, 1956. Foundation work started on the site on November 1, 1957, with the blasting of the first of the rocky outcrops, endemic to the site.

Another option considered before the deal was signed, to alleviate the demand for space in Geelong, was to relocate the tool room to Melbourne. The most likely site at the time, was the BOC Gases, previously CIG, Plant site in Bell Street Preston, ultimately rejected as the surrounding areas, already developed, prevented any potential expansion. Ford ultimately abandoned plans to relocate the tool room altogether.

The complexity and magnitude of the project would have been daunting even today. The detail of the planning was equally complex and detailed. Binder after binder was prepared, nothing must be left to chance. One whole binder was devoted to classification of the workforce. First there were those who were to stay in Geelong. A second group would transfer to Broadmeadows, their move subsidised by the company. This group of 'sponsored'

SLIM WESTMAN

'Slim' Westman retired in May 1955, after nearly thirty years in Australia. At a retirement dinner in Geelong, attended by twenty dealers and senior Ford managers, Slim was presented with the keys of a Zephyr Six to mark the occasion. Those attending included Hubert French, Charlie Smith, Lyn Hamilton, Alan Tyrer, E. Scott Inglis and his replacement Walter Follis.

employees would move in two stages: 300 in stage 1, the remainder at stage 2. A third group of payroll personnel, 'non-sponsored' employees, comprising 900 from Geelong and 100 from Ballarat would have to move to Broadmeadows or be made redundant. One hundred salaried personnel would have to make the same decision: transfer or accept redundancy. Many made the move. Almost up to the day that Broadmeadows plant commenced, there was a belief in Geelong that Ford would not leave. In retrospect, Ford did not leave Geelong; the move to Melbourne in turn expanded Geelong immensely over the years with Manufacturing, comprising Stamping, Engine Assembly and Casting Plants, later known as Basic Manufacturing Operations, (BMO), Product Engineering and the Proving Grounds.

Ford needed government approval for the expansion, due to the large amounts of currency involved, and made a detailed submission to the Commonwealth government in February, 1957 entitled:

> *A Plan for the manufacture in Australia of an Australian motor vehicle in middle horsepower range (20–26 h.p. range comprising three models, viz., Sedan, Coupe Utility, and Van.*

It was the plan that should have been submitted twelve years earlier. It detailed the Ford local content to date, the planned expansion and objectives, export potential, project timeframe and analysis of the automotive market by model. It assured the government that Ford would fund the project internally, but requested a temporary increase in import quotas, predicting the increase would be more than offset by the reduction in overseas currency requirements on completion of the project. Ford requested a number of other assurances from the government while the project was in progress. The government approved the plan.

ABOVE John McIntyre and Charlie Smith

One effect of the local content rule was the over-investment in capacity. It is of interest that Ford knew then that over-capacity of the automotive industry was going to be a problem. An analysis of the industry, attached to the Ford Business plan 1958/1 dated October 1958 contained the following capacity information and the forecast sales: [58]

TABLE 4.1 | AUTOMOTIVE INDUSTRY CAPACITY 1957-1961

Company	Capacity	Projected Capacity
	1957	1961
General Motors	120,000	147,000
Ford	41,100	89,500
British Motor Corp. (BMC)	48,000	48,000
Volkswagen	15,000	30,000
Rootes Group	18,150	18,150
Chrysler	12,100	12,100
Standard Motor	24,200	24,200
Industry Capacity – Total	170,550	368,950
Sales Forecast	230,000	237,000

Should the investment have been made? For Ford, driven by market leadership ambitions, yes. For GM-H, possibly, the remainder, no. The British automotive industry was already in trouble at home. Even in 1956, the Chairman of Directors of Standard Motor Company, A.F. Crosby, was telling his shareholders that if the existing sales tax rate continued, the reduction of sales 'would render further investment uneconomic'.[59]

The year 1958 was one of hectic, secret activity. Styling of the new Zephyr III began in Detroit, work started on the extensions to the tool room and stamping plant, and planning began alterations to the other assembly plants, timed for later. The major activity was in Geelong and Melbourne; the other plants had to maintain production.

In October that year Smith flew to Detroit with the key members of the Program Group, Brian Inglis, Alan Tyrer, Gene Chorolsky and Len Hamilton to review the final clay models of

FORD FAMILIES

Through the years, many family groups are growing within our Ford Community with fathers, sons and daughters teaming together in our activities. In fact, at one stage, we could claim a father, son and grandson—the Graham family, 'Pop', Les and Jack. With Les and Jack now at our Gosford, NSW dealership they can still be counted as part of our overall team. However here in Geelong the honour of a third generation is now vacant, but judging by the increasing number of fathers and sons in our community, a third generation won't be too far off. We also have a father and three daughters in our employ. Ralph Lindross and his daughters Helmi, Dawn and Elma are all employed in the machine shop.

the Zephyr III, of which tooling for the long lead-time stamping tools had already commenced. Rhys Sale and Theodore Emmett, President and Vice president of Ford Canada respectively, met them and together they reviewed the clay models for the Zephyr III and another vehicle, tentatively named Falcon, the first of the so-called 'compacts' for the American and Canadian markets.

When Smith compared the Zephyr III clay, only a facelift of the Zephyr II, with that of the Falcon, his comments were scathing. The Zephyr would never beat the Holden he said. From a weight comparison between the 1957 Holden Special Deluxe sedan and the Zephyr Mark II Deluxe, he knew he had a weight penalty of nearly 150 kg (330 lb) to overcome.

In addition, estimates put the assembly time for the Falcon at thirty-five hours, versus nearly fifty hours for the Zephyr, a significant cost penalty. The Falcon was lighter than the Zephyr, and had a new, low-cost 6-cylinder engine. An additional benefit was that Ford US would do most of the engineering work. Moreover, the Americans could help with the launch of the vehicle. Smith immediately told Emmett and Sale, 'That's the car I want for Australia.' Sir Brian Inglis said later:

> *...in that visit we decided to change from the Zephyr engine to a Falcon engine, reprocess the plants for Falcons and get into the tooling of all the Falcon sheetmetal, and just whack in a chassis plant which did the front suspension and spindles, and all those other terrible things. I have to say, when I look back (on it), we worked like dogs, 9pm every night, every day of the week, even some Sundays. It was a mad, mad scramble, we had to place (orders for) tooling all over the world, we were doing things which we were not trained to do...everything was new.*

While there were cancellation costs of £137,000[60] for the Zephyr tooling already commenced, the basic decisions were sound. The decision to make a single major modern plant with up-to-date facilities and equipment, including the paint shop, would pay off in later years when GM-H, with multiple, lower-volume plants would be unable to compete in later years on unit cost with Ford. GM-H would also face higher facility costs when updating or modernising the multiple plants with new technology.

The Geelong stamping plant had converted to the overseas practice of in-line presses to blank, trim, form and pierce in one facility line. Ultimately, this paid off when robots replaced the operators between the presses, transferring a product from one press to the next. The new chassis plant had modern, latest technology machining equipment purchased and installed. Members of the Program Group developed knowledge and expertise, later recognised throughout Ford, in stamping and chassis machining of relatively low volumes; Jack Hawke, Jack Kelly, Mick Penna and Norm Dalton, to name a few.

Late in 1957, three Ford Canada executives arrived to review progress of the enormous project: For Rhys Sales it was a trip down memory lane. Arriving in Australia for the first time with Hubert French in 1924, this was his third visit since 1946. Now, he was coming as President of Ford Canada. With him was Jack Dalton, Vice-president in charge of Overseas Operations, and another who would play a larger role in Australia in the future, Assistant General Manager of Manufacturing at the Windsor, Ontario, plant of Ford Canada, John McIntyre. While on the visit and during a newspaper interview, Sale announced that erection of steelwork for the new assembly plant would commence in February 1958. He declined to comment on the new Australian Ford car except to say, '...it would be like the Zephyr 6'.

The takeover of Ford Canada by Ford US was finalised in the late 1950s. The effect on the various overseas affiliates varied. For Ford Australia, it meant a greater managerial involvement. Canada had supplied the funds and left Australia to manage the company. The US style of management was more direct. They wanted greater input and consequently greater control. It wasn't necessarily a bad thing; the scale of the project in Australia, with its limited management size and experience, meant Australia welcomed as much expertise as it could. The problem was the quality of the Americans. Bill Dix said it was admitted, years later, that some of the eighty to ninety advisors sent to Australia, were deadwood, selected from American and Canadian assembly plants as a means to move them on.

Last Car off Geelong
ASSEMBLY LINE
23 OCT. 1959

One not in that category was a young Canadian, Ted Gardner, responsible for the establishment of the engine assembly plant in Geelong. Ted was later to return to Australia as Director of Manufacturing in 1976 to replace Bill Carlier as Director of Manufacturing. The Australians had to learn an entirely different vocabulary, terminology and culture. And the cultural differences were not just work related. Dave Brock of the Geelong toolroom recalled the wife of one of the US advisors at a party given to welcome them to Geelong, was overheard saying, 'We've been sent out to Australia to sort out the lazy Australians', which didn't go down well.[61] He also questioned the commitment of the Americans. They could go home whereas the Australians were more committed. Dave said he always believed there was better morale at Ford, with Australian management, than GM-H had with its US Managers. And while the Americans were running the shop, they were not teaching the Australians, a problem quickly recognised, but resolved more slowly.

The new plant at Broadmeadows was different to the other parts of the program. Ford was beginning with a clean slate. Everything was new. It was soon evident that such a project could not be adequately controlled from Geelong.

A project office for the Plant Engineering staff was established in Hardware House, Queensbridge Street, South Melbourne, close to the offices of the architect, Stan McConnell and his associates.

The group, headed by Geoff Madden, also known as 'The Silver Fox' included Ron Rau and Phil Jones.

Ron had joined Ford after finishing his Mechanical Engineering Diploma at the Gordon Institute in Geelong on a Ford scholarship. Ron, unsure of staying at Ford as a stamping tool designer, had swapped with Neil Shirley to join the project group. Having also studied and qualified as a Chartered Engineer, he relates with pleasure that he, not Geoff, had to sign the documents relating to the plants' construction.

Phil Jones joined the group in September 1957. He had started work at Johns and Waygood as a mechanical draftsman with his brother, but decided that designing lifts was too limiting. Deciding to spend a maximum of two years in any company, he worked his way through a contract drafting company, a white goods company, the GM-H foundry and a chemical engineering business before applying to join the group in Hardware House. He recalls his first experience of the Broadmeadows site. 'There were so many snakes in the grass on the site, we all wore heavy gumboots.' He was later to become Mechanical Engineering Supervisor in the plant under Geoff Madden and remained at Ford until his retirement, involved with the construction of most Ford plants in the Asia-Pacific region.

The new assembly plant, based on a 50 by 50 foot bay format, was so large, BHP actually altered and extended their rolling mills to increase the available length of the 'I' beams to accommodate the order. Understandable, given that the beams and columns totaled more than 10 km in length.

There was only one casualty at the construction site during the erection of the plant, when a crane dropped a wheel into a hole, breaking a roof truss which fell on a construction worker, killing him outright. Another did occur during the startup, when a janitor had his overalls caught in one of the conveyors.

There were plenty of near misses, however. Phil Jones recalls, like Stephen Mustica, the thick, black mud on the site and related one close shave. A worker was sealing the roof of the plant, walking backwards along the southern edge of the roof, watering can full of hot tar in hand, pouring it over the join in the bitumen sheets to seal the roof. Unfortunately, at the end of the building he kept on walking. Phil said he did a perfect somersault and landed flat on his back in the deep black mud. 'He never spilt a drop!', Phil recalled. 'He lay there for a minute stunned, then got up, shook his head and walked off, leaving a perfect 100 mm deep impression of himself in the mud.'

Brian Dummett believes he was the first permanent salaried person on the Broadmeadows site. Brian joined Ford Geelong in 1952 as a Personnel Clerk, and in 1957 applied and joined the 1957 Graduate Training Program as an internal applicant. On completion of the course, he was assigned to the Sydney plant as the plant's Training Officer for the next eighteen months before

STEPHEN MUSTICA

Stephen joined Ford in October 1959, three months after the Broadmeadows Assembly Plant began and worked there for forty years, retiring in 1999:

> *There was no medical centre then. I had to go to the Camp Rd. Clinic for my medical. I was just twenty-one. My first memory is of the mud; thick, black sticky mud, everywhere. I started as an inspector in body build, and then moved onto the water test and had to drive the cars through it looking for leaks. We built everything: Consul, Zephyr, Customline, Trucks, everything. The operators would open the crates and we would inspect the body components as they pulled them out. When I was an inspector on the Final Line, my General Foreman was Ewan Crocker, the father of Barry Crocker. He used to drive up from Geelong every day.*

OPPOSITE PAGE Last Zephyr off Geelong assembly line, 1959

OPPOSITE PAGE Ford Australia's first Managing Director Hubert C. French 1925–1950 (front left) and Managing Director John G.W. McIntyre (front right) were present on August 20, 1959 to watch the first vehicle to come off the Broadmeadows assembly line, a Fairlane 500

FLY SPECK OR TYPO?

The Geelong Community was shocked and disappointed at the news the new assembly plant was to be located at Broadmeadows, forty-five miles from the engine, chassis and stamping plants. The map included in the project binder proposing the location was so poorly drawn that any American familiar with an Atlas would have difficulty recognising the location of Geelong, Melbourne, Corio and Port Phillip Bays when comparing them. There is a rumour in Geelong to this day that the only reason the Americans approved the Broadmeadows site was those reading the project misread the distance as 4.5 instead of 45 miles. Was it a fly speck or a typo?

RIGHT John McIntyre (left), Prime Minister Robert Menzies (centre) and Premier Henry Bolte (right) at opening of Broadmeadows Assembly Plant

being approached to return to Melbourne, to assume the position of Employment Officer. Brian was pleased to move closer to his family although the facilities were spartan. Brian recalls his office was a small fibro shack located on the north-east corner of the plant site, which was, 'just a giant ballroom, no assembly lines or equipment'.[62]

His first two hourly employees, recruited in June, 1959, were a janitor and a boiler attendant. The area was a desolate place, he remembers, Ford was the first company in the area, the site a sea of mud, sand and screenings. Of the many Housing Commission homes the government had agreed to build in the area, some were to be reserved for new Ford workers, to lease or buy, an attractive incentive at a time when housing in Melbourne was still in short supply. As part of the agreement with the government, Ford had agreed to offer jobs to new immigrants. Sir Brian also recalled that Ford Employment Officers would go down to the wharves on the arrival of migrant ships and say, 'All you mob, come over here,' and offer employment to anyone:

> *Some of them were really from a peasant background, with no experience of machinery. At the time, there were more jobs than there were people available. We needed them, we had to have something…we had to have someone who actually had two arms and two legs.*[63]

The access to migrant labour was a double-edged sword. On one hand, Ford had access to labour in an extremely tight labour market. However, the lack of skills and Ford's underestimation of the training needs of the workforce became a real problem in launching both the new plant and, later, the Falcon. In the longer term however, many of those new employees and their families became in later years the middle management that helped achieve the success that Ford became. By comparison, labour supply to Ford US new plant startups had a far more homogeneous, integrated workforce, compared to Ford Australia's multicultural multi-lingual workforce, a problem not fully recognised at the time.

Geelong Plant Manager Jack Lavers, was the first Broadmeadows Plant Manager. At the same time, John McIntyre was appointed Deputy Managing Director, returning to Australia after his 1957 tour with Rhys Sale. Imposed on an ageing Smith by Ford of Canada, Charlie Smith and John McIntyre did not get on. Smith didn't want him and wanted nothing to do with him. They were totally different in tastes and character; Smith was an engineer, a doer, a creator, McIntyre was an administrator when, at this time of enormous change, Ford Australia needed a salesman.

Charlie Smith retired from Ford Australia in 1959 at the age of sixty-six, his job done, to be succeeded by McIntyre. Smith had transformed the company from a struggling importer to a company on the brink of a new 'Golden Age', revamped the management structure and introduced a graduate program to produce the next crop of Ford Executives.

After his retirement, Smith returned to Ford for the opening of the Broadmeadows Plant by Prime Minister Robert Menzies on January 27, 1960. Meanwhile, McIntyre was out of his depth with a new plant, new unskilled workforce and a bewildering model complexity. To make it worse, according to Bill Dix:

> *McIntyre micromanaged everything. He just couldn't cope. We had lots of meetings, but nothing seemed to get done.*

Finally, in August 1959, the plant was complete with a capacity to build 200 vehicles per day. The first car offline on August 20

FIRST VEHICLE OFF BROADMEADOWS
ASSEMBLY LINE AUGUST 20TH 1959.

RIGHT Final inspection of Fairlanes, 1959

was a Customline sedan, driven by Managing Director John McIntyre and watched by Plant Manager Jack Lavers, the newly retired Charlie Smith and the long retired Hubert French.

Slowly, Canadian and English passenger vehicles and trucks, even tractors, began to wind their way through the various sections of the plant, as much to debug the equipment and to train the workforce, as to build them. They progressed through body build, paint shop, trim lines one, two, three and four, then the high line and final line before being reviewed in the PD (pre-delivery) area.

Stephen Mustica started at the assembly plant in October that year. He had applied for a job there but had had to wait till he turned twenty-one to start. When asked to recall his first days at work, he said simply, 'The mud! The thick, black gooey mud that stuck to everything'.

The production control planning was vital to the success of the launch. To maintain production and therefore sales and revenue, it was important to maximise the production of all plants. Tooling was relocated, modified where required to suit the new plant's assembly line. Components had to be procured and sent to the correct assembly plant.

Finally, it all started to come together in mid-1959. The last vehicle down the Geelong assembly line was a Zephyr, on October 23, 1959.

Off-line assembly and balance out[64] of the English Commercial 15 cwt Chassis cab and Bus continued until the following February.

In November, assembly of the Consul and Zephyr vehicles began at Broadmeadows, followed in December through to February, of assembly of the smaller 7 Cwt and 15 Cwt English commercial vehicle ranges.

Also temporarily transferred to Broadmeadows were the Anglia and Prefect vehicles for six months, until the launch of the Falcon production. Thus began the greatest shuffle of production assembly of products in the history of Ford.

Now began the task of clearing the Geelong assembly plant, renovating it and installing equipment to transform it into an engine plant.

Adelaide and Fremantle plants increased their build rate of English passenger and commercial vehicles from late 1959 while Broadmeadows slowly built volume. Adelaide continued production until September 1960, slowly winding down until ceasing production in December 1961, converting to become a rectification plant before finally closing the next year.

Fremantle continued low volume production of Canadian passenger vehicles, offset by higher quantities of English passenger and commercials until the plant closed in November

1961, also converting for a time to a rectification plant.

The Sydney plant increased production of Canadian and English commercial vehicles during 1960, as Broadmeadows launched Falcon, continuing production of the complete range of Ford vehicles.

Brisbane, after completion of modifications to assemble Falcon sedans and wagons, also continued to build the full range at a reduced rate until early 1961 with the introduction of the Falcon commercial range.

After exhaustive research in the US and Australia, of more than 10,000 names, the Falcon name was chosen. Ford legend has it that the Falcon name was selected because the Falcon is one of the strongest birds in the world, is graceful and soars to great heights, an excellent analogy. In an interesting glimpse into the future, one of the names considered was 'Meteor'.

After his retirement, Charlie Smith remained in Australia, living quietly until his death on the Queensland Gold Coast in 1986 at age 92. He had had as much influence on the company, if not more, than his revered predecessor, Hubert French.

THE FREMANTLE RECTIFICATION PLANT

After cessation of assembly work at Fremantle, the plant was converted to a rectification plant, repairing in-transit damage from the long rail journey from Geelong or Sydney. The most complex and difficult of vehicle repairs in Fremantle involved the repair of bullet holes. The vehicles, in open rail cars were often used for target practice as the trains crossed the Nullabor Plain; vehicles arrived with a doors or fenders peppered with shotgun pellets. More accurate aim resulted in windows smashed, even high velocity bullet holes through one door and out the other.

LEFT Aerial view of Fremantle plant 1955

CHAPTER 5
1960—1969

THE FORD YEARS 1960—1969

Land adjacent to the Geelong property purchased from Shell for a new Chassis plant. The first Falcon, an XK sedan comes offline at Broadmeadows, June 28, first Falcon offline in Brisbane July 13. XK Falcon sedans introduced September 14, and station wagons in November, 1960.

1960:

1961:

Adelaide plant closed. Head Office moves from Geelong to the Shell building in Melbourne. Ford announces £15,500,000 expansion. Super Major tractor introduced in July.

Assembly operations cease in Fremantle. XL Falcon released. New $3 million, National Parts Distribution Centre opens in Broadmeadows. Sydney and Broadmeadows Assembly Plants extended. Zephyr Mark III released. XL Falcon released. Consul Cortina introduced.

1962:

1963:

Ford Sales Company Ltd established. First computer operations commenced using IBM 1401 computer for Vendor releases, using card based system. New Tractor and Implement Assembly Plants open in Fawkner, Melbourne and Punchbowl, Sydney. Consul Cortina G.T. released.

XM Falcon range released. Scott Inglis retires after 40 years. Head Office opened at Campbellfield, apprentice training centre opened at Geelong. First 2-door Falcon Coupe introduced. Ford US introduces the Mustang.

1964:

1965:

700 hectare Proving Ground opened at Lara. 70,000 mile Durability run at Proving Grounds. XP Falcon released. Cortina GT 500 released. LHD Mustangs imported from US, converted to RHD in Sydney. XP Falcon wins COTY award.

XR Falcon released with new V8 engine. ZA Fairlane production commences. $2 million extension to Brisbane plant. Industrial tractor range launched.

1966:

1967:

Australian designed ZA Fairlane introduced. XR GT Falcon released. Falcon GT's take first and second at Bathurst 500. XR wins *Wheels* COTY award. Mark II Cortina released. Tractor operations move to Broadmeadows. One millionth vehicle assembled by Ford Australia.

XT Falcon, ZB Fairlane released. US Model 8000 and English 6Y tractors released. Ford Australia wins team prize and manufacturer's prize in London–Sydney marathon, with Falcons placed 3rd, 5th and 8th.

1968:

1969:

XT wins Rothmans 12-hour race at Surfers Paradise. XW Falcon, ZC Fairlane, English based Capri Mark I released. XW Falcon GT-HO introduced. V series truck, precursor to Trader released. Computers switched from IBM to Burroughs.

In addition to the Falcon program, Ford confidently embarked on a building expansion of epic proportions. Recognising that managing the company 45 miles from its major plant and one of its largest markets was impossible, Ford decided to move the Head Office and Sales functions to Melbourne. They followed the Broadmeadows Plant program group, providing more room for manufacturing in Geelong. Space was quickly found in the Shell building at the corner of Bourke and Williams Streets in Melbourne.

While those outside the company perceived the move as another example of 'desertion' of Geelong, to Ford insiders, particularly those in manufacturing, the consensus was they would not be missed, rather 'more room for us' quipped Lindsay Sheppard. For those who had to move, it was not quite so easy lthough as Industrial Relations Manager Alec Hand recalls:

> *The train, which left Geelong about 7.30am, wasn't so bad. We operated a car pool to get us to the Geelong station and I used to cut it a bit fine. One day I picked up Bert Stark, a big guy, overweight, and we had to run to catch the train. When Bert eventually got his breath back, he abused me all the way to Werribee. Coming home by train allowed us to relax a bit, with a drink or two before it left, particularly on a Friday night.*

I am sure the rent paid at Shell house later became, in Ford terminology, part of the justification to propose the construction of a new Head Office building, north of the assembly plant.

The Falcon launch program was just as ambitious. The first Falcon 6-cylinder engine came off the new Geelong engine assembly line on April 19, 1960. Along with other engines, panels and chassis components, it was transported by goods train direct to the assembly plants at Broadmeadows and Brisbane.

The first Falcon sedan assembled at Broadmeadows assembly plant came off line on June 28, 1960, followed by Brisbane the next month. Then the wagon; launched in Broadmeadows in August, followed by Brisbane in September.

The Falcon utility and panel van followed in February 1961 at Broadmeadows, March and May respectively in Brisbane. There was little time for the new, still in training, workforce to get used to the Falcon build system. They were also assembling the Anglia, the Consul sedan, wagon and utility, Zephyr and Zodiac sedan, the Zephyr wagon and utility, the US designed Fairlane as well as the F100, F250, F500, F600, T and Thames trucks, even tractors. Seventeen unique, totally different vehicles. Brisbane had a similar complexity, with the Prefect and 7 cwt Escort Car until the launch of the Falcon Ute and Van.

PAGES 96–97 1968 XT Falcon

LEFT 1960–1961 Fairlane was assembled at Broadmeadows and Fremantle assembly plants

FIRST AUSTRALIAN-BUILT
FORD FALCON - JUNE 28 1960

FIRST FALCON

Allan Wembridge in 1993:

> *Neil Fox and I unpacked the first Falcon from USA in about 1958, a grey sedan. Harry Ruffin told us to take it for a drive. We went to Lorne, no security, no test track in those days; when we returned we told Harry it had 'clutch shudder'. Harry then uttered those immortal words, 'One swallow doesn't make a summer.' Later we had over 100% warranty on clutch shudder!*

There were problems with the Falcon design, specifically the front suspension. The Falcon, initially released with the US designed 'Boulevard Suspension ride' was just not up to Australian conditions. Despite the Falcon having been a runaway bestseller in the US and Canada for a couple of years, during the press drives the motoring writers all complained that 'the suspension bottomed out so hard it felt like it (the suspension) was coming through the floor'. As luck would have it Brian Inglis, after reviewing the equipment to manufacture the socket ball joints on one of his visits to the UK, had made the brave decision for that part to stay as an import from the US. In an interview, he later said:

> *I think if I had made that part I would have been fired…I was in England looking at the equipment to make the ball joint. It was different to how they made it in the US and I asked our agent looking after the equipment supply in Europe, Bob Page, what he thought. He said he was a bit nervous of the process. I agreed with him, so I cancelled the order, even though the equipment was half-built. Later when we determined the root cause of the problem and it was reported to Henry Ford (II), he reportedly went to John Dykesta and told him to fix it. John went to the Stirling plant where they were manufacturing it and found they were developing a stronger socket ball joint for their new Fairlane. We changed to that and the problem went away, although it cost us a lot of money and our reputation. Later when Henry asked me what had gone wrong and why we hadn't tested the Falcon to our conditions, I told him we relied on the US for testing, as we had no test facilities. His reaction was typical, 'I'll give you a test track; don't ever come back to me again with a durability problem'. And that's how we got the proving rounds at Lara.* [65]

The running change to introduce the US Fairlane ball joints fixed the front suspension but there were a lot of disgruntled owners, dealers and fleet buyers out there. The replacement program cost Ford dearly, supplying replacement parts under warranty but it also tarnished the Falcon image. Another problem not seen in the US was of clutches prematurely burning out. While not as frequent as the front suspension problem, it was a design problem that could only be fixed with a new design and model, the XL. The warranty costs and the assembly plant operating problems saw Ford losing money hand over fist. Losses in 1961 associated with the launch of the Falcon were $4.36 million, 1962 saw a profit before tax of $9.97 million, then a loss of $1.97 million in 1963, followed by another of $8.84 million in 1964.

While the Falcon wasn't perfect, it was more than competitive with the Holden. The Falcon looked better, felt more roomy, was 90 kg lighter, 120 mm lower, faster and the price was competitive. As Sir Brian said, 'GM-H didn't know what struck them'. Ford couldn't make enough to keep up with the demand. Combined output from Brisbane and Broadmeadows for 1960 was 12,597 sedans and 2,510 wagons, despite launching mid-year. The following year, 1961, Ford produced 31,161 Falcons, 17,609 sedan, 9,070 wagons, 3,690 utilities and 792 vans. The year of 1962 saw the highest output in the history of the company up to that time. The release of the larger 170 cubic inch 'Pursuit' motor in March 1962 as an option over the 144 cubic inch motor certainly helped.

The XL Falcon range was introduced in July 1962, with a redesigned clutch and gearbox, seatbelt attachment points, a 'Thunderbird' style squared roofline and the advertising slogan 'Trim, taut, terrific!'. That year, 66,861 vehicles were produced, of which 54,135 were (XL & XM) Falcons, 27,844 sedans, 18,406 wagons, 6,142 utilities and 1743 vans. While the vehicle itself was good, the image problems at Ford persisted, busily promoted by GM-H salesmen. Total Ford production in 1963 only dropped by 4,845 vehicles, but Falcon sales slumped by 10,468. GM-H, facing real competition for the first time, still had over 45% of the market with the popular EH Holden.

The 'Armstrong 500' Bathurst race held in October that year was notable for the success of the Cortina. The Falcon was not represented due to financial restrictions; the cost of two teams would have been prohibitive. The Cortinas competed in two classes, but the interest was in class 'C', where the Cortina GT competed against the EH Holden.

In a scene repeated only later with the Falcon GT-HOs, Car 20, driven by Harry Firth and Bob Jane finished first in a one-two finish with Car 13, a Cortina driven by Bruce McPhee and Graham Ryan. With lap times of three minutes thirty seconds, the laps were leisurely compared to those of today's specially prepared

OPPOSITE PAGE 1960 XK Falcon sedan. Assembled at Broadmeadows and Eagle Farm assembly plants. A total of 41,389 sedans were produced.

vehicles, but they completed the race with three scheduled pit stops, averaged 20 m.p.g. (8 litres per 100 km) and no tyre changes. It was reported at the time the Cortinas were coasting after fifty laps. The EH Holdens did not do well, plagued with breakdowns and were consistently lapped by the GT Cortinas.

If life in production had been tough during the depression, things changed for the worse on the industrial relations front once Broadmeadows plant started up. The combination of raw unskilled migrant labour, a complex vehicle mix in transition, inexperienced management, combined with a new, different vehicle was disastrous.

Plant Manager, Jack Lavers was out of his depth. He reported to John McCabe in Geelong, who used his contacts with the US and Canadian 'advisors' to operate a fifth column in the plant to white ant Lavers. Ken McDonald recalled in 2015, 'John McCabe frightened the hell out of me!'. With an ineffective Managing Director in McIntyre, the political atmosphere and insecurity at the top transmitted itself all the way down through the plant.

Turnover was more than 100% per year; i.e. replacing the entire workforce every year, making a mockery of any training, or ability to operate within a budget. Absenteeism averaged 25%; with no stable workforce, stable production was impossible. With management focused on their own in-fighting, industrial relations went out the window. Little consideration was given to the workforce; on any given day, if the daily output was not going to be met, the decision to work overtime would be announced fifteen minutes before knock-off, giving workers no time to make alternative arrangements for their families. The aggravation, in a

BELOW 1960 XK Falcon sedan

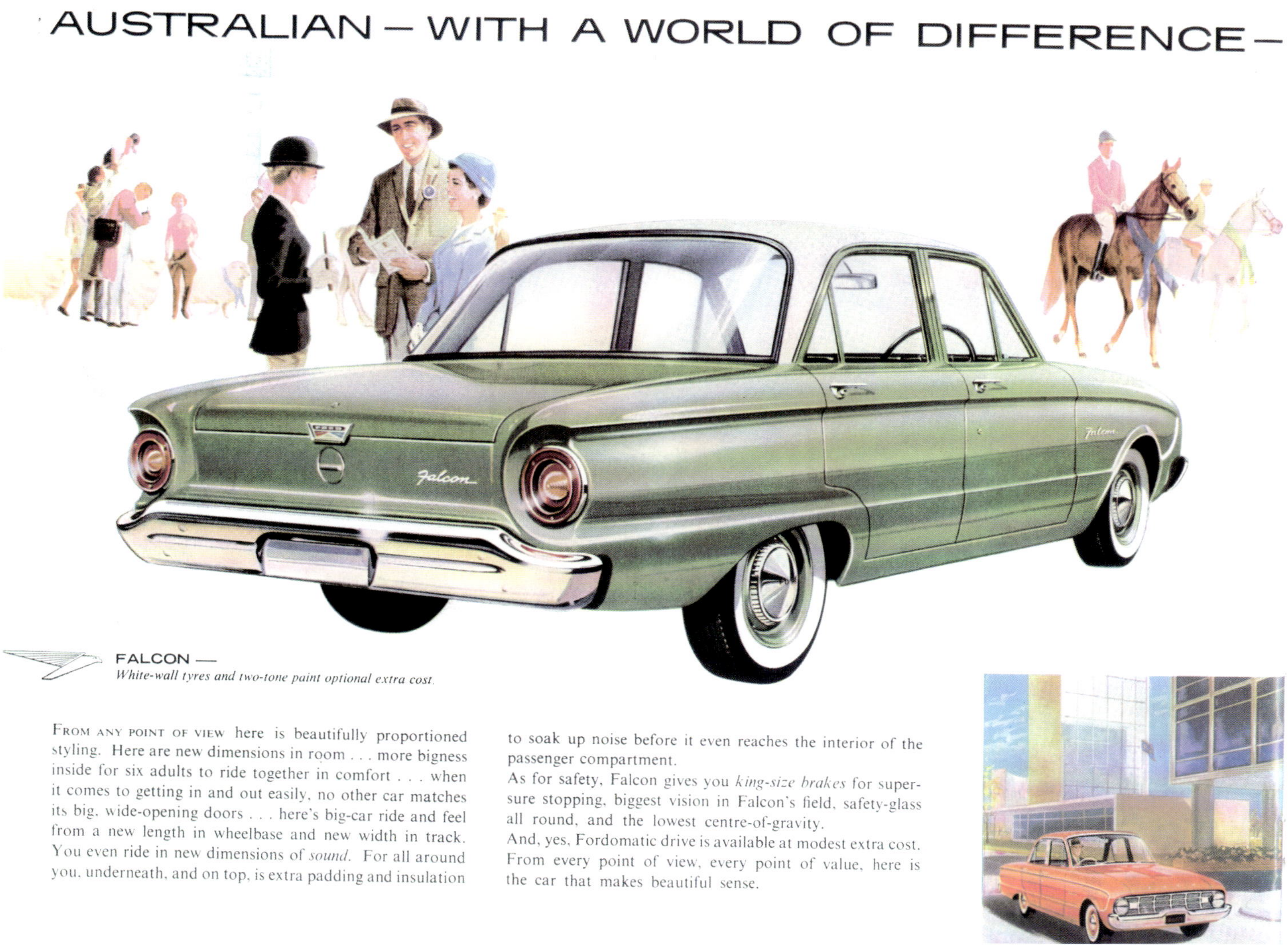

LEFT 1960 XK Falcon brochure

plant already with low morale, encouraged the VBEF who became more aggressive. The plant industrial relations staff was kept busy; negotiate, negotiate, negotiate, anything to keep the employees at work. The atmosphere inside the assembly plant, if not poisonous, certainly bubbled.

Outside the company, the 1960s were also a period of unrest and change. Politically, Australia was in transition with Robert Menzies nearing the end of his career. The 1961 election saw the Liberals returned with a substantially reduced majority after a disastrous budget by Treasurer Harold Holt resulted in a credit squeeze. Then in 1963 Menzies dissolved parliament claiming an unworkable majority. During the election campaign, a picture of Labor leader Caldwell and deputy Whitlam outside their Canberra Hotel, waiting for decisions on policy, was labelled by Alan Reid of the Sydney Daily Telegraph as 'The 36 Faceless Men' and greatly damaged the Labor Party. One issue of the 1963 election was Australia's involvement in the Vietnam War. Labor called for immediate withdrawal, but on the day, DLP preferences to the Liberals resulted in a crushing defeat for Labor. The public initially supported Australia's involvement, but opinion turned against the war when conscription began, and soldiers began dying in the conflict. Many of the protests against the war were led by students, particularly from Monash University and the University of New South Wales.

Harold Holt replaced Menzies in January 1966; during his visit to the US in July that year he made a speech that included

ABOVE 1962 XL Miss Australia Falcon Convertible, special build designed by Lewis T. Bandt

ABOVE Wallace Booth

the now infamous slogan, 'All the way with LBJ,' which jarred with many Australians, who disliked sloganeering and whose attitudes to the war were changing.

When United States President Lyndon Johnson visited Australia in October 1966, protests were widespread. In Sydney, protestors lying on the road stopped the cavalcade. The route of Johnson's Melbourne cavalcade was changed at the last minute, ruining the protestors plans; however, when LBJ arrived at a function in South Yarra later that day, a protestor lay in front of his car to stop it, while another threw red and green paint over his Lincoln sedan and his security guards. An urgent call to Ford resulted in delivery of LBJ's Lincoln Presidential Limousine to the Broadmeadows Plant that evening. Overnight, Ford cleaned and re-sprayed the vehicle, returning it to his hotel the next morning as though nothing had happened.

Protestors targeted Ford and other multinational companies with American parentage particularly on July 4, American Independence Day. Ford responded with tighter security and extra security guards at these times. Union organisations were also infiltrated by ex-student radicals, with ambitions of influencing or taking them over, sometimes with violent intent.

The company had grown too fast, was out of control and haemorrhaging money. Inevitably, heads had to roll. Most visible was that of Broadmeadows Plant Manager Jack Lavers, transferred to Sydney Truck Plant in January 1963, and replaced by an American, Earl Warner.

Typical of the many managerial shuffles of the time was John Marshall's experience. John had graduated from Melbourne University in Mechanical Engineering in 1952 and was one of the inaugural Graduate Training group in 1953.

As part of their training, in 1955 he was asked by Walter Follis to develop a Quality Rating System for the five assembly plants. After launching the rating system, he moved to Adelaide as relieving Plant Manager while Bill Hussey was overseas, before moving to Sydney as assistant plant manager in 1957.

Two weeks after his arrival, Plant Manager Alby Woodhouse suffered a heart attack and John became Plant Manager. On Woodhouse's return, John spent three months in 1959 at the prestigious Mt. Eliza Administrative Staff training college, before moving to Fremantle, replacing Duncan Norris as Plant Manager, who had joined the task force to 'fix' the Broadmeadows plant. John also joined the task force in 1960, in charge of the overwhelmed rectification department. As things slowly improved at Broadmeadows, he returned to Perth before moving back to Melbourne as Production Manager, again replacing Duncan Norris who was sent to take charge of the Brisbane Plant.

When the Paint Shop Superintendent Keith Mathews resigned, Warner and Marshall hired Don Deveson from Massey Ferguson in 1963 as his replacement. As John Crew said later:

> *Whatever you may say about Don Deveson, he was an absolute genius in spotting obstacles and logjams in production.*

Managing Director John McIntyre was recalled to the US in July the same year, where he left the company shortly after. Wallace (Wally) Booth replaced him.

Booth was born and raised in Chicago, and graduated from Chicago University, working his way through university, having previously served with the American army in Italy and Germany. He joined Ford and after eleven years, became Director of Finance for Ford Canada.

Promoted to Vice-president of Ford Canada, he was the personal choice of Ford US Executive Vice President R.J. Miller, who had worked closely with Booth in Finance. Booth came with the directive from Miller to 'fix it if you can, or close manufacturing in Australia'.

After spending some time looking carefully at the market and driving as many of the competition vehicles as he could in a month, Booth decided that, despite the losses to date and the £4.89 million loss for 1964, the situation was far from unrecoverable.

Booth was a shrewd judge of character and understood people; he was street-smart and understood finance. Moreover, he had the confidence of his management in the US. David Letford recalls he would demand to face-off with the person doing the job:

> *He had a unique style of management. His philosophy was, I want to talk to the man doing the job, not his boss or his bosses boss…I was a lowly supervisor, a grade 8 and he had me down for excess freight costs and food service costs…when he wanted to talk to me, as often as not it was in my small cubicle of an office.* [66]

One problem Booth saw immediately was of morale. David Letford went on:

> *…our morale was low. We had a bad product, we weren't making profits and we had all these overseas advisors who were really operating like an exclusive club…they talked amongst themselves and didn't do a lot of teaching. Booth's approach was 'I don't want overseas people running this company; I want local nationals to do it'. So he literally cleaned all the overseas advisers out of the company I think in the end there were only five.* [67]

BELOW 1962 XL Falcon sedan. Assembled at Broadmeadows and Eagle Farm assembly plants. A total of 38,646 sedans were produced.

HEAD OFFICE

When Head Office was opened in September 1964, the company recognised the isolation of the complex from 'civilization', allowing women employed at Head Office one shopping afternoon a month. Gwen Compt (nee Nelms), working at the Broadmeadows Assembly Plant remembers the angst felt by those working there, of discrimination by the company. Eventually, after some agitation, this privilege was extended across the site and the practice continued until the 1970s. For men, a barbershop had been established in the basement of Head Office; 'Bob the Barber' McQueen was also an agent for a drycleaners, sold cigarettes and magazines, some under the counter reputed to be of a 'racy' nature. Westpac Bank also operated a bank and a travel agency in the basement.

Other decisions by Booth once he began to pull manufacturing together, was to take up Henry Ford II's offer of the test facility in the You Yangs. And, as the product engineers needed to be housed near the manufacturing plants, the Annexe became the Product Engineering Office (PEO). In turn, the Parts and Service function moved closer to its market in Melbourne with a new building north of the proposed new Head Office site, and opened by the then Sir Henry Bolte on November 21, 1962. Then, in September 1964 the new Head Office building was completed. One effect of bringing more engineers into Ford— all were 'petrol heads'. You didn't work long in the automotive business unless you were.

For years Ford had supported motor racing worldwide and Australia was no exception. Sponsored and supported by Ford, Bob Jane and Harry Firth won the Armstrong 500 at Phillip Island in 1962 in an XL Falcon with Falcons filling the first four places. The Ford publicity machine went into overdrive: the question asked in bold print, 'How did the Holden's fare? Answer, laps behind'.

The next year, the race transferred to Bathurst and the same two drivers again won in a Cortina. A Ford Cortina also won

RIGHT Head Office Broadmeadows 1969

OPPOSITE PAGE National Parts Depot Broadmeadows, 1960s. Complete body shells were also available.

RIGHT 1962 'Compact' Fairlane

ABOVE W.O. (Bill) Bourke

the next two years, 1964 and 1965. Falcons, the new Anglias and Cortinas followed the Ford tradition in motor racing, winning rallies and economy runs during 1963.

After a tremendous amount of work, and only eighteen months after the introduction of the XL, the XM build commenced in Broadmeadows, December 1963, followed by Brisbane in January 1964, and launched a month later. The marketing people dubbed it 'The Golden Quality Falcon'. Naturally, one feature colour of the model was gold. Rustproofing was improved and service intervals were extended to 6,000 miles.

In addition to increasing the output of the existing engines, another engine, the 'Super Pursuit' 200 cubic inch engine became available as an option. The design was Australian; Ford Australia had ignored the US reskin of the Falcon and given the vehicle a new front end, new grille, bumper and headlight surrounds. The model range included for the first time, the B pillar-less Tudor, built only at Broadmeadows. Marketing Manager Max Gransden said later:

> *All of the problems from the XK and XL were fixed. It was a good, solid, honest car, it wasn't perfect, but boy it was a great improvement.* [68]

To round out Booth's program, he now turned his attention to marketing, asking for and getting one of the best in the business, Bill Bourke, as his deputy and Sales Director.

Bourke, born in Chicago, had worked for Ford US and more recently as Sales Manager of Ford Canada.

Naturally, Bourke brought some of his own staff with him, one of his picks being Bill Hawkins. While Bill Bourke was the marketing and sales genius, Bill Hawkins was a purist in marketing theory.

Booth and Bourke together made a formidable team; Booth supplied the wherewithal for Bourke to market the Ford product. Bourke reviewed the Dealer body and decided a new approach to sales was required. In the words of Sir Brian:

LEN PAPLEY & ROSSCO

You would think it impossible to finding your way around the two-and-a-half miles of passageways at Broadmeadows Assembly Plant for a blind person. This is not the case for Len Papley and his guide dog Rossco; in just a few weeks Len and Rossco mastered the layout of the plant. Len, totally blind, has worked at Ford for more than a year and works on the trim line. Before that he assembled brake and clutch pedals and can assemble complicated door locks, using special tools designed by equipment engineer Mike Linderman. Len catches two buses and a train to work with Rossco as his guide and feels nothing is more stimulating to a handicapped person than to be able to carry out a normal job.

Bourke said, 'We've got some very old dealers…and they aren't cutting the mustard. We have to get dealers strategically placed in the marketing areas. They are going to have the right facilities, not grandiose and we'll finance them.' He started a scheme where the Sales Planning people decided the best location. Then he went and bought the property. If there were ten houses, he bought ten houses and cleared them out. Then we'd build an appropriate facility with corporate colours, good signage, high visibility, a good workshop with parts and accessories and room for expansion. Then Bourke would look around for the right guy to run it. GM had lots of Sales Managers, people prepared to have a go. Bourke would ask them how much money have you got? They'd say, 'I haven't got much, but I could raise $30,000 if I mortgage my home or something'. Bourke would tell them, 'Do that, put the $30,000 down and this is your facility. You run it, you're the Managing Director and we will finance you. Then we will sell it to you at our cost.' In ten years, we made millionaires of them…they'd go in early in the morning and sweep the floors. They were really committed. It did wonders

LEFT 1964 XM Falcon two-door hardtop. A total of 2,565 produced at Broadmeadows assembly plant only.

ABOVE 1965 XP Falcon sedan. Assembled at Broadmeadows and Eagle Farm assembly plants. A total of 36,723 sedans were produced.

for our dealer body. We went to Bib Stillwell, GM-H's biggest dealer in 1965, made him an offer and he changed overnight to Ford. Psychologically, it was a real body blow to GM-H. They could not believe their biggest dealer would turn on them like that…and of course, we had other dealerships popping up all over the place, staffed by some of their best people. It was a rout![69]

Even more extensive development and engineering work went into the next model, the XP. Ford was determined to get the vehicle right. Two engineers brought out specially for the XP program in 1962 were Product Planning's Al Sundberg and Chief Engineer Jim Martin. Long range durability testing for the XP was the most extensive conducted to date. It even included Jim Martin who, on his annual leave, set off round Australia via Perth and Darwin solo on a durability trial. He completed the trip in ten days, handed in his report and the next day set off on another trip, a shorter one to Port Augusta and back. That was one way to see the country!

Between March 1964 and the release of the vehicle, more than 470,000 miles were travelled by test engineers and test drivers. Rumour has it that some of the potholes around Port Augusta were so bad, that Jim Martin had them photographed and measured for inclusion into the Lara test facility.

The Lara Proving Grounds, in the You Yangs, north of Geelong, were developed over a number of years. Purchased in

CHRISTMAS PARTIES

Christmas parties at Ford are a time of fun, rides and presents for the kids. In the early days, they were held at the Broadmeadows Assembly plant, so parents could show their children where they worked and the operation of the plant. That was until, despite all the checks, a couple of vehicles were left with the keys still in them. Two young lads found them, started the cars and ended up driving them through the PDA ovens and through the plant wall, damaging several vehicles in the process. After that, Luna Park was a far safer option.

1964, it would ultimately include a number of test laboratories and other facilities, skidpan, basic durability track and a constant high-speed test loop. The basic durability track was completed in time for the XP launch.

The XP Falcon tooling changeover occurred over the Christmas shutdown period of 1964–1965, the last time Ford Australia followed the Ford US practice and closed a plant for a model changeover. Future model changeovers would be done 'on the fly' while production continued. The new model XP was the last of the body style, refreshed and updated to give a more modern feeling, the side panel styling disappearing.

Although the engines did not change, the more responsive three-speed Borg Warner transmission replaced the two-speed 'Ford-O-Matic'. Structural improvements and larger 14 inch wheels added 25 kg kerb weight.

Concurrent with the release of the XP, was the demise of the US styled, longer wheelbase Fairlanes. The Fairmont name appeared for the first time, replacing the 'Futura' and 'Squire' nameplates. The Fairmont, an upmarket Falcon, came with the 200 c.i.d (3.3-litre.) 'Super Pursuit' engine, 3-speed auto transmission, front disc brakes, wider tyres, luxury seating, carpets, and more chromium trim as standard. While the launch of the XP was somewhat subdued, Bourke's *piece de resistance* was yet to come.

Early on Saturday morning, April 24, 1965, the new $750,000 Lara proving grounds were abuzz with activity as over 100 people

LEFT XP Falcon two-door Deluxe. A total of 3,838 two-door XPs were produced at Broadmeadows assembly plant only.

> **RIGHT AND BELOW** Five stock standard Falcons start the 1965 70,000 mile durability run.

watched Wally Booth flag five Falcons off at 8.28am on the start of the now-famous 70,000 mile (116,600 km) durability run around the 2¼ mile (3.62 km) track (31,100 laps). The vehicles, three manual, Pursuit 170 (2.8 litre) sedans, one 'Super Pursuit' 200 (3.3-litre), 3-speed auto-transmission sedan and a similarly equipped two-door hardtop, were all bog standard, as though straight from the showroom floor, the only optional extras fitted being seat belts, laminated windscreen and driving lights. The whole event was under the strict supervision of the Confederation of Motor Sport and was a race against the clock.

In attendance twenty-four hours a day was a whole army of support crew, working twelve-hour shifts, garage mechanics, pit crews, flag marshals, doctors, ambulances, breakdown crew. A corps of cooks was on hand to supply hot, three-course meals at any time, and there were fifteen caravans and marquees on site serving as dormitory sleeping and living quarters.

For the total mileage of the five vehicles to reach the target in time, each vehicle had to *average* more than 71 mph (118 km/h). The fastest lap time, by Harry Firth, was 1 minute 44.5 seconds —Ford had recruited twenty-two of the best professional and licensed amateur racing and rally car drivers, who were to drive in shifts, two hours on, four off, twenty-four hours a day, to achieve the target. The only stops were to be for fuel, tyres, brake pads and driver changes.

The drivers included such luminaries as Ian and Leo Geoghegan, Fred Gibson, Alan Moffat, Bruce McPhee, Barry Seton and Ken Harper, as well as volunteer drivers from Car Clubs and Motor Sport Clubs.

Many of the drivers, as they navigated the tight circuit, considered the durability run to be madness, but were prepared to give it a go. Most believed the vehicles would not survive the

LEFT Pit stops 1965-style

circuit with its series of twists, loops, 'S' bends and 1-in-4 gradient. The western side of the track where the pit area was located comprised five sweeping bends that rose 205 feet (63 metres) in 2.5 km. There was not one level, straight section of the circuit; it was designed to impose continuous strain on the whole vehicle, strain magnified enormously when taken at high speed.

To achieve the target, and allow for the downtime and all the changeovers, the drivers were doing more than 100 mph (167 km/h) on the 'straights'. In fact, tyres and drivers were the problems. The freshly laid, rough surface and high speed cornering shredded the Dunlop radials. Soon truckloads of tyres were regularly travelling from Melbourne and it is rumoured that tyres were even taken off new vehicles in the assembly plant.

The drivers, too, could not sustain the punishing pace; all suffered from fatigue. Ford had to draft in another ten drivers with rally driving experience to stand in with shifts. Driver error was the cause of two of the vehicles rolling over; one driver losing control rolling four times and sideswiping a massive boulder. Another rolled when a tyre burst at 90 mph and ended up in a gully. The trickiest session was early in the morning just before

RIGHT 1965 XP 70,000 mile durability run publicity release

RIGHT Henry Ford II at the 70,000 mile Mobil durability run

sunrise. Patches of fog would settle on the lower bends of the track, cutting visibility. Heavy dew on the track at night made the track treacherous. However, the large team of mechanics and helpers had all the vehicles, repaired in a makeshift trackside garage, patched up and back on the track within hours.

The endurance run had been announced in advance and the publicity it engendered, meant there was no going back, there could be no failure, things like driver error or the weather couldn't be predicted. It was crash or crash through management. The daily newspapers and fledgling television news coverage was enormous.

Lindsay Sheppard recalls one of the radios normally fitted to a forklift in the Stamping Plant was seconded to the proving ground. Alfie James would radio Lindsay each morning with an update on progress and events overnight. These reports were constantly relayed to Ford Geelong, Ford Management in Head Office, Public Relations and, in turn, to the media. Nightly footage on TV contained daily updates on the progress. The media went into even more of a frenzy when, in the middle of the reliability run, a helicopter made its way to the You Yangs site with none other than Henry Ford II on board. He only stayed a short while, giving only brief interviews to the media before returning to Melbourne. Not given out to the media were his comments about the run itself. When Ford US had given approval for the reliability run, they assumed it would be run on the yet-to-be-constructed constant high-speed banked loop. Bourke had not deceived them, he merely switched the venue to the basic durability course. After surveying the course and the progress, Henry Ford II departed, privately telling Ford management they were, 'Out of your minds, a bunch of damn fools.'

The vehicles and drivers survived. At 1.42am on May 3, all vehicles finished six hours ahead of the nine-day target, battered and dented, a stylist's nightmare, but mechanically none of them missed a beat. Ford proved the engines, transmissions, drivelines and suspensions could take the punishment. During the endurance run, forty-nine Australian time and distance endurance records were broken.

Ford made the most of the publicity, but the testimonials of respected, independent drivers counted much, much more. All were full of praise for the vehicles. 'The Falcon's not only a flier—it's a tough bird, too', was the consensus.

Shrewdly, Gransden went to the fleet buyers and offered to loan them a vehicle for six months, with the comment, 'At the end of six months, if you like it, buy it, and buy more like it'. The public and more importantly, the fleet buyers did like it and showed it by buying the XP. It didn't hurt either, that it was competing against the dated and dumpy-looking HD Holden.

That year, 1965, a Cortina won the Bathurst 500 and *Wheels* magazine named the XP Falcon 'Car of the Year'. Bill Tuckey,

LEFT Battered, bruised, but unbowed

LEFT Success! The first car crosses the finish line at 1.42am on May 3, 1965, establishing forty-nine Australian endurance records.

ABOVE Gold 1967 XR GT, only 596 produced

editor of *Wheels* magazine, called the durability run the 'Epic of the Year'. Ford was now a major force in the automotive market in Australia. In five years Ford total vehicle production had grown 38.5%, from 51,493 in 1960 to 71,309 in 1965. Market share had grown from 16% to nearly 21%.

Ford advertised and recruited worldwide for draftsmen and engineers with qualifications and experience, as both were in short supply in Australia. When Mike Alves arrived at Ford, after stints at GM-H and International Harvester, he recalled the styling studio, headed by Lew Bandt, comprised:

> *...two design draftsmen, and four contract draftsmen. Bruce Palamountain and I, looking after exterior and interior pre-program engineering respectively, sat at one end of the 'studio', layout tables were down the other end. Full body size clays were unheard of then, we still worked with clay, but modified existing bodies or components.*

Dave Cox and Don Dunoon were two recruits from the UK in 1965, Lindsay Dawson joined the next year. Under US Manager Don Wurtz and Design Engineer Al Bliss, and with Ron Game running the proving ground, these three were to play a vital role in the engineering development of the XR and subsequent models. Ford, accustomed to the many arrivals, had a well-established welcome program, which occasionally went astray. When Roger Clarke and wife Reta arrived, Bill Howard of Industrial Relations met them at the airport. After driving them to Geelong, he proudly proceeded to give them a complete guided tour of Geelong and its highlights, not realising that after a long twenty-four hour flight from the UK, all they wanted to do was sleep.

The Product Engineering Office staff grew by more than 55%—mostly young, enthusiastic engineers, particularly those with emission control experience. Led from the top by Booth and Bourke, a sense of purpose focused the group and extended throughout the organisation.

The success of the XP saw the confidence of the company rising in leaps and bounds. The styling for the next model, the XR, was well under way in the US even before the XP was released in Australia. The Ford US team who had designed the XP, Gale Halderman and George Schumaker, under the direction of design chief Joe Orso completed the clay of the XR in November 1963. They had made the styling leap of the Mustang, the 'hippy' or 'coke-bottle' design waistline that was to inspire a plethora of imitations in other manufacturers. The XR followed the styling theme of the Mustang, and the design was approved and transmitted to Australia early the next year.

Using the experience of the previous models, Ford Australia took the styling, but did all of the engineering. A styling studio of sorts was created in the Product Engineering building so that minor changes, badges etc. could be reviewed.

Based on research, Ford believed Australians wanted a larger vehicle, and they got it. The designers made the XR 92 mm longer, increasing the wheelbase by 38 mm to 2.82 metres, with a wider track both front and back to give more space inside the vehicle. The suspension was retuned; the front suspension with heavier coil springs, and a heavier rear axle. They added extra cross members for greater vehicle stiffness and increased the size of the fuel tank to 72 litres. To compensate for the 136 kg of additional steel, the base 2.4-litre engine was dropped. The 2.7-litre became the base engine, a larger 3.2-litre straight six was introduced, as well as a 4.7-litre fully imported V8.

The spare wheel, placed right in the middle of the boot, took up too much space in the US design. The product engineers walked across the road and with the Advanced Stamping Manufacturing people under Ivan Tan Sing, the short, irascible Jimmy Leason, Ern Millard and Graham Mould, redesigned the fuel tank, the top of which was the boot floor. They were able to position the spare wheel at an angle of 45 degrees, recessing the wheel into the tank. A complex operation, the first operation in the stamping press involved partially forming the recess in the steel blank to stretch the metal, reversing it and pushing the formed recess 'inside out' to stretch the metal further. After fully forming, the blank was then re-struck, to form the flanges of the tank, which was seam welded to the tank bottom. The US stamping plants advised the design was not feasible and the process wouldn't work. It did, substantially increasing the usable boot volume.

Product Planning added disc brakes as an option on all vehicles and, to simplify the assembly operation, 14-inch wheels became standard across the range. The result was a quieter, faster, better handling vehicle, particularly with Bathurst 500 in mind. The design also had the potential to be worked over and stretched to include a long wheelbase future model.

Another marketing manoeuvre planned by Bourke was to

LEFT XR GT Instrument panel

LEFT 1967 XR GT grille badge

LEFT 1967 XR '289' fender badge

RIGHT 1964 Mustang

RIGHT Mustang grille badge

RIGHT Mustang fender badge

POSSUM PROBLEMS

Living in the eastern suburbs of Melbourne, Brian Dummett had a perennial problem of possums getting into the roof of his home. With a euphemistically called 'wild cat trap,' (it being illegal to trap possums) Brian used to catch them and on the way to work, release them near the Yarra river. One morning he forgot the possum in the boot.

Arriving at work and not wanting to keep it in the car all day, he released it at the top end of the test track, behind the assembly plant. That morning about 11.15am, a massive power failure blacked out the plant and stopped production, the plant losing over thirty vehicles in production before power was restored. At lunch that day, Brian asked what had caused the blackout, Keith Tyack told him somehow a possum had got into the plants' main substation and shortcircuited the system, dying in the process. Keith could not understand where the possum had come from. Brian never told him.

import new Mustangs from the US and convert them to RHD. The plan was to locate one in every dealer's showroom to promote the XR with the advertising slogan 'The Mustang-bred Falcon'.

The first Mustang, a 1964½ model, was converted to RHD especially for Bourke by Bill Buckle Auto Conversions. The first 48 of the 1965 Hardtop Coupes were imported in July 1965 for conversion at the Sydney Plant, using some common Falcon components, including the steering box. Ford engineers in the US had said there would be no trouble converting the instrument panel from left to right-hand drive as the instrument cluster and glovebox were the same shape and would be interchangeable. When Bourke saw the first instrument panel he realised they were only interchangeable if fitted upside down. A retired engineer living near the Homebush plant was found, who converted the dash panels in his garage. A total of 208 Mustangs were converted at the Sydney plant. The 'Australian Mustangs' were the only factory Mustang-conversion by Ford worldwide. Rural dealer resistance, who felt a sports car was not suited to the outback, saw Bourke's original quantity pared back from the planned 400, but the marketing program was a huge success and the 'Mustang bred' XR was born.

As part of the XR launch, Director of Manufacturing Brian Inglis appointed John Marshall New Model Coordinator, Bill Carlier moved from Geelong, where he had been Tool Room Manager to become Broadmeadows Plant Manager, and Don Deveson was appointed Production Manager. When hepatitis sidelined Don for the last half of 1966, John returned as Production Manager for the launch. The XR commenced manufacture in Broadmeadows in June 1966 and was released in September that year, eighteen months ahead of the Holden. The XR set a new benchmark for the family sized vehicle and surprised the industry with the extensive range of options. It made the yet-to-be-released HK Holden look out of date even before it commenced production and forced a redesign. GM added 75 mm to the front end of the HK between the front door and wheel arch, which improved the looks a little but did nothing for the driver or passengers. In the words of Booth in an interview:

> *The XR was the culmination of a program to bring out a top competitor to Holden. We had to guess what the public wanted, which is often not what they say they want. We went for a larger car, it was a $35 million gamble. If it had not worked, we would have been in deep financial stress. But within a month the dealers were screaming for cars—and we knew we had a winner.*

The Falcon was an immediate success. Despite discontinuation of the two-door and a slow launch, as many XR Falcons were built that year as the XP. Manufacturing records for 1966 show the following:

	1966 Build | XP	1966 Build | XR
XP/XR Sedan	14,305	14,782
XP Tudor	1,227	--
XP/XR Wagon	6,208	6,367
ZA Fairlane	--	6
XP/XR Utility	3,774	2,579
XP/XR Panel Van	575	198
Total	26,089	23,932

In addition to the Falcon and derivatives, Ford also produced:

Canadian Galaxie Sedans	837
Mustangs (converted to RHD)	161
English Cortina range	15,111
Commercial Vehicles (various)	4,544

RIGHT 1967 Australian-designed ZA Fairlane 500—8,820 were produced

for an annual total of 70,513, only 796 shy of the most successful year, 1965. Then three months after the XR Falcon commenced production in Broadmeadows, production began on the longer wheelbase ZA Fairlane. Its unique rear styling and five-inch increase in wheelbase cleverly disguised its Falcon origins while adding legroom to the rear seat and increasing the boot to cavernous. Termed 'A marriage of strength and elegance' the Fairlane and the upmarket Fairlane 500, with power steering, extensive instrumentation and optional V8 and 'SelectShift' three-speed auto transmission, became the benchmark in luxury cars in Australia not matched for years by the other local manufacturers. Bourke had done it again.

As the shuffle of vehicle build locations continued with the introduction of the Falcon and Fairlane, the English origin vehicles were changing. The older, outdated model ranges of Prefect, Consul and Zephyr were phased out, and newer models were introduced. The Falcon replaced the Zephyr, Cortina replaced the Consul, even being called the Consul Cortina in the UK for a short period. New style 105E Anglias, with the unique reverse sloping rear window, replaced the Prefect and Popular. Most of the rationalisation of Ford Australia's product line coincided with the closure of Adelaide and Fremantle plants.

The Anglia, previously assembled at Adelaide, Brisbane, Fremantle, Geelong and Sydney, was consolidated temporarily to Brisbane, Broadmeadows and Sydney, then to Sydney alone with the introduction of the 105E. Similarly, the Consul and Zephyr, until their demise in 1962, were concentrated to Brisbane, Broadmeadows and Sydney. By end of 1961, only four assembly plants operated, Brisbane, Broadmeadows and Sydney's Homebush and Auburn Plants, the Auburn plant being leased premises for the assembly of trucks.

Brisbane, which had had similar complexity to Geelong before its renovation and expansion, had slashed its product range by the start of Falcon assembly in July 1960. Canadian Customline sedans and Mainline utilities ceased assembly by June 1959; English passenger vehicle assembly was progressively reduced as parts were balanced out, and by July 1961 all were gone, either discontinued or transferred to Sydney, as were the smaller English commercial vehicles and vans.

The F series vehicles, introduced to Brisbane progressively from July 1959, were all gone by September 1962, transferred to Auburn. The T Series truck was transferred to Auburn in December 1961 although the Thames Mark 1 series lingered on until the model changeover in July 1963.

LEFT FC Thames Trader

FAR LEFT Ford bus based on R Series chassis

LEFT F600 truck at Melford Motors, Melbourne

FAR LEFT Fitzroy City Council Thames Trader

With priority given to the Falcon products, and the plants to produce them, it fell to the Sydney plants to balance out the soon-to-be-superceded vehicles. Homebush specialised in passenger vehicles and in body build, building the truck cabs for the Auburn plant. Auburn carried out trim and assembly operations and assembled them to the truck chassis. Ian Craven remembers the plant carpenter built a seat from packing cases so they could drive the R Series bus chassis between the plants. The two plants handled between nineteen and twenty-one different models in the 1959–1961 period.

With the deletion of the English vehicles, and a recession, there was little work—a difficult time for the close-knit people of the Sydney plant.

Fred Bradd joined Ford in 1951, building Anglias. In 1961, he and a leading hand were the only people working in the seat trim area of the plant, which had been reduced to a total of twenty-six payroll employees. Ray Brewster joined Ford as a vehicle tester in 1953. The road tests were carried out up and down Parramatta Road—unthinkable today. Instead of losing their skills by retrenchment, Ray was one of the many employees sent out to work at dealerships until the economy improved; Ray worked at one for six months before returning to Ford.

The Customline and Mainline vehicles were deleted at the same time as Brisbane, in 1959, followed by the Anglia, Prefect, Consul, and Zephyr products in 1961, leaving only the new English Capri.

CORTINA FASTBACKS

Body Craft Industries in Geelong converted some 1965 Cortina 240/1500 and 440/1500 sedans to fastbacks. Brian Creer test drove one of the two doors and was impressed with the styling, in fact he was stopped several times on the test with people enquiring about the car. He found the body design improved air flow over the body, improving both top speed and fuel consumption. His comment on being told Ford had withdrawn any official interest? 'Fellows—you have made one heck of a marketing goof.'

(*Australian Motor* September 2, 1966)

RIGHT 1966 Cortina Fastback and Lew Bandt

The US Fairlane was launched in Sydney in 1962, to be followed by the Galaxie in 1964, as well as, for a short time in 1965–66, the US Mustang.

The smaller English commercials, the 7 cwt and 15 cwt series, were introduced in 1958 at the model change. The Canadian F100 and F250s later joined these in 1959, then progressively upgraded, 350, 500, 600, 700, 750 and F800 models until their transfer to the new Broadmeadows Truck plant when it opened in December 1971. The D, K, series and the R and V series English trucks, introduced to the Auburn plant in 1965 and 1966 respectively, also transferred to Broadmeadows Truck plant in December 1971.

In the middle of this shuffle was the introduction of the two and four-door Cortina in 1967, and the Escort range in 1972. The transfer of all commercial trucks in 1971 left the Sydney plant as an English light vehicle assembly plant, until its conversion to assemble the Japanese, Mazda sourced, Laser-Meteor range of vehicles in 1980.

The changes in the fortunes of Ford would not have occurred without the leadership of Booth and Bourke, the improvements to quality in the Falcon from the XK to the XR would not have taken place without the hundreds, even thousands of hours put in by dedicated professionals inspired by them.

Mike Alves recalled Brian Tredwell and Barry Warren, whose Quality Control Department introduced the Master Control Hole system. They pored over the bodies-in-white[70] on the inspection tables in the Technical Inspection area of Geelong, and later Broadmeadows, sweating over the many difficult decisions to resolve panel fit and finish issues and body/component coordination. Later, people like Brian Elstone at Geelong and Joe Tibaldi at Broadmeadows would carry on that work, often unsung but vital to support the standards set by Booth. Mike Alves said of Brian Tredwell:

> *You could almost see him put on a new personality, like a new set of clothes when he arrived at work. Outside the work environment, he was charming, relaxed. Arriving at work, a switch was turned on and he was intense, driven.*

On the styling front, Jack Telnack was sent from Dearborn on foreign-service assignment to establish a design centre in Geelong. He added a sense of professionalism to the fledgling studio, taking it to a new level, painting the studio white throughout. Six months into that assignment, in 1966, he recruited Brian Rossi from Ford of Britain to work with him on the styling changes to the US designed XR, and to design the XT. Travelling down from Melbourne to Geelong each day to the fledgling styling studio in Geelong, they managed to create a new look with a cleaner-looking front end while emphasising the Mustang lines with a chrome strip which followed the body's curves.

Before the release of the XR in 1966, Fleet & Leasing manager Bill Ludgrove had been involved with the Victorian police force on the development of a police pursuit vehicle. Bourke tasked Don Dunoon and Harry Firth to develop the vehicle. Don was the Supervisor of the Test section of Product Engineering, located at the Lara Proving Grounds, and in charge of engine development at the time. Harry Firth was the racing driver who had led the team of drivers in the 70,000 mile endurance run. Working together, they reworked the cylinder heads of the 289 cubic inch V8, increasing the compression ratio and added a four-barrel carburetor. They chose a manual all synchromesh four-on-the-

LEFT 1967 GT Cortina Mark II

floor gearbox, added wider tyres, bigger brakes with eleven-inch front discs and reworked the exhaust system to create a throaty roar. Don Dunoon was one of the drivers to take representatives of the police force on a test drive:

> *I would take three burly passengers on a lap of the basic durability circuit, keep it in third gear and particularly when going over the top of the 25% grade at speed, point out the front wheels were off the ground by wobbling the steering wheel. Then down the other side but never exceeding 90 mph through the curves. They always got out somewhat pale and shaken!*

After building eight, all Australian state police ministers were invited to Lara to test the vehicles with test drivers. Phil Jones, working in Fleet & Leasing at the time, put it more succinctly, 'I went on one circuit with the test drivers and I haven't been so s@#$ scared in all my life!'

Bourke liked what he saw, named them 'GT' purportedly for 'Grand Touring', in reality a street legal vehicle for Bathurst. Launched at Calder Raceway in May, 1967, Ford built 596 of the XR GT, all gold in colour, much more than the 200 required for Bathurst. They sold like hotcakes at the premium price of $3,890. An added bonus was the free publicity when the New South Wales Police Force selected them to use as high-speed pursuit vehicles.

The same year, 1967, Harry Firth and Fred Gibson won the Bathurst 500 in the XR GT, with another XR GT driven by Ian and Leo Geoghegan finishing second. Firth's GT broke the record for the event by twenty-five minutes.

It wasn't only the Falcons that were winning; brothers Ian and Roger Vaughan completed another successful year in their Mark II Cortina, winning the Cooper Memorial Trial, the last of seven trials in the Victorian trials Championship series. Winning this event clinched first place for Roger in the Navigator's Championship, and second place for Ian in the Driver's Championship, for 1967.

In 1967, Ford manufactured 88,135 vehicles to achieve 20.5% market penetration. Falcon achieved over 16% of total passenger vehicles, while Cortina was the top vehicle in the light car segment.

Fairlane	8,075
Cortina	15,005
Galaxie	440
Commercials	5,582
Falcon range (total)	59,033

To cap it off, The XR Falcon won *Wheels* magazine Car of the Year (COTY) Award for successive models, the first time this had been achieved. The cream on the cake was the pre-tax profit of $12.16 million

A number of changes to the management structure of Ford took place in 1967. That October, Wallace Booth announced his departure, and promotion back to the United States, as Vice-President of the Philco-Ford organisation. His replacement, on November 1, was his assistant Managing Director Bill Bourke. While Booth was justifiably proud of Fords achievements in his four and a half year term, he was particularly proud of the fact that:

> *When I arrived, there were more than fifty US and Canadians in management positions at Ford Australia. As I leave, there are less than five. All were replaced by Australians.*

Of these, four key appointments made by Booth in 1965, were those of Keith Horner as General Sales Manager and Eric Witts as General Industrial Relations Manager, both of whom would significantly affect Ford in the future and later become Directors of the company. Two other positions announced in 1966, were that of Brian Ingles, previously appointed a Director of Ford Australia in 1963, but appointed as Director of Manufacturing and Supply in October 1967, and Bill Dix, appointed Director of Finance.

OPPOSITE PAGE 1968 XT Falcon sedan. Assembled at Broadmeadows and Eagle Farm assembly plants, a total of 46,334 sedans were produced.

While Ford of Canada International Operations Division retained operational control of the Asian-Pacific Ford affiliates, the geographically closer Ford Australia now assumed an engineering support role for the region. This was later to be formalised when Ford US restructured their international operations and Bourke formed Ford Asia-Pacific, (FASPAC).

Brian Inglis wanted a Head Office Manufacturing group to oversee the expansion of manufacturing. After the successful launch of the XR Falcon in 1966, while on one of his usual Broadmeadows Plant morning walk-throughs, he tapped John Marshall and Geoff Madden on the shoulder to join him in Head Office as Assembly Engineering and Plant Engineering Managers for Australia and Asia Pacific. Just before his death in 2015, John recalled the move:

> *After the noise and bustle of the assembly plant, I suddenly found myself in Head Office: quiet, carpet and muzak. I couldn't believe it.*

Now Australians were involved everywhere in the Asia Pacific region. The Ford New Zealand assembly plant at Lower Hutt was complemented by the purchase of 100 acres of land at Wiri, South Auckland and the construction of a new transmission and chassis plant and spare parts warehouse. As well as handling the Geelong expansions, the Assembly Engineering and Plant Engineering groups were sent to build a stamping plant in the free trade zone at Mariveles and an assembly plant at Muntinlupa, near Manilla. Phil Jones was one of the group. He and John Marshall had the job of selecting the land in the free trade zone. After negotiation with President Marcos and his wife, Imelda, they flew to the zone to select the land, naturally owned by Imelda Marcos.

Twelve months later, Phil was one of the five members of an advisory group to select a joint venture partner for Korea. Until then, a local dealer had been assembling English Cortinas from CKD packs. Hyundai had approached Ford US with a view of assembling Ford vehicles and the group travelled to investigate opportunities. According to Jones, Hyundai were the only viable contender. Phil recalls:

> *Hyundai had started business dredging harbours and reclaiming land. At the time we looked at them, they were into construction in a big way, and were building the main Pusan–Seoul Highway. They built the highway with 2 km, straight stretches. The mountains on either side were bored out to create hangers for jet fighters which could use the highway stretches as a runway.*

John Marshall recalled the ceremony to commence the construction of the Ford/Hyundai Ulsan plant:

> *At the end of the speeches, Mr. Hyundai clapped his hands and 150 women poured out of the nearby building, buckets on yokes across their shoulders, to start digging the foundations. Twelve months later, the plant was operational.*

INDUSTRIAL RELATIONS

Geelong and Sydney plants had long serving Employee Relations Managers who contributed much to the successful, personalised atmosphere of their plant. Both 'Tunner' Kenworthy in Geelong and Wally Sinclair in Sydney were renowned for remembering the names of the people working in the plant, and enjoyed close working relations, not only with plant employees but with the unions, 'They weren't superior,' said Ray Brewster. Their personal relationships didn't mean they were soft. Ian Cramer remembers his employment interview with Wally before he joined the Sydney plant in 1964. 'You get two sick days a month,' Wally told him, 'But if you start taking them, you won't be here long!'

The Manufacturing and Plant engineering groups worked closely together, cooperating on projects. In Australia, integration studies conducted by Marshall's group on the possible in-house manufacture of high-cost or high volume products resulted in either cost reductions, as vendors, spooked by Ford's manufacturing capacity, or new plants, lowered their prices.

Integration studies were conducted on glass manufacturing, Bill Hanlon conducted a study on the integration of manufacturing hardware; the manufacture of the thousands of screws and fasteners used in every vehicle. The foundry integration study conducted by Stan Branch resulted in the eventual purchase of the Ensite Foundry in Geelong. Karl Ketonen, returning to Ford after a stint with Chrysler and Renault, studied the integration of heaters and air conditioners when Australian Design Rule ADR21 mandated the fitment to all vehicles. The return on investment of the Heater Plant project was so good it triggered another larger, study conducted by Neil Tompkins, Bruce Kelynack and Doug Wallace that resulted in the ultimate construction of the Plastics Plant two years later.

Bourke brought a new atmosphere into the company. Booth was a finance man, perhaps more guarded or cautious in his manner. Bourke, only forty when appointed Managing Director, was the marketer and salesman. Down to earth, he greeted everyone and got on well with everyone, but his army background showed. The corridors of the third floor of Head Office could echo with the language only a trooper could repeat, when he chewed someone out. And you only made a mistake once. He could be ruthless, even callous, if the need arose. But he engendered loyalty and created a rapport with journalists and the press alike—invaluable public relations for the company.

Production of the XT began in January 1968. That year, due to the launch, Falcon volumes dropped slightly, but were offset by higher volumes of the Mk2 Cortina, ZB Fairlane and Galaxie to produce another record year, 88,701 vehicles

Engines were redefined in litres, and increased for the XT, 3.1 and 3.6-litre, as well the Mustang 5-litre V8. Engineering wise, there had been much work on the engine head to improve

RIGHT 1968 XT Falcon Van

FAR RIGHT 1968 XT Falcon Sedan 500

RIGHT 1968 XT Falcon Wagon—15,728 were produced

FAR RIGHT 1968 XT Falcon Ute—10,030 were produced

ABOVE Jack Telnack

economy, boost power and improve engine life, while the all-synchromesh manual gearbox was another first, with the three-speed automatic an option. The overall result was a quieter more fuel-efficient vehicle.

Jack Telnack had changed the look of the front end, replacing the egg-crate design and three horizontal bars of the XR grille with eight strong horizontal ones. The chrome strip now followed the curve of the body at the waistline emphasising the length of the vehicle. Options offered were front brake discs, laminated windscreen and a vinyl roof. It contrasted very favourably with the GM-H Holden, the HK, which offered only an inefficient two-speed automatic option, the 'Powerglide,' which one motoring writer caustically dubbed 'more glide than power.'

General Motors-Holden, however, had also released the Holden Monaro GTS327. When both fronted up at Bathurst that year, the Monaro, with the larger engine and lighter body won. All the XT GTs suffered from overheating problems; the XT was slightly slower than the XR, and it showed.

ZB Fairlane production began in February 1968, one month after the XT. The Fairlane Custom had the 6-cylinder 221 c.i.d. engine as standard, while the 302 V8 was standard on the up-market Fairlane 500. The most chosen option was power steering (understandable) while it was standard on the 500, with power-assisted front disc brakes. Although the Custom was the lesser of

1968 Ford Falcon XT GT.
A total of 1,415 were produced.

RIGHT 1968 ZB Fairlane—10,708 were produced at Broadmeadows assembly plant

RIGHT 1970 Galaxie—622 were produced

the two, they were both streets ahead of GM-H's Brougham in comfort, performance and style.

Of the three major strikes in the history of Ford Australia, the first was in Geelong. The Australian Engineering Union (AEU) in the Geelong toolroom had traditionally been the more militant of the two major unions on site. This was particularly the case in September 1969, when the AEU, lodged a demand for a $45 per week wage increase to replace the PPP, the Plus Payment Plan, in effect an over-the-award payment for attendance and punctuality and performance. The unions were against such payments as the company could and did deduct the PPP for even the slightest infraction. Employees cynically called it the Private Penal Powers. At first, only the maintenance fitters went out on strike, supported financially by toolroom employees who initially remained at work. Eventually all AEU members went out but, as the VBEF members were not involved, production continued. Apprentices were not permitted to strike, so apprentices from the large Ford apprentice school were used to maintain the plant and keep it operating, supervised by the non-unionised plant personnel.

The strike dragged on for three months until eventually the workers, concerned that should the strike continue until Christmas, they would lose their holiday pay, returned to work, their claim rejected. The strike caused real hardship in Geelong,

CLAY MODELS

When 'where does clay come from?', most people would automatically answer, 'the ground.' In the early days, this may have been true, but not now. Modelling clay sets firm at room temperature, but unlike pottery clay, which hardens and is difficult to work with when dry, modelling clay must not shrink as it dries, and must be able to be 'shaved' and scraped with fine scrapers to finesse the shape the stylists are looking for. A full-size vehicle clay model can require up to a ton of clay for a full-sized vehicle model, supported by an alloy 'chassis' on wheels, and foam styrene blocks, with a skin of clay, averaging 50 mm covering the foam. Modelling clay is recycled, so it must become malleable again when it is heated. Like normal clay, it is sieved to remove any impurities then put through a pug mill. The modelling clay pug mill also has heating elements as well as a die in front of the mill to extrude a specific shape such as a body-side moulding. The exact formula of modelling clay is a closely guarded secret, but all styling studios use a mixture of clay, paraffin wax and special oils. Newer formula clays are now capable of being machined by a computer-controlled mill. This takes away some of the drudgery, leaving the modeller to finesse the final shape by hand.

and as usual, the innocent suffered. Ken McDonald recalls there were children attending primary school in Geelong with a note from their parents asking the school to give them breakfast, as there was no food in the house. Later, Laurie Carmichael one of the fiercest of union leaders, acknowledged that Ford was a tough negotiator, a point long remembered by the union.

As soon as the XT was released, work began on preparing vehicles for the inaugural London to Sydney marathon, an unbelievable endurance test of drivers, navigators and vehicles. The route passed through France, Turkey, Afghanistan and India, before the vehicles were to be shipped to Perth for the sprint across Australia to Sydney. A race of 10,500 miles, (16,800 km) across eleven countries in eleven days. As he had for the 70,000 durability run, Bourke decreed that standard vehicles only be used, with suitable options such as laminated windscreen and disc brakes, while retaining the four-speed manual gearbox. Ford Australia entered three XT GTs.

The Car 2 team was Harry Firth, veteran of the endurance run, Graham Hoinville and Gary Chapman. Car 24 comprised Ian Vaughan, of Cortina rally fame, Bob Forsyth and Jack Ellis, while Bruce Hodgson and Doug Rutherford, later plant manager of the new Truck Plant, crewed Car 29. The Team Manager was John Gowland, later Competitions Manager of FPV (Ford Performance Vehicles). Much of the preparation was organising sponsorship and supplies in checkpoints; Dunlop tyres, BP fuel, Ford spares, even food and water. Nothing was left to chance.

At last, the three vehicles were flown to London, at a cost of $8,000 each, to be checked by scrutineers before last minute fine-tuning. There were ninety-eight competing vehicles of all makes and models, over 300 competitors and officials. An unusually warm and sunny November morning in 1968 saw the vehicles head off towards Dover, but the good weather was not to last. By the time the first of the vehicles had arrived at Istanbul, the weather had turned bitterly cold, with heavy fog. The roads, until now bitumen, turned to gravel and, with the requirement of an average speed of 100 km/h, it was inevitable that points began to be lost. The route through Afghanistan was easier than expected although all were looking forward to the first official rest day of the London–Bombay sector at Kabul.

Servicing of the vehicles was carried out in the most primitive of conditions, exacerbated by the ever-present crowds of people milling around. Refueling the Falcons was equally hazardous; British Petroleum's John Price hand-pumping fuel from drums on the back of a truck. The sector through India was difficult, particularly through the mountain passes after Kabul and then trying to navigate through the crowds of spectators who, careless of their own or the crews' safety, milled around them. By the time all the vehicles were loaded on the *Chusan* at Bombay for the voyage to Fremantle, only seventy-two cars were in the race. All had lost points, but when the mechanics checked the Falcons, there was little that needed to be done.

Race Leader was Roger Clarke in a Lotus Cortina, while of the Falcons, Firth was seventh, Hodgson tenth and Vaughan eleventh. The betting odds now had the Ford Australian Team drivers, little known for their rally driving experience outside Australia, as equal favourites as they would now be on home territory. The nine-day voyage from Bombay allowed plenty of time for relaxation, but also for the rumours of the terrible conditions they would face in the Outback. All fueled of course by the Australians who never failed to exaggerate the size or frequency of kangaroos and the damage one could inflict on a vehicle as they made the mad three-day dash to Sydney.

Conditions varied from narrow twisting tree-lined tracks east of Perth, to the high-speed run across the Nullabor where the Falcons all averaged 145 km/h. Temperatures hovered consistently

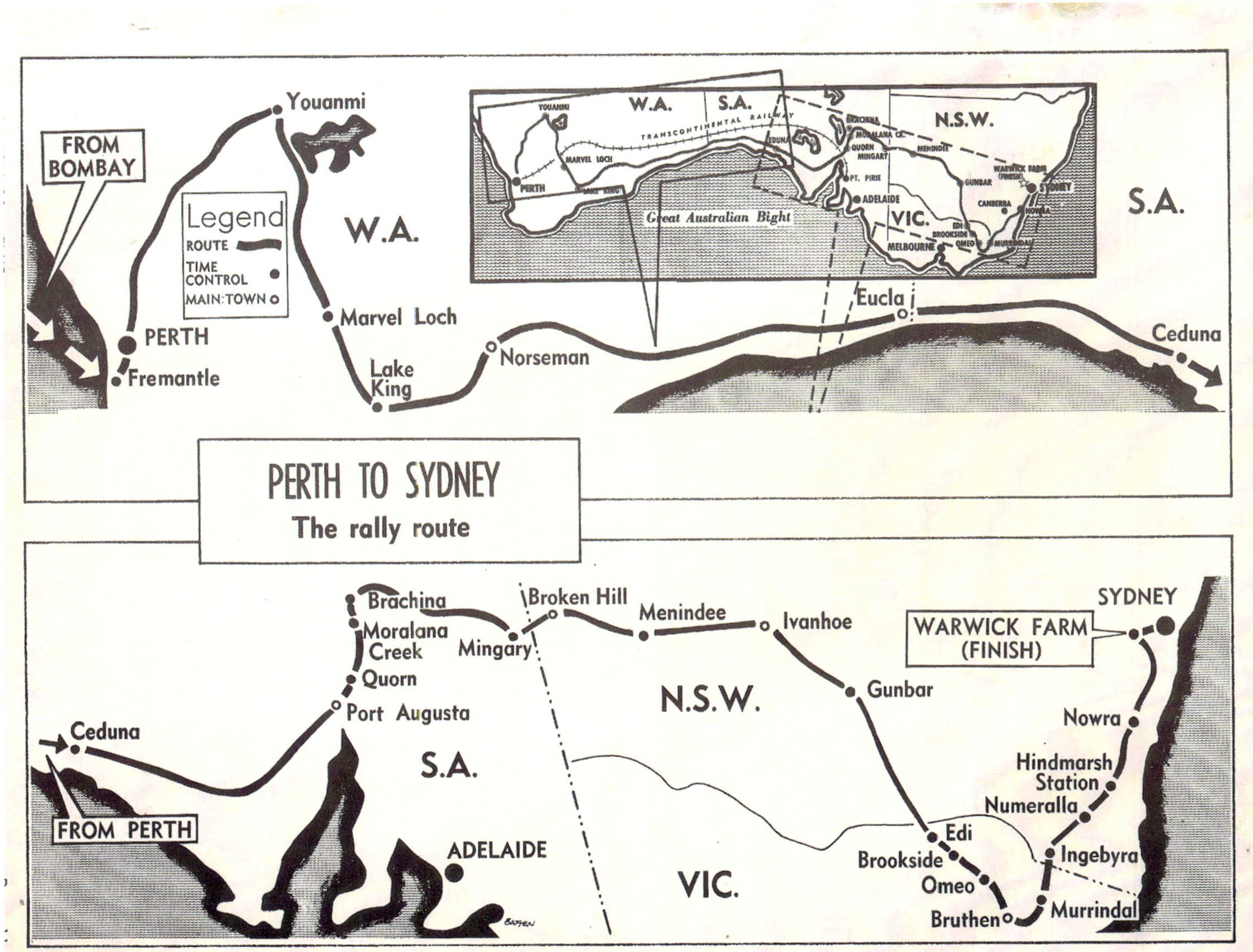

RIGHT London–Sydney route, Australian leg

in the high thirties as they made their way through a particularly tough section, the Flinders ranges, where the teams pushed the vehicles and themselves to the limit to make up time. As the cars made their way from Broken Hill, and through Victoria into the Southern Alps, the teams now found themselves in snow country, driving on roads covered with snow—a totally different set of conditions.

Finally, they wound their way to Sydney and an enthusiastic reception. Ford Australia won the team prize of $11,000, Vaughan and Forysth losing only sixty-two points and finishing third overall behind Cowan's Hillman Hunter and Hopkirk's Austin 1800. Hodgson and Rutherford finished fifth, Firth and Hoinville eighth. Of the fifty-six vehicles that finished the marathon, fifteen were Ford.

The success of the London-Sydney marathon inspired the public. The Australian Motoring writers found it difficult to devise enough superlatives for the XT, particularly the GT. Peter Robinson wrote:

> *It is one of the easiest high-performance cars in the world to drive, barring the fairly heavy steering (at parking speeds)...The reserves of passing power are incredible...I cruised the car at between 140 and 160 km/h...at these speeds the loudest noise was an annoying whistle from the driver's quarter vent window. This came in at 120 km/h and got progressively worse, only*

fixed with tape. Apart from this, it is one of the quietest cars around, like all Falcons…If you get the impression I liked this car, you are right. I reckon it is easily the best car made in Australia, able to hold its head up in any company. [71]

That same year, 1968, saw Ford profit increase again, to $17.04 million, although still paying for the investment in facilities and models, again Australia paid no dividend to the parent company; profits were invested in the new models.

By now, work was well underway on the next Falcon: the XW. Bourke had insisted Jack Telnack and Brian Rossi produce a more aggressive design. They came up with a Falcon more square in looks, with a revised roofline and a recessed back window. The departure from round to rectangular wrap-around tail-lights guaranteed a different looking rear-end, while the front incorporated an aggressive 'whale's mouth' grille treatment. Large, heavy looking bumpers completed the aggressive stance. The product planners added larger, ventilated discs and the 351 cubic inch Windsor V8. Competition was heating up in the engine stakes; GM-H had won Bathurst 500 the two previous years with a Monaro, and Chrysler had released the two and four-door Pacer, later to be replaced by the two-door Charger.

Production of the XW commenced in May 1969. Now Ford not only regained leadership in the engine capacity stakes, two months later they went one more and released the GT-HO (GT-Handling Options).

Harry Firth had left Ford to join GM-H, so Bourke had recruited Al Turner, an American specialising in performance vehicles, to develop the GT-HO—and win Bathurst. Hopes were high when GT-HOs won the Sandown Datsun three-hour race in Melbourne, filling the first three places and rose even higher when only seven Monaro GTS350s entered Bathurst, compared with fourteen GT-HOs; weight of numbers must tell, surely! But it was not to be; poor tyre selection by Turner cost Ford the race, which was won by a Monaro 350GTS, a private entry XW GT-HO coming in second. The factory GT-HOs finished fourth and fifth. Advertising by Ford after Bathurst led with the headline; 'We were deflated!'

While the tamer Falcons had a long list of options, including a GS (Grand Sports) package, a GT lookalike, the GT-HO with everything included had few options except colour.

The ZC Fairlane could not have looked more different. The styling, perhaps harking back to the earlier, US-designed Fairlanes, had twin vertically stacked headlights and wraparound tail-lights. Combined with the features borrowed from Falcon, it oozed style and luxury—a boulevard cruiser. But it was not only luxurious and comfortable; it was also fast; only dedicated sports cars could beat it over the standing quarter mile.

LEFT Car 24, KAG 002, departing London in the 1968 London–Sydney Marathon, driven by Ian Vaughan and Jack Ellis

LEFT Car 29, KAG 003, driven by Bruce Hodgson and Doug Rutherford, looking the worse for wear in outback Australia

THE CRYPTOLOGIST

David Lamb migrated to Australia from England in 1963. Previously a cryptographer in the R.A.F., David joined Ford as a Purchasing Analyst in Geelong before moving first to Hardware Street, South Melbourne, under manager Carter Bowen and his second-in-command Sid Adams, then to the new Head Office in Campbellfield, where he was promoted to Supervisor, Purchasing Analysis.

He was in the basement telecommunications area one day when a coded telex came out of the machine. Intrigued and against Ford policy, he took it home and quickly broke the code. He sealed the telex and the decoded message in an envelope and returned to work the next day, handed them over, saying the code was too simple, and offering to design a more complex one, appropriate for the company. All hell broke loose and paranoia reigned. After several meetings and, despite his protestations of good intentions, he was told to, 'Return to your desk, we won't fire you this time'. Offended his motives were doubted, David resigned, only to return six years later at the request of Bruce Burton who, convinced the introduction of the 'Matcon' program would be a disaster, asked David to assist. 'For all that', related David, 'the telex addressed to Wally Booth only gave share prices for Western Mining Corporation'.

The motoring press wrote rapturous reviews, then went into paroxysms of pleasure when the Phase II GT-HO was released later in the year. After extensive testing, motoring writers reported they believed the GT-HO was a more advanced and more sophisticated vehicle, and certainly faster, than the GTS 350 Monaro.

It had been a busy 1969 for Ford. Apart from the introduction of the XW Falcon range of all eleven models, the year had seen production commence on five F-series trucks, F100, F250 (two models), F350, F500 and F600, as well as the Mk1 Capri and the new Galaxie. Bourke, in what was to be his last annual meeting, was pleased to report record production of 97,843 vehicles and a record pre-tax profit of $25.86 million.

The Cortina was the top-selling 4-cylinder small car for the third year running and, in the large car segment, the XW now commanded 26% of the market, up from 22.4% for the XT and Ford now held 22% of the total vehicle market. The XW range was only in production for eighteen months, but in that time a total of 93,129 vehicles were produced, more than the XR range, 88,786 in twenty-one months, and the XT, 74,392 in twenty-one months.

Years later, Chief Engineer David Ford was to spend some time living and working in Dearborn. By sheer coincidence, he

BELOW Mark I Capri Deluxe—11,536 Capris were produced at Homebush assembly plant

LEFT XW GT flyer

LEFT 1969 XW Falcon Fairmont station wagon—18,685 station wagons were produced

FAR LEFT 1969 XW Falcon sedan—58,451 were produced

ABOVE XW concept drawing by Brian Rossi

RIGHT (Left to right) John Eastwood, Les Egan, Ivan Tan Sing, Tony Isherwood, Don Norman and Alan Gledhill inspecting an XW Instrument Cluster Fascia, for reasons which remain a mystery!

rented a house next door to Bill Bourke, who at the time was head of North American Assembly Operations (NAAO). Invited to dinner one night, David recalled Bourke reminiscing on his time in Australia:

> *'One thing I liked about Australians,' he said, 'They were very laid back. They didn't give a shit. One time I know, you told me to my face I was full of shit. And I was!'*

Bourke also said Ford US was 'chimneyfied', no thought of the management working together as they did in Australia. Without the support of his managers, he later left the company, Ford's loss.

FIRST MILLION VEHICLES IN AUSTRALIA

The one millionth vehicle produced by Ford Motor Company of Australia rolled off the line at the company's Broadmeadows assembly plant today (Monday, February 13). In a ceremony to mark this milestone, the car was preceded off the line by the first vehicle produced by the company forty-two years ago, a T model, now owned by Mr. George Cox, President of the Vintage Driver's Club of Victoria. The vehicle, a light blue Falcon 500 was driven off the line by Ford's Assistant Managing Director, Mr. W. O. Bourke. The ceremony was watched by Company executives and a large number of employees. Among them was Mr. George Hogg, a production supervisor in the Broadmeadows plant, whose father, former Police Sergeant T. Hogg of Preston, was the original owner of the first vehicle produced by Ford in this country.

LEFT 1967 One millionth Ford Australia built vehicle

LEFT 1967 One millionth Ford Australia built vehicle and the first Model T produced by Ford Australia

351-GT

CHAPTER 6

1970—1979

THE FORD YEARS 1970—1979

1970:

XW GT-HO Phase II released. Falcon takes 1st and 2nd places at Bathurst. XY Falcon, ZD Fairlane production commences. Phase III GT-HO announced. Research Centre opened at Broadmeadows. $45 million facility expansion announced. Ford Australia pop group 'The Going Thing' formed, managed by Athol Guy. Tyre and Trim store constructed at Broadmeadows. Ford Asia-Pacific formed, Bill Bourke becomes President. Brian Inglis becomes Managing Director of Ford Australia.

1971:

Falcon GT-HO's win Bathurst, placed 1st, 2nd and 3rd. XA Falcon and ZF Fairlane production commences. TC Cortina released, the first one built being the 1.5-millionth vehicle built by Ford Australia. New truck plant at Broadmeadows commences production. Ford Credit Australia formed.

1972:

XA Falcon Hardtop production commences. Crashtest barrier and emission laboratory commissioned at Lara Proving Grounds. New $4 million Plastics Plant announced. Ford Fiera announced for Asian market. The Blue Line tractor equipment range announced. Ford worldwide builds 4 millionth tractor, Australia builds the 4,000,010th. New computer system introduced, APDIS.

1973:

XB Falcon, ZG Fairlane, P4/ P5 LTD and Landau production commences. Last Falcon GT built. XA GT Hardtop wins Bathurst 1000 touring car race.

1974:

Ford takes passenger car leadership for six months. Falcon wins Bathurst, Ford withdraws from motorsport. Ford Employee Credit Union commences in Geelong.

1975:

Two-millionth Australian-built Ford vehicle produced. Louisville heavy duty truck range announced - the first righthand- drive versions in the world. 'Little Ripper' special value pack for 8 cwt Escort van released. Ford construction equipment range released. Ford Credit Employee Union opens in Broadmeadows and Sydney.

1976:

XC Falcon, ZH Fairlane, P6 LTD production commences. 250,000th Ford Truck produced. $72 million product and facility investment announced. 7A tractor range released. Brisbane plant converted and dedicated to build Fairlane, LTDs

1977:

One-millionth Falcon vehicle produced. 100,000th Fairlane-LTD produced. Expansion of Plastics Plant. Famous 1–2 win by XC GS500 Falcon Hardtops at Bathurst 1000 touring car race.

1978:

Japanese-sourced Courier, European Transit Van and D Series trucks announced. Last 400 XC Falcon two-door Hardtop vehicles marketed as Cobras.

1979:

XD Falcon, ZJ Fairlane, FC LTD production commences with the world's first plastic fuel tank for mass-produced vehicles. Brisbane becomes sole source for Fairlane, LTD. Trader truck and Econovan released. Ford Motor Company buys 25% of Mazda Corporation, Japan. Ford Australia celebrated the export of it 100,000th vehicle in April.

The XY Falcon, the last of the body style, commenced production in August 1970 and was released in October that year. It was too late for Bathurst 1969; Ford entered the XW GT-HO Phase II.

It was always going to be a tough racing year, with GM entering the XU-1 Torana and Chrysler the Valient Pacer, both very quick vehicles. But Ford had won Sandown and were optimistic for Bathurst. Qualifying saw GT-HOs fill the first three places, followed by three Toranas. The race was notable for a competitor pushing Bill Brown off the track at Skyline on the first lap. Brown, in ninth position in his GT-HO, blew a tyre, rolled several times in front of the pack and the resulting carnage wiped out several cars. Luckily, the marshals cleared the wreckage before the race leaders came round again three minutes later. The race continued comparatively uneventfully and the GT-HOs prevailed again, coming first and second, with the third place-getter an XU-1 Torana a lap behind. Superior speed, better handling and slick work by the pit crews had won the day.

The XW-XY change was more a refinement than the radical change that the XT-XW had been; nevertheless, the XY was a substantial model change. Under the skin, the XY contained significant engine and transmission improvements, as well as being notable for the release of the Phase III GT-HO. Engine capacity of the 6-cylinders increased to 200 and 250 c.i.d.,[72] while still offering the 302 c.i.d. and, of course the Windsor 351 c.i.d. V8s. The resulting increases in power and capacity in the sixes gave significant improvements in torque and power, while the new 7-bearing crankshaft with eight counterweights substantially improved smoothness. Increases in throughput to the oil and water pumps improved engine longevity, while the 3-speed automatic transmission was streets ahead of the Holden's power-sapping two-speed, or the 3-speed Tri-matic, dubbed by journalists as the 'Trau-matic' due to its reliability issues and service failures. Ford never publicly criticised GM's products, only too aware of their history and potential for disaster, the 'there but for the grace of God' or the 'thank God it's not us' syndromes.

GM-H released their 'little' 253 c.i.d. V8; Ford countered with a two-venturi 250 6-cylinder engine with exhaust extractors to keep ahead. Other options offered on the XY were an 8-track cartridge player, advanced for its time, a sunroof, alloy wheels and for the 302 V8, a lowered suspension. Falcons now had the edge over Holden for ride, handling and seating comfort. Heaven!

Looking for every advantage, product planning even came up with a 4-wheel drive version of the XY utility for the rural market. Brisbane plant produced 432 of them, mainly for the Queensland and Northern Territory markets, although the odd vehicle appeared in the other states.

PAGES 138–139 1971 XY GT-HO Phase III

LEFT 1970 XY Falcon GT. 1557 were built

RIGHT XY instrument panel

FAR RIGHT XY Falcon GT T-Bar Automatic

RIGHT XY Falcon GT 351 shaker

FAR RIGHT XY Falcon GT badge

In production for 17 months, the XY Falcon product range actually outsold the XW, producing 100,474 vehicles.

Released at the same time as the XY, the ZD Fairlane Custom and 500, had styling themes hinting of the Lincoln Continental, with full width grille, and rear decklid trim. Bucket seats were standard, and they were quieter and more refined; 12,797 were produced. The XY-ZD vehicle range was also profitable; Ford was able to report an increased profit for 1970 of $29.6 million.

With newer production facilities, modern state of the art engineering and test facilities, better-looking and better vehicles and a more aggressive sales force than GM-H, the future for Ford looked brighter than it had only five years previously.

But, it was not all good news. Ford US had advised early in 1968 they were dropping the Falcon and developing two new models, the smaller, 2-door Maverick, and the new, larger Torino. There would be no more reliance on the US for design and development.

On a cool autumn May morning in 1968, Jack Telnack, Brian Rossi and Alan Jackson left Melbourne to spend a long, hot and humid summer in Dearborn working on the next model Falcon, the all-

ABOVE 1971 XY GT-HO. Only 300 were built

Australian XA. Much preparatory work had already been done before they left.

Telnack and Bourke lived near each other in Toorak and they met regularly at the Toc-H centre in Toorak Road for coffee on Saturday mornings. Bourke had flown to Dearborn as soon as he learnt of the US plan to ditch the Falcon for the Torino and he didn't like what he saw. While he and Jack met regularly at the Toc-H, planning the next week's work, Brian Rossi was busily sketching design themes to take with them to Dearborn. Perhaps not as bluntly as Charlie Smith, Bourke had told the US that the longer Torino was not for Australia. It was too close to the Fairlane in size, and the Fairlane was large enough. He didn't have to be as blunt as Smith; he had the runs on the board. Nevertheless, the American designers pushed for the Torino design to be accepted. After much discussion, the Australians developed a clay using the Torino design, chopping off the longer front and rear overhangs. The result created was just that; a snub nose, short-arsed vehicle that even the US designers rejected.

The Australian team was eager to demonstrate their credentials. 'This was our chance, and nobody wanted to blow it,' said Rossi. They worked long days over that summer, six days a week, often seven when Bourke was to fly in the next day for his fortnightly review with Ford President, Semon 'Bunkie' Knudsen. Knudsen and his entourage viewed their work regularly at their weekly design review meetings where the clays, wheeled out into the courtyard of the design centre, were examined in the early morning light. 'We got nothing but support and encouragement from them,' said Rossi. 'They were very interested in what we were doing.'

To speed up the decision process and allow comparisons of different design ideas, often one side of the clay would have a different design to the other. The Falcon design theme did contain influences of the Torino, particularly the 'coke-bottle' theme of the hip line, but was uniquely Australian. By the time they returned to Australia in October that year, they had completed the designs for the Falcon sedan, wagon and Fairlane. The utility and panel van clays would be completed in Australia as would Bourke's pet project, the two-door hardtop. One of Rossi's sketches of the hardtop, exaggerating its width and fattening the design, was later to become a classic. The work of the team impressed not only the US designers, 'Bunkie' Knudsen gave Bourke the green light, saying, 'go out and build yourself a design centre, but make sure it's close to Head Office'. The shortage of clay modellers continued but now they had help. Mike Alves recalled:

> *We had lots of clay modellers from the US come out to work with us. They taught us a lot about modelling and body design.*

ABOVE 1970 XY Fairmont sedan. A total of 62,602 sedans were produced.

Boy, were they dedicated. We used to call them 'ghosties'; they'd pull an 'all-nighter' just to finish off a clay, to get a style or design just right for the Design Committee meeting the next day.

Even though the hardtop clay was finished later than the others, in April 1969, the entire range was completed in time for tooling to commence. The clever marriage of parts reduced complexity and cut costs considerably. The wagon wheelbase was the same as the Fairlane; the hardtop used the front end of the sedan and wagon and the longer doors of the utility and vans. Much of the mechanicals were from the XY, the effort went into the new body design. Perhaps the only disappointment with the hardtop was it was released with skinny tyres on the base model, and looked under done, but provided room for the wider wheels and lower profile tyres used for the Bathurst campaign.

Bourke had not wasted any time taking up Knudsen's offer of a styling studio. As soon as the design team returned to Australia, he announced plans to build a styling studio behind Head Office. In almost no time, it was completed and Victorian Premier Sir Henry Bolte opened the Research Centre, as it was then named, on April 22, 1970. As usual, he took the opportunity to lambast his critics for selling the Broadmeadows land to Ford.

While Bourke was busy building the Australian operation, he continued to be involved in Asia. In great secrecy in 1970, he tasked John Marshall, Noel Woodford and Don Gillies with finding and fitting out to Ford standards, a new sumptuous, office space in Melbourne, near St Kilda Road. On its completion, and timed with the restructuring by Ford US of its overseas operations into three regional groups, he announced the formation of a new company, Ford Asia-Pacific, to assume responsibility for all Asia-Pacific operations, of which Ford Australia was but one division. FASPAC had five directors, John Sagovac, Finance, Bill Hawkins, Sales and Marketing, Bill Hartigan, New Business, Bill McGuiness, Product Development and John Marshall, Manufacturing and Supply, as well support staff, mostly Australian.

The frenetic pace continued as the company geared up for the next phases of capacity increases. The September 1970 issue of *Ford News* carried the announcement of a $45 million expansion program for both Geelong and Broadmeadows.

For Geelong, a new chassis plant for machining components, brake drums, wheel hubs and door hinges, amongst other components, the stamping plant was extended to incorporate five new press lines to stamp 500 panel sets a day. The engine plant was extended to build the V8 engines locally, complementing the 6-cylinder plant already in operation, while a new canteen to accommodate the estimated 300 new workers was to be erected.

Broadmeadows plant was extended by a whopping five acres to a total of twenty-eight acres, adding additional assembly lines

NEW MANAGER FOR RACING TEAM

Howard Marsden joined the Special Vehicles Office at the Research Centre in July 1971. In charge of the company's Rallycross and Circuit events racing teams, Howard has prepared cars, drivers and teams to race on the world's most challenging circuits, including Monte Carlo, Le Mans and Indianapolis. Howard said he was looking forward to the coming season when Alan Moffat and John French will be driving Phase III GT-HO Falcons at Sandown before competing at Bathurst.

LEFT 1970 XY wagon—18,997 were produced

LEFT 1970 XY ute—13,920 were produced

LEFT 1970 ZD Fairlane

to increase the plant capacity to 400 vehicles a day, fifty an hour. A new satellite tyre and trim store, to remove a fire hazard and to free up area in the assembly plant, was built. Three new automated electrocoat paint systems were announced, to improve paint quality, coverage and corrosion resistance, the first electrocoat systems in the industry. Also announced was the construction of a new truck plant north of the assembly plant, capable of building forty trucks a day, replacing the older leased, truck plant in Auburn, Sydney. The same issue of *Ford News* also carried an article about the company's new Managing Director, Brian Inglis. With Bourke becoming President of FASPAC, he had had no hesitation in recommending his fellow director to replace him. So it was with much pride that employees learnt their next Managing Director would be an Australian, one of their own.

The year 1970 saw an increase in volume of nearly 21,000 vehicles over 1969. The increase was all in passenger vehicles, commercials reducing by a mere 564 vehicles. It was the start of the second golden age for Ford. Except for the years of 1981–82 and 1988, the next twenty years would become the highest output years in the company's history. It was also the year when, after declaring a profit before tax of $29.56 million, the company began repatriating dividends back to Ford US.

The popularity of the XY Falcon and ZD Fairlane continued during 1971 as the company tooled up for the XA/ZF range. The Bathurst campaign that year could not have been better; Sandown had been disappointing, with brake pad problems, which Ford hoped were fixed for Bathurst. It was immediately obvious the GT-HOs were in a class by themselves. With Alan Moffat on pole

1971 XY GT Phase III

ABOVE 1970 Mk1 Escort GT—only 806 were produced.

position, GT-HOs occupied eight of the top ten places on the grid, Valiant Chargers taking eighth and tenth places. The nearest XU-1 Torana was next, on eleventh. The XY GT-HO Phase III Falcons swept all before them finishing one, two, three. Alan Moffat, leading the charge, won by a lap, followed by Tony Skelton and Rob McKay, with five of the first six being GT-HO Falcons.

Another crash by Bill Brown on the forty-third lap in his GT-HO marred the race. His vehicle blew a front tyre at McPhillamy Park and rolled several times along the Armco railing, almost cutting it in half. Amazingly, he walked away almost unscathed.

Bourke's mantra, 'Win on Sunday, sell on Monday', certainly held true for the XY Falcon.

The company was brimming with confidence during this period; sales were up, the company was profitable. The parent company was happy; dividends were flowing again and the product range was covering the market.

Don Deveson, production manager of Broadmeadows transferred to Sydney plant for the build of the 1970 model Escort, launched in January and February. It had been well received with 12,145 vehicles assembled that year, and hopes were high the new TC Cortina would sell better than the Mark 2 which, while selling 11,692 vehicles, was down from the previous year. There were insufficient English Capris available to satisfy demand and the

increase in Falcon sales meant every plant was working overtime, often seven days a week. The heady atmosphere was palpable; like the advertising jingle of the era, 'Going Ford is the Going Thing'. With the growth in sales volume, came growth in employment. By 1971, employment was past 14,000 and rising, the organisation expanding in all directions.

The Truck Plant began production quietly in October 1971; first vehicle was the V series, followed by the multi-model F series, F100, F250, F350, the D series in January 1972, and the K series in February. The Heater plant commenced production to coincide with XA, supplying heaters, air conditioners, demist nozzles, gloveboxes and the right and left hand exterior rear-view mirrors that with the clever use of spacers, was fitted to all Ford passenger vehicles, and became known as the corporate rear-view mirror.

Mid-1971 saw the launch by Chrysler and GM-H of new models, the VH Valiant and the HQ Holden, and the motoring public eagerly awaited the launch of the XA/ZF Falcon and Fairlane. Both sedans commenced production in Broadmeadows plant in December 1971. The wagon followed in January, after the Christmas shutdown period, the month that Brisbane launched both Falcon models, by now fitted with mandatory seatbelts. It had been a successful year; Ford recorded a A$16.1 million profit for the 1971 financial year; sales had increased, and Ford now had a 22.3% share of the Australian market as well as exporting the

ABOVE 1972 XA Futura sedan—there were 78,404 four-door sedans and 8,686 two-door XA hardtops produced

1972 Ford XA GT Falcon

RIGHT 1973 XA 302 c.i.d. Superbird

Falcon to forty-two right-hand-drive countries. A dividend of A$3.5 million was repatriated to the US.

The slogan for the XA/ZF range was 'The Great Australian Road Car'. While many felt the Fairlane was too close to the Falcon in profile, acceptance by the public of both models was good; many felt the cockpit-style instrument panel and interior styling superior to both competitors and the now famous coke-bottle exterior styling was praised. The utility, panel van and two-door hardtop commenced assembly in June in Broadmeadows, one month after the launch of the TC Cortina sedan.

Ford celebrated its 1.5 millionth vehicle built in August, a Cortina, only four years after celebrating its one millionth. The TC wagon followed in October.

The cost of reskinning the XA/ZF series had meant most of the mechanicals were carry-over from the XY, something not appreciated by *Wheels* despite their raptures with the XY. While they wrote that the styling was, 'An appealing halfway house between the big car look of the Valiant and the smaller, chunky appearance of the HQ Holden',[73] they controversially withheld the 1972 COTY award, much to Ford's displeasure. But there was no time to waste. By the release date of the XA, the XB facelift program was already firmed up and work had begun on tooling.

While Ford waited for the COTY award that did not come, the Ford US board approved the project to build the Plastics Plant, in April 1972. FOA released the following news release on April 4:

ABOVE A Carlton United Breweries 1972 XA Ute

LEFT 1972 ZF Fairlane

LEFT 1972 XA Panel Van

Ford Australia is to spend nearly $4 million on a new plastics plant at its Broadmeadows headquarters in Victoria. The 87,500 sq. ft. building will be erected adjacent to the company's head office administration block on the Hume Highway. Building of the plastics plant is expected to start early in May and should be completed by September. Ford Australia's managing director, Mr. Brian Inglis, said today that the new plant would manufacture a wide variety of plastic components for the company's range of products. He said the decision to build the plant was made after the successful trial of a small pilot plant, which began operations 18 months ago. Ultimately it will employ about 130 payroll and staff members, and should be fully operational by the first quarter of 1973.

The production departments in the manufacturing and assembly plants operated differently; the manufacturing plants operated on a batch process, where machines, production lines or product assembly lines operated, stopped and changed tooling, dies, or fixtures to make another product or series of products. The facility operated on a daily, weekly, monthly cycle or longer, depending on the run quantity and the length of time for changeover. Traditionally, the smaller the quantity, or longer the changeover time, the longer the production cycle. Later, Japanese production concepts of 'Kan-Ban,' just-in-time, and 'Muda,' the elimination of waste would challenge this and become the accepted practice in the 1980s. Daily production plans began in the afternoon, for the next day's production. With the shift starting, at 7.30 am, the

DON DEVESON LETTER

Mr. W. W. Sinclair,
Industrial Relations Manager,
Homebush
18th February, 1970
I wish to draw to your attention that with my breakfast this morning, which was brought to my office, there were 2 salt shakers and no pepper. Also the bacon was not cooked enough and was rather greasy because of this. I would also like you to contact Schweppes on Official Ford letterhead about the flat lemonade in their tin pack.
(signed)
D.F.Deveson
Plant Manager
P.S. Also, the canteen did not send a cup and saucer on the tray to my office.

FIRST INTERVIEW

The first employee to be employed from outside the company to join the Plastics Plant Integration group in August 1970 was Doug Wallace. After an interview with Fred Adams, he was asked to stay for another interview, to be confronted by a panel comprising, John Marshall, Neil Tompkins, Karl Ketonen and Bruce Kelynack. After a grueling half hour interview he left, to be offered the job several days later. A few days after commencing with Neil Tompkins in Geelong, Doug commented on how knowledgeable the group had been. Neil hooted with laughter, 'We were asking all those questions because we didn't know!'

production and material control supervision would be in the plant early, checking stock and monitoring attendance as employees clocked on at the time clocks. By 7.25, the General Foremen of each area had a good idea of the absenteeism in their department for the day. In the next five minutes, decisions on which machines to run, which lines to temporarily close pending latecomers, which areas to shut for four hours or to close for the day, would be made. By 7.32 am, it was all over; the plant was up and running, adjusted later if necessary.

An assembly plant has no such flexibility. At the start of the shift, the production line had to produce vehicles; cars had to be built. At 400 vehicles a day output, every 1.13 minutes produced a vehicle. Conversely, every 1.13 minutes the line did not run was a vehicle irretrievably lost, in the 1970s approximately $5,000 per minute. The pressure to produce was enormous, the potential for losing production equally enormous. The Production Manager knew within ten minutes of the shift commencing if the day was going to be a good one, or a disaster. One Production Manager summed it up; 'You can't win, but you can't afford to lose.' One of the biggest effects on meeting production, and therefore budget, was absenteeism or lateness, which is why most automobile companies with an assembly line were willing to pay a bonus for consistent and timely attendance, even back in the 1920s.

Successful control of costs and elimination of waste in any form are key drivers in the automotive industry. The Cost Accounting and Finance departments kept tight control on the budget. The imposition of overtight controls or incorrectly applied objectives stifled performance. John Crew put it succinctly:

> *Head Office didn't care about you if you were in production. They only cared about your output. Broadmeadows Plant was 8% of the operating cost of Ford in the 1980s. The Production Manager who missed his Direct Labour budget by 2% lost his job. That's 2% of 8% of the company's expenses!*

The pressure to perform affected people in different ways. Some couldn't cope with it and left. Others stayed on, failed and lost their jobs. It is believed, that the divorce rate in the production management areas in the automotive industry was higher than for the rest of the population. However some found a way of avoiding the pressure, creating working relationships with their people.

John Crew was put in charge of the trim area of the plant in the 1970s, a department of which he knew nothing. His General Foreman had good people skills, planned and ran his department well but, under pressure, was seen as a poor performer. John allowed him to get on with the thing he was best at, running the Trim department while John attended all the meetings, took the flack and provided the buffer. These partnerships produced the best results, others became ruthless with the very people they relied on to produce the product; the hourly paid, payroll people. The result was a sausage machine that could chew people up and spit them out. Unfortunately, the tyrants often produced the results and were promoted, perpetuating the image of production at Ford being a harsh regime.

In 1973, the VBEF on the Broadmeadows site made a claim for higher wages on the company. The mantra of Industrial Relations to negotiate, negotiate, anything to keep them at work, failed; nothing was going to stop the employees going out on strike this time. As usual, as soon as the workers went out the door, Ford Industrial Relations personnel became hard and tough negotiators, as the Unions had found previously. After three long weeks of negotiations, agreement was reached between the shop stewards, the union and the company on an outcome that was put to all employees at a mass meeting, held at the Broadmeadows Town Hall the next day. There was much discussion, much of it acrimonious, but when it was put to the vote, a slim majority accepted the settlement and voted to return to work. However because little of what was said was translated into other languages, many employees really didn't understand exactly what they were voting for; and that was when the trouble started. A number of Greek workers, dissatisfied with the outcome, met and in conjunction with a number of agitators, decided to blockade the plant.

The next day cars and barricades blockaded the main gate before most employees arrived to start work. As soon as it appeared there would be trouble, the security staff had closed all gates to the plant and office area. Many employees, unable to begin work, were confused, thinking the company had locked them out. Confusion reigned outside the gate, watched by the Plant Management inside the fence.

As the morning wore on, tempers frayed amongst the crowd, and scuffles broke out as those wanting to work, clashed with the protestors, while managers looked on, powerless. Then, right in the middle of the fracas, a delivery truck loaded with fruit and vegetables arrived, headed for the canteen. A golden opportunity. The fruit was delivered all right; the strikers raided the truck, emptied it and pelted the management, building, everyone and everything in sight as they vented their frustration. Ken McDonald recalled he had tomato stains on his shirt for weeks. Things rapidly deteriorated when the crowd noticed the company taking photographs of the protesting workers and late in the morning the violence escalated. One group of agitators started pushing the cyclone wire fence near the gatehouse. Another, more violent group, broke open the fire hoses in the carpark and using poles, posts, anything smashed the windows of the south end of the office block, where the computer centre was located. Directing the fire hoses through the windows, their objective was to cripple the company by putting the computers out of action.

The company had called the police in when the first scuffles broke out but up to this stage, had not been involved. Aware of the escalating violence they had in turn called out the police horses, who had gathered on the other side of the plant, at the Sydney Road gate. They galloped around the plant and worked their way through the downed fence. Meanwhile about thirty or forty protestors had managed to get into the plant. They ran riot through the pre-delivery area and up and down the aisles, damaging vehicles as they went. Each one was hunted down, often gang-tackled by staff members and frog-marched out of the plant. As the police horses worked their way through the violent fray, several attempts were made to unsettle the horses but the horses prevailed and the crowd soon melted away. The day ended with a standoff.

In the light of the situation, which had clearly got out of control, Laurie Carmichael of the AEU and Len Townsend subsequently reneged on the agreement with the company and the strike resumed. It would be another nine weeks before it ended. Subsequent to the riot, the photographs taken were analysed by the company. Production staff verified the worst agitators and rioters were not Ford employees. The AEU and the VBEF, also embarrassed by the outcome, which had clearly wrong-footed them also verified they were not union members. Finally, the company consulted the police and one of the security forces. Ken McDonald recalls the police and security people made only verbal reports to the company, to the effect that they believed that student-radicals from Monash University were involved.

LEFT 1972 apprentice workshop Geelong

Nothing good came out of the strike. Senior police were severely embarrassed they had allowed the situation to deteriorate so badly before they intervened. Ford, clearly believing they were the injured party went on the offensive. They took out two page advertisements in all the Australian national newspapers. The advertisements included some of the photographs taken during the riot with the text, 'Is this what unionism is in Australia?', seeking to put pressure on the ACTU to assume control of the strike and seeking public support. The campaign failed spectacularly. Bob Hawke, head of the ACTU was no help. He was not even in the country, at an International Labour Organisation (ILO) conference in Geneva. The Federal Labor government backed the unions. McDonald remembers the Federal Labor Minister, left winger Clyde Cameron, when interviewed on the ABC's *AM* program and asked to comment saying, 'If Ford are involved, they're in the wrong!'

When the Unions, led by Carmichael and Townsend, recommenced negotiations they changed tack, demanding 'meaningful negotiations', whatever that meant. Finally, the dispute was brought before the Conciliation and Arbitration Commission, and after several fruitless discussions, the unions made the claim that, in total, 'Ford paid less than General Motors'. To compare the two different awards, with differing rates, over-award payments, attendance bonuses, merits etc., was like comparing apples and oranges.

The standoff was broken eventually when Ford, who knew the GM-H award as well as their own, got their staff in the Finance Department to work over a weekend. With the agreement of the union, they calculated the amount that every employee at Ford would receive if they were on the GM-H award and presented it to the Commission. The Commission ruled on the result and at a mass meeting, the unions put a vote to the workforce with a recommendation to return to work. After three months on strike, they returned for an increase of between $1.20 and $1.30 a week.

Sometime during 1969–70, Bill Hartigan had proposed that the Asia-Pacific region develop a program that would involve all Ford affiliates. Designed to provide transport for the masses, the 'Basic Concept' vehicle, shortened to 'B.C.' then nicknamed the Bullock Cart by the Australians, the homologation plan called for the various affiliates to manufacture some components and export them to the others. In return, they would import components and assemble vehicles; the concept that the value of imports would equal exports, and be duty-free to all. It was an ambitious plan, simple in concept, complex in implementation. Taiwan would cast engine blocks and build the Escort 'Kent' engine, New Zealand would supply spindles and transmission components, Singapore would build rotating electrics i.e. starter motors and alternators, while the Philippine stamping plant would supply simple brake-press stampings. Various countries would make the tooling, Taiwan and the Philippines the tooling for left-hand-drive vehicles, Thailand the tooling for right-hand drive. Australia would provide the technical expertise. Among those joining FASPAC from FOA and working in the Mariveles Free Trade Zone or Muntinlupa, near Manilla were Jimmy Leason and Bruce Kelynack from Geelong, Bob Taylor, Phil Lumb and Ron Stein from assembly engineering.

As part of the homologation plan, Phil Jones was given the task of rejuvenating the old Japanese assembly plant built on eleven acres of land at Koyasu, halfway between Tokyo and Yokohama. Ford US had set up the plant in 1924, to assemble vehicles imported from USA in CKD[74] packs. Some of the vehicles assembled in this plant were then re-exported to China and Korea, in SKD[75] format. In the 1930s Ford bought a further 91.5 acres of undeveloped

NEW TRUCK PLANT

The new Truck Assembly Plant, to be built on a five-acre site between Head Office and the main assembly plant, will cost $5 million and is planned to be complete by September 1971. Equipment will be transferred to the new site from the Auburn (Sydney) plant and, with new equipment, will have a capacity of forty vehicles per shift. Truck lines produced will be the Ford D, F, K, R and V series. The plant will provide the most up-to-date and flexible truck production facilities and equipment for on-site truck engineering. The first trucks are due off the assembly line early in 1972.

RIGHT A Tip Top Bakeries, Ford V Series Transit van

reclaimed land on Tokyo Bay at Tsurumi for (then) US$100,000, with plans to build a large assembly plant. General Motors and Chrysler had also applied for permits to build assembly plants, but MITI (the Japanese government), wanting to protect the fledgling Japanese automotive industry, refused permits to all three. After Pearl Harbour, the Japanese government seized the Koyasu plant and gave it to Nissan, who used it during the war to build trucks. One of the older employees later told Phil that during bombing raids by the US Air Force on Tokyo, civilians would flock to the plant with its distinctive 'Ford' water tower and large roof area, believing that Americans would not bomb their own property. Later, in the US, Jones related this to an ex US air force pilot. He laughed and said it was partly true, but only to the extent they used it as a navigation beacon; get to the Ford factory and water tower, turn left and bomb Tokyo, turn right and bomb Yokohama.

After the war, the Japanese government returned the plant to the US government as described by Jones, 'plus a bag of gold'. The US government and McArthur used the plant as a warehouse during the Korean conflict, and later returned it to Ford ownership in the fifties. No word on the bag of gold. The plant lay idle for many years, rusting and rotting until 1971 when, as part of the Asian-Pacific homologation plan, the Japanese gave the go-ahead to renovate it and use it for a warehouse, at a cost of US$5 million.

The B.C., by now named the Fiera, was based on a design concept from Dearborn, modelled and pre-program engineered at the Research Centre at Broadmeadows. FOA built the prototypes at Geelong and tested them at the Lara test track. Market research had shown the region wanted a low-cost, revenue-producing vehicle with versatility to develop from a simple cab-chassis to a flatbed truck, a pickup, a high side truck, an enclosed van and a people carrier. To keep cost to a minimum, the design concept was to use only simple manufacturing equipment, brake presses (a single action mechanical stamping press) and guillotines. With a price of US$1,000 and low-cost finance, the primary target was the 'Jeepney'. Since WWII, Jeepneys had been a principal source of Philippine transportation; usually decorated with tin animals and festooned with streamers, the Jeepneys packed ten to twelve people together on seats along the sides. Originally cobbled together from war surplus jeeps in Manila backyard workshops, they later became specialised vehicles, produced with local bodies and imported engines and transmissions.

The Fiera was released to the public twice. The first was at the Ford Pavilion of the '72 Transpo exhibition, held at Dallas, Texas in May 1972. The announcement by Bourke at the release highlighted the ruggedness of the body and the reliable 4-cylinder 1.1 and 1.3 litre engines, suited to the poor road conditions, as well as the ability to remove the rear wheels and use it as a power take-off source for other equipment.

LEFT Bill Bourke, President, Ford Asia Pacific Inc. beside the new Fiera

LEFT Fiera styling drawings by Griffin

The second release of the Fiera was with great fanfare in Davao City in the Philippines on August 10, 1972. Motoring writers from around the Asia-Pacific region flew to Manila to attend the launch and conduct test drives, to be duly reported in the *Manila Times*, and other regional newspapers. Those attending the launch included T H Mecke Jnr, R W Dewey of FUS, Ray Kennedy and Al Turner of FASPAC and C Allan Foran, President of Ford of Philippines. The mayor of Davao City declared August 10 to be Fiera Day. Foran told the gathering he hoped to sell 12,000 Fieras in the first twelve months and, pitching his speech to the local industry, said the Fiera Jeepney would cost an estimated 4,000 pesos (US$597) less than the current Jeepney models, use half as much gasoline and be easier to maintain. Much was made of the

ABOVE Bill Bourke and Brian Inglis

fact that Ford had supplied tooling to forty local suppliers and that 487 vital components were sourced locally. He said he was not trying to run the local Jeepney builders out of business, but rather he said, he believed they might want to return to their original tasks as 'body builders', using the Fiera chassis for their platform.

A brilliant concept, with altruistic motives as well as a shrewd business opportunity, the Fiera fairly quickly began to run into problems. The Japanese vehicle industry sensing an opportunity, began exporting vehicles produced in their plants, vehicles more sophisticated in styling, more complex in manufacture but cheaper due to the high volumes they were producing. The Japanese vehicles satisfied the aspirational ambitions of people in the region who refused to be perceived as backward, using basic transportation although they continued their love affair with their cobbled together, flamboyant Jeepney. Internationally there were difficulties; Singapore and Malaysia, for a time a united nation, separated and the concept of electrical manufacturing in Singapore and assembly in Malaysia fell apart. The Singaporeans saw themselves as high-tech, not vehicle assembly workers. Then Ford of Britain bought into the battle for supply. Fed up with the poor quality of Lucas supplied electricals in the UK, they successfully managed to have the manufacturing of the electrical components transferred to a manufacturing plant in Ireland.

Four new models of the Fiera were released over the next ten years, each time with increasing engine size and modified body; version three introduced a 1.7-litre diesel engine. The fourth model of the Fiera, released in 1980 was based on the Mazda Courier. More complex stamped panels were added to the 'brake press and guillotine' vehicle to improve the styling somewhat. Engines were expanded to a choice of four; a 1,500cc petrol engine or one of three diesels, one from the Mazda R series, the others supplied by Izuzu. Eventually FOP and FASPAC found themselves operating at a US$600 penalty per vehicle to the Japanese, unsustainable and in 1982, ceased production. Even today, John Marshall believes that in individual markets, the concept would have worked, but Ford US pulled the pin and the stamping plant in the Philippines was abandoned to the jungle. Australian involvement virtually ceased from that date. FOP resumed assembly of CKD vehicles in 1989 until 2013 when that also ended.

The XB Falcon was a minor facelift; mechanically the changes that missed fitment to the XA were implemented in the XB. Ventilated front wheel disc brakes became standard across the range, which were still an option on rival base models. The GT now had 4-wheel disc brakes as standard. The same feature was an option on Fairlane and LTD models with the 351 V8. The Ford engines, by now the 200 c.i.d and 250 c.i.d. 6-cylinder and the local 302 V-8 and the two-barrel carburettor Cleveland V-8, were superior to anything offered by GM-H or Chrysler. The styling of the XB was sharper, with squared-off front end and wraparound tail-lights.

Bourke's influence even from FASPAC had prevailed. He had always hankered after a luxury two-door, and with the XB/ZG range, he got it. Ford went upmarket again with not only the Custom and Fairlane 500, but now with the LTD; the four-door P5 LTD and on Bourke's insistence, a two-door P4 Landau. The P4/P5 LTDs were designed as though they were bespoke vehicles. Leather, carpet and woodgrain was everywhere. The crash pad and console were padded vinyl, the seats were leather and carpet covered the hard plastic cowl panels. Externally, unique taillights differentiated them from the Fairlane and, in a unique front end treatment, the headlights were concealed behind lift-up covers, similar to the US Mercury Cougar. A padded vinyl roof with stylish C pillar badges completed the look.

RIGHT 1973 P4 Landau

RIGHT 1973 P5 LTD

Bourke never saw the P4 Landau in production; in mid-1972, he was appointed President of Ford of Europe. His successor at FASPAC was Robert B. Alexander, an American, previously Vice-president of Ford Latin America. Jack Telnack head of styling at the Research Centre also headed for Europe before returning to the US, replaced by Duncan McRae, while Don Deveson returned from Sydney plant to take charge of his old plant, Broadmeadows. Production commenced on the LTDs in May 1973, the Fairlane and Falcon sedans were launched in June, followed by the van, hardtop, and utility over the next five months. The XB Falcon range remained in production until June 1976 and a total of 211,981 were built, the highest volume model built by Ford Australia. The ZG and LTD volume, at 26,831 were the second highest LWB quantity, only beaten by the next model, the ZH.

ABOVE XB Falcon and ZG Fairlane

FORD
GT
VIC
LLF·485

1973 XA Falcon GT with RPO 83

RIGHT XB Wagon

FAR RIGHT 1973 XB Falcon 500 GS two-door hardtop

RIGHT 1973 XB Utility

FAR RIGHT XB Standard Panel Van

The XB enabled Ford to lead the passenger car market for six months over GM-H and brought Ford up to within 4.5% of GM-H. Pre-tax profit for 1973, 1974 and 1975 was A$23.0 million, A$12.9 million and A$29.8 million respectively.

The Bathurst campaign for 1973 was notable for the negative publicity received when the Sydney *Sun Herald*, carried banner headlines on June 25, 1972, screaming '160 mph "Super Cars" soon', an article criticising carmakers for building vehicles considered too dangerous for the public to drive on the open road. This article sparked the NSW Transport minister, Milton Morris, to join in and the resulting furore saw carmakers denying the dangers. Of course, Ford had started building the Phase IV GT-HO, and with Holley carburetors, exhaust extractors and a high 3:1 ratio differential, it could potentially reach the speed. But, the publicity was enough to force CAMS[76] to scrap the Group E Series Production Car rules that required road registered vehicles, and replace it with Group C which allowed modifications for race special vehicles. Immediately Ford scrapped plans to build the Phase IV after building four vehicles, followed by GM-H and Chrysler abandoning their Group E programs.

While not as dominant as the XYGT at Bathurst, nevertheless the XA GT hardtops still managed two more Bathurst wins, first with Alan Moffat in 1973 then, in 1974, with John Goss and Kevin Bartlett. That year saw Ford announce their retirement from active support of motorsport, much to the disgruntlement of Ford fans everywhere.

However while one breed of Falcon was retiring, another was being created. The 'Ford Falcons', a soccer team sponsored by the Broadmeadows Social club was formed in 1974 and accepted into the third division of the Metropolitan Industrial League. The team was sponsored by Plant Manager Don Deveson who, in one of his gardening exercises, created their home ground at the

XB GT racing at Bathurst

assembly plant. The team was organised by Anton Lazarenski of the Broadmeadows Industrial Relations office and coached by Joe Ardia of the Plastics Plant office. They began training three times a week in preparation for their first match on April 7 against the ANZ bank, and won two of their first three matches. They went on to win the Adidas cup that year, beating the Ericsson team 3-0 in a decisive victory, and as a reward were treated to a slap up dinner by their greatest fans, Plant Manager Don Deveson and Director of Manufacturing Bill Carlier. 1974 also saw the return of Ted Gardner to Australia as Director of Manufacturing and Supply, after a ten year absence overseas. He had previously been in Australia to oversee the establishment of the 6-cylinder engine plant in Geelong. Later appointed Director of Manufacturing and Technical Operations in April 1981, he retired back to the US in March 1983.

RIGHT 1976 ZH Fairlane Marquis

Sydney became the CKD assembly plant, assembling Escorts while the Cortina was shared with Broadmeadows, the high volume plant which produced the majority. Sydney built the Cortina two, four door and van for Mark II, then the TC four door and wagon until the TD, which was solely built in Broadmeadows. As Escort volumes ramped in the 1970s, Sydney operated on one shift plus overtime, often working seven days a week from 1973 as a single model plant with a capacity of 128 UPD (units per day).

RIGHT 1976 P6 LTD

Born out of the Heater Plant, established to make Falcon heaters and air-conditioners, mandatory fitment with the introduction of ADR21 in 1970, the Plastics Plant commenced production in 1972. As soon as the roof was on and floor poured, the first of the injection moulding machines, from Meiki, Japan were delivered. As the Program Group, brought together to build the plant, wound down, Neil Tompkins, Program Group Manager returned to Geelong, while others, Karl Ketonen, Gwen Nelms, Ron Tyack and Doug Wallace transferred to the plant, complemented by staff recruited from throughout the company, among others, Alan Coutts from SQA[77] as Quality Manager, Bill Pidding from Material Control Head Office, as Material Manager. Others were recruited from the Plastics industry; Alex Rae from F&T Plastics, as Manufacturing and Plant Engineering Manager, while the Plant Manager Geoff Thornton, was recruited from Michaelis Bayley Plastics in Hawthorn, as was Nick Greiner, Production Manager.

To generate income and get production experience in a new plant, Thornton used his contacts in the industry to supply tools for the plant to produce products unrelated to the automotive industry, income while automotive production tools were integrated from suppliers. The plant became known for its production of drainage channels and red plastic chairs until the plant was filled with Ford products, and they were no longer able to be produced. Current model products and new model components were introduced into the plant daily, and the plant struggled to launch products and meet assembly plant volumes.

As with all new plant startups, there were production and personnel problems with inexperienced staff; several were unsuccessful and became casualties, leaving the plant or the company. With an ambitious plant manager, the plant aggressively pursued the manufacture of every plastic product the company used. The XB Falcon and ZG radiator grilles were the largest early components supplied by the plant. Exterior components supplied by the Plastics plant included some difficult to supply in steel; the rear quarter panels and quarter panel extensions for Fairlane and LTD, compression moulded from SMC.[78] Another SMC product, the LTD front end was found, after tooling trials, to be too large for existing presses and continued to be manufactured and imported

1977 SILVER MONARCH LTD

Stuart McMurtrie remembers Peter Gillitzer commenting on the 'Silver Monarch' LTD, 'Never underestimate the bad taste of the buying public.'

from the US. The new design, ADR21 compliant Cortina heater/air-conditioner was added to the range as well as any carryover components to the next model, the TD Cortina. Tail lamps, turn signal lamps and most of the interior plastic components for the Falcon and Cortina ranges were also to become components supplied by the plant, which had gained a poor reputation as a supplier to the assembly plants. Gradually, as the plant quality of supply improved, plans to expand the plant grew.

As the plant stabilised, Karl Ketonen developed a project to manufacture foam seating in the plant. Traditionally, seats had been fabricated by cutting and gluing polyurethane foam blocks to the shape required, a complex operation. Bayer Pty Ltd of Germany had developed a process for casting the foam cushions and seat backs in one piece using specialised moulds and equipment. The new process, significantly improved seating consistency and quality. Another benefit was the substantial space saving in the assembly plant and cost savings; direct labour was reduced by over 70%. The equipment was sized to manufacture both Falcon and Cortina seats and installed in time for the TD Cortina production launch of July 1974. At the launch of the TD Cortina, Product Planning Manager Peter Gillitzer wrote the following:

> *Improved front seat comfort is achieved with the adoption of moulded front seat pads replacing the previously fabricated pads. The moulded pads provide a more consistent seating package less susceptible to variations in comfort levels and which will also allow a better fit of seat covers to be achieved.* [79]

The establishment of a working relationship with Bayer was to become a fruitful one for both companies.

The Federal government mandated a reduction in vehicle emissions, resulting in ADR27A scheduled for implementation effective July 1, 1976. Maintaining a policy of continuous improvement, in 1972 Ford began investigating ways of meeting the emission standards while improving engine economy and performance. The existing 6-cylinder and V8 engines would not meet the new standards due to uneven fuel flow and fuel/air mix between the cylinders.

In great secrecy, a number of engineers in the Product Engineering Centre in Geelong began working on the problem. The group, headed by Dave Cox included Alex Mishura, David Head and Darrel Hawthorne. They developed the concept of locating the intake manifold on the other side of the engine to the exhaust manifold, creating a cross flow of fuel through the cylinders. The cylinder heads were redesigned with angled valves to allow the use of larger valves, also improving the fuel mix and flow. Revised carburetion and other refinements designed to equalize the flow of fuel/air mix to all cylinders added to the complexity, they were designing a whole new system. Despite the piece cost penalty over cast iron, the group settled on aluminium die-cast intake manifold designs produced by Castalloy in South Australia; the die-cast manifold would give weight savings, improve idling and reduce engine roughness. The complex design was easier to manufacture and, with the addition of water heated by the engine and piped through the manifold, would warm up faster than a cast-iron manifold, heating the fuel/air mix and improving emission control.

One of the design problems involved the design of the push rods. Too large a diameter added weight; at high speed the inertia of the heavier push rods overcame the valve springs and affected valve performance, valve bounce. To resolve the issue the engineers used the main frame computer in Head Office to determine the optimal length to diameter ratio.

Tooling commenced as soon as designs were completed and a number of engines, 6-cylinder and V8s were built to the modified

LEFT 1976 P6 Silver Monarch LTD—342 were produced. This was a special edition which included silver paintwork, a unique silver vinyl roof, red crushed velour trim and whitewall tyres.

Modellers and modelling
bridge, Research Centre

RESEARCH CENTRE OFFICIALLY OPEN

Victoria's Premier, Sir Henry Bolte, officially opened the top-secret Research Centre on April 22, 1970. He recalled, 'Fourteen years ago I was criticised for supporting the company's bid to buy land at the present Broadmeadows site. Now everyone can see how right we were to back Ford,' he said. The $2 million centre heralds a new generation of design and vehicle safety in Australia.

design. Before they could be put through the stringent testing program, the new design engines needed to be run a number of hours, a task beyond the limited resources at the Proving Ground. A program was developed to fit the new engines to the lease cars of the test engineers, and were driven around Geelong by family members for a number of weeks, unaware of the changes under the bonnet. The first engines failed. The group went back to the drawing board, to evaluate the problems and repeat the process. As time went on, it became a very real possibility that Ford would have no engines to meet the design rules, but with only weeks to spare after a four year program, all engines passed the tests. The A$16 million program paid off. The 6-cylinder Falcons did not gain extra power, but GM-H, who had merely added extra plumbing to meet the regulations, were left with an engine that idled lumpily and lost power at high revs, a significant disadvantage to the smooth pulling Falcons. The better performance of the Falcon became a distinct selling point over the Kingswood.

While classed as a mid-term facelift by Ford, the XC became a major program for the Plastics Plant because many of the interior and exterior components to be changed were plastic. These included not only the inevitable radiator grilles and rear lamps, but also much of the instrument panel, which for the first time was designed across the full width of the vehicle.

Also changed were the instrument clusters and binnacle, the centre finish panel for the radios and heater controls, and glovebox

LEFT Research Centre at Broadmeadows under construction.

Ford

Max Gransden, Edsel Ford II and XC Falcon 500 (left), XC Fairmont (right) and ZH Fairlane (rear)

ABOVE 1978 XC Falcon sedan, X-Pak

RIGHT 1976 XC Fairmont wagon

assemblies. The Falcon grille tooling was cleverly designed as one tool, with inserts to enable the production of the three variants, the single headlight GL, the rectangular head-lighted Fairmont and Ghia, and the GT with driving lights. The ZH Fairlane grille was in three parts, while the P6 SMC front end and die cast grille remained carryover. The new instrument panel allowed a completely new styling approach to that of the XB/ZG, the flat panel look across the vehicle giving a roomier, spacious effect, while still integrated with the new centre console.

Styling-wise the three models, Falcon, Fairlane and LTD were now distinctly different to each other. The upper market was now served by Fairlane, Fairlane Marquis and LTD, the sports market, while disappointing GT fans, was satisfied by the Fairmont GXL, which could be optioned up to GT levels without causing conniptions from the insurance companies.

The XC/ZH/P6 range of vehicles commenced manufacture from May through July 1976 and were to remain in production for two and a half years while the company began tooling up for the next major model, the XD. Over that time, 171,080 XC Falcons

WHOSE CAR IS THIS?

It was a hot February day in 1971 and the Styling Centre personnel anxiously awaited Ford 'Royalty', Henry Ford II and his entourage, to arrive and inspect the clay models of the XC Falcon range, due for release in four years. They lined the tall glass windows, in air-conditioned comfort as they watched as the entourage, all clad in the management uniform of dark suits and ties, walk through the high walled courtyard, which acted like a suntrap, baking show vehicles and entourage alike. It was a relief when Henry took his coat off; a trigger for all present to instantly remove theirs. As Henry prowled along the row of cars, like royalty inspecting a guard of honour, he continually demanded, 'Whose car is this? Whose car is this?' Eventually some minion meekly spoke up and told him they were all Fords. 'I want to see the Ford Oval on the front of every damn Ford vehicle,' was his response. That is why the front end badging on Ford vehicles went from F.O.R.D. and F.A.I.R.L.A.N.E. on the XB range to the Corporate Ford scripted oval on the XC. Mike Alves said he believed 1971 was the start of the 'Badge Wars', ever increasingly large badges on the front of vehicles.

ALBERT JOHNSON

When fifty-nine year old Albert Johnson has to move a car, he pushes it. For throughout his forty years in the car industry, (thirty-three with Ford, he joined in 1937), Albert, who works on the rectification line at Homebush plant, has never learnt to drive. And he says he doesn't want to start now!

and derivatives were produced, number five in the Falcon top selling model list, while the 28,878 Fairlane-LTDs produced at the same time made it the top selling luxury model of all time for Ford Australia.

Don Deveson transferred to Geelong in 1976 as Basic Manufacturing Operations (BMO) manager, the announcement of which was greeted by staff at Geelong with mixed emotions. Interviewed in 2015, Lindsay Sheppard and Terry O'Brien both had many stories of Don. No doubt he was a bully, a martinet and enjoyed the terror some felt at his very presence. But Lindsay said he was like a fresh broom:

> *He cleaned up the place; he forced us to get rid of old, damaged stock, enforced a perimeter aisle around the plants, even cleaned the windows. If it didn't move, it got painted, he put glass walls in the oases, introduced rock gardens into the grounds, which were quickly dubbed 'Devhenge', but he made the plant a better place.*

The radio communication system in Geelong was open, all could listen in and overhear. The problem was, so could Deveson, and Don had an uncomfortable habit of suddenly appearing to investigate any production holdup or breakdown. The plant management quickly developed a radio code to communicate whenever Deveson left his office, a warning system. Manufacturing Engineering Manager George Radovanovic, sick of having Don suddenly appearing at every plant problem and 'overseeing', managed to get a separate radio channel for his department. It took two months for Don to work out why he wasn't hearing of any problems except through George.

Brian Inglis was knighted in 1977 for his services to industry and technology, and gained a trainee Assistant Managing Director from the US.

Henry Ford's great grandson, Edsel Ford II graduated from Babson College in 1973 and, after a brief management training course at Harvard, joined Ford in January the next year as a product planning analyst. For the next four years he worked in both the Ford and Lincoln-Mercury Division sales offices.

In 1978, aged thirty, he moved to Australia to get experience and exposure to the company's international operations. Ford Australia was chosen, after much consideration, because of its small, by comparison, market; a mentor with a wealth of experience, Sir Brian Inglis, and a country with a 'safe' reputation. He still came with his own bodyguards; kidnapping and being held to ransom was, and is, a very real fear for the Ford family. Edsel's companions went everywhere with him. Used to this environment, Edsel thought nothing of it, although many who worked with him found it oppressive.

One incident during Edsel's time in Australia was that he was supposedly staying at the Sydney Hilton at the same time as the CHOGM conference was being held there. On February 13, 1978 a bomb exploded in a garbage compactor outside the hotel.

ABOVE Sir Brian Inglis

COB-019
VICTORIA

OPPOSITE PAGE 1978 XC Falcon Cobra. Limited production of only 400, each uniquely identified with a badge mounted in the glovebox. Numbers 00002–00031 were option 97, Cobra Bathurst Specials. Numbers 00001, 00032–00400 were option 96, Cobra Special Value Pak.

LEFT 1978 XC Falcon Cobra brochure

Apparently Edsel was rushed out the rear of the hotel, by his bodyguards, through the kitchen, sans luggage and flown direct to Melbourne on a private flight.

As Assistant Managing Director of Ford Australia, Edsel was responsible for car product planning and sales and marketing as well as truck operations. It may have been a case of young bull and old bull, but Max Gransden and Edsel did not hit it off. In fact it is rumoured Edsel lobbied hard for the dismissal of Gransden, but Sir Brian refused and Henry backed his experienced Managing Director's judgement.

As the XC neared the end of its life it became apparent the love affair of Australians with two-door vehicles was fading. Hardtop sales lagged the rest of the range. There were 400 two-doors to be built to balance-out the model, and they weren't selling. Edsel's idea, a stroke of marketing genius, was to option them up to GXL level, paint them all white, slap Cobra badges on the fenders and two great blue stripes the length of the car and call it a Cobra Special, after the original Shelby Cobra Mustangs in the US. They sold out in a week and remain a classic to this day. Edsel also inspired others with his marketing 'nouse'.

At a speech he made in 1978 to Geelong managers, he showed them a picture of a tractor which had been slow in selling and was about to be discounted to quit the stock. General Manager of Tractors, Noel Howard decided to take a lesson from car marketing and create a 'GT' version. He added air-conditioning, a turbo charger and then got Andy Jacobsen in styling to design a lively colour scheme. It sold out overnight; the dealers and farmers loved it. Edsel said Ford US were not too impressed, they had been very skeptical but as he said, 'If it turns a bad loss to a good profit, you've got to admit it's a good idea and worth repeating'. [80]

Ford continued its profitability; pretax profit for 1976 was A$34.11 million, but as the cost of tooling the XD program began to bite, profit sank in 1977 to A$3.01 million, and in 1978 to A$5.81 million. There was a lot riding on the XD.

With Sydney ultimately to become a one-vehicle plant with the Escort, building the TC Cortina at Broadmeadows as well kept production rates up at the larger plant, giving economies of scale. But the introduction of the TD Cortina worried Sir Brian, who asked the product planners to look at options to improve local content of the TD. The result was the introduction of the Falcon engine and transmission to the Cortina, improving local content substantially. Buyers liked the reliability of the 200 and 250 c.i.d. Falcon engines and transmissions over the smaller 4-cylinder engine. They liked the performance better. The 6-cylinder TD

THE SCHEDULING MEETING

Like all production-scheduling meetings, the one in the Stamping Plant, just after plant startup in January, was tense as the staff tried desperately to satisfy all the back orders. No one noticed the figure in the background, who had quietly entered the in-plant office while the meeting was in progress. With an off-white towelling hat, bright shirt, shorts flopping below the knees and wearing thongs, obviously in holiday mode, he stood out. As the meeting was concluding, he spoke for the first time. 'What's running on press line fourteen?' he asked. All turned to the inquirer, eying off the obviously out of place stranger. 'And who the F!@#$ are you?' snappishly asked Supervisor Ashleigh Creighton. 'I'm Brian Inglis', was the calm reply.

Cortina could be a potent weapon in the wet, particularly the wagon which had a 'twitchy' rear end. Production of the TD sedan and wagon commenced in July 1974 and continued with the 76 Cortina, a minor facelift to meet the ADR27A emission requirements.

The introduction of the 76 Cortina sedan and wagon resulted in the majority of Cortina build moving to Broadmeadows, although Sydney's involvement didn't end until the launch of the TE Cortina in May 1977. The popularity of the Falcon and Cortina combined now resulted in a capacity problem in production; and it didn't look as though it would reduce in the short term. Ford urgently reviewed their options and, rather than return Cortina to Sydney, in November 1977, subcontracted the building of Cortina wagons to Renault, located in West Heidelberg, Melbourne. Of the 86,298 TE Cortina's built from January 1977, to July 1980, 17,649 wagons were assembled at the Renault plant.

RIGHT Wayne Draper in design studio

The Product Planning group released the Red Book[81] for the 1978 XD Falcon, codenamed 'Blackwood' in 1973. Late that year the price of petrol doubled from 30 cents a litre to 60 cents, the first of the 'oil shocks'. For the first time since the WWII, the Federal Government introduced petrol rationing into Australia. The global uncertainty triggered the stock market crash of 1974 and suddenly, the future of large vehicles with high fuel consumption became doubtful. Then Ford obtained intelligence from overseas that GM-H planned to replace the full-size Kingswood with a new, smaller vehicle based on the European Opel Rekord. Ford considered a design based on the smaller, European Ford Granada to replace the Falcon but clinic after clinic held with the public rejected a mid-size car in preference to the larger vehicle so, with much trepidation, the larger Falcon program continued and a major weight-saving campaign began, to put it on a diet and improve fuel consumption.

Another hotly debated decision was which styling theme to follow. One early decision was easy, to reskin the XC for a new design completely. There were two themes on offer; to follow the Granada European styling or that of an American vehicle shortly to be produced. Sir Brian recalled he spent many hours in the styling studio looking at two clays, comparing the American and European styles. The heavier-looking, American-styled clay was rejected by the public in styling clinics, supporting the concepts pushed by the product planners, headed by David Ford and stylists Peter Arcadipane, Wayne Draper, Andy Jacobsen, and Brian Rossi. Sir Brian said he favoured the more European-style Granada, originally penned by UK designer Trevor Creed. They ended up with a vehicle 136 mm shorter but with the same wheelbase, 41 mm narrower and 14 mm lower than the XC, while improving head, shoulder and knee room. The XD Falcon vehicle had 120 mm more shoulder room than the Commodore; it not only felt roomier, it was. Sir Brian related how he was not happy with the high belt line of the Granada and pondered how he could lower it without changing the windscreen. He said he discussed it with Jack Telnack in the US, who said he wished he had done the same with the Granada. Their solution? They put a mirror over the intersection, completely hiding it. The result was a lower belt line, a 20% increase in glass area, and a much prettier looking vehicle.

With the Falcon now thought to be at a substantial weight disadvantage to the Commodore, improving fuel consumption became imperative. A number of proposals resulted in a far greater involvement for the Plastics Plant: moulded foam seating, polyurethane bumper bars, crash pads and head restraints, a new plastic instrument panel, the usual interior trim components and a plastic fuel tank. After representations from Managing Director Sir Brian Inglis, Ford U.S. gave Ford Australia approval to fund the weight savings program, over and above the program costs, of approximately A$130 million.[82] The engineers from the Plastics Plant, now recognised for their skills, together with Thornton and his management lobbied hard to have the major components manufactured in the Plastics Plant.

The result was a massive expansion of the plant; it more than doubled in area. New presses and equipment were ordered for the bumper bar and integral skin components, crash pads, and head restraints. New tooling was required for the seat foam production, making it the largest polyurethane plant in the southern hemisphere. A new blow-moulding machine for the plastic fuel tank and an injection moulding machine for the instrument panel

XD Falcon design sketch by Wayne Draper

Preparing an XD sedan model for wind tunnel testing.

1980 XD ESP (European Sports Pack) sedan

LEFT 1979 XD Sundowner panel van

FAR LEFT 1980 XD GL station wagon, Alloy Head upgrade

LEFT Falcon XD introduced wool seats for the first time

FAR LEFT 1979 ZJ Fairlane

made the plant one of the most advanced and complex plastic plants in the world.

At the same time, tooling also started on the components for the TE model Cortina, scheduled for introduction in January 1977. A mid-cycle facelift, it had a similar flat panel look instrument panel as the Falcon, requiring new instrument panel components, as well as a new radiator grille and other components. Thirty engineers, some recruited from the plastics industry worked on the programs, in a plant still suffering from production problems. Nevertheless, with all the optimism and brashness of a new kid on the block and an ambitious plant manager in Thornton, the plant took on the Blackwood and TE Cortina projects.

One of the better internal moves was that of Ron Tyack to Manufacturing and Plant Engineering Manager, after the resignation of Alex Rae. An electrical apprentice at Ford, he had worked on program groups for a number of years, including the Broadmeadows Plant expansion and the Plastics Program groups before being promoted to Production Manager at the height of the management purges. It was an inspired choice by Thornton. Later, Tyack went on to become the most successful plant manager in the plant's short history, and was promoted eventually to BMO, Geelong.

All the innovative products and processes had their origin in Germany and Ford turned to the best companies there with experience in their field. The crash pads, instrument cluster binnacles, head restraints and steering wheels were made from a self-skinning polyurethane (PU) foam pioneered by Otto Bock, Germany, used in the manufacture of prosthetic limbs for soldiers. The bumper bars were also polyurethane, a denser formulation designed by Bayer especially for the purpose. The PU bumpers were backed up with light-weight moulded glass reinforced polyester beams designed to absorb impact damage,

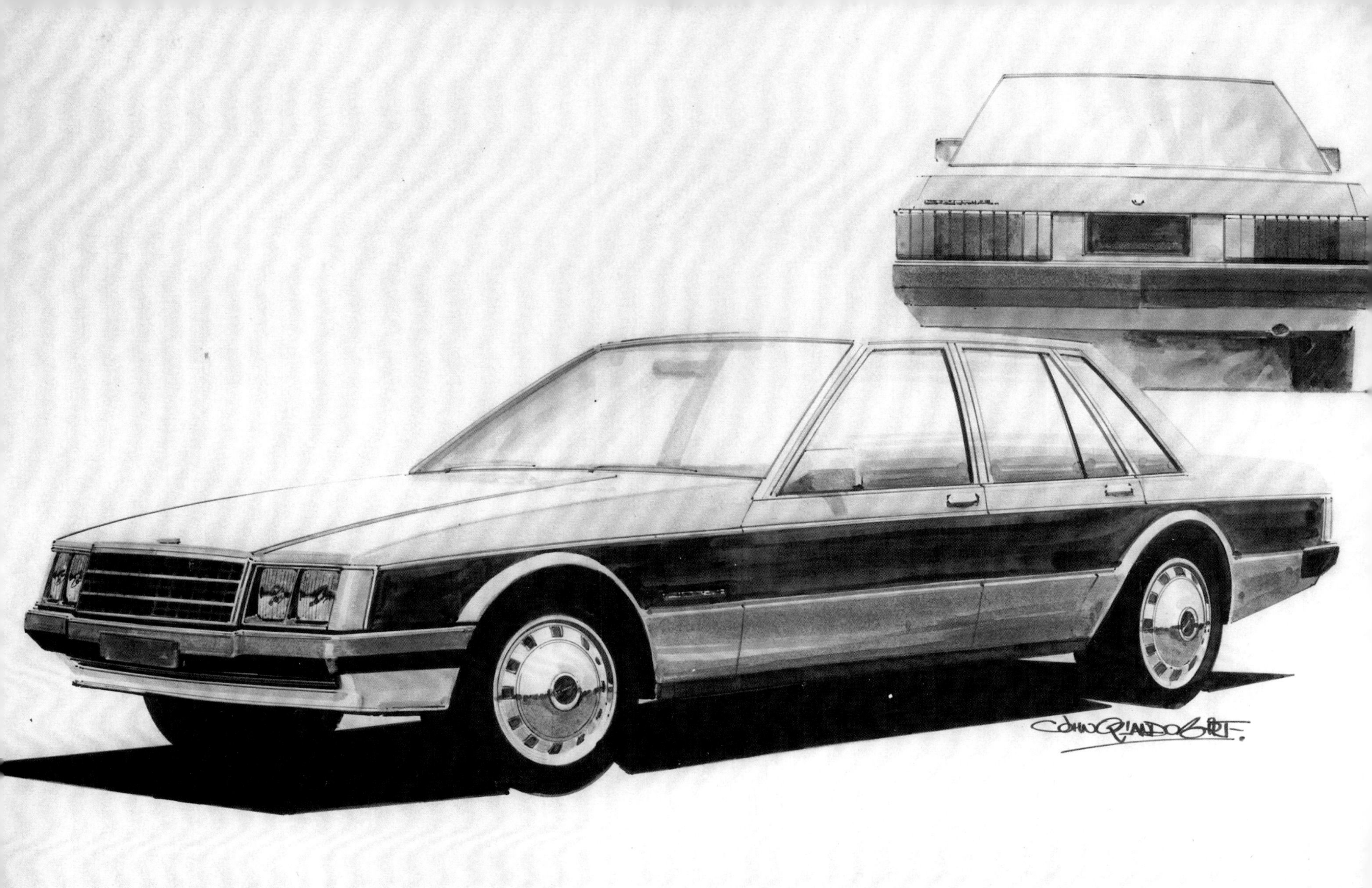

ABOVE 1979 ZJ Fairlane sketch by John Birt

the test requirement being 5 mph without damage extending to the vehicle body.

The most innovative material was a unique specialised polyethylene material developed for use in fuel tanks by BASF, already in use in Porsche racing cars and soon to be used in the VW Golf. Ford US had also begun work on a plastic fuel tank using a similar material with an American supplier but were extremely cautious. A few years before, Ford US had released the Pinto vehicle, designed with the metal fuel tank behind the rear axle. As was common practice, the fuel filler neck was a fabricated steel tube, fixed to the body at the rear quarter panel and fitted to the fuel tank with rubber sealing grommets. Analysis of a number of rear end collisions found that when the fuel tank was shunted into the rear axle, the filler neck speared through the metal tank, spilling fuel which ignited, the ensuing fire incinerating the vehicle occupants. The resultant court cases and adverse publicity forced Ford into a vehicle redesign. For their new vehicle, Ford US were conducting two prototype programs for their vehicle, one in steel, one in plastic.

The Falcon was designed to have a rear entry fuel filler pipe, but the blow moulded plastic fuel tank had an integral filler neck, designed to deflect with a rear end collision and not leak fuel. The tank attaching mechanism could also allow the tank to detach from the vehicle in one piece, minimising fuel spillage. The design

POKER GAMES

Like any large organisation whose finances are tightly controlled, paperwork is king. A prime example was in Capital Expenditure projects, 'Capex' projects. Every capex project required supporting documentation to justify the dollars to be spent. In the 1970s the cynical view in manufacturing was the Finance group measured the worth of a project by the thickness of the binders containing the backup. The original Plastics Plant project in 1971 requested $4.1 million; sure enough, the thickness of the binders supporting the project totaled four inches. David Ford recalls attending a series of project approval meetings in Dearborn where FOA was in danger of losing the XD utility and van. Ford Chairman 'Red' Poling wanted full accounting of costs and profits by model. David and Kevin Bensted knew the business case for the commercials would not standup to this close analysis and losing the commercials could jeopardise the whole XD model business case. The meeting spent the first day reviewing the sedan and wagon costs, and then adjourned to the next day, when they would analyse the business case for the commercials. David and Kevin fronted up to the meeting the next day, piling binder after binder on the table as supporting documentation for the project. The US group, eyeing the feet-high pile of binders, decided to keep the meeting brief and signed off on the total XD program, not wishing to be involved in what was obviously going to be a lengthy and detailed presentation. What they didn't know was that several of the binders piled on the table actually were Dearborn telephone directories re-covered to appear as Ford Project binders.

also allowed the engineers to utilise all available space, maximising fuel tank capacity, a design feature not possible with a steel tank. Ford Australia had only one prototype program, in plastic; no fall back design.

The prototype program was conducted in Germany and samples provided to the Product Engineering Office in Australia for validation. There being no Australian standard for plastic fuel tanks, Ford used the European Community standard, ECE34. Of the many tests in ECE34, three were crucial; the ambient drop test, the –40° Celsius drop test, and the fire test.

The ambient temperature drop test was designed to test the integrity of the fuel tank. At room temperature, a tank was filled with water and dropped 6 metres. The hydrostatic water pressure in the fuel tank would find any weakness in the structure. The tank must not leak. Likewise the –40° Celsius drop test was designed to ensure a vehicle in cold weather could survive a rear impact test. A tank, filled with propylene glycol, was chilled to –40° Celsius then dropped six metres and must survive with no leakage. Ford used the German standard despite the tank being larger, 80 litres, compared with the 40-litre German tank, a test twice as severe. The fire test was designed to simulate a number of vehicles in a carpark catching fire. A vehicle with the fuel tank 50% full of fuel had a bed of burning coals pushed under it for a two minutes and allowed to catch fire. A diffuser was then pushed under to spread the heat while maintaining it, allowing the tank to burn for a further two minutes, at which point the fire was extinguished. At the end of the test, the tank must not have leaked fuel. Inevitably, the vehicle tyres caught fire, burned more fiercely and burnt the vehicle out. The plastic fuel tanks all passed the tests: significantly, steel fuel tanks would not, but with no such comparable test standard, and based on forty years' of use, this was not considered a problem.

The weight savings of the new materials was significant. The weight reduction of the Falcon, Fairlane and LTD sedans was in excess of 43 kg, the wagon and commercials with a steel fuel tank, between 20 and 23 kg. respectively, contributing mightily to the final sedan reduction of 116 kg., and substantially improving fuel consumption. The reduced vehicle length, by reducing the overhangs, and the lighter bumper bars and fuel tank, improved handling. The Product engineers redesigned the front end structure with the stamping plant engineers and by eliminating the torque boxes, improved vibration throughout the vehicle.

While the Geelong tool room was fully committed to the stamping tool program, the impact of losing the bumper bars and fuel tanks to plastic affected the stamping plant. It allowed the now to be under-utilised bumper bar chrome plating plant to be relocated, relegated to supplying Parts and Service bumpers only, and reduced stamping press workload.

Not all things went according to plan. The integrity of the fuel tank was so important that non-destructive tests were done on every fuel tank to ensure its integrity. In addition, selected destructive tests were carried out to ensure the shift's production was acceptable. FOA management were understandably nervous; by the time preproduction build of the XD began, Ford US had backed away from their plastic tank and Ford Australia was going it alone.

Just before the XD launch, senior Ford US executives visited Australia to review progress. One of the demonstrations for them was a drop test of a fuel tank; to everyone's horror, the

ABOVE Ron Tyack

ABOVE XD Job 1 offline with (l to r) Fred Herr, Ted Gardner, Edsel Ford II and Plant Manager Phil Staley

tank leaked at the neck, a technical failure and the repercussions reverberated round the company. Test after test was done, entire shifts of production were tested or scrapped and a taskforce was established to determine the cause before vehicle production began. Despite thousands of tanks being tested or scrapped, the failure could not be replicated.

The final report was indecisive, but one rumour was that Plant Manager Thornton, wanting everything to be perfect for the Ford US visitors, had already drop tested the same tank. Tanks regularly passed three such tests but the decision to use a previously dropped tank, if so, was folly, but as the major participants are no longer living, the cause will never be known. No other production tank ever failed the test, before or after, but it was a jittery management which watched the first XD production vehicles go on sale.

The word got out in the industry that the XD had a revolutionary fuel tank. A competitor began a whispering scare campaign of the dangers of buying a vehicle with a tank made from 'plastic that burns' and questions were asked in Federal Parliament.

In responding to a question from Senator Gietzelt on September 25, 1979, asking if the Commonwealth Fire Board had raised concerns about a fire risk posed by Ford LTDs to be purchased by the Commonwealth, the Minister for Administrative Services, J. E. McLeay replied on May 22, 1980, saying he had requested the Fire Board to further investigate; this had been done

PRODUCT PLANNING

Total tooling cost was always a problem in any new model program; there was never enough money to go round to include all the desired features. This was the situation with the Blackwood (XD) program. There were no funds left to pay for tooling of the wagon load bay interior trim. Solution? Take the design and manufacture the plastic components using the vacuum forming process. Peter Fry, 'The tooling was cheap, the piece cost outrageous. And the next year we had a ready-made cost reduction for the budget; injection mould the same components, a high tooling cost, but a low piece price. Perfect! A vehicle piece cost reduction for the Finance group to approve.'

MAYOR 'TUNNER' KENWORTHY

Councillor 'Tunner' Kenworthy, Mayor of the City of Geelong West for two years, handed over his robes and chain of office to his successor in September 1970. 'Tunner', a personnel officer in Geelong's Plant 1 joined Ford thirty-five years ago as an assembler in the spring department. For years, he has been involved in community affairs both as a politician and as someone interested in local charities. He admits he enjoys being well known because of the satisfaction he gets from being in a position to help people. Most people remember him as a boxer; he turned professional in 1932 and fought several bouts in the Geelong West Town Hall. 'I always said I would make a comeback, but I didn't think it would be as Mayor,' he said.

and after reviewing the test data, the board was satisfied there was no fire risk in carparks; additionally, enquiries to insurance companies overseas had elicited no concerns. He did report that, in discussions between the Fire Board and the research arm of Telecom Australia, Telecom had suggested the addition of an another antioxidant to ensure tanks in the tropics would further withstand higher operating temperatures and ultra-violet radiation. McLeay advised the House that Ford had already modified the formulation. Ford tests had indicated any degradation would be negligible, but with Government sales at risk, had no problem complying. The opinion of the German supplier BASF, was that with the harsher drop test and over-the-top UV protection, the Australians were mad. Ford also quietly let it be known through the backdoor they had video (they did) of one of their competitors' US sedans with a steel tank undergoing the same fire test. The unvented tank exploded, exiting the vehicle through the sunroof. It is doubtful that Ford would ever have released the video publicly, as the XD wagon and commercials still had steel tanks, but suddenly there was no more chatter.

It should be added here, there has not been one instance of failure of a plastic fuel tank, nor a fire involving plastic fuel tanks in Australia. Most European vehicles sold in Australia now have plastic fuel tanks, as does Ford's major competitor. But Ford was first. The fuel tank was later tarnished with an unrelated problem of fuel gauge malfunction until corrected by a post-job one fix.

The Product Engineering drafting area overwhelmed with the workload, used contract drafting services, mainly in the US. Product Engineers and Manufacturing Engineers spent many months overseas, working in the US and Germany. As the program developed, the product planners excelled themselves, designing a vehicle for everybody.

The base vehicle, the GL with the 3.3-litre engine and four-speed transmission actually ended up slightly more economical than the Commodore. Even a bench seat was offered to provide a genuine six-seater vehicle, another differentiation to the Commodore which had only bucket seats.

For the sports enthusiast, the Falcon S; for the upper end buyers, the Fairmont, then the Fairmont Ghia, with everything as standard, although for the first time, leather seats could be optioned. The choice of cloth seat trim, with carpets and velour seat trim for the high series vehicles was a point of contention. Would the public accept it, or insist on being able to, in the words of one manager, 'hose their vehicle out'. Luckily vinyl mats were only fitted to the commercial vehicles. There was no change to the 6-cylinder engines and transmissions, the V8s were improved with electronic ignition and the fitment of a viscous clutch fan.

For the long wheel base Fairlane and LTD, the 4.9-litre engine was standard, the major options power windows, alloy wheels and the 5.8 litre engine.

In the interval between the release of the GM-H Commodore and the XD release, Ford started an advertising campaign showing

ABOVE John Marshall

RIGHT Falcon XD Sundowner brochure

RESI GRIMWOOD

To improve space in the Broadmeadows Assembly Plant, foam seat manufacture was relocated to the now defunct Heater Plant in Mahoneys Road, Thomastown. Soon after the shift had started, General Forelady Resi Mack (nee Grimwood) was concerned to see a tall, solidly built grey haired man with a somewhat military bearing step out of a vehicle and stride purposefully through the plant, stopping now and again to observe the activity around him. Conscious of the need for security, Resi boldly walked up to him and demanded to know what he thought he was doing in the plant, did he have any identification and what was his name. She was shocked and taken aback when he delightedly introduced himself as Sir Brian Inglis, and he was the Managing Director of Ford. Resi recalls she blanched, stammered her apologies for not recognising him and offered to conduct him around the plant. Somewhat amusedly, he graciously declined her offer and returned to his car, Resi now noticing the chauffeur. An urgent phone call to Plastics Plant manager Geoff Thornton's office interrupted the morning's management meeting, which was abandoned moments later, by another: 'Mrs. White here, Sir Brian for Mr. Thornton please'. A phone call not to be declined. To Thorton's surprise, a delighted Sir Brian praised the plant's security and particularly Resi, (he had asked her name) for her initiative, boldness and security awareness, reinforcing Sir Brian's reputation for courtesy and affability.

a slowly melting block of ice 'We've got your new car on ice' was the slogan. As time went on the ice slowly melted revealing the new model.

The XD was launched at the Sydney Opera House on March 20, 1979, at a ceremony with the precision of a military operation. It was attended by Henry Ford II, who had already toured all the manufacturing facilities. At the launch lunch he joked about the Sydney traffic. 'I've just had a good long look at your beautiful city,' he quipped, 'the driver was awful slow.' At the launch Edsel spoke of the XD, which had rated the highest of any Ford vehicle in consumer reaction studies worldwide.

The XD/ZJ were revealed at the 1979 Melbourne motor show with great fanfare, as was the stylish Escort RS 2000, scheduled for release in September. Initially the smaller Commodore sold well, as it had against the XC, but slowly customers came to appreciate that despite GM-H stressing the efficiency of the Commodore, the Falcon was nearly as good. Why get a small car that costs as much as a big one was the rationale and the buyers bought it. The Commodore 3.3-litre was less efficient than the 4.1-litre Falcon. Similarly, the Statesman, with its 5.0-litre engine was unfavourably compared with the 4.9-litre Fairlane and GM-H had no answer for the 5.8-litre option. As fuel rationing ended and the public got used to the higher cost of fuel, the Ford choice of a larger vehicle was seen to be inspired, but there had been much soul searching and nervousness around the decision.

The Plastics Plant's supply problems severely affected the company's ability to build vehicles. Sir Brian sourly commented to John Marshall the plant had cost him a million dollars in lost profits that year. Despite that, Ford still managed a pre-tax profit in 1979 of A$20.02 million

---

Having spent so much on the body, no funds were available for mechanical improvements, a point noted by *Wheels* magazine.

EDSEL FORD II AND PARA PORT

The launch of the ZJ Fairlane was held in the Barossa Valley of South Australia. All the journos were there with the Ford Management, including Managing Director Brian Inglis and his assistant M.D., Edsel Ford II. One of the lunches at the launch was at the Seppeltsfield winery, makers of the renowned Para Port. At the lunch, one of the owners of the winery asked Edsel the year his grandfather had started Ford Motor Company. As they were leaving, he returned with a bottle, which he presented to Edsel, telling him the liquor had been made the same year his grandfather had launched the company, 1903. Edsel was overwhelmed at this generous gesture and stammered, 'I don't know what to say.' Sir Brian, 'Thank you very much, would be nice.'

PLANT TOURS

Visits by Ford senior management were always an excuse to clean the plant, painting everything that didn't move. On the news that Henry Ford II was coming to visit, efforts redoubled, and months were spent ensuring the Broadmeadows Assembly plant would be pristine clean and sparkling. The day came. Unfortunately, Henry and wife Christina had just had a spat. She had flown off to Hayman Island, and he was in an ugly mood. John Crew remembers Henry, driving the buggy himself, sped through the plant, the tour over in ninety seconds, the plant's annual budget blown.

While taking a dig at GM-H's 'world car' and parochially acknowledging the XD was: 'A great step forward for the local car industry because it was conceived and developed in Australia and not part of a world car program, editor Ian Fraser was scathing of its performance '…sloppy on the road, unresponsive and dead to the touch.'

Others were not so critical. After two days driving the XD on test drives in outback South Australia, Mark Fogarty in the *Motoring Reporter* said, 'The XD Falcon shouldn't drive anywhere near as well as the Holden Commodore—but it does.' He went on to say while he rated the Falcon behind the Commodore, it was so close in handling that the average driver wouldn't be able to pick the difference. Many at Ford felt the most technologically advanced vehicle in decades deserved better treatment from *Wheels* and were even angrier when, in the March 1980 issue, *Wheels* again withheld the COTY award, depicting a large lemon on wheels on the cover. Peter Robinson and Phil Scott, past editors, claim even today they withheld the award because they owed a duty to their readers. Edsel Ford is not so charitable. The lack of the award still rankles him today, saying it was a cheap shot, designed to sell more magazines. However revenge is a meal better served cold. In a brilliant response three months later, Ford replied with a full-page advertisement in the same magazine depicting thirty-one lemons, labelled with all those vehicles that had entered the COTY award with the by-line, 'There are times when being a lemon is not a bitter experience at all.'

In its model life, 200,849 XD vehicles were produced, the sixth most successful product range in Ford Australia history.

CHAPTER 7
1980—1989

THE FORD YEARS 1980—1989

1980:

750,000th English-derived Ford vehicle produced in Australia. Ford announces $300 million investment program, and a $13 million upgrade for Homebush plant. Alloy head engine introduced for XD range. TF Cortina production commences. Introduction of 1000 series and 8401 tractors.

1981:

XE Falcon, ZK Fairlane, FD LTD production commences. New F-Series and Bronco released. Cargo trucks replace D Series. KA Laser and GA Meteor production commences in Sydney plant. Dick Johnson and John French win Bathurst, and Australian Touring car championship with XD Falcon. MATCON 1 computer system introduced, Sir Brian Inglis retires, Bill Dix becomes President of Ford Australia. New Unimate robotic underbody line installed at Broadmeadows.

1982:

KB Laser, AS Telstar production. Henry Ford II retires on October 1. MATCON II computer system introduced.

1983:

Three-millionth Australian-built Ford vehicle produced. GB Meteor production commences. First use of CAD/CAM at Product Engineering, Geelong. PM Bob Hawke opens new $70 million 4-cylinder plant in Geelong. Ford wins Australian Design Award for Falcon, Fairlane, LTD range. AR Telstar wins *Wheels* COTY award. Last tractor assembled in Australia at Brisbane plant.

1984:

XF Falcon, ZL Fairlane, FE LTD production. $13.7 million automated high pressure mould line for Geelong casting plant opened.

1985:

New $1.4 million Apprentice training centre opened in Geelong. Local assembly of LTL 900 truck commenced. New mileage record set by Ford engineers—5,107 miles per gallon, (0.55 L/100km).

1986:

ADR 37 Emission standard implemented. Force 11 tractor range introduced. KE Laser production commences, Meteor name deleted. Brisbane plant begins conversion to truck plant.

1987:

Henry Ford II dies September 29 in Detroit. EA Falcon, NA Fairlane, DA LTD production commences. Maverick introduced into Australia. EA Falcon wins Australian Design Council award. New Training Centre and $62 million satellite paint facility opened at Broadmeadows. Fremantle Rectification Plant closed.

1988:

LTS 9000 truck released. $15 million extensions to Plant 2, SA Capri production commences. $1.5 million extension to Plastics plant. Dick Johnson wins Australian Touring Car Championship, John Bowe second in Ford Sierra's. EA26 Falcon, Fairlane and LTD range wins 1988 Australian Design Council awards. Ford Australia wins Australian Business/IBIS Top 500 Award as 'The Most Improved Enterprise in Australia'. Plastics Plant becomes 1st Australian Plant to achieve quality Q101. Ford is market leader for seventh consecutive year. Max Grandsen retires, replaced by Bill Hartigan. New EI centre opened in Sydney Plant.

1989:

Former Managing Director, Charles Smith dies April 17. EA2 Falcon production with 4-speed auto transmission commences. Two millionth Falcon rolls off assembly line at Broadmeadows plant. BMO announces $40 million expansion. Ford announces model-sharing agreement with Nissan Australia. Corsair introduced into Australia. Capri II commences production. LTA9000, LTS8000 and 9000 heavy trucks released. Geelong Casting Plant achieves Q101 status. Ford Aluminium castings for the CVT transmission exported to Europe for the Ford Fiesta, worth A$14 million in 1989. Ford Motor Company purchases Jaguar in England.

The decade started with a bang as Ford announced an A$300 million investment program, and an A$13 million upgrade for the Sydney plant to manufacture a new vehicle, the Laser.

The story of the Laser began in 1974. Ford Asia Pacific still owned the unused plant at Koyasu near Tokyo which Phil Jones had renovated in 1971, and the land at Tsurumi, now valued at US$1million per acre which Japan Airlines (JAL) were interested in purchasing and developing as an airport. With serious pollution problems in Tokyo bay, Yokahama City Council had decided they wanted the Koyasu land for remediation purposes and indicated they were prepared to commence legal proceedings to assume ownership. Protracted negotiations between the Ford Office of General Council and Yokahama City Council had dragged on from 1974 to 1978 and identified capital gains tax as being a major problem for Ford.

Then, Ford was advised of an obscure Japanese tax law, that a sale of an asset sold to a government or semi-government authority was tax-free if the funds were reinvested in Japan within twelve months. Should Ford sell to JAL, capital gains tax would be about US$80 million. So, Ford sold the land to the Yokahama Council for US$83 million, picked up US$11 million on the exchange rate to the Japanese Yen, put in a further US$10 million and went looking for an investment in Japan. Toyota were not interested, Nissan wouldn't even meet with Ford representatives. Mr. Honda of Honda Motor Company was wined and dined in Detroit, but eventually declined as he feared Honda would (quite rightly) lose their identity. That left Fuji Heavy Industries, makers of Subaru, and Mazda, then known as Toyo Kogyo Motors.

Mazda were in financial trouble and owned by the Sumitomo Bank, so Ford swapped the money for shares in TK and paid no capital gains tax. It was a great investment. The first year's return alone on the investment in Mazda was US$32 million. The Koyasu plant became a Mazda Product Development Office. A press release on May 18, 1979 from Philip Caldwell advised the managements of Ford and Toyo Kogyo were meeting to discuss an arrangement for Ford to take up a 20% shareholding in TK. By

PAGES 184–185 1988 EA GL and Ghia sedans

LEFT 1981 KA Laser Ghia

ABOVE January, 1981 Job No: 1— front-wheel drive Ford KA Laser rolls off the production line at Ford Australia's Homebush Assembly Plant in Sydney

2000, Ford owned 33%. Nowadays with the repatriation of funds back to Ford US, the Ford shareholding is down to about 3%.

Sir Brian Inglis always credited Frank Erdman, head of FASPAC in 1976, with the strategic decision for Ford Australia to abandon Europe, convincing Bob Lutz, the head of Ford Europe to accept the change in source of products to Japan. The decision was financial; Erdman believed FOA couldn't compete with competitors trading in Japanese Yen, while Ford dealt in European currencies for their products. In addition, while the Cortina and Escort vehicles had improved, they weren't competitive with their Japanese sourced rivals, which were lighter and easier to produce. This, then is the scenario that led to Ford Australia's cooperation with Mazda and the birth of the Laser.

In the interim, the Cortina had to hold the small to medium car market for FOA until the Laser and later, the Telstar. Production of the TE Cortina had been 26,696 in 1979, but volumes dropped rapidly and by May 1980, only 8,723 were built. The TF replaced the TE that May, the most visual exterior change being the all-black Rim Polyurethane bumpers. Only 4,303 TF were built that year, a combined volume half that of 1980. The final year of production of the TF, 1981, saw little change in the volume produced. The wagon ceased production in November 1981, the sedan a month later. Laser couldn't come fast enough.

The Sydney plant, already a single vehicle plant with the Escort, was the logical choice for a small vehicle plant but needed extensive modification and renewal to achieve the projected volumes. The topography of the Sydney plant was difficult. Bounded by a railway line to the west, any extension had to be eastwards, where the land fell away quite steeply. The engineering team took advantage of the slope and built the plant extension on

ABOVE KA Laser advertisement

two levels. Export boxes arrived at the plant and were stored at the rear. Body components were unpacked in the original building for body build, the engine and transmission received on the ground floor of the extension. Trim and final components were unpacked in a warehouse at the rear of the main plant. Apart from the new extension, approximately A$6 million was spent on a new world-class, state-of-the-art paintshop, conversion of the electrocoat to the new cathodic system and drying ovens, built on a mezzanine floor of the old building. All facilities to the assembly lines were mounted overhead, leaving the floor clear—a significant work space improvement, and eliminating trip hazards for the operators. To improve cleanliness, the plant was repainted inside and out and the floors epoxy coated to seal them. Lighting was improved, as well as re-glazing many of the windows.

With staff of Ford of Japan (FOJ) acting as liaison and translators when needed, teams of Ford Australia engineers, stylists, finance, production supervisors, plant managers and logistics staff, travelled to Mazda plants at Hofu and Hiroshima to design the Laser, as it was to be called, to study how the Mazda 323 was built and establish systems and procedures for working with each other. Members of the VBEF[83] also visited Hiroshima, at Ford's invitation.

Apart from the differences in culture, the differences in philosophy of vehicle manufacture and assembly shocked the Australians. John Marshall said when he saw the process sheets, the instruction sheets for the operators to use for assembly operations, he thought they had been sent a sample, but was assured these were all that the operators required. Instead of detailed instructions on how to fit a door glass for example, the only instructions were the positioning of the winder handle, to ensure a screw was not cross threaded and the torque on the gun to fasten a screw. How to fit the glass into the channels and the mechanism were left to the operator. Investigation into Mazda operations revealed every operator was trained for three weeks before even starting on the production line, and then mentored and supervised. All employees at Mazda were high school graduates or better; and a totally different work philosophy and environment existed. A new phrase now entered into the Ford vocabulary, Process Intent.

The logistics personnel had similar experiences. Requests for how Mazda would handle returns, rejects, requests for credit and single item orders for replacement parts were met with bemusement. You wanted a complete vehicle set of parts, you got one. There would be no damaged parts, therefore no returns, no need for credit notes and no requirement for orders of single replacement parts. If the vehicle required six screws for the assembly of a part, you got six, not a bag of 100 or 1,000 thrown in the case. Of course there were issues, but eventually the system was nutted out between the Australians and their Japanese opposite numbers. Plant Manager Brian Tredwell wrote the following as part of the 1987 Laser Meteor facelift launch program binder:

> *Since Laser was launched with Toyo Kogyo…many methods of operation have had to be learned and assimilated, such as (a) new part numbering system, process sheet presentation, minimum information on drawings, KD lot system and engineering changes…Generally speaking it has been necessary to conform to TKK procedures and practices, rather than have them change to ours. TKK have, however, introduced a number of improvements in documentation and in packing over the last few months…The experience gained and the lessons learned are proving to be of value to those planning the introduction of Laser (and Meteor and Telstar) into Broadmeadows.*

An example of the different philosophies of the two companies was engineering changes, changes to a product design. Excluding new model engineering changes, Ford averaged about 500 production engineering changes a year. Mazda changes were often 200 a month. The sheer volume of documentation alone forced Ford into a rethink in the administration of Product and Manufacturing Engineering, Purchasing and Material Control.

From their experiences at Mazda, the engineers used the Sydney site to advantage in assembling the Laser, as well as incorporating the latest technology. After painting, the vehicles were carried by clam shell jigs on overhead conveyors, passing into the new extension for assembly. The engine, transmission, even the exhaust were assembled on the ground floor, before being raised on a scissor lift directly under the painted, trimmed body and assembled in place. Seat fabrication was similar, seats were assembled on the ground floor and raised on a lift on each side of the line at the assembly point. The extensions and improvements reduced the plant to a one-shift operation with only a slighter lower rate, 110 UPD. Assembly time for a Laser and Meteor hatchback and notchback was twenty-seven hours, three-quarters that of a Falcon.

The first Laser, the KA, commenced production in January 1981 and was launched shortly after. It was an instant success. While some of the media murmured about badge engineering, the Laser was sufficiently different in looks, trim and pricing to the Mazda equivalent not to bother the motoring public. While 1981 was not a notable year for sales, the Laser notched up production of 60% of Falcon volume, 25,019 vehicles versus Falcon sedan production of 41,686. Production of English derived passenger vehicles had ended the same year, 1981, with production of 12,578 Cortina sedans and wagons and 289 Escorts. Their demise was more than adequately covered the next year. The GA Meteor hatchback commenced production in January 1982, complementing the Laser. Combined production for the two in 1982 was 46,249.

The relationship with Mazda also sparked off a design exercise which, similar with Misubishi and the Magna, would see a Mazda 626-design based vehicle widened to replace the Falcon. A design exercise, codenamed Capricorn, developed both a notchback and hatchback vehicle and even developed clays for the interior designs. However, market research conducted as part of the program showed the public preferred the longer and wider rear-wheel-drive Falcon and the program was terminated. The exercise was not wasted however; one outcome of the program and the work with Mazda resulted in the birth of the Telstar. A clone

PRIME MINISTER OPENS ENGINE PLANT

Prime Minister Mr. Bob Hawke opened Ford Australia's $70 million 4-cylinder engine plant in Geelong on October 14, 1983. The plant has a capacity of 90,000 engines a year and will soon be manufacturing 1.6 and 2.0-litre engines for Australia and exports, initially to New Zealand.

of the Mazda 626, design work on the Telstar started after the commencement of work on the Laser/Meteor. Destined to be built solely in Broadmeadows, the sedan commenced production with two built in December 1982, followed by the hatchback the following March. As part of the expansion of the Plastics Plant, large injection mould machines had been procured to manufacture the Falcon instrument panel. Automatically it became a task to fill the capacity of the machines. Introduction of the KB and GB Laser and Meteor in December 1982 became a suitable model breakpoint for the Plastics Plant to integrate the manufacture of bumper bars. The Japanese used a rubber modified Polypropylene (EPDM PP) injection moulded material which quickly proved to be the more appropriate material compared to others; cheaper, recyclable, and quicker to produce. The same material was used for the AS Telstar bumpers in 1985, when they were also made in Australia. This material would later influence future Falcon designs.

Instead of Bill Dix returning to Australia after a stint in Ford of Europe (FOE), he was offered the position of President of Ford Japan (FOJ). Henry Ford II and Don Petersen's negotiated change in the relationship with Mazda, to owning equity in Mazda, had to be implemented; Bill was tasked with overseeing that transition. Working in Japan, he saw first-hand the relationship of Mazda and its employees. In his 1988 interview with Professor Lewis, he said, in part:

ABOVE 1983 KB Laser S —66,139 KB Lasers were produced at Broadmeadows and Homebush Assembly Plants. All Laser production was moved to Homebush in April, 1984.

LEFT Capricorn design project, 1981

ABOVE Job No:1—AR Telstar sedan, December, 1982. Pictured among others: Bill Dix and Plant Manager David Thursfield

RIGHT 1983 AR Telstar Hatchback

The Japanese, individually and collectively, are probably a more independent and confident race than most…it was my appreciation of the strength of the Japanese, the dedication of their people. Everyone you spoke to, spoke well of the company and their product, were loyal to the end. That was something I was not used to. We are a race of knockers in Australia…We had people working for the company that would knock the product… would only speak up for it at a pinch. For Australians, it was a job for which they were paid, not a matter of loyalty.

Dix had already seen the benefits of worker–company consultation and cooperation, and was determined that Ford

Australia must improve its relationship with its people. He had also seen the first attempts in Ford US, in 1981, to introduce Employee Involvement and Participation Management development programs.

On the completion of his term as President of Ford Japan, Dix returned to Australia as President of Ford Australia, a month before the third long industrial dispute at Ford, at the Broadmeadows Assembly Plant in July 1981. It began in unusual circumstances. Unbeknown to Ford, a number of employees had joined the company with the intention of overthrowing the existing leadership of the Federal and Victorian state branches of the union, now known as the Vehicle Builders Union, (VBU).

Highly educated and intelligent, they had ingratiated themselves with the workforce for more than a year and been elected as shop stewards. Their particular targets were Federal Secretary Len Townsend, who was always very well dressed, and Assistant Federal Secretary Sandilands. Espousing opinions, 'The union doesn't represent us any more, they are in the pay of the company,' and 'They don't run the union—we do,' they won support of many of the workforce.

Without approval of the union, the stewards created a dispute over pay and planned to go out on strike the next day. The last thing Ford wanted was another strike like the 1973 dispute. Alerted at the last minute of the details of the strike proposal, Ford scrambled to identify the ringleaders. On the morning of the stoppage, Ford called them into an office and fired them all, escorting them from the premises. Inevitably, there were threats, table thumping, and violence threatened, 'Ford will suffer the consequences', but as they were dismissed before the stoppage, their dismissal was not part of the dispute, and with no support from the union, any unfair dismissal claim could not proceed.

Even so, the strike would drag on for another six weeks, a fight with anarchists that Ford could not afford to lose. Townsend was in a difficult position. He and Sandilands were fighting for their jobs, even their careers. They wanted Ford to win the dispute but couldn't be seen to be supporting, or even cooperating with the company, else be guilty of exactly what they were accused of. There followed a number of farcical meetings followed, with two, even three agendas; the union membership, the union leadership and the company. Quietly, a hint was passed to the company that the Federal government had recently passed legislation permitting voting by secret ballot on resolution of disputes. Ford applied and won the approval of the Conciliation and Arbitration Commission for a secret ballot for a return to work. The Victorian Electoral Commission conducted the ballot, supervised by scrutineers from the union, shop stewards and the company and was the first secret ballot held under the legislation in Australia. It was not unanimous but it was a resounding decision to return to work immediately.

DOING BUSINESS WITH JAPAN

It had been a long two weeks in Hiroshima and the trip looked like it was a waste of time. Mazda was philosophically committed to doing business with Ford, but some individual managers were still unconvinced. How to persuade them to give you information for the Plastics Plant to make components for the Telstar which would result in Mazda losing A$1 million worth of business? Doug Wallace had been meeting with various Mazda managers and this was his final meeting, on his last day in Japan. Small talk had been about family, children, photos shown, oohed and aahed over, all very polite, but business? Forget it. Finally he decided to play the Japanese at their own game. He called the Ford of Japan secretary, Micki Ikada into the office and in front of his three Japanese hosts, told her to cancel his flight home, and to rebook in two weeks' time. Polite consternation from his hosts. 'But what of your family? They will be waiting for you!' Distressed look on face. 'If I go home without the information, I will lose much face at Ford and my career will suffer. My family must wait.' Silence; a protracted conversation in Japanese, then in English, 'We have to go to another meeting', Japan speak for 'we don't want to meet with you any longer', then a surprise. 'We will meet again in one hour.' One hour later, meeting reconvened. For the next hour, two weeks' worth of information was shovelled across the table, enough drawings, specifications and information to fill a small suitcase, borrowed from FOJ for the purpose. FOA Plastics got all the information to make the Telstar components and the flight wasn't cancelled.

Having been in the job for a month, Dix, speaking of the strike, quipped, 'It was not a good look for a new President!' He went on:

> *I spent a disproportionate amount of time analysing the issues in Ford Australia and working with my people to find a better way of dealing with our employees. I wanted to get some of the Japanese type philosophy ingrained in our people and merge that with US Participative Management concepts.*

One outcome of the strike was that Ford's market leadership plans were thrown into disarray. Ford had led for five out of the nine months of the year to September. The strike effectively handed market leadership in 1981 to GM-H, but it was to be only a temporary setback.

It took some time for Dix to work through the process of introducing Employee Involvement to the company, but Percy Worsnop, a teacher in a previous career, and Tom Pettigrew embraced the philosophies, and were instrumental in introducing them in the smallest of Ford Australia's assembly plants. The assembly process of the Mazda source vehicles lent itself to be an ideal way to launch the new management concepts. Another perception was that the VBEF in New South Wales would be more receptive to change, than the more radical elements in Broadmeadows.

In 1982, Sydney Plants' first Employee Involvement facilitator Charlie Murphy and senior shop steward Graham Coakes visited Ford US. Other personnel also travelled to both Japan and Dearborn to study and compare the principles involved and to develop a system based on the experiences of these countries, but unique to Australia. Their visits culminated in the construction of a new Employment Involvement Centre in Sydney, opened by Sydney Plant Manager Brian Tredwell and senior shop steward Zaid Youssef that year.

Before production of the Laser began, plant management were introduced to the concepts at a seminar in Gosford, NSW. Bill Dix and Ken McDonald were among others to address them, stressing the importance of the process and to demonstrate to those doubters of the system, and there were some, that there was no choice, no option, no fallback system, and the senior management of the company supported the new process. After extensive discussions with the union one of the first innovations was a new employee induction scheme. No longer a quick few hours' induction, employees were now to spend five days being introduced to the company, in stages. A Company and Plant induction which included occupational safety, employee benefits, and the company rules and regulations was followed by a a second phase, 'Assembly Skills Familiarisation'. Then a 'Section Induction' with the employees' supervisor. The final three days were for 'On-line Training' with direct supervision. A final question and answer session completed the process. The whole process substantially improved communication between an employee, his supervisor and the company, and fostered a 'team' spirit. One immediate indirect benefit was to be a reduction in employee turnover and absenteeism.

Employee Involvement (EI) was launched in the Sydney Plant on March 1, 1983. Production was stopped and all employees addressed by Plant Manager Geoff Norcott, VBEF (NSW) State Secretary Joe Thompson, Senior shop steward Graham Coakes and members of the plant EI Steering Committee, to introduce them to the EI process. It (the process) received a warm reception; over 50% of employees joined EI Groups and a new era in Ford was born.

While it was hard work at first, most employees, managers and supervisors eventually realised that improved personnel relationships actually improved the work place. Work groups were formed in all areas of the plant, and were trained in problem solving techniques and basic statistical techniques. Training was also carried out in understanding the various styles of decision-making. A steering committee, comprising shop stewards, group leaders and management was formed to guide the process and to listen to proposals and ideas from the work groups. Minutes of the meetings, as well as results and achievement of the groups were published on notice boards around the plant for all to see. The monthly company newspaper, *Ford News* publicised the achievements, carrying photographs of the groups, leaders and information, and played a crucial role in disseminating the commitment of the company and all its employees to the new process. It took time, but gradually with many small steps, the tortuous process of changing the company ethos began to gather its own momentum.

The period 1982 to 1988 was to see an extensive training process begin around the company. While Percy Worsnop oversaw the complete transformation process, Tom Pettigrew, aided by Alan Long and Steve Martin were instrumental in conducting in-plant seminars and training courses. With the success of Sydney Plant, ACTU Secretary Bill Kelty endorsed a statement of EI principles and the VBEF sent a senior delegation to the US to meet with their counterparts in Ford, the United Auto Workers, (UAW). At Broadmeadows plant, the assembly line was stopped in order for employees to attend briefing and training, a process unheard of in prior days. Every operation of the company followed Sydney's lead. There was total commitment to the process. Plants introduced the process to employees in various ways. Plastic Plant's Senior Standards Analyst, Ray Hawryluk, ran a small business filming weddings and other events. At the suggestion of EI Facilitator Ted Lavender, and the plant EI Steering committee, he filmed interviews with Bill Dix, Plant Manager Ron Tyack, VBU's Len Townsend and the shop stewards John Carter and Felix Mondon, who described their experiences with EI. When completed, the video was played on television screens over the three-shift operation of the plant for two days. On the third day, all employees received personal EI booklets and an invitation to attend a meeting with EI group leaders the next day. Over 50% of the employees joined EI groups, one of the highest levels of participation.

PILFERAGE

Pilferage was (and is) a constant problem. When the Sydney plant was operating two shifts and struggling to meet demand for Lasers, inventory checks showed stock went missing on the afternoon shift. Ian Craven recalls he and a compatriot, in great secrecy, spent long nights in the darkened PABX room in the front of the plant, equipped with night vision glasses to observe any illegal action. Only one other person, the security supervisor, knew they were there. They were surprised however that the security guard on his rounds would stop at the office window, tap on it and wave to them. The supervisor had briefed the security guard. Ian saw nothing on his shifts, but the culprits were ultimately caught. You guessed it; one was the security guard, the other the afternoon shift maintenance foreman.

Or the story of the enterprising lad who stole four special racing tyres from the Research Centre and fitted them to his car, which he proudly drove to work. Trouble was the security staff, who regularly checked the employee carparks, knew these were specially imported—there were no others in Australia. Oops. And then there was the enterprising lad who glued those small 'Ghia' badges all the way along the body side protection mouldings on both sides of his car.

EMPLOYEE INVOLVEMENT

Sign on the wall of Advanced Stamping Plant Engineering Manager Ivan Tan Sing's office: 'Be cooperative—do it my way!'

It was not only Ford that had to change. With over 68% of Ford's revenue paid to suppliers, their role in improving quality was vital and not neglected. During December 1983, senior managers from over 500 suppliers attended seminars given by Ford at the National Science Centre in Melbourne. They were addressed by Bill Dix, Tom Pettigrew, John Marshall, David Stobart, David Lamb and David Ford. Each group was told the ability of Australian vehicles to compete against the best imported German or Japanese vehicles, rested on exceeding the customers' experience in quality, durability and service. The attendees were then shown Ford's New Approach to Quality and the importance of Process Intent and the integral part an operator played in achieving quality. The seminars concluded by emphasising the need for cooperation between their respective companies and with Ford.

Changing the culture of an organisation takes time, commitment and effort. At a subsequent Management Seminar, held at Sovereign Hill for Senior Management and Suppliers, Tom Pettigrew outlined the task of each of them:

> *Employees must understand the depth of change needed in our approach to Production, he said. We are starting a program which may take seven years to implement. We're not in this to make a big noise and disappear. The changes must occur throughout our supplier companies as well as within Ford.*

Some employees and managers found it difficult to accept the new work environment and decided to leave.

The rewards from all the consultation, Employee Involvement and cooperation came in 1988. After nearly six months of consultation and work by shop stewards, the unions, the company, and more than twenty working parties and 100 meetings, a joint presentation was made to the Arbitration Commission with over eighty-one pages of efficiency improvements achieved without industrial action. Commissioner Smith had no hesitation in granting the requested 4% increase in wages, while Ford undertook not to increase prices. The Industrial Relations press and newspaper editorials were effusive in their praise of Ford and the changes wrought over the period.

The September 1988 issue of *Ford News* carried a message on its front page from Bill Dix titled 'Quality—The key to our future'. He was blunt. The goal was to produce the best vehicles in the world, but first we had to earn that reputation locally. The process of continuous improvement meant continuous change and he challenged the attitude and commitment of every employee. He linked the processes of Employee Involvement and Participative Management and committed the company to continue the already significant education and training programs. He concluded:

> *Ford Australia is committed to this continuing process of improvement...with your help and cooperation we can do it.*

Meanwhile the Federal government, under Prime Minister Bob Hawke had, late in 1988 helped organise, through the Directorate of Industrial Relations (DIRD) and the Automotive Industry Authority (AIA) a Tripartite Study mission comprising twenty-six members of the government, employers and unions to travel overseas to study how the Australian automotive industry could become more competitive through restructuring. They returned with the conclusion that the Ford process was heading in the right direction, a process that continues today.

In the decade following 1982, there had been only two full days lost in industrial action. There had been stoppages; some shop stewards, taking advantage of their position, abused it. Max Kenworthy, son of 'Tunner', was also an industrial officer in Geelong and the Broadmeadows plant. He said it took time for people to get used to talking to each other:

> *On my second day in the Broadmeadows plant, we had to speak to an operator in the paint shop. The whole paint shop walked out. That nearly got me transferred back to Geelong!*

Another shop steward would call a stoppage and refuse to discuss the problem until a Vice-President of the company came to see him. Then, in an office, he would literally break down in tears about how he was doing his best to help. Or the senior shop steward who had an office next door to the industrial officer, and would spend all day there talking to other shop stewards. Max also recalled one employee returning to Geelong from a meeting in Broadmeadows, relating how the 'Plant Manager' had been thumping the table at the meeting, only to be told, 'he's not the plant manager you !@#$%, he's the senior shop steward!'

But one of the most significant but small changes, Max believes, was trust. It became possible, even promoted, that managers and supervisors talk to people on the production line without having to talk to a union official first.

Probably the biggest breakthrough came in 2000. One of the senior shop stewards had ordered a vehicle and knowing the SIDO[84] number, influenced or 'persuaded' a number of people on the line to upgrade it, from a base to a top-line model. An alert security guard at the shipping gate picked up the discrepancy of the vehicle to the SIDO and, after an investigation, the company fired the shop steward. The other shop stewards and the union called a mass meeting, insisting the plant go out on strike until he was re-instated. At the meeting, the workers backed the company, rejected the union and the shop stewards' demands and returned to work.

The XE and ZK/FD Falcon/Fairlane/Ltd vehicles were launched in Broadmeadows and Brisbane respectively in December, 1981 and February, 1982. The model change could have been unremarkable, with the usual revised bumpers, grille, tail-lights

BELOW 1982 XE Falcon station wagon

etc. But the XE wasn't that. If not completely new, it was a considerably revised and improved vehicle with the addition to the sedans of the six-link Watts Link rear suspension. With that suspension also came tapered coil springs, powder coated to reduce NVH, while the wagons and commercials retained what many journalists derisively termed cart springs, but they were better for load carrying, despite whatever might have been written. The continuous improvement saw the introduction of Ford-designed, Honda Japan manufactured alloy heads with dual throat Weber carburettors on the 6-cylinders and four barrel Carters on the V8s, which improved performance without affecting fuel economy. Product Planning had really done their homework. The Fairmont Ghia was distinctive and classy, while the 4.1-litre ESP Falcon continued the tradition of a European sports touring sedan. The Fairlanes and LTDs also benefited from the engine and suspension refinements. There were minor trim changes to the interiors. *Wheels* response to the XE was perhaps a peace offering and recognition of Ford's efforts:

> *The XE is the car we hoped the XD was going to be. This is a fine car and has nothing to do with lemons.*

Still no COTY award though!

By 1982, all the pieces started to come together. The A$13 million extension and modifications to Sydney Plant were complete and the KA Laser and GA Meteor had commenced production. The XE and ZK/FD Falcon/Fairlane/LTD vehicles, were selling well. As volumes climbed, so did the overtime. The industrial unrest which had doomed Ford's ambitions for market leadership in 1981 had been settled and an embryonic era of cooperation and working together was slowly developing with Employee Involvement.

Meanwhile, GM-H were planning the launch of the Camira, which, along with the Gemini, was to go head-to-head with the Laser/Meteor. They planned an ambitious launch for the Camira, and reduced the build volume of the Commodore during the launch phase. It was a disaster. As the market took off in the second quarter of the year, they were caught short, unable to build enough Commodores to satisfy the market, who turned to Ford. The May ADAPS registration figures, released in June, showed Ford had again hit the front and was the market leader, not just with Falcon. GM-H trailed again in June and July, and even in August with the launch of the Camira, still trailed Ford. The Camira, with production problems, later also gained a poor reputation for quality in the industry.

To respond to Ford, in September GM-H began offering dealer incentives. Ford responded with 'The Great Race' sales campaign, but their leadership was still halved by September end, to 3,180 units. Then in October, 1982, with cash incentives Ford increased the lead to 5,878. Then as the market softened and sales slumped–, other manufacturers jumped in with their own incentives. Everybody began offering discounts; Nissan slashed prices on the Bluebird, Toyota joined in with discounts on Corolla, GM-H even began discounting the Camira, Ford offered cash incentives across the board. By November end, Ford were leading by 4,908 units and many thought the race was over.

By now, both companies had turned their company fleets over at least once so there was little room to manoeuvre. Then the Dandenong registry office registered 2,660 vehicles in one day; GM-H maintained it was only 1,100 and they were all employee lease vehicles. On December 13, GM-H reintroduced the cash incentives with specific quotas for dealers and suddenly Adelaide registrations were twice the normal average; dealers in Queensland and South Australia were registering but not selling vehicles. After complaints and an investigation, nearly 500 Holden vehicles were quietly de-registered in early January 1983. GM-H disowned their

NEW HONOUR FOR BRUCE BURTON

Congratulatory messages poured in for Director of Supply, Bruce Burton, who was awarded the CBE (Commander of the British Empire) in the Queen's New Year honours list for 1982. Bruce's award was for service to the Australian motor industry. His principal contribution to the industry has been as a delegate to the Federal Chamber of Automotive Industries, (FCAI). Bruce has served as treasurer, vice president and president on this body, which liaises with the Federal government on behalf of all businesses associated with the motor industry. He joined the Chamber a year after he joined Ford Australia in 1953 as division head of Customs and Traffic, having previously served in the Commonwealth Government Department of Customs and Trade. Appointed Director of Supply in June 1971 and a lover of horseracing, golf and photography, Bruce has led a colourful life. In World War II, he served in the distinguished RAAF No. 3 Squadron as a pilot, flying Kittyhawks and Mustangs and was based in Canada, England, the Middle East, and completed an operational tour of duty in Italy.

MYXESP

XE Falcon Fairmont Ghia ESP (European Sports Pack), features striking gold latticework alloy wheels, two-tone paint treatment, integral driving lights and front air dam extension.

ABOVE 1982 XE Falcon X-Pak sedan and wagon

dealers' actions but significantly, did nothing about discounting the vehicles registered.

The period of December was a poor one for Ford. GM-H registered vehicles at an astonishing rate, anything to regain the lead. This was rapidly whittled down from 4,823 on December 22 to 449 by January 13. Even some at Ford thought it was lost. Twenty-four hours later it was down to 201, then 151, then 136. An error found by ADAPS saw the lead soar up to 345, then back to 145 after the correction. It was nail-biting stuff.

Wheels motoring writer Phil Scott had organised with Ford to be with Max Gransden over the final days of the registration period and challenged Gransden in an interview whether Ford had followed a similar registration rort, albeit legal, as GM-H. Gransden merely pointed to the near empty storage yard at the rear of the assembly plant, but agreed he had had approval from Bill Dix to extend the incentive program for the dealers to move their stock. GM-H were desperately trying to sell enough vehicles to maintain their, until then, unbroken thirty-year record of leadership, but on January 21, 1983, the final moment came. Grandsen, nervous, tapping his foot, was being interviewed by Scott when Owen Cook, dressed in a tuxedo adorned with 'Ford No. 1' badges, presented him with a silver platter on which lay a single envelope.

Phil Scott recalls:

Gransden is caught mid-sentence and splutters '...oh, for Christ's sake...Jesus.' He reaches for the envelope amid cheers and catcalls from the Ford execs now crowded into his office. Gransden stands up, a smile breaking across his face: 'OK are you all listening? Here are the results for 1982. Ford 139,318 for 22.6 percent. GM, 139,18...' The last figure is lost in an uproar of raucous cheers. Like a politician playing to an audience of party faithful, Gransden lets the noise die, and continues reading. 'Now let me give you some of the other numbers, Falcon, 66,849, a lead of 2,171 over Commodore...' Again the noise and cheering erupts. He waits again, choosing the perfect moment to continue: 'Laser at 27,865 leads Gemini by 364. Laser the top-selling small car...' More noise. 'So we're market leaders, we're top with Falcon and top with Laser. Meteor at 12,204...did that beat Cortina's 1981 figure?' he asks. Nobody knows, and few, one suspects care too much at the moment. 'Oh boy, how about that, eh...We knocked 'em off.' Champagne appears, complete with flutes. The company rule about no alcohol on the premises has gone by the board. Gransden cuts across the muzak to deliver the news on the office PA system. On his way back to his office he pauses for a chat with the switchboard girls. The next calls to Broadmeadows are answered with the words. 'Hello, Ford, Australia's Number One'. The call to Dearborn is made, a statement is made to the press and telexes go out to Sir Brian Inglis in Taiwan and every Ford dealer in Australia. Bill Dix, on holidays at St. Leonards is on the line. 'Hello, how are you Bill?' says Gransden, 'well we've won. We won, Bill!'

The final margin was 137 vehicles, but retail sales tell a different story. Ford sold over 6,000 more vehicles than GM-H. A congratulatory fax from Philip Caldwell, Ford Chairman, and sportingly, a fax from Chuck Chapman, Managing Director of GM-H:

> *The ADAPS registrations are out and the final result is in. Naturally, we at Holden's are disappointed that we lost the race after a tremendous effort in December, but I think it is only fitting that I congratulate Ford Australia on a tremendous job.*
>
> *Chuck Chapman*

Reflecting on that time, Dix said in an interview for this book:

> *I was asked by (Ford Chairman) Philip Caldwell if I needed to register extra vehicles (like GM) but I said no, we were far enough in front. It was close, way too close. I think I would have been sacked if we had lost after saying that'. Ford remained market leader for the next sixteen years.*

The election of the Hawke Labor government in 1983 brought into power three of the great thinkers of the era, Prime Minister Bob Hawke, Treasurer Paul Keating and Senator John Button, Leader of the Senate. When asked his preferred portfolio, Button chose Industry and Commerce because, as he said, 'he had seen some very bad factories and he thought it would be a challenge'. Button said he had no pre-conceived ideas on tariffs and protection but in 1984 he travelled to Sweden on a parliamentary study tour. There he found a similar political environment but found the government had a better relationship with industry, there were no tariffs but the government assisted industry with research, development and restructuring.

Back in Australia, their three objectives corresponded, Button with industry restructuring, Hawke greater global integration while Keating wanting economic efficiency. In his plans for revitalising industry, Button believed management relied on high levels of protection. In a 2002 interview with Andrew Leigh, he said:

> *For the whole of my time as Industry Minister, I was less than enchanted by the quality of Australian management and largely attributed this to the culture of protection in which they had been cocooned. I actually remember using the 'iron lung' analogy for protection in the motor industry.'*

The outcome was the Passenger Motor Vehicle Plan—'The Button Plan'. The objectives of the plan were to abolish quotas on imported vehicles, progressively reduce tariffs, and give incentives via an Export Facilitation Scheme. This allowed companies to accumulate export credits to offset against import

LEFT XE Falcon Fairmont Ghia ESP (European Sports Pack)

EO·190
FALCO

Bill Dix and Denis MacInerney of Denmac, Brisbane with the first V8—the model B18, the first GT—the XR Falcon and the last locally produced V8 engine—an XE Falcon Fairmont ESP

WORLD RECORD!

A team of Ford Geelong engineers shattered the world fuel economy record when their home-built, cigar-shaped vehicle achieved 2,948 miles per gallon at Sydney's Amaroo Park motor racing circuit at the 1983 Shell Mileage Marathon. Casting Plant apprentice Shane Thomas drove the lightweight car to victory for the second year running, using a 13 cc model aircraft engine, larger than the 10 cc engine used in 1982. Looking forward to next year, the team are considering fuel injection for the next engine. 'But it may not be a viable proposition for such a small engine,' said designer Clive Humphries.

duties on vehicles or components. It also created rationalisation by promoting viable volumes, productivity and quality. The Button Plan was introduced in 1985. One effect was the sharing of models between three of the major manufacturers: Holden and Toyota with the Commodore and Lexcen, Nissan and Ford with the Pintara and Corsair, the Falcon Ute and Nissan Navara and, to a lesser extent, Ford and Mazda with the Laser and 323, Telstar and 626, and the first generation of the Ford Ranger and the Mazda BT50 utility.

However the badge engineering exercises were unpopular in the marketplace, and agreement between the various manufacturers on common componentry protracted. Even after exhaustive consultation agreement was limited. Two of the few successes were the design of an interior dome light and the paint colour library available from Dulux Paints.

Ford desperately needed an export program; the 1985 Button plan demanded it in order to gain import credits. GM-H had a large export program; 4-cylinder engines to Taiwan, they had also negotiated with General Motors to forgo their Middle East market in favour of an export program for the Commodore and the larger Caprice, a market barred to Ford Australia by Ford US. Not that Ford US cared about it, the volume was small; they generated few specific programs for the region, unlike GM-H who fostered it carefully, supported and encouraged by General Motors in the US.

One Product Planning concept was the export of left-hand drive Fairlanes to Ford US, to be sold there as the Crown Victoria, a Ford US sacred cow. The Fairlane was an attractive proposition as, with an estimated annual US volume of 30–40,000 vehicles it would be, to Ford Australia, a high-volume, high-profit vehicle, using existing componentry and sheet metal; a low-cost investment and with a shorter lead time than an entirely new vehicle. To test the waters, Product Planning had a vehicle built and sent to a clinic in Chicago, at which the new Lincoln Town car was being researched. Peter Gillitzer recalls clinic feedback was that it was seen to appeal to a younger buyer with its more European styling, with many respondents saying their children would like the car—'an East/West (coast) car'. Peter recalls:

> *The clinic was stacked against us by holding it in Chicago, which has an age profile dictated by the Town Car. The truth was the Product Development group didn't want our car competing in what they thought was their territory. They even played cheap tricks by adding very bright wheel covers at the last minute to add appeal to their offering; it was war. Our Fairlane drew some potential sales from the town car, and that was all it took to sink the program. I'm sure the Fairlane would have attracted a whole new class of buyer to Ford and we would have exceeded our objective volumes. But, so much for the idea that the corporation makes logical business decisions. Our toughest competitor wasn't in the marketplace, it was in-house!*

Resistance came from everywhere. With the Fairlane program barely on the drawing boards, Chief engineer David Ford travelled to Dearborn. At one of the meetings, he bumped into Charlie Knighton, Vice-President of Product Development for Ford USA. Charlie was bristling, 'David, I'll fight you tooth and nail over the Crown Vic. It will cost jobs in the US, I won't let it happen. You can have the Capri, but we'll keep the Crown Victoria.' And so, as in any family squabble, Ford Australia lost the argument with the parent company, and a major export opportunity.

Earlier, interest had been sparked by the good results in a customer-review clinic of a stylish, pert, two-seater convertible penned by Ford-owned Ghia of Turin and exhibited at the 1983 Frankfurt Motor Show, named Barchetta, Italian for 'little boat'. Head of Ford of Europe and car enthusiast, Bob Lutz had wanted to produce an affordable latter-day Porsche speedster and commissioned Ghia to design one. The result was the Barchetta. But he could not find a way for the program to be viable. When he was appointed Vice-President of International Operations, he suggested to Alex Trotman, head of FASPAC, by now renamed APAO (Asia-Pacific Assembly Operations) that Alex look at the Barchetta as an option for export by Ford Australia. But even the Ford Australia feasibility study of building a Barchetta for Europe didn't stack up economically. However the exercise did point to a niche market for a small front wheel drive convertible, based on the Laser platform. Not economic with Australian volumes alone, the concept looked doomed until, Trotman and the APAO

Finance Director, John Devine reviewed the Barchetta project and decided an option could be for Ford Australia and Mazda to cooperate in the project. Again the major market was the US, the target market being US college kids.

The original Barchetta concept, while a good idea, nevertheless was again considered too small. Additional modelling work by Ghia to produce a larger vehicle for the US were not successful. They had lost that cute, sporty image. With Australia fully committed to the EA26, other options had to be pursued. So, in 1984, Trotman established a small group to be headed by David Fewchuck, comprising Alan Thompson as principal engineer, Jeff DuComb, a US product planner, and Larry Mamos, a retired US engineer to develop a new design based on a Laser, codenamed SA30.

Trotman had met Fewchuck previously while working as a product planner at Lincoln-Mercury and Fewchuck, a graduate trainee there on assignment. David's parents were Canadian and American, with Ukrainian and white Russian ancestry. Working as missionaries to white Russians, they lived for a time in Argentina, where David was born. Called to a ministry in Sydney, the family migrated to Australia in 1952. David was granted a scholarship and graduated in Mechanical Engineering from the University of New South Wales. He was a practising Christian and it showed in his relationships, both personal and professional. Interested in cars, he joined Ford on graduation but quickly discovered his engineering abilities were not as good as his conceptual and persuasive abilities, which were more suited to product planning. After stints in the US and Australia, he transferred to APAO[85] under Trotman and moved to the Philippines, where he was responsible for the fourth iteration of the Fiera, based on the Mazda Courier. He returned in 1981 to Australia as head of Ford Products Company in APAO. Three years later, Trotman asked him to take on the Capri program. Fewchuck was not convinced the project would succeed:

> *...I had an excellent job with the company and here I was being asked to trade a job with real substance for one that may have no substance at all. I held out for about a month telling Trotman that I was not convinced the idea (the Capri Program) had any merit. He got very upset...in the end I relented but I wasn't comfortable. I was also bothered because this bizarre proposal only had one sponsor, Bob Lutz, but I respected and trusted Trotman.*[86]

He would spend nearly six months a year overseas for the next five years.

After much negotiation, Ital Design in Turin was contracted to develop the design. The first thing was to scan the designs

LAST TRACTOR ASSEMBLED IN AUSTRALIA

There was a twinge of sadness around the Brisbane plant in October 1983 as Jan Wojciechowski drove the last tractor off the assembly line. The Series 10, 6610 tractor rolled off the line ending an era of tractor assembly in Australia. The tractor assembly line had been operating at Eagle Farm since 1969, after moving from nearby leased premises, occupied for six years.

LEFT Advertisement celebrating sixty years of Ford tractors

1982 Louisville truck brochure

OPPOSITE LN Series Truck through truck wash at Eagle Farm

PLANT MODIFICATIONS—DEVESON STYLE

When Don Deveson wanted something, it had to happen to his timetable, no one else's. It didn't always work out. With the installation of the die-casting presses in BMO, Don decided he wanted the external walls in that section of the plant replaced with glass. Not a bad idea actually, extra light in the plant, replacing fifty-year-old walls. Trouble was, Don wasn't prepared to wait the quoted three months for the glass and frames to be delivered. The next week, in the middle of winter, contractor and friend Paddy Hoare arrived and at Don's direction, proceeded to knock down the walls. Uproar as workers throughout the plant felt the cold Corio Bay winds whistling throughout the plant. Rapidly and at significant cost, temporary plywood walls were erected until the new glass walls arrived, yep, three months later.

and ensure they would fit the Mazda floorpan and drivetrain. Fewchuck said later:

> *Ford's relationship with Ital was never easy because they had a different cultural outlook to working practices than we did. Here were a bunch of Aussies in effect asking an Italian company to use a Japanese engineering database to produce a car using outside companies to do the tooling and Australia or Taiwan to make the final product. They thought it was a dog's breakfast.*[87]

In 1985, after more designs and more clinics the design was firmed finally up, with an Ital-designed interior and the exterior designed by Ghia. It was time to sell to Ford US management the concept of a sporty runabout designed in Europe, manufactured in Australia and sold in the US. The program group also sought manufacturing partners in Japan and Australia to assist with the design and engineering.

Then the Ford US N.I.H. (not invented here) factor kicked into high gear. In 1985, Mazda were only beginning to set up assembly operations in the US. J.D. Power, an independent authority for reporting on the American public's attitude to quality of vehicles was, at the time, consistently reporting a low image of Mazda vehicle quality. So, while Mazda and Mazda-built Ford vehicles were two of the highest-rated vehicles for quality in Australia, in America the equivalent product was considered 'a lemon'.

This is surprising; typically, in Australia, imported vehicles are seen to benefit from the 'halo effect'. Owners of imported vehicles accept the quality of their vehicle, perhaps they have no recourse; the dealer rejects the problem or the owner shrugs the problem off as 'one of those things'. In any case, generally, imported vehicles are regularly reported as having higher quality levels than the comparable Australian vehicle. This is not a unique Ford issue; GM-H has had the same experience. There are specific examples of Ford vehicles which were regularly reported with higher 'things gone wrong per hundred vehicles, three and six months-in-service' than the corresponding Mazda-badged vehicle built at the same time, in the same plant. Similarly, when a European branded vehicle, with a reputation for quality was measured by Ford, using the Ford standard for quality, it rated worse than the Falcon. One could argue that Ford must be measuring the wrong things in assessing quality, but exactly what Ford and GM-H owners would complain about, would exist in the European vehicle and owners would not even rate, or mention in surveys. Quite an enigma.

So Ford Australia had the task of selling the concept of a Mazda-sourced vehicle to a dubious client, Ford US. Yet when two different Capri clays, produced by Ital and Ghia, were presented to the American public in clinics, competing with vehicles considered the logical American competition, the Fiat X1/9, Honda CR-X, Nissan EXA, Toyota MR2, as well as the Mustang and the GM Pontiac Fiero, both clays were preferred by more than 50% of the attendees over the other vehicles, particularly the popular GM Fiero, which ran a poor third. Largely influenced by the Ford US dealers, who preferred the Mustang, the Ford division rejected the Capri. Ford US management recognised a market niche existed and accepted a proposal by Edsel Ford that the Capri be marketed by the flagging Lincoln-Mercury Division (L-M), who were desperate to improve the performance of that division. The Capri would be sold alongside the Tracer, the US version of the Laser. The image of a typical L-M customer at the time was their next vehicle would be a hearse. Unfortunately, L-M also had little experience of handling importation of, what was to them, a low-volume vehicle. So the Capri had two strikes against it before it was even launched; but two years after pre-program engineering work commenced, Ford US gave the SA30 program the green light in October, 1985.

Processions of Australian, Japanese and Americans now regularly visited and worked in Turin and the four languages and accents blended as they worked on the program. One word in Italian which became part of the Ford terminology was the 'Capote',[88] the cover over the convertible top when folded down.

One of the regular visitors to Turin was Laurie Roberts. A long-term employee of Ford who had started his career in Geelong and Broadmeadows in systems engineering, he was a no-nonsense, tough negotiator with experience in procurement purchasing.

Another was Jim Leason. Short in statue but a real scrapper, Jim Leason was a tin-bender from Geelong from way back. A veteran of the Fiera program in the Philippines, he was not one to take a step back when the arm waving began and became well respected by the Italians for his knowledge of steel stamping. Others seconded to the program were Rod Greer, a specialist engineer from the Plastics Plant and Barry Warren from Head Office, who handled the administration and documentation. Negotiations with Ital and suppliers all over the world meant long hours and the fanatical five or six key personnel were permanently jet-lagged. Alan Thompson recalls much of his time was spent handling the volatile personalities and rivalries of Giorgetto Giugiaro and Aldo Mantovani of Ital on the one hand, and Filippo Sapino, Ghia's Chief Designer on the other. Another problem was the Japanese, who were aghast at the emotion and arguments that went on between the Italians at meetings; to Japanese culture this was totally alien. After one such high drama meeting, with much arm throwing and shouting, several Japanese decided to return to Japan. Roberts remembers he and Fred Irie of Sumitomo took them to dinner that night and plied them with plenty of good Italian food and wine to convince them to stay. Eventually the Japanese got used to emotional Italian meetings, but it was always interesting!

It wasn't only the technical meetings that were interesting. The signing of the final, centimetres-thick agreement between Ford and Ital demanded a ceremony, with senior personnel from everywhere. The table placings at the formal dinner alone, held at a restaurant in the Turin Castle on the river Po, were a nightmare. Attendees included Bill Dix and Merv Manning from Australia, Edsel Ford and others from the US, the top designers of the world, Giugiaro and Sapino from Ital and Ghia, Kopka and Telnack from Ford, many with wives, a total of forty people seated around a gigantic baronial table.

The next day, at the formal signing ceremony, while group photographs of the dignitaries were being taken at one end of the room, Laurie Roberts was at the other, still negotiating the last details of the already signed, agreement.

LEFT First export Lincoln-Mercury Capris

RIGHT Clubsport Capri with crash test dummy. Even the dummy had a sense of humour

THE MARTY FELDMAN HEADLIGHTS

Having spent A$1 million developing the system of pop-up headlights with Hella Germany, the Capri was undergoing one of its regular reviews with Ford US management. It was before the design of today's more efficient, high intensity headlights. The operation of the pop-ups was fine, but when they opened, the bulbs had a disturbing unfocused look about them that the Capri engineers quickly nicknamed 'The Marty Feldman headlights'. Ford US were not impressed and ordered them changed. The only lights that fitted were smaller, rectangular off-the-shelf motorcycle headlight, hence their heavy black surrounds to fill the space and A$1 million wasted.

The first setback came when Ital began engineering the Capri around a Laser platform that was to become superseded partway through the design phase, forcing another redesign. They also designed a body lacking the Ford Australia system of 'master control holes' which ensure relevant components relate, and would fit each other. This was a crucial error, for which Ford would pay dearly later, when designing the hardtop roof.

There were also issues with the design capability of the Ital product. The original design contained examples of spot-welds through four thicknesses of sheet metal, a no-no for weld integrity and quality assurance. To accommodate the load-through fold-down rear seat feature for ski storage, a feature considered essential for the US market, the body required extra reinforcing and bracing over the original design, to maintain torsional rigidity and prevent scuttle-shake. Double-sided, zinc-coated steel was used on all skin and other critical panels to resist corrosion from the salt used on the US roads in winter, as was underbody wax and corrosion resisting lacquer in the engine compartment.

Eventually most design problems were resolved, and by February, 1987 the first of the fifty-five prototypes had been built and were being tested. Three prototype programs were conducted, for right- and left-hand drives. Specialist Jackie Stewart evaluated and praised the handling and braking capability. In the US, corrosion protection testing was conducted at the Arizona proving ground, air conditioning in Houston and Phoenix, high altitude testing in Colorado, cold testing in Minnesota, road testing in Florida and Los Angeles, and crash testing in Detroit. Body stress and torsional stiffness was tested by Mira in the UK, wind tunnel testing in Turin, Italy, emissions testing at the You Yangs proving ground and cooling development at Tennant Creek in Australia. A truly international program.

The second setback came when Ford US decreed that the vehicle be redesigned to incorporate airbags, in line with the pending legislation. The original position that a vehicle being developed could remain under the existing legislation was now rejected by Ford US management. It forced the SA30 program group back to the design board, and caused an additional US$70 million program expense. While a legitimate business and marketing decision, this was a change in policy over previous situations and one cannot but suspect ulterior motives by Ford US. Long, seventeen-hour days to fully utilise the Honda sled test facility near Marysville Ohio, and crash testing at the Ford Dearborn proving grounds, resulted in over 150 crash tests, an inordinate number for a vehicle program, many having to be repeated because of the airbag introduction. The frequent shuttling between Italy, Europe, where component suppliers like Hella, who designed the pop-up headlights were based, Japan for body tooling and stamping, Australia for assembly and the US for marketing began to tell. Alan Thompson recalls the time well:

> *At least four round-world trips a year as well as innumerable shorter trips, living out of a suitcase. My wife can't get me to go anywhere near an airport nowadays!'*

Mazda were building the MX5 sports car at the same time, and despite the similarities, Alan said the cooperation between the two program groups was excellent. The vehicles were targeted at two different markets, but Mazda wanted the Capri to do well, as it

FRANK WILEY AND QUALITY

One of Vice President Frank Wiley's fetishes was quality. Lindsay Sheppard recalls one seminar at Geelong where Frank harangued his managers for more the three quarters of an hour over quality. At the end of his address, he told everyone in the auditorium to stand. As the people stood, the squab of each of their seats returned to its upright position. Suddenly, a voice from the depths of the theatre, 'Hey I've got $20 taped to the underside of my seat!' At which Frank responded, 'That's the message I've been giving you today. If you're serious about quality and get off your *!@#$%* arse, you'll find a dollar in it!'

would be good business for them. 'Yeah, we both peeked over the design studio wall at times to see how the other was going,' Alan recalled, smiling.

However, with all the delays, the Capri was launched at least a year later than the MX5. Fully committed to the EA26 program and with their own workload problems, David Ford's product engineers could offer little help, but David's gloomy original observation, 'This turkey ain't goin' to fly', proved all too prophetic.

Another issue was the testing and approval of the prototypes to the CVRM[89], which had been subcontracted to Ford's OPEO[90], based in the US and staffed by Americans. They insisted that the Capri had to be assessed by their criteria, whereas Mazda-designed Ford vehicles had been accepted against the dissimilar Mazda criteria. Whether this was due to the US 'not invented here syndrome' or US concerns after the EA26 experience is not known. But OPEO insisted on fixes for problems they had previously accepted on Mazda origin vehicles and they failed to see the double standard. In all nearly 260 vehicles went into the three prototype programs and scuttle shake, a perennial problem for convertibles was a persistent issue, resolved with extra steel reinforcing, adding 25 kg.

Differences of opinion also emerged with the suspension and OPEO refused to allow the existing suspension to be used. Their design was rejected by Australia, and a standoff threatened. Eventually an Australian suspension engineer, Elvin Guillam, flew across to the US and 'helped' the US engineers discover a suspension superior to the US design and acceptable to the Program group. Alan Thompson recalls:

> *One of the OPEO ride and handling experts spoke wonders of the Crown Victoria. That's a barge as far as I'm concerned, and someone who thinks it's a great car shouldn't have even been working on a sports car suspension!*

By March, 1989, after the sign-off of the hundreds of test requirements in three countries, right-hand-drive vehicles began production a month later in the renovated Broadmeadows Truck Plant, now called Plant 2, using the same clamshell carrier system introduced into Sydney for the Laser. The left-hand-drive vehicles commenced production in November the same year. The engineering and development costs to develop both versions by now had totaled A$100 million, while investment in new presses in Geelong, the new facilities at Plant 2 and startup costs were an additional A$150 million, never mind the airbag engineering costs.

The first of the regular monthly shipments of left-hand-drive Capris left Australia in January, 1990 but were poor in quality. As they arrived at the US port of entry, Bernicia, near San Francisco, a temporary assembly line in marquees was established on the waterfront, manned by nearly 100 people, to carry out late engineering changes, partially strip the vehicles and check bolt torques, do complete water tests and road test on each car. In-transit damage and seagull damage were particular problems, the seagull droppings damaging the paintwork worse than that ever seen with birds in Australia. The Capri was released with great fanfare, both in Australia and later in the US, but quality problems, specifically relating to the soft-top persisted. The Italian design of the soft-top was fiddly; it required ensuring the roof fully engaged with the channel around the lower edge when it was raised. It really required two people to raise and fasten it properly, which rarely happened. Failure to do so allowed the soft-top material, inferior in quality, to shrink and ultimately the roof to leak. Despite a facelift and two new models, the latest being the much-improved SE in May 1993, sales slowed to a trickle. As Ford knew too well, poor quality is death.

The deathblow was administered, not only by quality however, but by currency exchange rates. Always susceptible to the problems of two exchange rates, the Japanese Yen to the Australian Dollar and the Australian Dollar to the US Dollar, rate changes did the job. The vehicle ended up just too expensive and combined with the poor quality image, the Americans were quick to say, 'I told you so'. The failure of the Capri reinforced the image that Ford Australia's quality was poor, and permanently damaged Australia's reputation in the eyes of Ford US. The Capri was expensive even in Australia; Ford knew it but had to defend it.

When a motoring journalist asked Bill Hartigan, Sales and Marketing Director, Ford Australia, 'Who would pay $28,000 for this vehicle?' he snappishly replied, 'Someone with $28,000!'

However, the exercise, started with so much enthusiasm and hopes, ended in tears, when the SE Capri ceased production in May 1994.

Meanwhile, the XF Falcon sedan had commenced production in June 1984, the wagon in December. Externally the vehicle was given new RIM bumpers, grille and tail-lights. Internally a new dash with switch gear on the binnacles were an added ergonomic feature as well as upgraded heating and air conditioning. Fully painted front bumpers differentiated the XF from the previous models and substantially improved production of the RIM bumpers. Most of the improvements were in the addition of the EEC-IV electronic control module which, among other things, controlled the air-fuel mix and spark timing better, and even allowed a limp-home facility. The engine upgrades resulted in the 4.1 EFI engine being almost as good in performance as the old 4.9-litre V8. The other major change was the addition of powder-coated progressive rate coil springs all round and revised suspension bushes. Improved sound insulation added to the NVH improvements.

The influence of the Mazda connection, sponsored by Bill Dix also improved inventory management. With the introduction of the XE Falcon, the Plastics Plant, under Ron Tyack began assembling the instrument panels and, with the aid of a teleprinter link to the assembly plant and dedicated truck, trailer and stillages, began deliveries on a thirty-minute delivery cycle. A similar system was later employed for the coloured XF bumpers. These changes alone, reduced inventory and indirect costs by A$2.6 million. This was quickly followed by BMO. Terry O'Brian and his department spent months analysing the production cycles of press lines to reduce the downtime and increase productive press time. Changing tool designs to reduce press adjustments on a six-press stamping

RIGHT 1984 XF Falcon GL sedan, there were 175,988 XF Series I and II sedans produced

FAR RIGHT 1984 XF Panel van

RIGHT 1984 XF utility

FAR RIGHT 1984 XF Fairmont Ghia station wagon

In 1985, Falcon celebrated its 25th anniversary with a limited release Silver Anniversary XF Falcon—2000 were produced

COA-353

Ford XF Falcon Fairmont sedan

ABOVE Job No:1—25th Anniversary Falcon. Among those present are (l to r) Roger Wiggill, Max Gransden, John Marshall and Bill Dix

line and new equipment to speed die changes, implemented by Peter Watson and the die change crews, further reduced inventory. The cost implications were enormous, the opportunities endless.

Lindsay Sheppard had collaborated with Vicrail to improve rail car delivery in the 1970s; now, with changing semitrailer design and the introduction of B Double trucks, rail delivery became too slow and expensive. Kim Murphy and John McGlynn found they could implement hourly deliveries of body panels and engines from Geelong to Broadmeadows more reliably, while substantially reducing inventory. Gradually, traditional systems were found to be the blockers to inventory management and were forced to change.

Ian Dalton, of Material Control in Head Office attended a meeting organised by the FCAI and FAPM[91] at Toyota where Barry Budge, an ex-Ford graduate who had moved to Toyota, presented a paper on the elimination of 'Muda', Japanese for waste, and Toyota's Kan-Ban system, also known as Just-in-Time. Doug Wallace, Material Control Manager in Plastics at the time, obtained a copy of the paper and after much planning, and discussion with the stockmen in the plant; an ideal Employee Involvement exercise, implemented a Kan-Ban system for delivery of Instrument Clusters to the Plastics Plant with the supplier, VDO Instruments. Within weeks, the inventory was reduced by five days, an immediate saving of over $480,000.

Encouraged by this success, it was extended to other suppliers, ultimately throughout the plant, affecting every major assembly produced and delivered to the assembly plant. One indirect saving was to halve the storage area required in the plant. The extension of Kan-Ban delivery of raw materials actually eliminated one warehouse entirely. In 1984–5, when Bill Dix announced a profit

PRODUCT ENGINEERING TEST RUNS

PEO design validation test runs were designed to test vehicles to practical limits that few would normally experience in the field. But they gave good feedback to the engineers. Occasionally things went wrong. There was one outback trip, when a Mazda 929 and a Falcon test vehicle were being tested and compared. The support back-up vehicle was a Ford Bronco. As it happened, the rear axle of the Bronco broke. By the side of the dusty track, the engineers (who better available to do this?) jacked the Bronco up and removed the rear axle. Putting the axle in the back of the 929, they drove the 250 km to Alice Springs and rang the Ford Dealer, who was at a Sunday BBQ. Sorry, no Bronco in Alice Springs, except one on the showroom floor. No problem. On a promise to send a replacement axle, they commandeered the showroom, the vehicle, and the workshop, stripped out the axle from the new Bronco and returned that night to the stranded vehicle, replaced the axle and continued the run.

for Ford Australia of $90 million, Director of Manufacturing John Marshall took great pleasure in reminding Bill the reduction in inventory in the manufacturing divisions that year alone had been that amount.

The XF continued to be a market leader for Ford from June 1984 to December 1985, with production of 114,889 vehicles. It also included a twenty-fifth anniversary special edition sedan to celebrate twenty five years of Falcon. The XF continued with only minor changes with the introduction of ADR37, the design rule limiting vehicle emissions, the main test of which was the 2 gram S.H.E.D.[92] test. This test required that a vehicle, soaking in a sealed, heated room for 24 hours, not emit more than 2 grams of fuel vapour. To meet this standard, a fluorination process was required to reduce permeability of the plastic fuel tank. This involved the introduction of Fluorine gas into the process of moulding the tank to produce an impermeable surface on the inside of the tank.

Nine months after the introduction of ADR 37 on the XF, the XFII began production; apart from the extra plumbing added for ADR37, Ford also added four-wheel disc brakes and power

ALISON NICHOLLS TWENTY-FIVE YEAR AWARD

Alison Nicholls outlasted three Plant Managers in her twenty-five years at the Brisbane Plant and in 1989 is currently looking after her fourth. The XM Falcon was being assembled at Brisbane when Alison joined as secretary to Plant Manager Duncan Norris, in June 1964. When he retired in June 1983, John Crew took over. Dick Standfield replaced John in June 1984, when the present Plant Manager Rob Alderman took over. Alison said she couldn't remember exactly how many Plant Controllers there were during her time but reckoned it was more than a dozen.

steering as standard equipment, further distancing themselves from GM-H. The XFII continued until December 1987 when the EA26 would begin production. The popularity of the XFII was so high, it forced a rethink on assembly locations, in preparation for the EA26. Truck assembly was transferred to the Brisbane Plant, in December 1987 in preparation for the Fairlane and LTD to return to Broadmeadows, now known as Plant 1, and the Truck Plant, renamed Plant 2 was renovated. Body build of the XFII utilities and vans was carried out in Plant 1, then assembled in Plant 2. Assembly of the XFII utes and vans would continue in Plant 2 as stand-alone models until March 1993, long past the introduction of the EA26 in Plant 1. The long run of the commercials meant the three-model series, (XF, ADR37, XFII) would become the second highest volume model produced, 322,778, only sixty vehicles behind the most popular vehicle, the AU series Falcon.

The success of the Japanese design bumper bars in production was such that it became the material of choice for the EA26 bumpers. Whereas Australia and the US used RIM Polyurethane, the Japanese bumpers were made from EPDM-PP. Ford of Europe were using another injection mouldable material, a modified Polycarbonate material named Xenoy. The material selection for EA26 had been carefully researched in Australia, announcement of the choice inflaming the debate already raging in Europe; Doug Wallace found himself between two warring factions at a meeting in the Ford of Europe Product Engineering Centre in Brentwood, London when the Australian choice became

ABOVE 1985 XF silver anniversary Falcon brochure

known. Significantly, FOE followed FOA's decision some months later, shortly followed by the resignation of at least one FOE engineer. As part of the Kan-Ban philosophy, the Laser bumper moulding machine in Plastics was later moved in 1987 to Sydney assembly plant, reducing inventory and transport costs.

The EA26 was to be the model that had it all. Employee Involvement was flourishing and 'The New Approach' used; seventeen System Control Groups were established, responsible for overseeing the development of every part of the car. Reporting to them were cross-functional design teams, comprising the design engineers, manufacturers, in-house or vendor, purchasing and logistics. Most teams worked well, a few did not. The design teams led by Brian Rossi, Clive Potter, Steve Park and John Birt produced a design which hardly changed from the original concept, it was so good the vehicle won the Australian Design Award in 1988. It was acknowledged throughout the world for its style, preferred in customer clinics over Mercedes Benz, BMW and Opel. The 'green house', the amount of glass was increased over the XF, the windscreen raked lower, the base pushed forward. The result was an impressive performance in wind tunnel testing: a Cd of only 0.34. An all-new SLALS (Short and Long Arm, Long Spindle) front suspension similar to the Mercedes Benz S class was included, as was a new rack-and-pinion system which at last reduced the vehicle turning circle.

RIGHT Steve Park sketch of EA26 wagon

FAR RIGHT Full-size clay model of EA26 in wind tunnel

RIGHT Debbie Raimondo and Don Thompson selecting fabrics and colours for the EA26 interior

FAR RIGHT 1988 EA26 Fairmont Ghia station wagon

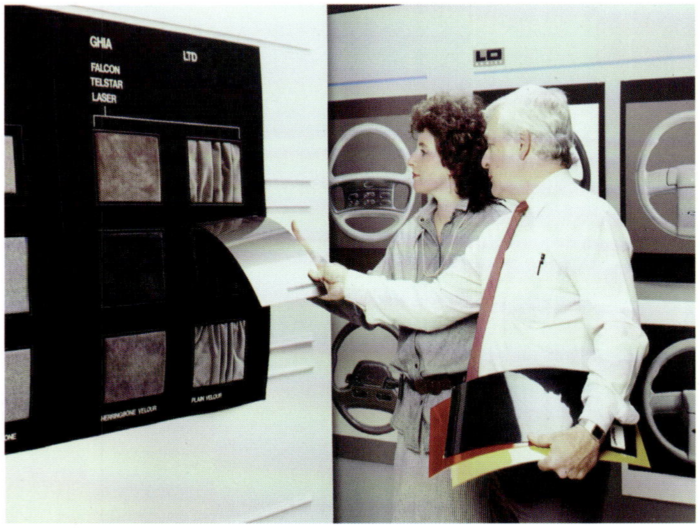

Job No:1—EA26. Among those attending include (left of vehicle) Tom Pettigrew, Bill Dix, (right of vehicle) Dick Van House, John Crew, Ian Vaughan and Don Pearce.

ABOVE Australian Design Council Award, 1988. (l-r) Brian Rossi, David Ford, Bill Dix, Dick Van House and (far right) Max Gransden

The EA was to be better in every way, faster, smoother, quieter, more comfortable and more elegant than any previous Falcon. The Fairlane and LTD were totally different models with the same mechanicals as the Falcon. Hella Australia supplied ultra slim headlights, the Fairlane to have a body coloured grille, the LTDs to be chrome plated.

The biggest problem turned out to be the Borg-Warner 4-speed transmission. It didn't work. Prototype after prototype failed durability testing; some didn't even make it off the assembly line. Once it became obvious Borg-Warner could not fix it in time, the choice was stark; no vehicle or stick with the 3-speed. Ford stuck with the 3-speed and tried to make the best of it, bringing in Jackie Stewart to convince the motoring press it was the correct choice. Even though the old transmission worked well, it wasn't the optimum, the journos knew it and some canned Ford accordingly, quite unfairly. It may, in hindsight have been better to have limited the pre-release publicity, hosed down the great expectations both within and outside the company and not tried to spin the media. In the rueful words of a one manager, 'We read too much of our own mail!' Most initial test reports praised the EA. Peter Robinson wrote in the February 1988 issue of *Wheels* magazine;

> *Ford's mission to build a Falcon for the 90s has succeeded brilliantly. Yes there is no doubt the car would be improved with*

a four-speed automatic, and we hope the wind noise dilemma can be overcome quickly. But the rest of the car is highly competitive and will undoubtedly represent one of the best value-for-money buys of '88. With that level of performance, the improved economy, roadholding and handling, combined with the roominess and style, and the improved equipment levels and standard of finish, this is one very competent car.

Other problems surfaced with time that affected the image of the EA26, however. There were front suspension problems with the ball joints failing, overheating was a problem and there were paint quality problems. Production of the sedan began in May,

SYDNEY PLANT TO MAKE BUMPERS

Plastics production came to Sydney in April 1988 with the installation of a huge 2,200 ton clamp Battenfield Injection Mould machine. Capable of producing a Laser bumper bar every two minutes this machine produces all the stock required for assembly as well as service parts for national distribution. The machine is equipped with a roller transfer table for quick changes of the thirty-tonne dies. Manufacturing in Sydney reduces inventory, component damage, and eliminates transport and dunnage return costs from the Melbourne plastics plant.

1987, the wagon in September, while the LTD and NA Fairlane began in October and November respectively. As the production problems became more widely known, sales slowed and for the first time in six years, the VN Commodore overtook the Falcon, although Ford remained industry leader. Ford weren't alone with quality problems, they were just more public. *Wheels* magazine began a series of quality audits on vehicles sold in Australia in 1991 and ranked the Falcon at fourteenth out of the twenty vehicles examined. The Commodore ranked seventeenth.

The restructuring within Ford continued. One of the most beneficial was the system of scheduling rostered days off, RDOs. One of the trade-offs of having ten RDOs per year, was the ability for the company to negotiate the timing of them, even changing them to suit circumstances. Traditional high absenteeism days, religious holidays or national days, were now declared as RDOs, largely eliminating high absenteeism days such as Chinese or Vietnamese New Year.

Similarly, stand-downs caused by supply shortages from suppliers did not result in lost wages for workers. RDOs were changed, even pulled forward by months to ensure stand-downs without pay were reduced or avoided. The Production Manager's life, while never easy as John Crew had said, became easier. The improved personnel relations between the various national groups who celebrated each other's national day brought a closer understanding of their cultures, while the Christmas plant breakup days, became social events, almost a marathon for production

LEFT Making of the Falcon EA26 advertisement. Rising from a lake? No, it's sitting on pontoons in the middle of a pool.

Ford

THE LAST TRAIN

The last train load of parts for the Broadmeadows Assembly plant left Geelong on December 22, 1988. From 1959, BMO had been supplying body panels, and chassis components by rail. During 1988, the number of rail trucks per day had dwindled to sixteen, making road transport more viable. Five new Louisville prime movers, to take the total to thirteen, will each do the 170 km round trip in four hours and twenty-two minutes between Geelong and Broadmeadows. Each plant will have automated loading bays and the trailers, the Tautliners will ensure the components are protected at all times. Ron Smith, Traffic Operations Supervisor estimates the twenty six drivers will travel more than 3.7 million kilometres each year.

HISTORIC FORD—UNION AGREEMENT

Historic and innovative agreements reached in September 1989 between Wayne Blair, Chairman of the VBEF, Iain Ross of the ACTU and Ford have resulted in big pay rises to Ford employees under the 'Structural Efficiency Principle'. Negotiations began August 1988 with a two-day seminar for all shop stewards of all unions, held under the joint auspices of the ACTU and Ford. Out of these negotiations came the Vehicle Industry Certificate for employees, a training and education program for all employees.

LEFT 1988 Design Centre staff celebrate the launch of the DA LTD

LEFT XE Alloy Head badge

management as they were welcomed by each national group to celebrate with their national dishes and illicit national alcoholic toasts.

With exquisite timing Bill Dix retired; he had joined the company in 1941 in the mail room at Geelong and retired in 1989 as President. While not the initiator of EI, he should get the credit for the successful application, the change in culture, and after the 1981 strike, a near perfect record in industrial relations.

'The Father' of EI, Percy Worsnop later wrote a book of his experiences, *Human Resource Management-Employee Involvement in Ford Australia.* In what may become a textbook on the theory and practice of human relations in business, the Los Angeles based Pacific Western University granted Percy a Doctorate of Philosophy for his thesis of the same name. Dix had also taken Ford to market leadership and record profits in the 1980s. He was to be replaced by another Australian, Jac Nasser.

Nasser had joined Ford at age twenty-one as a financial analyst. After transferring to International Operations and several promotions, he was appointed Vice-President of Autolatina, a joint venture between Ford and Volkswagen in Argentina and Brazil in 1987. Promoted to become President of Ford Australia, he joined a company scrambling to recover from the fiasco of the EA26, with falling sales and climbing warranty claims.

To add insult to injury, the VN Commodore had overtaken the Falcon for the first time since 1981. The EA26 quality slowly improved, it had good bones mechanically, with award-winning styling, but badly needed the Borg-Warner 4-speed transmission.

FORD TAKES OFF RAAF STYLE

How do you bring all of Head Office to a standstill? Simply arrange for the RAAF to land one of their huge Chinook helicopters a few metres from the front door. The occasion was the special delivery of a new Telstar to the Alfred Hospital for a major prize for the Cancer Centre Appeal raffle. The RAAF was asked if it could stage a spectacular delivery of the car to get TV coverage and the crew obliged. The twin-rotor Chinook swept out of the overcast skies and neatly landed in the small car park in front of Head Office, where the fierce blast from the engines and rotors set off the foyer fire alarms. The car was supplied by Ford and Melford Motors. Bill Dix handed the car over to the RAAF, who loaded the Telstar into the cavernous interior of the Chinook and delivered it to the Albert Park Cricket Ground, where Melford Motors MD, Col Paige, presented the car to Cancer Centre Appeal chairman, John Gandel.

SYDNEY PLANT & LASER WIN QUALITY AWARD

The Prime Minister Mr. Hawke presented the 1989 Australian Quality Award to Vice-President Dick Van House and Sydney Plant Manager Brian Tredwell at a ceremony at the Hyatt on Collins in Melbourne. Laser vehicles are the highest quality vehicles in Australia, with the least number of faults of any locally assembled vehicle.

This came in August 1989, after 118,819 vehicles and thirty months, with the introduction of the EAII.

The EAII was everything Ford had wanted with the EA26, a transmission for which the engines had been tuned, a vastly different, and improved suspension and a much needed superior fit and finish. And just when the EAII was hitting its straps, the Australian stock market collapsed on October 29, 1989 and the biggest recession since the 1930s rocketed in and spoiled the party.

BELOW 1987 Chinook helicopter and Telstar

1989 2 millionth Falcon driven by Ita Buttrose

FAIRLANE GHIA

CHAPTER 8
1990—1999

THE FORD YEARS 1990—1999

First shipment of Capri convertibles to USA in May. Two-millionth Falcon vehicle produced. Ford celebrates 30-year Falcon anniversary. KF Laser, Corsair hatchback,Capri II released. New range of heavy trucks introduced including LTS9000, LTS8000 and 9000.

1990:

1991:

EB, NC Fairlane and DC LTD introduced with V8 engine option. New Festiva introduced. Tickford Engineering (TVE) joint venture formed. Four millionth Australian-built Ford vehicle produced. First Enterprise Agreement in the Australian automotive industry negotiated with Unions. EB II Falcon, NC II Fairlane, DC II LTD production commences in December with ABS brakes.

Falcon top-selling vehicle in Australia. Geelong Casting Plant wins A$30 million export contract with Mazda. Ford Plastics plant achieves Q1 quality award, first plant to do so. AS Telstar wins *Wheels* COTY award. EB II 30th Anniversary GT released by Tickford. WA Festiva introduced. SC Capri released.

1992:

1993:

500,000th Laser/Meteor/Telstar vehicles produced. Falcon again top-selling vehicle in Australia. Festiva Trio introduced into Australia. LPG factory-fitted option released on Falcon. SE Capri production commences. Ford wins Australia Quality award. Ian Vaughan in XT Falcon KAG002 competes again in London-Sydney marathon. Imported vehicles achieve more than 50% of total vehicle sales.

EF Falcon production with airbag as standard, wins Australian Design award. Geelong Stamping Plant receives Q101 Quality rating. Capri production ends at Plant 2. Probe vehicle introduced into Australia. Dick Johnson and John Bowe win Toohey's 1000 at Bathurst. Ford Aeromax 120, and Transit trucks introduced into Australia. Homebush NSW plant closes.

1994:

1995:

President John Ogden replaced by David Morgan in November. 1997: Jack Telnack, designer of the XT, XW and XY Falcons in Australia, retires as Global Vice-President of Design, September 1997.

EL Falcon, DL Fairlane and XH utility released.Taurus introduced into Australia.

1996:

1998:

AU Falcon, ER Fairlane-LTD production commences.

Falcon panel van production ceases. Cougar, KA vehicles introduced into Australia. Bill Ford appointed CEO of Ford Motor Company. Henry Ford crowned by America's 'Fortune' magazine as 'Business man of the Century'.

1999:

If the previous decade had been one of exuberance and confidence, the winds of change began blowing strong headwinds. The economic reforms introduced by the Hawke-Keating Government, including the floating of the Australian dollar and the deregulation of the financial system quickly exposed Australia to the international economy. In an eerie reminder of the 1930s, with the collapse of economies overseas, wheat and wool prices collapsed; rural communities went into decline. Treasurer Keating initially insisted the economy would have a soft landing, but later argued '...this is the recession Australia had to have'.

As the recession deepened, interest rates climbed to unsustainable levels; home loans reached as high as 17%, credit card interest rates even higher. The Reserve Bank attempted to support the Australian Dollar, but after spending A$2 billion, could not prevent the Australian Dollar collapsing to 51 cents US. Suddenly, corporations and banks built on financing were exposed; the State Banks of Victoria and South Australia and the Pyramid Building Society collapsed.

There was also a political price to pay; John Cain resigned as Premier of Victoria, to be replaced by the hapless Joan Kirner, who was swept from office in 1992 by Jeff Kennett. John Bannon resigned as Premier of the South Australian Government and in Western Australia, Premier Brian Burke was replaced by Carmen Lawrence and then ultimately jailed for his role in the WA Inc. affair. Unemployment climbed rapidly, reaching 11%, the highest since the 1930s.

Despite the recession, Senator Button was unable to persuade the government to slow the rate of tariff cuts, which were inexorably reducing from 57.5% in 1987 to 27.5% in 1995. The automotive industry began to lose money as car sales dropped to their lowest in twenty years. For Ford, 1992 was the volume low point.

Ford responded by increasing the frequency of models, adding features to vehicles as incentives. Where the EA26 had been in production for 30 months, subsequent models were cycled more quickly.

The financial cost was enormous. From a pretax profit in 1989 of A$220.8 million, Ford crashed to a loss in 1990 and succeeding years were no better;

Year	Pretax loss (A$ Millions)
1990	A$134.0
1991	A$185.8
1992	A$ 57.9
1993	A$ 57.4 [93]

Accumulated losses over the four years were A$434.9 million. Was Ford prepared to commit A$700 million to a loss-making division to produce an entirely new vehicle, due to come on stream in 1998 and stay in production until 2008, sixteen years away? Or invest in Asia which was forecast to expand rapidly? The 1990–1992 business plans had to include closing manufacture in Australia and reverting to import. Manager of Government Affairs from 1990 to 1992, Ian Vaughan could only report the news from Canberra was bleak, at best. It was almost as though both major political parties were trying to outdo each other in the race to end manufacturing in Australia. Ross Garnaut, economic advisor to Prime Minister Hawke in 1989 was advocating reducing tariffs on all goods to zero by 2000. The 1990 Industry Commission inquiry into the car industry led by Bill Scales, also an 'economic dry' recommended tariffs be reduced further, followed by the 1991 Labour Government Economic statement which accelerated general tariff reductions from 15% to 5% by 2006; then the government car plan, released in 1991 was revised again, reducing car tariffs from 25% to 15% by 1996, far in advance of the original Button Plan. The Liberal Party opposition, led by academic economist John Hewson, 'Captain Zero', was advocating, and went to the 1992/3 election, on a policy of zero tariffs by 2000. No wonder Ford US, who was watching Canberra closely, was receptive to Nasser, with a reputation for cost cutting, to first slash jobs, and then proposing if there was no improvement, to close manufacturing. Ian Vaughan had regular dealings with the bureaucrats of government as well as both sides of politics. When interviewed for this book he dismissively termed those he dealt with in Canberra as:

> *...the Canberra School of Economics, he sniffed, adding, They didn't want to listen to us or the industry, they wouldn't listen to advice, they knew best.*

From 1989 to 1992, Falcon production dropped 26%, Laser/Meteor production 19%, Fairlane/LTD dropped 32% while exports of Capri dived 50%. Nasser had little choice. Employment was reduced from 14,550 to under 9,600, earning him the sobriquet of 'Jac the Knife', from *Wheels* editor Phil Scott, a nickname Nasser disliked intensely.

In an interview with The Age's Craig McGregor, in July 1992,[94] Nasser defended the automotive industry from the economic rationalists who queried whether Australia needed a car industry at all. Eerily, he predicted the future saying,

> *The days of a single manufacturer dominating the market were over. In Europe the difference between the market leader and number five in the industry is only 3–4%. The market is*

PAGES 226–227 1995 NF Fairlane Ghia

fragmenting; it's going to be model against model. It's going to be tough.

Year	Total Ford Production	Falcon, Fairlane — LTD production
1990	132,789	104,706
1991	104,939	79,145
1992	94,476	78,309
1993	102,469	86,102
1994	102,440	92,577
1995	103,047	103,047

Model	Production Start date	Model Build (months)
EAII	August 1989	23
EB1	April 1991	11
EBII	December 1991	20
ED	June1993	14
EF	June 1994	15
EFII	August 1995	13
EL	July 1996	13

Publicly he said the Government had to make up its mind if it wanted a car industry. But Canberra's mind was made up; in hindsight the automotive industry was doomed from 1990.

The retrenchments were deep and savage. An entire generation of experience, technical ability and loyalty disappeared in a sweeping program that left few employees in the company over fifty years of age. The redundancy packages were better than many, but in an economy where more than one in ten were unemployed, who would employ an older worker? The brutal fact is many never worked again. Those who remained were those whose expertise would help Ford survive, but many were given a Hobson's choice; move to another department, plant, interstate, or even another country. That or take a package. For an older skilled manager, a move overseas could be attractive; the life of an expatriate would top up the superannuation nicely, but family life had to be a consideration. Dozens of employees moved overseas. Bob Stephens and his wife were sent to Ford of India. Styling staff and designers moved to Ford US.

As Ford Australia slowly sank in a sea of red under the weight of losses, they were not alone. Nissan lost A$125 million and closed its assembly plant in 1992, Mitsubishi in Adelaide lost A$23.8 million. Toyota barely broke even while GM-H made a miniscule profit.

Nasser would not stay long enough to implement the closure of Ford. Not wanting to spoil the record of a rising star, President of Ford of Europe Lyn Halstead, at sixty-one, was tapped on the shoulder to retire, effective January 1993. Nasser was abruptly transferred in October 1992 to Europe as his understudy. His replacement was John Ogden. Ogden had joined Ford in 1965. With qualifications in mechanical engineering and an MBA, he had risen through the NAAO[95] ranks within Ford until he was appointed Managing Director of Ford of Mexico in 1986. After restructuring that division, he returned to the US as Director of NAAO Car Programs. Ogden joined FOA as President, aged fifty-three; much better to have an old, loyal hand to go out to Australia, close the place and then retire quietly into obscurity, than have a rising star with that blot on his record.

While Ford US pushed for closure they underestimated two crucial factors, the resistance within Ford Australia to losing manufacturing, and John Ogden's rational personality. The vehicle of choice to replace the Falcon, imported from the US, was the Ford Taurus. Scheduled for production from 1996, the early generation of the Taurus had been designed by John Doughty. Later versions were purported to be designed by Jack Telnack and followed the 'New Edge' design, based on an oval. Everything was rounded, from the bumpers to rear window. The interior featured an oval shaped 'Integrated Control Centre' panel. Considered too radical, even the American public turned away from the design. Fleet sales were the only reason for the Taurus' success in America; the majority of sales in 1996 were to rental fleets. Ian Vaughan, by now Vice President of Large Car Product Planning raised a number of arguments against the Taurus. The Taurus was smaller than the Falcon, narrower and shorter. Shoulder room and leg room would be compromised. Don McAllister, a member of the Project Eagle team recalled, 'the marketing clinics we ran with the Taurus all said it was a dog of a car.' Memories of GM-H's disastrous flirt with the smaller Commodore was invoked.

A number of other issues were also raised. One was the 'halo' effect of manufacturing in Australia. Even though Volkswagen, and later Nissan, remained in Australia after ceasing manufacture, both lost almost half their market share, also experienced by Mitsubishi in March 2008. For Ford to revert to the Toyota Camry and Mitsubishi Magna size vehicles would abandon the large car market to GM-H. There would be no utility or panel van, no Fairlane/LTD, over 13% of Ford's volume in 1992, a sizable market to lose to competitors. The Taurus market penetration in the US was 6% versus the Falcon's 26% in Australia. The Taurus was front wheel drive, well suited in snow, the Falcon was rear wheel drive, a highway and outback vehicle. Despite the

THE DOWNSIZING OF AUSTRALIA

It was a small part of Australia's biggest downsizing exercise in the 1990s but when Ford closed the gates on the last car plant in NSW, it was still an emotional moment for the 417 men and women who worked there. Some of the Homebush staff had been there for forty years. 'If we could turn back the clock, and Homebush started again, I reckon 99% of the blokes would be back there without a doubt,' said one senior worker. 'It was very hard for Ford to make the decision to close the plant because of the strong culture and the part it played in the company culture,' said David Ahern, a senior manager at the plant. Workers departed over two days with each team or group leaving at the same time. 'We tried to make sure they could say goodbye as a team. On Saturday, they came back to the plant with their families for a family day, barbecue and circus rides for the kids. A specially designed, personally numbered, china plate commemorating their years at Homebush was presented to each employee, there were speeches and the last car off the line was raffled.'

(Sydney Morning Herald, October 20, 1997)

FAX TO SYDNEY PLANT

The annual Xmas dinner will be held on Thursday at lunchtime with the Ford Motor Company providing a free luncheon for all its employees. The entertainment will be provided by the popular group, 'Henry Ford and the Multinationals' singing their famous tune, 'Leaving Ford is the going thing'. Following that, Santa in person will not only provide us with gifts, this year he will go so far as to even let us have his very own sack. The Plant Management will then start a quiz show with the motto, 'Guess who gets it.'

(Anonymous)

success of the FWD Laser and Meteor, who were competing in a different market, Falcon owners used their vehicles for other uses. For instance, nearly 69% of Falcon owners fitted tow bars; the Taurus was only suitable for light towing duties. Finally, the redundancy payouts for the workforce and the remediation costs of the Geelong and Broadmeadows sites when the plants closed had to be considered. Ford had turned the corner economically, announcing a profit in 1993 and would go onto make record profits in the next two years. Did Ford US really want to lose two thirds of their business and forgo those profits?

As Director of NAAO Car Programs Management, one of the programs Ogden had overseen was the 1992 Taurus and he could have been accused of bias. But he listened and, while reluctantly accepting the logic of Ian Vaughan's arguments, he had his own demands. The redundancy program must continue, core staff moved to cover vacancies. Every aspect of the business in Australia was to be put more closely under scrutiny than Nasser had done and assets sold. Vehicle programs would only continue if they were viable. Falcon would be no exception. In line with the One Ford philosophy, the Taurus from the US, and the Mondeo from Europe would be imported to Australia, to test the acceptance, or otherwise, of a smaller vehicle. But he agreed to the establishment of a task force, Project Eagle, to determine if the Falcon could pay its way and survive.

Nothing was spared. Groups were established with the sole task of disposing of assets. Phil Spender moved from Plant 1 to replace Tom Pettigrew as plant manager of the Plastics Plant while Tom headed up a group charged with the task of selling the Plastics Plant, one of the drivers of manufacturing innovation in Australia.

LEFT Homebush Assembly Plant, Sydney, 1989

RIGHT 1993 London to Sydney Marathon, KAG002 which came 2nd outright driven by Ian Vaughan and Barry Lake

Tom, seen as the 'Godfather' of EI, SI and PI,[96] had replaced Ron Tyack as plant manager when Ron moved to BMO. He had been the coach and driving force behind the Plastic Plant becoming the first Australian plant to be awarded Ford's quality status QS9000 in 1992; the same year the Plastics plant had won the Australian Quality Council's 'Subsidiaries and Divisions' section of the Australian Quality Awards. Neville Glennan joined Tom when the Matrix management system eliminated the Manufacturing Engineering Managers position. With a background in accounting, data processing, material control and manufacturing, Neville, tall, urbane with greying hair, had worked in the plant for more than ten years and knew the plant intimately. Ford chose Consulting group Bose Allen to advise them on the sale of the plant and a number of prospective customers were canvassed, Australian and overseas. After an eighteen month negotiation period, a second tier plastics supplier to Ford US, Venture Plastics headed by Larry Winget, who had ambitions to become a major supplier to the Australian automotive industry, bought the plant in June 1995.

One of the few highlights of this depressing time was in 1993; the 25th anniversary of the London-Sydney marathon. Restricted to pre-1969 vehicles and teams reduced to a driver and a navigator, organiser Nick Brittan persuaded twenty-one of the original competitors to enter, amongst a total of 106 teams from seventeen countries. Once again there were three 1968 Falcon XT GTs entered. Ian Vaughan and Barry Lake in Ian's 1968, second-placed KAG002, Bruce Hodgson in a replica of his 1968, 6th-placed vehicle KAG03, partnered by Ray Lawton, and Ross Dunkerton and Harry Mansson in another XT GT. The political climate in Iraq and Afghanistan forced some route changes to the 16,000 km rally, although the remainder of the route through Europe, Turkey and Australia was largely unchanged. Other changes included the introduction of sprint sections timed to the second, rather than the longer endurance sections of 1968 timed to the minute, more rest periods and airlifts of the vehicles in two giant Russian Antonov cargo planes, between Ankara to Delhi via Tashkent, and from Bombay to Perth, instead of the nine day sea voyage of 1968.

Harry Firth, Graham Hoinville, Garry Chapman and KAG001 in India during the 1968 London to Sydney marathon.

END OF THE ROAD FOR FORD VETERAN

'When I was a little boy, I would go past the (Sydney) plant with my father. I would think, 'That looks like a nice place.' Of course I didn't know then that I would end up working there,' said Ray Brewster. When the last car rolled off the assembly line at Ford's Homebush plant yesterday, it also brought to an end a career that spanned forty-one years. Ray said he was taken aback when they were told to finish up on Wednesday morning, believing they had until Thursday to say goodbye. 'I had my lunch all packed up from yesterday – but we finished up before I had time to eat it!'

(Sydney Telegraph, September 2, 1994)

EMPLOYEE REWARDS

Almost 300 Ford Australia employees from Geelong and Melbourne were rewarded with a special night at the 1993 Ford Australia Tennis Open. The 'Perfect Attendance' tennis nights were suggested two years ago to reward employees who had worked for an entire year without being absent or late for work. Employees enjoyed a meal in the corporate marquee followed by a night of tennis. Ford President John Ogden congratulated the employees and praised them for their efforts. *'It is pleasing to see the number attending has grown from 96 in 1990 to more than 300 in 1992,'* he said. Sydney employees will enjoy a harbour cruise, while Brisbane plant is planning a day at the races.

The rally left London on April 17, 1993, headed to Ypres in Belgium for the first night's stopover. The second day almost ended the rally for Vaughan. Navigating a tight corner on a rural road in Belgium covered in cow dung, Vaughan found himself sliding off into a deep ditch and had to be levered out by several burly Belgians. With damage limited to panels and pride, a nearby friendly Ford dealer soon had them back in the rally. The rest of the journey through Europe was relatively uneventful, except for the traffic in Istanbul where some crews actually hired taxis to guide them through the narrow streets and seething traffic. Dunkerton and Mansson had had less luck, hitting a rock and having gearbox problems. Vaughan recalls:

> *India was hell on earth, high forties temperatures, dust, rough roads, swarms of people, carts doing 1 km/h, tractors 5 km/h, trucks 50 km/h and all coming at you from everywhere. And the dreaded 'Delhi Belly'. We put up with the heat and dust, threaded our way through the throngs, and beat 'the Belly' with our diet of Aussie freeze-dried hiking food, dried fruit and nuts, 'Astronaut' icecream and about 10–12 litres of bottled water each per day.*[97]

As planned, Vaughan and Lake arrived in Perth in seventh place, better than his 1968 eleventh. While many of the other competitors suffered punctures as they raced across the Nullabor, Vaughan and Lake had no such problems, despite losing control in a deep creek washaway, going bush and flattening several large saplings in the process, and later dispatching a large kangaroo in the rugged Gawler Ranges in South Australia. By Port Augusta, they were fourth. By the time the rally reached the Snowy Mountains the rally had changed, the leaders now driving to protect their positions from those hard-charging drivers behind them, notably the three Escorts of Roger Clark, New Zealander Graham Lorimer and the Britain's Colin Short. The alpine snow near Suggan Buggan was treacherous. Vaughan had just passed rally leader Tuthill in his Porsche 911 and found how slippery virgin snow could be, even for a 2-tonne Falcon, when Clark, a driver with plenty of rally experience in European snow conditions appeared, passed them both and slalomed off into the distance. Despite the impressive display, Clark finished fourth, behind Tuthill and Vaughan, with Kirkland's Peugot 504 in third place. Vaughan wrote later, 'third in 1968, second in 1993, roll on 2018. KAG002 will be ready, will I? You bet!'

The quality problems and poor sales of the Capri in the US meant the export credits were falling. Quality issues kept the Capri volume low in Australia as well and, as one of the victims of the cost reduction programs, the Capri had to go; it ceased production in May 1994. The small area used for Falcon commercials in Plant 2 was expanded to take up the whole of the plant becoming, in effect, a light commercial plant. The hard-nosed approach also affected the Sydney Plant. Despite the plant having the reputation as the best quality automotive plant in Australia, for some time, the

ABOVE Capri Clubsprint developed by Tickford Vehicle Engineering

LEFT 1992 Capri Clubsprint interior

FAR LEFT Capri assembly line

RIGHT 1990 KF Laser

FAR RIGHT 1992 Tickford XR 4x4 KH Laser

RIGHT 1991 KF Laser wagon

FAR RIGHT Imported 1995 KJ Laser Lynx

ABOVE Falcon 30th Anniversary badges

cost of CKD vehicle packs had equaled, or exceeded, the cost of importing fully assembled vehicles. The increasing costs, reducing tariffs and loss of export credits with reducing Capri exports to the US eliminated any advantage over fully importing the Laser. The Meteor had been an early casualty. Changing market tastes and falling sales doomed the GE Meteor, which ceased production in March 1990, the KF five-door Laser picking up the slack, remained in production until October 1991. The replacement, the KH Laser did not do well, and in production for only 12 months, was replaced by the KI in June 1992.

Despite the small vehicle segment being the largest market in Australia, one of the decisions was to close the Sydney plant, import the next Laser, the KJ Laser Lynx and import small vehicles. The last Laser came off the assembly line on August 31, 1994. It was a sad day but celebrated in typical Sydney fashion. All the employees, family and friends, 1,500 in all, were back three days later for a family day and farewell barbecue at the plant. There were rides, and entertainment for the children and the two Lasers used throughout the plant, having been completely refurbished were raffled, one raffle restricted to those with a perfect attendance record in the last month. The other was raffled to aid the Rwanda Famine appeal and raised more than $11,000. Each employee was presented with a numbered, commemorative plaque, designed by the employees, depicting the plant façade, the first car built, a 1936 Ford V8, and a list of all the models built at the plant. The plant was stripped and decommissioned by December, the clam shell jigs and useable equipment sent to Plant 2.

In between the EAII and the EB1 model change, there was an upgrade in October 1990, the 30th anniversary Falcon in Australia. As much to celebrate the milestone as to reinforce to the market the continuous improvement in technology of Ford,

1991 Ford KH Laser GLi Series I

Imported 1996 Ford KL Laser

TIBBE DOOR LOCKS

It is a tribute to the forethought of the Product Planners of the time that this feature was added. The November 24, 2015, edition of the Melbourne *Herald-Sun* reported that apart from Nissan Pulsars, the vehicles most likely to be stolen in Victoria in 2015 were the 1997–2000 VT and the 2006–2013 VE Commodores.

the 30th anniversary model was identified by the 'Falcon in flight' badges, but was more than badging. As part of the upgrade, Ford released the 'Smartlock' Tibbe lock system designed to prevent vehicle theft and allowing a remote keyless entry system, a first for an Australian-built vehicle. Apparently the South Australian Police employed experienced car thieves and challenged them to break into one of the Tibbe lock vehicles. The story is they gave up after four days.

Six months later came the EB1 Falcon sedan and wagon, which commenced production in April and May 1991, a minor facelift from the EA, but with equipment levels upgraded even more, and at little cost. One major change was the return of a 5.0-litre V8,

RIGHT 1992 EB Falcon Ghia sedan rear

FAR RIGHT 1992 EB Falcon S wagon

RIGHT 1992 25th Anniversary EB II GT—only 265 were produced

FAR RIGHT 1992 EB GT engine detail

the small aluminum block Windsor engine lifted from the Mustang in the US, which was 90 kg lighter than previous iron block V8.

The same improvements were given to the NC/DC Fairlane/LTD which commenced production in June the same year. Then in December 1991, Ford began building the EBII with the option of ABS braking on all vehicles except for the S-XR8, Fairmont Ghia, Fairlane and LTD, where it was standard fitment. The Bendix LC5 ABS system had been designed to work even on dirt roads, and wrong–footed the opposition completely. Also included were redesigned seat belts, with lockers to limit movement and a 'rip-stitch' system, designed to stretch during an accident. To reinforce the continuous improvement and safety message from Ford, the turret (roof) was strengthened to withstand a 3-tonne load to protect passengers in a roll-over accident. NVH was further improved and the national standard of adding a seventeen digit identification number to the vehicle and chassis was adopted to reduce vehicle re-birthing. The EBII was to remain in production for 20 months.

The combination of retrenchments and cost reductions in 1992 lowered the company's break-even point; the pre-tax loss for the year was A$57.9 million, an improvement over the whopping A$185.8 million loss the year before. An upbeat Ogden was careful not to report the loss in the May 1993 issue of *Ford News*, stating only the company was operating profitably for the first quarter of the year. The only reference to the financial difficulties still being experienced was that while borrowing costs had reduced, Ford had still paid $284 interest on borrowings for every vehicle sold. He continued, reporting that Ford had remained passenger car industry leader in 1992, with a 0.2% increase in market share, to 23.3%. Falcon had regained leadership over the Commodore, the release of the EB Falcon contributing greatly to the turnaround, being the recipient of many awards. The imported Telstar had won

ABOVE 1992 EB Series I Falcon 4.1-litre Sedan. There were 36,337 Series I produced and a further 84,874 EB Series II produced.

1992 EB Falcon GT. This Silver Anniversary GT was limited to 250 for the local Australian market and fifteen for export to New Zealand. All individually numbered, the first ten were numbered P01–P10, then GT001–GT240 for Australia and NZ01–NZ15 for New Zealand.

1993 NCII Fairlane Sportsman. 'A Sportsman this good only comes along once in a blue moon.'

Ford
HAVE YOU DRIVEN A FORD...LATELY?

MIKE JARVIS & THE NC FAIRLANE LAUNCH

Public Affairs Manager Mike Jarvis well remembers the launch of the NC Fairlane in July 1991. Part of the launch was held at the Lara Proving grounds to show off the new vehicle and the introduction of ABS braking as standard on the range. With a car load of journalists and a Ford driver (Ford didn't trust the journos on the high speed loop), they set off. The plan was to get to speed, the driver slam on the brakes and maneuver round a set of cones. Unfortunately, instead of smoothly navigating the course, as the driver hit the brakes, there was an almighty bang and all the airbags activated. White powder floated round the vehicle as the dust settled on some very red Ford faces. Mike found out later the engineers had been testing some more sensitive sensors on the test vehicle and had forgotten to replace them. Oops.

RIGHT Presentation of Australian Quality Award to Ian Vaughan, Vice President of Product Development, Ford Motor Company of Australia

RIGHT Imported 1992 AX Telstar TX5 Ghia

Wheels COTY award, the Plastics Plant had received the prestigious Australian Quality Award, the Capri Plant had been commended, and an independent survey by the Automotive Industry Authority found the quality of the Falcon family of cars had improved 52% over the last four years to 1992. A contract to export engine blocks to Mazda in Japan had been won and to re-affirm the improving quality, Ford had implemented a two-year, 50,000 km warranty on all cars and light commercials. Buried, three pages further on in the same issue was the fact that Toyota, with imports of commercial vehicles had assumed industry leadership for total vehicle sales in 1993 and would remain leader for two years.

The recovery began with the EBII; 48,435 sedans and wagons were produced in 1992, followed by 36,402 sedans and wagons in 1993. And then the ED; 31,274 sedans and wagons in 1993, followed by 41,297 in 1994. The company returned to profits in 1993 and the good news continued in 1994 when Ford won the Australian Quality Award. At a ceremony at the Melbourne World Congress Centre, the Federal Minister for Industry, Technology and Regional Development, Alan Griffiths presented the award to John Ogden and his management. The awards continued with the company winning the Australian Design Award for 1994, once again Ogden and designer Steve Park accepting the award. It was the recognition of nearly ten years of work by the company.

Employee involvement and participative management and the drive toward total quality continued to pay off in 1994 when the Engine and Casting plant under Ron Tyack was granted Q1 award status in April, joining the Plastics Plant which had won accreditation in 1992. The competition between the remaining plants had been intense and the event was celebrated with great pride, as they beat the Stamping Plant under John Crew, and the Broadmeadows Plant 1 under Murray Gilbert, by a month. Even with the building blocks in place, it took three to five years to be certified to the Ford Q1 status.

The drive to quality was not the province of Ford alone. Now the philosophies of the company focused on the vendor body to improve their quality performance, the objective that only suppliers with a Q1 rating would remain as suppliers. With

1993 ED GLi Sedan and Futura Station Wagon. Ford produced a total of 54,729 sedans, and 17,842 station wagons.

RIGHT 1993 Tickford ED Falcon XR8

RIGHT 1994 Tickford XR6 Ute

the reduction of employees within Ford, by late 1994 below 8,000, came the outsourcing of product design, development, certification, manufacturing and supply of assemblies to suppliers. It carried with it considerable risk, but if confidence was there that the supplier had the systems and processes in place, there were considerable benefits as well. Relinquishing design and manufacturing control enabled Ford to tap the resources of a wider range of designers and specialised manufacturers; invariably the labour and overhead costs of the supplier were lower than Ford. The supply of more complex assemblies to Plant 1 resulted in less in–house labour, lower costs and overheads. This process, begun under Dix, began to bear fruit with the EF Falcon series. Henderson Automotive designed and manufactured a new front seat system for the EF which prevented 'submarining' of the occupant in an accident, as well as being easier to operate. PBR Automotive designed a new central-mounted park brake assembly with 70% less components. Both were award-winning designs, PBR Automotive later selling the new system to Chevrolet in the US and Ssang Yong in South Korea.

Back in 1992, subjective feedback from some customer surveys had reported a 'performance feel' problem relating to a perceived lack of performance and fuel economy of the EBII engines. In typical Nasser fashion, Jac had obtained the names of the Geelong-based design engineers responsible for engine design and 'invited' Alex Mishura and his supervisor Greg Harbutt to a breakfast meeting at the Head Office management dining room. Alex recalled he didn't realise it wasn't a meeting for a discussion, it was more a 'you listen, then fix it' sort of meeting. While Nasser was

AURORA Q1 ON SHOW

The record-breaking Aurora Q1 solar car was a special guest at the 1994 Sydney Motor Show. The Q1 team, consisting mainly of Geelong based Ford Australia engineers, supported Aurora as it travelled from Perth to Sydney in eight days, smashing the previous solar record of 20 days, held by Hans Tholstrup and Larry Perkins. The successful trip was in preparation for the 1996 World Solar Challenge and to help raise money to compete in the event. Aurora was the top Australian entry in the 1993 World Solar Challenge, finishing in the top five, despite a budget only a fraction of many of the other competitors.

AURORA 101 = 101

The ill-fated Aurora 101, the Ford-sponsored solar car which crashed at the start of last year's World Solar Challenge is back in action. During a recent test at the Ford Proving Ground, the 101 averaged 101 kph for fifty laps. The race last year was won at an average of just 89 kph by the Honda Dream. During the test Aurora's driver for the first two hours was Melbourne University Electrical Engineering graduate, Kate Holroyd. Kate, who joined Ford this year as part of the company's graduate training intake has been involved with the Aurora team since December 1995 and works on the telemetry.

talking, Alex kept interrupting Jac to explain some of the issues while Greg frantically tried to hide under the table. Finally Nasser had had enough, looked Alex in the eye and said, 'You go away and do what you have to do. Give me a call if you need anything.' Returning to Geelong, Alex, Greg, and later, Gowan Cook from BMO took him at his word and, in conjunction with other engine engineers and the Commonwealth Aircraft Corporation developed a new manifold using gun drilling machines to drill long, 8 mm holes. This locally developed technology was a work of art and a first for Ford worldwide, later copied by Ford US and other manufacturers.

The design, later called 'The Ford Falcon Resonance Intake Manifold' incorporated both long and short manifold runners and resulted in reduced air/fuel induction noise, better acoustics and performance, and was instrumental in achieving the 4% improvement in fuel economy. Oh, and it also fixed Jac's 'performance feel' problem. The design later went on to win one of the 1995 Australian Design Excellence Awards.

This innovation, along with a new designed crankshaft with twelve counterweights and hydraulic engine mounts, improved NVH even further. The new six-cylinder 4.0 litre CTC 'Computer Torque Control' engine with the EEC-V fifth generation electronic control system now matched the V8s for power, torque smoothness and fuel economy. These continual improvements of the engine and management systems resulted in fuel consumption improving from the EA26's highway usage of 10.0 litres/100 km to become the vehicle average of city *and* highway.

The rapid vehicle model changes resumed with the production of the ED Falcon in June 1993, followed by the major mid-term facelift EF. Where the ED had minor upgrades to specifications and safety performance enhanced with improved side intrusion beams, every panel except for the doors was restyled on the EF, along with a completely new interior which integrated the instrument panel so it flowed into the newly designed door trims. As a further safety measure, driver airbags were introduced as standard on all vehicles. In addition, the research into better and more efficient engines had continued and yet again the engine engineers had tweaked extra performance from the 4.0-litre I6 engine to bring it closer to the 5.0-litre V8.

The new sheet metal for the EF allowed the designers to create three unique front end treatments to differentiate the models with new front bumpers and bonnets; a low sloping bonnet for the Gli which flowed into the bumper, no grille. The higher series vehicles shared a bonnet with a raised centre section with unique grilles and bumpers. Driver airbags were now standard across the range, while once again, TVE provided performance options.

Then, only 14 months later in August 1995, Ford released the EFII, boasting a new low Cd performance of 0.31 and refinements to the front and rear suspension, following criticism that the rear suspension changes implemented with EF had been a retrograde step. Also introduced was the front passenger airbag (standard on the Fairmont Ghia and Fairlane) in response to the GM-H's standard fitment on the VS Commodore. Trim and paint options varied slightly.

Ford regained the total market leadership flag from Toyota for the first time in five years and the EF and EFII gave Ford bragging rights in 1995 of most popular passenger vehicle, with 21.5% and 24.3% market share respectively.

An Australian Motor Vehicle census taken in June 1993,

1993 Tickford Assembly line
with ED XR6 vehicles

Tickford options, sunroof, sports wheels and body styling kit fitment to this 1994 EF Falcon XR6. Note the gas fitment to a taxi in the background.

ABOVE 1994 EF I Gli, Fairmont and XR6 Falcon sedans. A total of 74,062 Series I sedans were produced.

revealed 2.2 million Ford vehicles were on Australian roads, 13,000 more than GM-H, a fact gleefully reported by Ford Public Affairs in February the next year.

The Fairlane and LTD came in for an upgrade in March 1995 with the production of the NF/DF series. Reviews of the range concluded, 'A car of refinement', with the new frontal treatment, the grille flowing into the bonnet, polycarbonate plastic slimline headlights and 'jewel effect' taillights. Despite the decreased overall length, interior space had remained the same. The new handbrake position won compliments as did the digital and analogue car phone aerial.

The turnaround in Ford fortunes helped Project Eagle's chances. The small group, representing all areas of the company, included Barry Ashton, Davis Elliot, Chris Lidis, Les Price, Brendan Quirke and of course Ian Vaughan and Don McAllister. Apart from designing a completely new vehicle, based on the current Falcon, they took a fresh approach to the vehicle costs. Analysis showed that 70% of the cost of a Falcon was in purchased components. The Eagle team approached twenty-six suppliers who represented 50% of the 70%. After some negotiations, all agreed to implement productivity savings to reduce costs, over and above that normally asked by Ford each year of suppliers. Ford costs were also analysed by the team. Don McAllister:

> *We had only had computers for a few years and they made a world of difference. Quirky (Brendan Quirke) was able to design spreadsheets that allowed us to calculate the total vehicle cost if, say, purchased prices went up 2%, or there was a wage rise in the*

third quarter of the following year. It really helped convince the US we knew what we were doing.

Ian Vaughan said one of the problems was the US believed we were biased against the Taurus. Of course we were, but with good reason. They wanted the Global Car concept across the world, but even the US public thought the ovoid concept of the Taurus was too avant-garde. Chief designers Steve Park and Graham Wadsworth gradually evolved the AU design theme, with some compromises, while Marcus Hotblack worked on the interiors. The ovoid rear window style of the Taurus was included in the Falcon design. The sharp trailing edges and triangular shape of the head and tail lights followed the style. The Research Centre completed full-size clay models of what would be the AU Falcon

ABOVE 1996 NF Fairlane Ghia Sportsman. A total of 3,745 NF Fairlanes were produced

LEFT 1995 DF LTD

THE AIR-BAG COMPATIBLE 'ROO BAR.'

Some suppliers called on Ford for assistance in testing products supplied as original equipment or for the aftermarket, particularly where facilities were not available or not able to be tested in real-life conditions. One such test was to assess the performance of an airbag compatible front bumper 'Roo bar'. A simulated test was developed and conducted at Lara with an artificial 'Skippy'. Skippy survived several such test as did the 'Roo Bar'.

RIGHT Bragging rights in 1995

RIGHT The 100 kph 'Skippy' 'Roo Bar' test

by Christmas 1993 and subjected them to customer clinics against the Opel Omega, destined to become the 1997 GM-H Commodore. In clinics, participants complete a questionnaire to determine their classification, i.e. Conservatives or Progressives. Their rating of the various cars were then scored on a scale of one to ten. The results?

Vehicle	'Conservatives'	'Progressives'	Average
AU Falcon	6.2	6.8	6.5
Opel Omega	6.5	6.5	6.5

People rated as progressive liked the AU Falcon better than those ranked as conservative, while both ranked the GM Omega the same. The average of both vehicles was identical, an indication they were both acceptable. And then along came Project 2000.

Ford 2000 was the baby of Ford Chairman, Scotsman Alex Trotman who divided the world into vehicle development centres instead of geographic regions; it aimed to restructure the company on global lines rather than regional lines. The first stage of this globalisation process was to take place in the US in January 1995, when the American and European automotive operations were merged. Eventually all automotive operations NAAO, EAO and ACG[98] would be merged into one entity, Ford Automotive Operations (FAO). The intent was to eliminate duplication. Newly appointed US President Ed Hagenlocker, said at the launch;

> *Our chief competitors are no longer local companies operating within the same boundaries we are...Most of our leading competitors, including Toyota, operate more globally and in some cases more efficiently than Ford.*

ABOVE 1995 EFII Fairmont Ghia sedan

The intention was to reduce the duplication of the company's systems globally, reduce model complexity and the number of components, to create 'global' cars such as the Mondeo and the Taurus. Cars could be sourced from anywhere in the world for a market. For example, the most expensive component in a vehicle, the floorpan was unique in each vehicle and market. Commonising this component alone would reduce tooling costs worldwide by millions.

The Australian launch of the Ford 2000 program was on December 3,1994, when Ogden chaired the first of the management meetings at Flemington Racecourse. In introducing the program, he said, in part;

> *In 1991, Ford was considered a 'loser' with product difficulties and financial losses and questions over the long-term commitment. We launched Ford Today introduced Lately magazine to new car owners and sponsored Rugby, Golf Commonwealth and Olympic Games. Today Ford is seen as more community and environmentally minded than Holden or Toyota. A higher percentage of people (61%) would definitely or probably consider a Ford over Holden or Toyota.*

One early effect of the new structure had been the closure of the FASPAC office in Japan the previous July and the reporting of Ford Australia to Wayne Booker, head of International Automotive Operations. The long-term implications for Australia were ominous; with only one of two rear wheel drive vehicles in the Ford world, the other being the Ford US Crown Victoria, the Falcon was in danger of becoming an orphan.

Project 2000 delayed Project Eagle by three months, but Vaughan persisted. The economics hadn't changed and the close marketing clinic result reinforced the fact that combined, the Falcon and Commodore accounted for one-third of all cars sold in Australia. Vaughan hammered that point home every chance he could:

> *I kept asking them how the Falcon, the best-selling car in Australia, could command 16% of the market here when the*

FORD ACHIEVES CORPORATE ISO9001

Ford Australia's design, manufacturing, purchasing, and marketing and sales operations have now been assessed as meeting the quality standard ISO9001. With Australia now joining Ford operations in South America, New Zealand and Taiwan in reaching this goal, Ford Motor Company has become the first major automotive company to achieve ISO9001 worldwide.

(Ford News, January 1997)

> *Taurus, number one in the USA only 6%. The Corolla is number one in Japan with 5.5%, the Golf in Germany is only 9% and the Escort in the UK is 7%.*

One of the hard tasks Vaughan faced was getting a commitment from Sales and Marketing to sell the volume needed to make the program viable. As he said in a later interview:

> *This business is about volume and unless you can make 80,000 to 100,000 cars a year off one set of components then you can't make money.*[99]

Project Eagle still had to overcome substantial prejudice. The Project Eagle team held seventeen meetings with Ford US over the AU Falcon. The Americans doubted the ability of FOA to deliver high–quality, low-cost cars, given the problems with the EA26 Falcon launch and the cancellation of the Capri program. A lot had been riding on trouble-free launches of the ED and EF; fortuitously both went well, the first glitch-free introductions in a decade. Confidence was restored with the Falcon regaining best-seller status and FOA again profitable.

In 1994, FOA returned to profitability with a bang. While write-offs had helped in 1993, 1994 was different; a record pre-tax profit of A$205.6 million, smashed again in 1995 by a profit of A$259.2 million, although that would come after the project Eagle decision. The profits certainly helped the chances. Other pieces of news which helped Project Eagle was the cost comparison that showed Geelong stamping plant was more efficient than Atlanta, the plant used for producing Taurus body panels. Geelong was able to produce an equivalent component at a lower cost, a point consistently pointed out to Ford US.

The culmination of good news, market leadership and excellent profits created sufficient doubt in the minds of Ford US management, that in May 1995, before the final decision was to be made, Vice-President Booker travelled to Australia for the launch of the EF Falcon, to review Project Eagle and to visit Canberra. At a crucial meeting in Canberra on May 3, between Prime Minister Keating and Booker, Keating convinced Booker the government wanted a viable motor industry. Booker also sought assurances from the Opposition Leader John Howard, who had replaced the unsuccessful Hewson, that the coalition car policy would not differ substantially from the existing plan, which had tariffs reducing from 27.5% to 15% in 2000. Phil Scott reported in The Sydney Morning Herald on July 13, 1995, that 'Mr. Booker left Canberra "pleased".'

Even with Booker's recommendation and news from Canberra, approval was always going to be a fifty-fifty chance. Eventually the board decided that while the Falcon didn't fit into Alex Trotman's vision, the volumes wouldn't affect the overall strategy. Not an endorsement, but the positives outweighed the negatives; the Australian volume was too big to abandon. The final, qualified decision came down to 'If they want it, they can pay for it'. There would be no funding from the US for the AU program. Ford US Board approval was announced by Ogden on July 13, 1995. Even then he qualified the decision for the AU:

> *I came here wanting to do a corporate car, I'll be quite honest. I think it makes more sense, I still do. The problem we've had is we haven't found one from somewhere else that fits...Back home everybody worried about the conclusion being driven by emotional issues. The attitude right along has been (from Ford US) 'Show me the facts'. We spent a long time doing that.* [100]

One interviewee for this book quipped of Ogden, 'We Australianised him!'. If so, John Ogden paid a heavy price for sticking his neck out and supporting the Australian operation. On the completion of his term of office he returned to America, where it is believed he was sidelined and retired not long after. The fact that he and Vaughan were right was beside the point, you don't cross the Board of Directors. The decision was headlined in the Australian press and widely applauded. Vaughan was rightly praised for his tenacity, foresight and faith in the Australian car industry. Affable and unassuming, he never let it go to his head. As he said in an interview with The *Australian Financial Review*'s Craig McGregor; 'All I've got to do now, is make it work'.[101]

The Taurus was launched in February 1996, and the Mondeo in

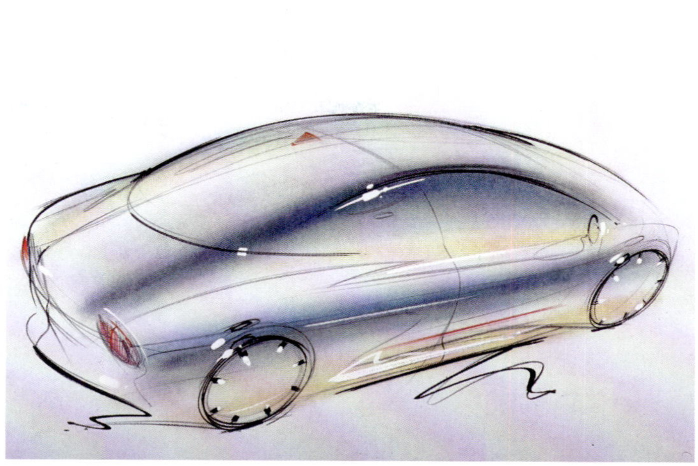

LEFT 1995 design sketch by Mark Richardson

FAR LEFT 1994 design sketch by Graham Wadsworth

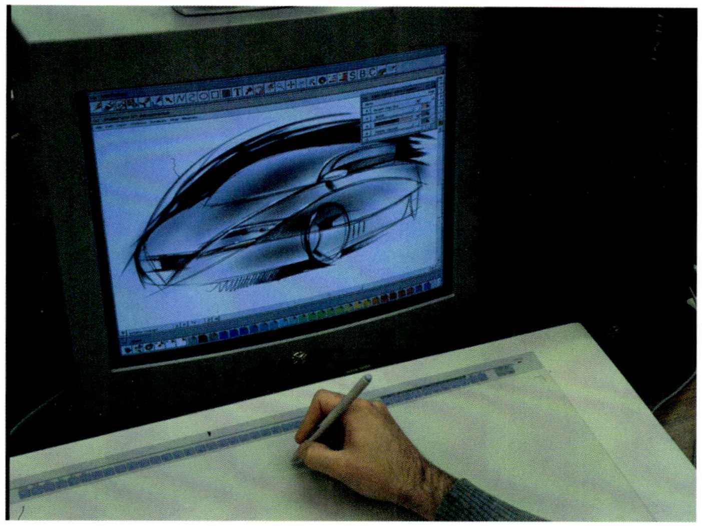

LEFT 1998 doodling on the computer

FAR LEFT 1997 design sketch by Mike Peruzza

November the same year. Despite their higher specification level over the Falcons of the time, as had been predicted, both failed and were withdrawn within two years after disappointing sales.

Meanwhile as tooling for the AU began, the launch of the ED product and the success of the KI Laser had taken the total 1993 Ford vehicle volume to 102,469. Combined volumes of the ED and EF in 1994 then reached 102,140. The closure of Sydney and the loss of the Laser to imports could have affected total volumes, but the success of the EF, then the EFII, launched in August 1995, took volumes even further to 103,047, then in 1996 to 103,675, the highest since 1990.

The ED resurrected the Futura name plate, a vehicle slotted between the GLi and the Fairmont, aimed at the 'user-chooser' novated lease market. ABS was now standard on the Fairmont and Futura, while an air-conditioning upgrade included the introduction of the more environmentally friendly R134A refrigerant. The door side intrusion beams were also improved to achieve a protection level 30% over that required of design rule ADR29. The release of the Futura separated the performance vehicles from the standard range of vehicles. This was reinforced by the establishment of a small assembly line at the Tickford Vehicle Engineering (TVE) plant, located not far from Plant1.

The XR series, XR6 and XR8, were assembled at Plant 1, then shipped to TVE for assembly of the unique, four-headlamp front end and bumper, sports suspension and other options. In addition to the XR series, TVE also assembled the first factory-fitted LPG system, available as an option on the GLi auto Falcons. The December 1993 edition of *Ford News* related a report by the

30th Anniversary EL Falcon GT
—only 272 were produced

NRMA that no Falcon fitted with the Tibbe lock system had been reported stolen. The edition also reported the graduation of the first twelve MBA graduates from the RMIT University/Ford joint venture, in addition to hundreds of non-trades employees graduating with their Union/Ford sponsored Vehicle Industry Certificate (V.I.C.).

John Ogden's term of office ended in November 1995, the same month that Ford Australia (FOA) was absorbed into Ford Automotive Operations (FAO). He was replaced by an Australian, David Morgan who had joined Ford Australia as a graduate trainee in the 1959 intake after completing a Bachelor of Commerce at Melbourne University. After time spent in market research, sales and marketing and regional and divisional sales management, he had been appointed to FASPAC as Director-Sales & Marketing in 1983, based in Melbourne. Transferring to Ford Taiwan (Ford Lio Ho) as Director of Sales and Marketing from 1985 to 1987, he returned to Australia as General Manager of Parts and Service and was appointed Vice-President of Sales and Marketing in 1991.

Work started on the 30th anniversary Falcon EL GT during January 1995. It was to be more a Grand Touring vehicle than a hot sports car with handling options. TVE boss David Flint headed up a team of engineers and the plan was not just to change the badges; four prototypes were built to develop and test their innovations and race car driver John Bowe was employed as test

ABOVE 1996 EL Falcon Gli. A total of 107,464 EL sedans were produced.

RIGHT 1997 EL undergoing the cold test

ABOVE Ivan Viduka

driver and consultant. Designers Steve Park and Mark Wright had a simple objective. 'It has to be instantly recognisable from any angle at 50m as a GT'.

After developing the design themes, Millard Design studios were contracted to develop the clay. Wheel arch flares were added, as were body-side cladding, bonnet scoops and a new bumper with in-your face driving lights, and Darth Vader-style radiator grille. Wind tunnel testing, conducted at Monash University, supplementing testing done five years earlier on the EB GT, resulted in the rear spoiler being placed 35mm higher than first designed, to reduce lift by 70% over a spoiler-less Falcon at 100km/h. Steve Hoinville and Bowe worked on upgrading the EL suspension and tyres to GT standards, while Rolf Glenk worked on the US-sourced 5.0-litre GT40 engine and engine management system, adding a TCU to the existing EEC-V Falcon system, then revising the air induction system for more power.

While Glenk was revising the engine, Ivan Viduka worked on the drivetrain, selecting a heavy-duty US sourced Valeo clutch. The stiffness of the 3.25 inch aluminium tube driveshaft used on earlier EB GTs and police vehicles, was increased by wrapping it in carbon fibre to withstand the higher engine torque and to reduce NVH. Apart from the major reworks to the front suspension, shock absorbers and spring rates, brake specialist David Orchid took the expensive, but correct decision to add twin piston brake calipers and larger brake discs to reduce fade and improve stopping distance.

The interior, designed by Sharon Vukic of the Design Centre, was largely carryover from the Falcon Ghia, but with LTD woodgrain, and discrete GT badging. The 272 vehicle production run began in September 1996 and went to June 1997; all were sold before production began.

Production of the EL/NL/DL Falcon/Fairlane/Ltd range began in July 1996, a A$40 million upgrade and the return of the Falcon GT.

Suspension engineer John Mole had previously helped Tickford (TVE) fine tune the rear suspension of the XR6 and XR8 series.

LEFT 1996 EL Fairmont sedan

FAR LEFT 1997 EL Falcon XR8 sedan

LEFT 1995 NF Fairlane Ghia

FAR LEFT 1995 NF Fairlane Ghia

Now, using the BMW 5 Series as the benchmark, he revised the Watts linkage rear suspension of the EL following criticism of the EF rear suspension changes. His efforts were so successful, *Wheels* journalist Tod Hellenbeck rated the suspension and ride as more stable than the BMW or Commodore.[102] Also thrown in were speed sensitive wipers, integrated wiring for car phones and vanity mirrors. The product planners revised the bonnet, grille, bumper and headlights of the GLi and Futura models to attract younger buyers.

If 1995 was a record-breaking year on all fronts, 1996 was a mixed bag. As commitments to fund the EL Falcon wound down and those for the AU began, it would have been difficult to top the record-breaking profit of A$259.2 million of 1995 but 1996 came close; profit dropped to approximately $229.0 million. The total quantity of vehicles manufactured increased by 628 to 103,675 vehicles. While Falcon sedan, wagon, the XG and then the XH1 utes and vans increased slightly, these were more than offset by a 21.2% drop in Fairlane-LTD volumes to 4,811 vehicles, and a 28.8% drop in truck production to 935. In fact, the 6,106 Fairlane-LTD assembled in 1995 were the highest volume for five years and the start of an irreversible decline. While Falcon production barely changed that year, the release of the VS Commodore in April 1995 by GM-H was a fresh face and was soon clearly the market preference over the EF and EFII.

Ford retained overall market leadership in 1996, thanks to imported vehicles while the VS Commodore took the honours of best-selling vehicle, beating Falcon by over 5,166 vehicles.

In a first for a local manufacturer, Ford announced a three year warranty for all vehicles, effective January 1, 1997. As GM-H and Toyota followed later that year with similar warranties, there was no immediate effect on sales.

Ford News were very happy to report that Ford had won back the double crown in 1997 of market leadership and total passenger vehicles, with sales of 130,215 vehicles and a 20.3% share of the market, a drop of 1,990 vehicles from 1996. However, it was the imported vehicles—Taurus, Mondeo, Laser and Explorer—

XR6

Tickford EF Falcon XR6

that sustained Ford; it was a disastrous year for manufacturing at Ford. Australian production dropped by 14,172 vehicles. Falcon sedans and wagons were the worst performers, dropping 12,222 or 13.9%, although reductions were across all segments.

Worse was to follow in 1998. In a year which saw the overall market expand by nearly 13%, Ford stagnated. Total vehicle sales for both Toyota and GM-H grew by more than 30,000 vehicles each. Even Mitsubishi, who had had a growth spurt in 1997, managed to hold their sales volume. Ford actually lost sales, recording a drop to a mere 128,814. Strong commercial sales in 1998 saw Toyota finish 4,701 and 29,476 ahead of GM-H and Ford respectively, while the VT Commodore took honours as the top passenger vehicle. Hopes and expectations for the AU, to be introduced in August 1998, were high. It couldn't come soon enough.

The AU Falcon began production in June 1998 and was released that September to general acclaim from the motoring journalists as far as performance, features and engineering, when the full range and scope of the program was revealed. The Falcon range of vehicles included seven different engines. Four six-cylinder engines gave various levels of performance, one using LP gas, while there were two V8 engines. There was the option of three rear suspensions, Watts linkage, independent rear suspension (IRS) and the wagon leaf spring suspension. There were two different bonnets to differentiate the models and suit the four unique front ends, and two instrument panels; the Fairlane and LTD would be released six months later.

Tickford had been involved from the start and developed the XR sports range, as well as the LP gas factory-fitted option, now actually fitted by Tickford. The option of factory-fitted LP gas was a first. No more backyard fitment and murky dealer warranty

AU—HARD WORK

As an example of cooperation between Ford, the unions and its people, prior to the launch of the AU Falcon, Ford management called for volunteers from the salaried ranks of the company to work on the assembly line at the Broadmeadows Plant to free line workers for training to build the new vehicle. Fitness assessments and the plant gym were used to ensure the new workers were suitably fit and able to carry out their duties. Michele Cook was one such volunteer and was assigned to install the left-hand front door glass and rear view mirror for two weeks, under the watchful eye of the line foreman. Michele recalls she quickly developed a new respect for the line workers as at first she had difficulty keeping up with the speed of the line and quickly found muscles she didn't know she had. The training was successful, the AU launched and the program further broke down barriers within the company. While the jobs were chosen with the abilities of each worker in mind, the choice of some jobs raised eyebrows. The head of the Ford Credit Union spent some time down in the pit installing the front suspension and engine assembly.

RIGHT Applying Dynock finish to AU clay

FAR RIGHT AU Instrument Panel clay

1998 AU Falcon Series I Forte. A total of 95,775 sedans were produced.

RIGHT 1998 AU Falcon Series I Forte

FAR RIGHT 1998 AU Fairmont Series I Station Wagon

RIGHT 1998 AU Falcon Series I XR6 VCT

FAR RIGHT 1998 AU Falcon Series I Forte with waterfall grill

problems with LP gas, the Tickford engineered system was fully integrated with the EEC-V engine management system. Project 2000 had linked Australia and Ford US in an organisational relationship from which Australia gained much; the AU was the first fully designed CAE[103] vehicle, whereas the EL designs had only been checked on the computer after completion.

AU Body Structures and CAE Supervisor Mario Brandini and his engineers took full advantage of their new access to Dearborn's powerful Cray computers, overseen by Vaughan's US based staff director of Large Vehicles, Ken Kohr. Kohr, knowing the Australian engineers understood Australian conditions better, focused his people on assisting them with access to design teams working on the Mustang, Aston Martin, Jaguar, Lincoln and Crown Victoria vehicles. The CAE programs reduced the need for the traditional quantity of prototype vehicles by 40%, releasing funds, while improving body stiffness by 20% and cutting NVH. This reduced weight and eliminated the need for costly sound deadening.

The main engineering features of the program centred on the variable camshaft timing (VCT), a new double wishbone front

1999 Ford AU LTD

RIGHT 2000 AU XR8

RIGHT 1998 XR6 badge

FAR RIGHT 1998 XR8 badge

PEOPLE BUSINESS

Ford bussed 2500 workers to Moonee Valley for launch day of the AU Falcon. It was a motivational day. They had inspirational speakers like Eddie McGuire, Sam Newman, Dick Johnson, Leigh Mathews and Glenn Seaton. There were so many people they couldn't all get in one area so they had different inspirational speakers in every room, so you could have a bit of this one and a bit of that one; go from room to room to get inspired. There was music; ukeleles broke down the racial divide and Vietnamese food was served. Max Kenworthy said later, 'The people all got back to Ford as high as a kite. You have to look after people!'

(The Sunday Age, November 22, 1998)

OUTSTANDING APPRENTICE

Fourth-year Fitting and Turning apprentice Naomi Parker won the 1998 'Outstanding Woman of the Year' award for an apprenticeship in a non-traditional area, at the National Centre for Womens' national awards. The award is designed to encourage and recognise women working in non-traditional areas, and to demonstrate to other women how wide their choice is of career options.

suspension, and independent rear suspension. IRS was standard on the Fairmont Ghia and an option for all other vehicles. While adding many kilograms of weight to the rear end, and conceding that many drivers would not feel the difference between that and the Watts linkage system, Vaughan said, in a pointed barb at GM-H, 'I didn't want to do a trailing arm (suspension) twenty years after everyone else'.

The IRS concept, heavily modified from the original Mustang design to give more wheel travel over bumps, kept the tyres squarely grounded, reducing wear, a notable criticism of the Commodores of the time. Ford again defended the modified traditional leaf-sprung rear end on the wagons as the best for carrying loads, criticized as usual by the journalists.

The six-cylinder engines underwent the most dramatic change. The evolution of the EEC-V engine management system now allowed a limp-home, a coolant loss detection system and prevention of the starter motor engaging when the engine was running. The Tickford developed VCT system adjusted valve timing to flatten the torque curve of the engine, giving better torque at lower revs, while improving fuel consumption. The new aluminium sump, although heavier than the usual pressed metal sump, became a structural member, stiffening the bottom end of the engine and reducing NVH. Using Jaguar's design experience, larger crankshaft bearings and redesigned counterweights were incorporated to give better balanced and smoother running engine at low and high-speed. The results from the virtually new engine surprised even the design engineers. 'We didn't believe we could get as good a result as we did,' said Falcon Vehicle Line Director Lindsay Dawson. The V8 engines were less seriously worked over, but enough to improve power, performance and extend the intervals between services.

The motoring writer's enthusiasm for the engineering aspects were more muted when it came to the styling. Jack Telnach's new edge design theme, his last before his retirement, was seen as too radical worldwide, as was Parks' and Wadsworth's interpretation on the AU. Global Design Chief J Mays defended the style on one of his visits to Australia saying,

> *The VT Commodore is a form car. You have to get within five feet of it to see all the design detail. The Falcon is a graphic car. You can see it a hundred metres away and know exactly what it is.*

He got that right! But the results of the clinic held in early 1994, in hindsight, were correct; the polarising and divisive design was too confronting. People talked about the Falcon but the safe, conservative, familiar market leader was the Commodore, so they bought a Commodore.

The AU was a damn fine vehicle and technically superior to any other local vehicle, and many imported ones as well at that, but it had its compromises. The dull argent (silver) painted Lincoln-style waterfall grille of the Forte looked cheap; the 15-inch wheels were too small for the wheel arches, designed for the larger 16-inch wheels and tyres of the higher specification vehicles. While the curved roof design had increased headroom, the same style and high curvature of the decklid as it swept down to the jewel-like taillights created a 'saggy-bum' effect that even the decklid hugging rear spoiler could not soften. The XR front end, while suitably aggressive with its four-headlight configuration took time for people to accept. Perhaps it was the sum of the parts rather

EA GT RESURRECTED

A prototype vehicle is usually destined for the crusher at the end of its life as a development vehicle. However, staff at the Proving Ground were so impressed with the 1990 EA GT vehicle, that it was put under wraps and 'lost', thus avoiding its fate. It was 'found' again in 1999 and restored by students of the Gordon Institute of TAFE before being presented to the Geelong Discovery Centre by Engineering Director Brian Williamson.

than the individual design features that were the problem; the new edge design themes would influence automotive designers and manufacturers worldwide for some years. Ian Vaughan reflected philosophically:

> *For instance, the C series Mercedes Benz had the same triangular pointed taillight design as the AU and nobody criticised them!*

Within Ford the design had been expected to stimulate conversation amongst the buying public, and then be quickly accepted. It wasn't. Ian Vaughan, in a later interview, said the marketing should have been much more aggressive:

> *We should have pushed the concept of the Commodore as stodgy and conservative, and promoted the Falcon better as a more modern design.*

Certainly looking at the vehicles fifteen years on, the Commodore body style over that period is difficult to distinguish between the models, while the AU Falcon is distinctive. Perhaps to make it worse, despite the development costs, marketing dropped the price of the AU over that of the EL, a move immediately perceived in the marketplace as a sign of weakness and desperation.

The problem for Ford was not only the AU Falcon, it was also one of timing. The drop in sales of the ageing EL in 1996 against the newer, fresher VT Commodore allowed the VT to build up a head of steam and many buyers followed the market leader. The AU was seen to be a failure in the market because, in the increasing market, it didn't recover the sales lost with the EL, and Ford continued to lose market share. Sales of the imported vehicles also failed to make any headway in the marketplace and Ford quickly became the also-ran to Toyota and GM-H, who continued their successes in 1998 and 1999, dominating the market while Falcon sedan and wagon production remained relatively static in 1998, then dropping in 1999 to 71,899 for the year, entirely due to a drop of 4,057 in wagon production. The AU was a failure.

The Fairlane and LTD range fared little better. Volumes had steadily declined from 1996. In fact, by 1998, with the introduction of the AU range, volumes had declined a further 38%, to a mere 3,410 and 338 respectively. The introduction briefly spurred production to 5,408 in 1999, but halved the next year to a mere total of 2,556 vehicles and the range was clearly in decline.

Niche model after model was produced in attempts to boost sales. A special value pack 'S' sports sedan with the Tickford suspension spoiler, alloy wheels and sports seats was released with the ugly grey waterfall grille now painted in body colour. The 1-tonne utility with custom tailored tray was released, but with a Courier type grille; nobody wanted that awful waterfall grille under any circumstances.

With the special value packs, higher features and reduced volumes, profitability dropped dramatically from the 1995 peak. After-tax profit declined each year from A$201.7 million in 1996 to A$57.0 in 1999 and was a bare-bones A$16.1 million in 2000.

Utility and panel van production reduced from 14,728 in 1989, to 4,230 in 1992, under the onslaught of Toyota commercial imports. The release of the XG series freshened the range and volumes climbed from the 1992 low to 8,429 in 1996, when the XH1 series began production.

The XHII series began production in 1997 and continued in production until the introduction of the AU utility in April 1999.

RIGHT 1999 AU Falcon FD-S show car

The panel van, with volumes dropping from 1,245 in 1996 to 906 in 1998, was always going to become an endangered species; the cost of tooling for the unique roof and rear doors alone were prohibitive. The low volumes in Plant 1 enabled utility production to be transferred there and, with the introduction of the AU series, the panel van was consigned to history, as was Plant 2. The last XHII panel van production was in April 1999, the XHII utility on May 12. Plant 2 was closed as a Ford plant and leased for a time to Air International before being sold.

One of the few highlights of the period 1996 to 1999 was the opening in early 1998 of the new Plant 1 paint shop by the Prime Minister, John Howard. The A$80 million investment, using water-borne enamel paint technology that does not evaporate volatile organic compounds into the atmosphere, made it the country's most environmentally friendly automotive paint facility.

Another highlight was the win in 1999 by the Geelong Casting Plant of the *Geelong Advertiser* Business Excellence Award, technology category, with the introduction of robotic fettling, the process of removal of excess metal from a casting, in this case

ABOVE 1997 XHII Tickford XR8 ute

LN Truck final line, Eagle Farm assembly plant, Brisbane

LTL series truck

OPPOSITE Commercial utility and van production moved to Broadmeadows Plant 1 with sedan and station wagon

MILLION MILE TRUCK

Dear Sir,
On November 30, 1973, you sold a Ford F-100 to G.C. Blakey & Co. For the past seventeen years it has been in my care and is about to clock up 1 million miles. (1.6 million kilometres) It has recently had a complete rebuild with a new engine, brakes and paint job (it was originally white). I thought you might be interested that the vehicle you sold is still going strong and in the hands of a proud owner.

(Signed)
F. Schoen,
Thornlie, QLD.

HENRY FORD III PATRON OF DISCOVERY CENTRE, GEELONG

A significant link with the Ford family was forged in April 1999 when the great-great-grandson of Henry Ford agreed to be patron of the Ford Discovery Centre in the original building where Ford Australia commenced production. Henry Ford III was with his father Edsel Ford II to open the Discovery Centre in April 1999. One of the features of the museum will be the original desk used by his great-great-grandfather.

crankshafts, camshafts and the front and rear exhaust manifolds. The robots were contained in a soundproof facility, reducing dust and noise and improving employee safety. Iron and Aluminium Casting Plant Manager Kevin Brown said the win was a credit to his casting plant team, who developed the process in conjunction with ABB Flexible Automation's Robots Division.

David Morgan retired in May 1999 after 40 years, having overseen the introduction of the Ford 2000 process, a profit drop of 70%, and one of the most disappointing decades of production for Ford since the Great Depression. He was replaced as President by Geoff Polites. Born and raised in Melbourne, Polites had graduated from Monash University with first class honours in Economics and joined Ford as a Product Planner in 1970. He joined the Ford graduate program in the US, where he spent nine months in product and market planning, before transferring to FOE Product Planning. Returning to Australia in 1975, he was appointed Marketing Plans and Research Manager, then General Sales Manager in 1985. In July 1988 he was appointed Dealer Principal at City Ford Sydney, Australia's most successful dealership and was named Dealer of the Year three times. He returned to Ford with excellent marketing credentials and contacts with the Dealer body, having served on the National Dealer Council for five years, and as its chairman in 1988. His unenviable task of resurrecting the company was to be helped by an ugly-duckling looking vehicle in the bowels of Product Development that looked like a wagon on steroids.

RIGHT 1-Tonne Ute launch and Geelong football club

Ford
Final XH Commercial
Utility & Van Produced at
Broadmeadows Plant 2
MAY 1999

GT

CHAPTER 9

2000 — 2016

THE FORD YEARS 2000—2016

2000:

Ford organises 'The Ford Rally' celebrating 75 years in Australia. Ford launches the first dedicated Falcon LPG sedan and wagon. GST introduced into Australia.

2001:

Five-millionth Australian-built Ford vehicle produced.

2002:

BA Falcon production commences.

2003:

Three-millionth Falcon vehicle produced. EU Fairlane-LTD production. Ford Motor Company (US) celebrates 100th birthday. Marcus Ambrose and Stone Brothers Racing win V8 Supercar Championship.

2004:

SX Territory production commences. Tom Gorman appointed President and director in April 2004. Marcos Ambrose and Stone Brothers Racing win V8 Supercar Championship for second year running.

2005:

BF Falcon, EV Fairlane-LTD production commences. Russell Ingall of Caltex Racing wins the V8 Supercar Championship to make it three years in a row for Ford and a clean sweep with Ford taking the top three places with Craig Lowndes second and Marcos Ambrose, third.

2006:

BA GT Falcon of Craig Lowndes and Jamie Whincup wins Bathurst. Ford Australia announces new strategic direction for the company, including investment in new projects and facilities totaling over A1.8 billion over the next decade. The Product Development Team is to become an Engineering and design "Centre of Excellence" for the Asia Pacific and Africa region.

2007:

Fairlane-LTD production ceases.

2008:

FG Falcon production. Ford Escort name plate replaced worldwide by Ford Focus.

2009:

BF Falcon of Craig Lowndes and Jamie Whincup wins Bathurst for second time. Fiesta wins three 'Best Car' Awards for best car. Ford Australia announces first after-tax profit since 2005, of A$13 million.

2010:

Ford celebrates 50 years of Falcon production. FG (SY) Falcon sedan production commences, Falcon wagon production ceases.

2011:

4-cylinder 2.0 litre eco-boost engine introduced on Falcon. SZ Territory introduced.

2014:

FGX Falcon and SZII Territory production commences. Chaz Mostert and Paul Morris win the Bathurst 1000 from last place on the starting grid.

2015 - 2016:

Ford Australia celebrates 95th birthday. Ford invests $300 million in Australia. UA Everest, 2016 Mustang introduced. TF Kuga MKII, UA PXII Ranger, Mondeo, Ecosport released. Lara Proving Ground celebrates 50th anniversary.

As soon as the tooling could be completed, the AUII was rushed into production, in February 2000. The unlamented AU had lasted a bare eighteen months, less two holiday shutdown periods. In an interview with *Ford News* in May 1999, Polites had promised change and a nimbleness in the market place. In a typically frank assessment, Polites conceded Ford had got the strategy and styling wrong. Gone was the waterfall grille, consigned to history and replaced by a single horizontal bar. Also dropped were the small 15-inch wheels, that looked lost in wheel arches designed for larger wheels. Gone also was the price decrease. Polites said the perception had been that as prices were lower, Ford had stripped features out of the vehicle. He said that wasn't the case, but that had been the headline and Ford had to live with that.

Now, for the AUII, the interior was upgraded and features, previously listed as options, were now standard fitment. NVH was improved by laminating the firewall and in response to fleet owners' criticism, the taxi option brakes were fitted to all vehicles. But it came at a cost. Pre-tax profit, A$57 million in 1998 had improved slightly to A$82.3 million in 1999, but crashed to A$16.1 million in 2000 as Falcon volumes dropped further. The static sedan volumes of the two previous years declined to a new low of 54,221, while wagons barely moved. Unusually, after the cessation of the panel van production, utilities enjoyed a resurgence, almost doubling the 1998 volume to 15,297, while Fairlane and LTD total volumes halved.

Just when things couldn't get worse, they did. Even with a vehicle acknowledged as an equal or better quality vehicle than the enormously successful VT Series II and VX Commodores, Ford failed to reduce Holden's lead in the marketplace. With comprehensive wins on the racetrack, including Bathurst, the higher volumes gave GM-H significant cost and volume advantages, consolidated further by the release of the VY Commodore in September 2002. Winning only twice on the racetrack and with lacklustre sales, Ford reported a pre-tax loss of A$33.6 million in 2001.

Despite the production of the AUIII in October, Falcon sedan volumes crashed to 42,283 that year, the lowest in 35 years. Utility volume increases offset wagon losses, but Fairlane and LTD sank further with 2,473 for the year, barely ten a day. The best AUIII feature was the Windsor V8 alloy heads that made the XR8 the best of the AU group. The shortened manufacturing cycle ended with the release of the BA series in July 2002. The four-year model cycle of the AU series body was the shortest in the Falcon's manufacturing history; sales of imported vehicles like the Festiva and Ford Escape had been the only highlights.

PAGES 274-275 2008 FG Falcon Series I GT number 881

LEFT 2000 AUII Falcon Classic sedan

ABOVE 2000 steering wheel design drawing

Ford Global Design Chief Mays returned to Australia in 1999 for a brainstorming session to start the redesign process for the BA with designers Scott Strong and Simon Butterworth. The return of such a senior figure was perhaps a recognition of the damage the new edge design concept had done to Ford worldwide. They started by raising the rear decklid 20mm and flattening the radius, while at the same time moving the rear quarter panels and tail-lights outboard by 40mm. The effect squared off the rear end, a more conservative look than the AU maybe, but one that, in Strong's words didn't look as though, '...it had appeared from outer space'. The headlights and grille were raised, similar to the rear end, to give the vehicle a more upright look; every panel except the doors was changed; the roof was flattened. While the effect was a more conservative looking vehicle, it was a cleaner, better proportioned and sophisticated design.

Styling, however wasn't the only change. The 'Control Blade' independent rear suspension (IRS) system of the smaller, front-wheel drive Focus, was developed for the rear-wheel drive Falcon by Alex de Vlugt, in conjunction with Dana Australia, resulting in a lighter, less expensive assembly which could be tuned to each model, while adding rigidity to the body. A Garrett turbocharger added to the 6-cylinder engine took power of the 'Barra' 24T engine to greater output than the 'Boss 260' V8; even the base DOHC[104] straight six outgunned the Commodore 3.8-litre V6. All auto transmissions now came with Tiptronic sequential shift. The interior was revamped with a more European look, following the trends of the imported Fords, with new seats and trim.

Technically, a new multiplex wiring system reduced weight and improved electrical reliability while in another industry first, an electrically adjustable pedal box allowed for pedal as well as steering wheel adjustments. Other features added were the 'fly by wire' accelerator pedal, no mechanical linkage, as well as an optional satellite navigation system. NVH again improved, but it was the styling of the BA which was the winner.

Production commenced in July 2002, the vehicle released in September. The effect was immediate. The 170-a-day daily production rate of the AU nearly doubled with the BA to over 300. That wasn't all. *Wheels* were so impressed after testing all versions of the BA against the newly released VY Commodores, and finding the BA superior in all respects, awarded the BA Falcon the 2002

RIGHT 2002 Job No:1—BA (Barra) Falcon, among others attending (left to right) Stuart Rowley, Trevor Worthington, Trevor Negus, Geoff Polites, Louise Teasdale, Brenda Richardson, Tony Simpson, Vin May.

ABOVE Russell Christophers

LEFT 2002 BA Falcon XR8

LEFT 2002 BA Series I GT—744 were produced

ABOVE Trevor Worthington

COTY award. The rewards were also financial. A pre-tax loss of A$36.64 million in 2001 was turned around in 2002 to a A$14.85 million gain, followed by a whopping pre-tax profit of $204.23 million in 2003. The BA wagon did not share the same success but volume did increase in 2003. The utility was now aligned with the sedan range; there had been three models produced in 2002. The AU2, 3 and BA, saw a 16% lift in production as well as an increase of the Fairlane volume to 2,849. LTDs also increased to 166 for the year, still far too few to be viable. Neither of the Ford's luxury range was as lively, nor as fuel efficient as the GM-H Caprice, though *Wheels* rated the Ford suspension as superior.

Coincident with the release of the BA, was the takeover of Tickford by Prodrive in the UK, the Australian arm now to be named Ford Performance Vehicles.

2002 Final inspection

FPV BA MKII GT-P

RIGHT 2002 door assembly line

FAR RIGHT 2002 wheel assembly

RIGHT 2002 Falcon console fitment

FAR RIGHT 2002 rear bumper assembly

ABOVE 2002 Falcon BA brochure

Back in 1999, Ford had begun a number of research clinics unrelated to specific vehicles. The sales trends of the 1990s were telling Ford the long term future of large sedans and wagons were bleak; but what were the options? New Falcon Vehicle Line Director Russell Christophers knew 4WD sales were a growth area, but what did people really want?

To find out, Ford carried out the research clinics in Sydney and Melbourne with detailed questions, and listened carefully to the responses. Their conclusions were that people did not want a sedate sedan, an expensive-to-run 4WD, or a dull, functional people-mover; they wanted all three, or the features of all three. Christophers, Dawson and Polites took their research back to the US with a proposal that Ford Australia should look at an alternative design vehicle to supplement the Falcon. Support came from an unusual source; Ford CEO Jac Nasser liked the concept. Lindsay Dawson recalled:

We were lucky Jac Nasser saw the potential and got the pre-program approved with a minimum of discussion in the US. Without his help, we would have come under much more staff scrutiny, particularly given the poor reception of the AU, I don't think it would have seen the light of day.

Given the blessing to move forward, a number of styling themes were developed, and rejected; the ugly-duckling Falcon wagon on steroids looked just that, and a design based on the Fairlane wasn't much better. Scott Strong, who had designed the BA, commenced working with the computer engineers to develop a design which, in the words of Christophers, 'would have the feel of a premium quality sedan with some of the ruggedness of a 4x4'. By 2001, the design of the vehicle, ultimately to be named Territory, was close to complete and computer simulated testing had begun. However, before the design was completed, Strong was promoted back to

Dearborn, his position filled by Simon Butterworth, who had previously designed vehicles at Jaguar.

Final approval from Ford US, to spend A$500 million on the program was, Polites knew, going to be a tough sell. He decided it was so critical, he should lead the team to the US, but also they needed some pizzazz.

Out of the cost-reduction programs, Ford had developed a system of building clay models 40% of the full scale vehicle. Polites asked the styling studio to make him a complete model of the Territory to 'show and tell'. It took three months to build the clay, cast the fibreglass mould and produce a body shell. Built from the inside out, the interior, seats and steering wheel were all fitted in place before the plastic windows were fitted. Every exterior detail was there, down to windscreen wipers and wheel nuts. Steering wheel badges became the exterior front and rear badges. The completed model, weighing over 150 kg, was airfreighted to Strong in Dearborn, who was charged with ensuring the model was in perfect condition for the meetings. Polites, Christophers and Engineering Vice President John Shelton, flew across to the US for a week of meetings and briefings before the final presentation at the Dearborn Design Centre. They treated it as though it was a new model launch. Polites presented the business case, they revealed the model and Christophers then took them through the details. Polites said he couldn't believe the reception they got at the end of the presentation, from hard-bitten automotive management, accustomed to high-pressure presentations:

> *...at the end, they all stood and clapped. I knew we were home and hosed. I think they were shocked at how good our model was. They were doing their own research...But we were months ahead of them. We literally pulled this thing out of its box and said 'here it is'.*

It was the ultimate sales pitch from the supreme salesman.

Now the real work began. While Butterworth and Graham Wadsworth finalised the exterior details, Marcus Hotblack and Sharon Gauci worked on the interior trim and colour schemes. Under Vice-President Product Development Trevor Worthington, Graham Pearson and Bruce Priddle worked on the engineering details and testing programs. All along the manufacturing and assembly engineers sat next to the designers and worked out how to build the RWD and AWD Territory down the same line as the Falcon. The emphasis was on innovation; find an innovative solution. The resources of Ford worldwide were certainly drawn on in the design, manufacture and testing of the Territory, but in its simplest terms, the Territory is a prime example of Australian engineering and manufacturing excellence. Time and again the motoring fraternity, when later testing the Territory, used the words, 'the Europeans should be worried', but it was never intended to replace the BMWs, Porsches or Mercedes Benzes of Europe. It was intended to be a unique vehicle, one Australians would want, suitable for all the climatic conditions in this country, available at a reasonable price. Ford used the best resources available to test the Territory; from winter testing done at -15°C at the Bosch test facility on a frozen lake at Skeut, outside Arjeplog in Swedish Lapland, to over 40°C at Arkaroola in South Australia. The engineers tested the vehicles, fitted with all the modern acronyms available (ABS, TCS, DSC and HDC[105]) to their limits. Both pre-production Territories and Falcon mules (Falcon vehicles with Territory mechanicals) were tested. And this was apart from all the computer-aided simulated crash test programs that had been run. Their objective was to create a vehicle unlike any other.

Vice-president Trevor Worthington, when asked by *Wheels* how did the Territory compare with the other vehicles Ford benchmarked it against, replied:

> *It's unlike anything else, and that's its greatest strength. There were other vehicles we benchmarked it against that we really liked, but there was to be no compromise. Territory is a no-compromise car.* [106]

The regular features of the BA Falcon were the starting point for the Territory, but literally thousands of hours went into creating an AWD or RWD vehicle that was different to any other on the market. The chain-driven transfer box was to be quieter

SYDNEY DEALERSHIPS JOIN FORCES

One of the largest Ford dealerships was created when fifteen dealers combined with Ford to create a joint retail venture, covering most of suburban Sydney. The venture covers nineteen sites in Sydney, has 1,400 employees and represents 74% of sales in Sydney. 'We want to offer customers a purchase and ownership experience that will grow Ford's market share, and offer greater career opportunities for dealership employees,' said new venture CEO Ian Dale, adding that dealer partners will run and control the operation.

than the gear-driven GM-H Adventra, although retaining the same 62% to 38% rear-front drive bias. A new front suspension was devised. Side curtain airbags were fitted as standard on the Ghia and TS models, optional on the TX; all seatbelts had pre-tensioning systems. The second row seats were placed higher than the front, theatre style, for improved passenger visibility; a third row seat system was designed. Both second and third row seats could fold flat with minimum effort to create a flat load floor. There was more computing power in the control systems than most businesses. Yet with all this, nearly 25% of the stamped components made in Geelong were common to the Falcon. The body assembly area of Plant 1 was modified to allow the body to be assembled down the same line; barcode readers scanned the build sheet, automatically changing the programming of the robots, the Falcon body assembly jigs swinging out of the way. Watching a robotic body assembly line in motion is to watch a large mechanical ballet, with a cacophonic musical background. Poetry in motion.

It all came together in February 2004, when the first of the Territories came off the assembly line at Broadmeadows, and were released to the public in May. The exterior design had been revealed some months earlier, so there were few surprises but the reception was excellent. In 2004, 18,266 Territories were made, making it the segment leader for six months and earning it the title of top-selling SUV. More than 8,300 Territories were also exported to New Zealand and South Africa in 2004, low volumes compared to the exports of Holden and Toyota but timely.

While Falcon sedan and wagon sales dropped by 10,497 in 2004, lost to the Territory, there was a net gain in sales. The success of the BA Falcon, the Territory and then the minor facelift to the Falcon, the BAII, in June and September for the sedan and wagon respectively, was a huge morale boost for the company. Total production in 2004 was 111,009 vehicles, an almost 30% volume boost over 2002. And the rewards were also monetary. Ford Australia's pre-tax profit, a bare-bones A$14.8 million in 2002, soared to A$204.2 million in 2003, to be followed by an even

RIGHT First preproduction Territory built at Broadmeadows Assembly Plant 1, with (left to right) Trevor Negus, Vin May, Trevor Worthington and Geoff Polites

better result of A$265.5 million in 2004, then A$175.98 million in 2005 when 107,974 vehicles were produced. An A$30 million dividend was also paid to Ford US. Others were not so fortunate. Mitsubishi, who had been struggling financially for years, closed their engine plant in Adelaide in 2004.

The successful recovery of FOA resulted in the promotion of Geoff Polites to Ford of Europe as Vice President, European Sales, before moving in 2005 to become CEO of Jaguar Land Rover. He was replaced by an American, Tom Gorman.

Ford now focused on refining their vehicles. Unusually, both the BF Falcon and the SY Territory were upgraded in the same month, August 2005, with minor facelift changes, except for the introduction of the Tremec six-speed manual for the XR series. The Dynamic Stability Control system, so successful on the Territory was now fitted as standard on the BF. Perhaps the biggest news was the option of fitting the Garrett turbocharged 6-cylinder 'Barra' 24T engine to the Territory, distinguished by the bonnet air scoop and diamond mesh grille. The option automatically included the larger, dual piston caliper brakes of the XR series.

Petrol prices began an inexorable rise in 2005. The December 2004 average unleaded petrol price of A$0.94 per litre had increased by the September quarter of 2005 to A$1.12 per litre and prices looked like they would continue rising. Soon fuel economy was on everybody's lips and sales of large cars began dropping; sales of the factory-fitted LPG powered Falcon, by now in-house at Plant 1 (instead of built by FPV) some months were running at 25% of Falcon build volumes.

With their tight control on inventory, Ford quickly began reducing production rates, and by September, the production per day had dropped nearly 100 per day. Production dropped even further in 2006 as the public turned dramatically to smaller vehicles, and an industry which relied on volume suddenly had enormous problems. Ford domestic production dropped 30% to a lowly 81,467 vehicles; Falcon sedan crashed to 34,983 vehicles, wagons to 8,443, the utility to 16,298, while Fairlane-LTD volumes

LEFT 2004 Territory wheel assembly

FPV BF Falcon GT Boss 300

2005 BF Falcon Series I Futura station wagon

halved to 1,120. The domestic reduction was offset by good sales of the imported ranges: Fiesta, Focus and Econovan.

The new models had to keep coming; GM-H released the VE Commodore, Ford responded with the BF2 in August 2006. The ZF six-speed automatic transmission, linked with dynamic stability control, from the Territory, became an option on the sports pack, Futura and Fairmont. But the good times were over. Ford reported a loss of A$73.98 million for 2006, a good result compared to others. Holden, after reporting a post-tax profit in 2004 of A$300.9 million, crashed even harder, reporting a net loss of A$144.6 million, despite exporting 60,518 vehicles the same year. Some of the loss was attributed to the elimination of one shift in the Elizabeth plant, redundancies costing A$89 million.

Overseas the news was not much better. Ford US was busy closing assembly plants and selling off the support divisions. One such division to be sold was the Plastics Development Centre in Detroit, the centre for much of the technology development of plastic materials in Ford vehicles. The sale process would continue for some time as Ford US first sold Aston Martin in 2007, followed by Jaguar and Land Rover in 2008, then Volvo in 2010. Ford US was not alone in closing plants and selling assets. General Motors, Chrysler and Toyota were also closing plants and retrenching workers. Ford Worldwide lost US$12.7 billion in 2006. One bright spot for Ford Australia was the engineering development work for other countries. At one stage, nearly half of Ford's product development engineers were working on overseas projects, proving Australia's value within the corporation.

October 2006 saw the opening of the new R & D centre in Geelong, behind the Stamping Plant, by Executive Chairman Bill Ford. Gone was the old Product Engineering centre, the annexe used for the manufacture of WWII mines, the site sold, to be replaced by a Bunnings hardware store. The new centre was a part of the new strategic direction announced by Bill Ford the previous May, along with global expenditure of $1.8 billion over the next decade. The centre was built with financial support of both the Victorian and Federal Governments, who tipped in a total of A$52 million. The subsidy was criticised by many in the press, but Premier Steve Bracks defended the investment, saying it would boost the Victorian economy by A$120 million a year and create 273 new jobs directly and 1200 indirectly, in a manufacturing sector which had shed 15% of its workforce in the previous two years. The centre's primary role was to be the development of vehicles for Australia and overseas. At the opening, Bill Ford said;

> *'This new Research and Development Center will allow Ford Australia to continue developing world-class vehicles for Australia and overseas markets. The centre will house 350 engineers, and incorporate new test and development areas, including engine development laboratories and prototype facilities. It will complement the company's Design Studio and Engineering and Technology Centre and the Proving Ground at Lara. It will play an integral role in successfully delivering the design and Engineering role we (Ford Australia) has secured for a new light commercial vehicle range that will eventually be sold in more than 80 countries worldwide.'*

The Technology Centre was ACART, the Advanced Centre for Automotive Research and Testing, and the vehicle was to be the Ranger light truck. Perhaps the period 2006 to 2008 is best summarised by an article in the *Sydney Morning Herald* in November 2006:

> *The Falcon versus Commodore battle has raged for the better part of thirty years...unstable petrol prices get most of the blame*

LEFT 2005 BF Falcon Series I utility XLS Cab Chassis

FAR LEFT 2005 BF Falcon Series I XR8 Styleside utility

vodafone
DEXION
DEWALT
Havoline
vodafone
Orrcon
Steel Tube Pipe
DUNLOP
Orrcon
FALCON

2007 Bathurst car 5, Mark Winterbottom leads the way

THE FORD RALLY

More than 2000 vehicles met at the Broadmeadows assembly plant to participate in Ford's 75th anniversary celebration. After a plant tour and breakfast, the convoy drove to the Lara Proving Ground for lunch and tours of the high speed and durability loops before moving onto the Geelong Waterfront where the cars were put on display in one of the biggest single car displays ever held. Events were located along the Geelong Foreshore and more than 80,000 people attended the five music stages, demonstrations of extreme sports hydroplanes, Moomba skiers and yachts.

FORD FIRST FOR SAFETY

The new FG Falcon is the first Australian-made car to achieve the maximum five–star safety rating in independent crash testing by the Australian new Car Assessment Program (ANCAP), scoring higher points than many premium European vehicles known for their safety. The comprehensive active and passive safety features are supplemented by the integrity of the new body structure, including the use of Boron steel and load paths to direct crash forces away from occupants. During its development, the Falcon was subjected to more than 5,000 simulated and 90 fully instrumented crashes of prototype vehicles.

for the recent decline in large-car sales but the reality is they have been falling for more than a decade...for some time Ford and Holden have been battling the popularity of novated leases and the improved affordability of imported cars thanks to a strong Australian dollar and falling import tariffs. Ford buyers haven't been defecting to Holden or vice-versa, they've been fleeing the large car market altogether in favour of Hondas, Subarus, BMWs, Audis and Mercedes Benzes...The last thing Ford and Holden want is Toyota taking an interest in the large car market, with the Aurion... [107]

Jac Nasser's prediction for the industry in the 1992 interview with *The Age's* Craig McGregor was proving to be correct. The industry was fragmenting. It would be model versus model, not manufacturer versus manufacturer and there would be casualties.

The first was Mitsubishi. In a year when one million vehicles were sold in Australia, Mitsubishi announced the closure of their Adelaide Tonsley Park assembly plant, and plans to become an importer in 2008, because of poor sales of the 380 sedan. Their production had slumped from 59,000 in 1997 to 10,744 in 2007. Market leader Toyota built 130,000 the same year, 2007, exporting half. Holden built 107,000, and exported 46,000. Third-placed Ford built 68,582 vehicles. The top three manufacturers had built barely 30% of vehicle sales in the country. Ford announced an operating loss in 2007 of A$132.5 million and further retrenchments. The next year, 2008, the last tyre manufacturer in Australia, Bridgestone, announced the closure of their plant in Australia. Now it became a case of the automotive companies supporting their suppliers as dropping volumes threatened their survival. Ford and Holden had to bail out hardware supplier Ajax Nettlefold, having previously been involved in a million dollar bailout of parts supplier Coghlan-Russell Engineering in 2007.

What became known as the Global Financial Crisis (GFC) had begun with US company Bear Stearns announcing problems with their mortgage-backed securities. Interest rates began to rise and in March 2008, Bear Stearns collapsed, followed by bankruptcy of US company Lehman Brothers. Global financial markets were in danger of collapse until governments responded by guaranteeing bank deposits, reducing interest rates and stimulating economies by fiscal stimuli, printing money. Home prices collapsed in the US as unemployment rates climbed nearly 10%, higher in Europe.

One of the most tumultuous years in automotive history finally closed in 2008 with General Motors, and then Chrysler LLC filing for Chapter 11 protection from bankruptcy, and the announcement of the US government making available short-term loans to both companies. Toyota Motor Corporation of Japan announced a billion dollar operating loss, its first in seventy-one years. Ford submitted its business plan to the US Government, detailing aggressive restructuring plans and a plan to return to profitability by 2011. Amongst other items were plans to build six small European vehicles in American assembly plants and the introduction of the fuel-saving Eco-boost engines into the Ford product range. Ultimately, the line of credit was not needed.

The Australian economy was less affected than those of other countries, but was not immune. Following the Reserve Banks advice of 'go hard and go early', the Federal Government began a series of financial stimulating programs, including a 30% investment allowance on purchases. The Australian economy slowed to about 0.5% and the unemployment rate rose to 5.75%

by November 2009. Of the three areas of industry employment that contracted during this period, the highest was Manufacturing, by 4%. Equity markets fell and the Australian household wealth declined by nearly 10% to March 2009, half of which was recovered by the end of the year.[108]

In the middle of the GFC, Ford began assembly of the FG Falcon in February 2008. Planned from 2004 when Simon Butterworth first penned the design, it had again been touch and go whether the Falcon would be based on an American design, but sometime in 2005, the final decision was made the BA platform would survive, at least for another generation, with the FG. Before the design could be finalised however, Butterworth returned to Jaguar, with the designs to be finalised by Scott Strong.

The vehicle was designed to be best-in-class for interior room. The curvature of the side windows was reduced and the rear doors made larger and reshaped; the redesign, with less intrusion of the wheel arches, allowed them to open wider. The result was more headroom, greater shoulder width, added rear legroom, while achieving an increase in-boot capacity. The instrument panel was redesigned and the centre console raised to create a more user-friendly interior. To match the newly released VE Commodore and Toyota Aurion, chrome highlights were added to lift the exterior.

BELOW A preproduction FG Falcon, testing DSC (Dynamic Stability Control) measurements and calibration—on the VDA (Vehicle Dynamics Area) at Lara proving ground

ABOVE Falcon undergoing heat test

The objective was for the FG to be best-in-class for ride, handling and brakes, and was largely achieved. Fuel efficiency was improved with a reshaped combustion chamber and a plastic inlet manifold for the non-turbo 6-cylinder. For the sports enthusiast, manual XR6 turbos featured a launch-assist system and a front bumper with a double-scallop cutout for the headlights for a racier image. Lastly, the four-speed auto transmission was replaced by the Ford US-designed, French-made, 5-speed 5R55 transmission. In a clean sweep with the past, G6, G6E and G6E Turbo nameplates replaced the Futura, Fairmont and Fairmont Ghia names.

Perhaps the saddest news was the end of production of the Fairlane LTD. Despite various special value packs and upgrades, with three models in 2005, the BA, BA/2, and BF, sales of both vehicles had continued to decline. Sales had halved from 1999 to 2003, to 2,849 vehicles. They dropped again in 2004 then marginally improved in 2005, but plummeted with the release of the BF series to a mere 1,069 Fairlane and 51 LTD. There could be no justification for the expenditure of tooling for such low volumes and in 2007, both models ceased production, the LTD in November and the Fairlane in December, after 34 and 41 years respectively, for a total 274,278 vehicles.

The demise of the LWB range of vehicles also heralded the beginning of the end of the Falcon wagon, which used LWB common components. With the introduction of the FG sedan, the wagon, in fact an upgraded BFII, was designated FG for the sake of clarity.

TABLE 9.1 FORD PRODUCTION VOLUME 2008–2010

Product	2008	2009	2010
Falcon Sedan			
BFII	5,764		
FG	23,520	27,813	13,137
EU			17,382
Subtotal	29,284	27,813	30,519
Falcon Wagon			
BFII	1,642		
FG	5,212	4,630	3,133
Subtotal	6,858	4,630	3,133
Falcon Utility			
BFII	4,500		
FG	8,306	10,927	10,896
Subtotal	12,806	10,927	10,896
Territory			
SY	12,791	2,232	
SYII		8,948	13,203
SZ			22
Subtotal	12,791	11,180	13,225
Total Vehicles	61,735	54,550	57,773

LEFT In December 2007, Ford Australia produced the last long wheel base, a BF Fairlane. The last LTD came off line the prior month.

LEFT Plaque commemorating final BF Fairlane

Gorman stayed in Australia an extra year to see the FG model into production in February 2008 before returning to the US, where he left Ford to join the board of the Chep group of companies. He was replaced by Bill Osborne.

Born in Detroit, Osborne had joined Ford in 1990. He was appointed President and CEO of Ford Canada in 2005 before being appointed President and CEO of Ford Australia. The move to Australia wasn't to his liking; barely eight months into the job, at a press conference announcing the retrenchment of 350 personnel and a reduction of 80 units to 285 a day at Plant 1, he announced his own plans to return to the US and leave Ford.

The GFC was affecting everyone in manufacturing; plants were closing everywhere. GM-H axed 1,100 jobs in Melbourne and

FPV Powertrain testing at Ford's test facility, Lara Proving Ground

Cornering stability testing at Ford's test facility, Lara Proving Ground

brembo

RIGHT FG Falcon XT, XR6 and G6E

THE ULTIMATE DAY OUT

Fifty Ford enthusiasts, winners of the Ultimate Ford Experience competition launched on the 'Ford Falcon turns 50' Facebook page had an unforgettable day in August 2010. Arriving at the Broadmeadows Head Office, they were welcomed by President and CEO Marin Burela before tours of the Design Studio and Assembly Plant. Lunch was held at the Ford Discovery Centre at Geelong, hosted by Burela, Dick Johnson and Alan Moffat, who took questions over coffee and dessert. After a tour of the Stamping and Engine plants, the fans were taken to the You Yangs Proving ground for a tour of a number of secret facilities few people get to see; the Anechoic Chamber, Engine Lab, ACART (Advanced Centre for Automotive Research and Testing) and the Wind Tunnel. The day ended with professional drivers taking the group for a spin around the Proving Ground, the Durability Test Track, the High Speed Constant Circuit and the Ride and Handling Track. One of the winners, Peter Arthur later said, 'It was one of the most awesome days of my life!'

Adelaide in August 2008, Mitsubishi cut a further 100 jobs as well.

Ford announced in September 2008 that Osborne's replacement would be Australian Marin Burela. One of the Graduate Training Program intake of 1984, Burela had spent his early years in the Geelong stamping plant and the last ten years overseas, where he held manufacturing positions at Jaguar and Land Rover in the UK before rejoining Ford of Europe in 2004. Burela spoke regularly of Ford Australia's plans and the problems the industry faced, particularly that of volume:

> *Chinese automotive production in 2008 exceeded 9.3 million vehicles; more than double that of Germany and the US combined and more than double that of five years earlier.* [109]

Australia's total vehicle sales at the same time were one million vehicles; Australian manufactured vehicles a mere 305,000.

Wagon sales continued to decline as the success of the Territory ate into its market. Finally, in March 2010, Ford announced the cessation of the Falcon wagon. The last wagon came offline in Plant 1, in September 2010. Over the previous fifty years and one month, 714,982 wagons had been produced. One month later Ford announced the end of the 4 and 5-speed automatic transmissions. The only auto available would be the best one, the excellent ZF 6-speed, tied to the Euro-IV compliant engines; the 6-speed manual would still be available.

Similar to GM-H, sales of the C/D size vehicles continued to lose market share to smaller imported vehicles. Ford production records for the period 2008 to 2010 are shown in table 9.1.

While sedan and Territory manufacture had stayed relatively static over the period, wagon production had halved in three years.

To comply with increased CO_2 emission requirements, known

LEFT 2010 50th Anniversary FG Falcon Series I XR6 Turbo

FAR LEFT 2008 FG Falcon Series I FPV F6 interior

LEFT 2008 FG Falcon Series I XR6 Utility

FAR LEFT 2008 FG Fa con Series I G6 sedan

as Euro IV, the FG was upgraded to the FG EU designation in January 2010, with a new catalytic converter. The Product Development group continued to improve the efficiency of engines and transmissions. One innovation came in late 2011, with the release of an LPG optioned Falcon, the EcoLPi, fitted with a new liquid–phase injection system, designed and produced by the Orbital Engine Company for Ford, which developed slightly more power than the ULP engine. Teamed with the now standard ZF 6-speed transmission, fuel economy improved over the previous model, but was still more than the ULP vehicle. With LPG prices linked to just over half that of ULP, it gave operating cost savings of approximately A$500 a year, although at a higher annual depreciation cost than a small vehicle. With the LPG tank replacing the standard plastic fuel tank and spare wheel well, the spare wheel occupied a third of the available boot space but more importantly still allowed the spli-fold rear seat. This spare wheel was usually replaced by taxi drivers with a puncture repair kit. As expected, with economy, power and performance substantially better than the Commodore, most taxis remained Ford vehicles. For tradies, the LPG option was available on the utility.

In a move reminiscent of the Nasser-Ogden changeover, Marin Burela was promoted in November 2010 to head the Ford China joint venture: Changan Ford Automobile Company Limited, located in Chongqing. His replacement was Bob Graziano, a thirty-year Ford veteran of Ford US and South America, former CEO of South Africa and CEO of the Ford China joint venture for the previous two and a half years. He would be charged with the task of closing manufacturing in Australia, and the transition program from manufacturer to importer.

The SZ Territory began production late in December 2010, and was released early the next year. From being market leader shortly after it was released in 2005, with a market share of 33%, additional entrants to the segment at the time of the SZ introduction had reduced its market share to 14%. The SZ was designed to recover that ground. Retaining the RWD and AWD options, the most anticipated feature of the new model was the introduction of the 2.7-litre common rail turbo diesel engine. Ford Australia had debated the merits of offering a diesel engine for some time; the issue of NVH being the major issue without major reinforcement and perhaps a double skin firewall. Brian Williamson resolved the issue shortly after launch of the SY Territory, by fitting one with a Landrover 2.7-litre single turbo diesel engine and proving to the NVH engineers their fears were unfounded. It took Australia nearly two years negotiating with the Ford engine plant in Dunton, before supplies were to become available for the SZ.

The SZ interior was tidied up and refreshed. The 'Human Machine Interface', and 'Interior Command Centre', the fashion names for intuitive and user-friendly controls, were redesigned with a new LCD screen, and access to Satellite Navigation, Bluetooth, MP3, iPod and USBs were available. Rear seat passengers had DVD entertainment modules as standard on both Platinum models, while the third seat, optional on the base TX, was standard on the rest of the range. The exterior featured a new bonnet, front end and bumpers. New headlights, tail-lights, driving lights and LED running lights on the Titanium model completed the package.

MARIN BURELA'S LEASE CAR

Way before becoming President and CEO of Ford Australia, Marin was promoted and became eligible to lease a company vehicle. Of course it had to be a white LTD. He parked it in the roadway between the plants at Geelong and as the shift was ending, drove carefully through the crowds, everyone admiring his new acquisition. He was so busy acknowledging the greetings of the 1,000-odd workers as they finished their shift, he failed to notice that Don Deveson had rearranged the concrete planter boxes in the roadway. The result? One LTD towed away for repair, an embarrassed Marin retiring to his office.

The GT came home to Plant 1 in 2012. They had initially been assembled by Tickford, renamed Ford performance Vehicles after Tickford Vehicle Engineering in Australia and the UK were

RIGHT 2010 New Territory design sketch

YFF·200

RANGER TRUCK RELEASED

Combining durability and power from the award-winning TDCi diesel and contemporary exterior design, the new Ford Ranger, designed in Australia's Product Development Centre and built in Thailand and South Africa, blends strength and style. Inspired by the Ranger MAX show truck revealed at the Thailand International Expo last November, the new Ranger is finding its way to markets in the Asia Pacific and Africa region, and will be exported to 130 markets around the world.

RIGHT 2011 Ranger truck on TASE test, Thermal and AERO Systems Engineering test, in ACART (Advanced Centre of Automotive Research and Technology) facility.

taken over by Prodrive. Now, as volumes dropped, they were to be assembled by Ford again, with special treatment. The 5-litre V8 'Miami' engines were now assembled down a single assembly line at the Geelong engine plant by one of only six specialist technicians. Each engine was hand-built by that technician and hand-tuned to perfection, before they personally inscribed their name on the engine. The vehicle body began its life through body build as a normal Falcon, but after paint, was taken to a special assembly area to be assembled by a small, nine-person, highly trained, FPV team, simplifying the assembly process. The intention was to return the GT to the bespoke era of high-class automobiles.

As the Global Financial crisis slowly faded from memory, fuel prices did not. Small imported vehicles continued to dominate the market and large vehicles continued to lose market share. The 2010 production of 57,773 was the last year Ford would produce that volume. Sedan production plummeted by 42% in 2011 to 30,519; with the exception of 2009, the lowest since 1961. Utility sales dropped 47%. The increase in Territory production to 15,282 hardly registered.

Another innovation was the introduction of the Spanish-sourced, 4-cylinder turbocharged EcoBoost engine to the Falcon in January 2012. A concept used in Europe for years, the increasing quantity of European imports meant it was no longer unusual to Australia, but it was alien to the traditional Falcon buyer. This was the first application of an EcoBoost engine in a rear-wheel drive vehicle, and it allowed the Falcon to compete on equal terms with most medium-sized competitors, with a fuel consumption of between 8.1–8.5 litres per 100 km, a 12–14% improvement, and CO_2 emissions of 192 gram/km. Like all medium vehicles, towing capacity was reduced to 1,600 kg, only seen as detrimental

FORD TO GET $52M TO HELP DESIGN NEW VEHICLES

The Federal Government announced in February 2006, it had pumped an additional $52.5 million into Ford Australia in return for a promise to design all-new Falcon and Territory models that can be exported. In turn, Ford will invest about $1.8 billion over the next decade to put the new models onto the market, extending the life of its Broadmeadows and Geelong plants. Of the Government money, $12.5 million will be used to build a new design and engineering centre at Broadmeadows. This will be used to develop a light commercial vehicle for global markets, a project Ford Australia won from Ford divisions around the world. The extra grants to Ford, which are in addition to any benefits the company may derive under the $4.2 billion Automotive Competitiveness and Investments scheme, have come as manufacturing has been under pressure from swelling Chinese imports and a strong dollar, which makes exporting difficult.

(The Age, Saturday May 7, 2006)

GEOFF POLITES

The untimely passing of Jaguar Land Rover CEO and former CEO of Ford Australia in April 2008 has robbed family, friends and colleagues of a dedicated, focused and determined man who was an inspiration to everyone he met. Despite battling ill health for the past two years, Geoff never lost sight of his goal to return JRL to profitability. Geoff was a VFL umpire, umpire's advisor before moving to Sydney where he acted as a runner and Team Manager of the Sydney Swans. Geoff was also an avid V8 Supercars supporter. As tributes, all Sydney Swans players wore black armbands as a mark of respect to a great supporter and all V8 Supercars racing at the Barbagello racetrack on 9–11 May will be adorned with a black oval bearing the name 'Geoff.' In his time at Ford Australia he had a major involvement in V8 Supercars and was responsible for the development of various champions, including Marcos Ambrose and Craig Lowndes.

compared to other Falcons. The 60 kg lighter engine allowed a different suspension setup and lighter steering system. The vehicle was noticeably quieter, using technology developed for the Territory and low-rolling resistance tyres.

There was little fanfare when the EcoBoost Falcon was launched. Amazingly, despite having introduced a vehicle that competed in fuel efficiency with smaller vehicles, and with emissions low enough to satisfy any 'greeny', Ford failed to advertise the advantages of the EcoBoost Falcon over smaller, less roomy vehicles, preferring to promote the imported EcoBoost Focus and the ECOnetic, diesel-powered Fiesta instead, as alternatives to their hybrid competitors. With a similar price tag as the 6-cylinder Falcon and no advertising, it is no surprise that sales of the EcoBoost Falcon from start of build in February 2012 to June 2015 totaled just 2,266 vehicles, and a low in June 2015 of barely 1.6% of sedan build. With little advertising of Falcon at all, manufacturing declined further. Losses continued to mount and manufacturing began the death spiral from which there is no recovery. Consciously or not, Ford management had decided to quit the Falcon, and by inference, manufacturing in Australia before 2011.

On May 23, 2013, President Bob Graziano announced the closure of manufacturing in Australia, effective October 2016, along with the news that Ford had lost A$141 million after tax in 2012, and a total of A$600 million in the previous five years. He continued;

> *Our costs are double that of Europe and nearly four times that of Asia. The business case simply did not stack up, leading us to the conclusion that manufacturing is not viable for Ford in Australia in the long term.*

Advertising of Falcon, little as it was, ceased immediately with the announcement, with predictable results. Buyers deserted Falcon. Total production for 2013 was just 29,685 vehicles, an immediate drop of 21% over 2012.

In the light of the pending closure, the launch and production of the Falcon and Territory FG-201X series of vehicles in September 2014 was low-key. Program funds were limited and Ford were unwilling to commit funds to an ageing vehicle, unlike GM-H who, with higher sales to protect, put more funds into upgrading the Commodore interior. While probably the best vehicle produced by Ford in Australia, the Falcon was seen, and labelled by comparison, by the media as ageing and out-of-date, a label noted by the motoring public. The first three month's sales of the new model were disappointing as, with more attractive smaller vehicles and advertising, they turned to imported vehicles at a greater rate, accelerating the rate of decline of the Falcon.

Despite the release of the 201X series, total production for 2014 of 20,456 vehicles included a mere 7,052 sedans, 2,750 utilities and 10,654 Territories, a 45% drop in two years. An

ABOVE Robert Graziano

LEFT 2010 Falcon's 50th anniversary

JOE HINRICHS

Joe Hinrichs, at 29, was the youngest plant manager at General Motors. At 40, just six years after joining Ford in 2004, he has become the youngest vice-president in the company. Now at 42, he is group vice president and president of Ford Asia Pacific and Africa Region (APA).

indication of the changing market, Territory overtook Falcon production volumes in 2012, a situation which continues today.

Holden cut 500 jobs from its South Australian and Victorian workforces one month before Ford's May announcement. Then in December 2013, Holden CEO Mike Devereux also announced its closure of manufacturing in Australia, at the end of 2017, citing the sustained strength of the Australian dollar, the high cost of production, the small domestic market and the most competitive and fragmented vehicle market in the world. Toyota followed suit in February 2014, announcing the closure of the Altona plant, also to end in 2017, ending manufacturing in Australia. Toyota had lost A$1.75 billion in the previous ten years.[110] The same article reported the high Australian dollar had resulted in Toyota losing nearly A$2,500 on every Camry it exported. So much for exporting to survive.

The blame game began in earnest in Canberra at Holden's announcement on December 2013. Independent Senator Nick Xenophon slammed senior government ministers for forcing Holden's hand. He told reporters the tipping point was the reckless comments made in the Parliament by Treasurer Joe Hockey when he was reported as saying 'either you're here or you're not!' Former Labour Industry Minister Kim Carr jumped on the bandwagon,

RIGHT 2014 FGX Falcon and SZ II Territory Job 1

saying the government had taunted GM and abused its executives.

In reality, it was all grandstanding; the decisions had been made months, if not years before. In the months before the closure announcements, Ford and Holden sales had each been overtaken at some time by Mazda, Hyundai and Nissan. Former GM boss Mike Devereux put it succinctly when he supported the closures, saying high wages, low import tariffs and more suitable imported cars and a strong currency, made it impossible to export cars; better to rip off the Band-Aid and start repairing the damage now, he said, and start retraining workers and find out what Australia can do well—apart from being a farm, a hotel and a quarry.

Despite maintaining his position that he would continue at Ford Australia until closure in October 2016, at age 55 Graziano announced his early retirement in April 2015, and his immediate return to the US. The rumours began circulating immediately; one that Ford US had effectively retrenched him because he had refused to close manufacturing early, as volumes were dropping faster than forecast. Another was there were personal issues or issues with the renewal of his three-year contract in 2013. 'We are on track with our plan for manufacturing transition in October 2016,' was all Public Affairs Director Wes Sherwood said in reply, and as production at the low rate continued, the rumours died.

Graziano was replaced by Englishman Graeme Whickman, who had been head of sales and marketing for Ford Australia since October 2013. Ford announced further daily rate cuts in 2015; a plant which had produced more than 400 vehicles a day was now to produce less than 80. As of August 2015, total production for the year will be 10% lower than 2014.

Through the last, difficult two decades, one issue is clear. Notwithstanding the insecurity that redundancies inflict, industrial relations harmony has persisted. The legacy of Bill Dix, Percy Worsnop, Tom Pettigrew and countless other committed employees and union officials is alive and well.

LEFT 2016 FGX Falcon XR8 Sprint

EPILOGUE

The Button plan became effective January 1, 1985. Senator Button on his announcement of the PMV (Passenger Motor Vehicle) plan said in part;

> *The plan was from the outset a key element of the Government's approach to industry policy. It was established to provide the framework for the necessary transition from a high-cost domestically oriented industry towards a more competitive internationally oriented industry supplying Australians—and the world—with better quality automotive products at more reasonable prices...we set up the Automotive Industry Authority and asked it to embark on a strategy with the following elements:*
>
> - *Rationalisation of the Industry, and*
> - *An increase in competitiveness to become an area of strength of the Australian economy rather than a weakness.*

His vision was to create a leaner, more sophisticated, highly skilled automotive industry, putting pressure on local manufacturers to lift their quality, rationalise their models and improve their efficiency. It worked. The automotive industry responded, becoming efficient, rationalising, automating and better utilising the skills of its workforce. Ford used the multifaceted approach of Process Intent, Statistical Inference, and Employee Involvement. Process Intent encourages operators to achieve measurable outcomes required of their activity to achieve zero defects—forever. Statistical Inference is the use of techniques developed by Dr. D. Edwards Deming, and applied so brilliantly by the Japanese, to identify and eliminate problems. Employee Involvement is the participation of employees in decision-making and problem solving within their area of competence. Other companies used similar techniques. The result; quality and reliability of Australian vehicles is now equal or better than many from other countries, truly world-class cars.

In 1986 the industry employed or supported, directly and indirectly, 240,000 workers, 6.2% of total manufacturing employment. By 1995, with increases in efficiency and falling local sales, the industry had shrunk to 137,000 employees, of which the automotive industries themselves employed only 30,000. The balance, 4.75 times those directly employed, were of suppliers and sub-suppliers from a whole range of industries, die casting foundry, fasteners, glass, paint, steel, aluminum, rubber, textiles and plastics. There was pain involved. Over the same period, as the import duty rate fell from 57.5% to 27.5%, vehicle imports grew from 15.5% to 55% of the total market.

Over the years, successive Governments of all persuasions had tinkered around the fringes of the industry. Between 1965 and 1981 alone, there were a total of twenty-four significant amendments to the car plan. All the time, there were calls for reduction of tariffs for the vehicle industry, yet primary industry and farmers continued to enjoy direct and indirect subsidies when drought, floods, economic factors, etc. affected them. They supply an essential item to the country: food. The industry supported the Button plan, if only because it gave long sought stability and direction to the industry. The pretax profit of all the Australian manufacturers over the high volume six-year period of 1980–1986 had been a loss of $111 million. Government Affairs Manager Graham Barber later wrote in his presentation to the Automotive Industry Industrial Mobilisation Course;

> *In developing the plan, the Labour Government was conscious of the need to allow the industry time to restructure and modernise, while the proceeding towards long-term efficiency goals which would permit survival against unrestricted imports by 1992, but protected only by tariffs on imported cars.*[111]

What Senator Button did not agree to and would not live to see, was the process of tariff reductions continuing towards 5%, then zero by subsequent governments, to the end of automotive manufacturing in Australia. The stability required for the massive investment did not come. As far back as 1929 the Brigden Report, established as an independent inquiry into the economic effects of Australian Tariffs, stated in part;

> *It is quite certain that without the tariff it would be possible to obtain a larger National Income per Head—but for a considerably smaller population. The maximum income per head for Australia would probably be obtained by reducing it to one large sheep run with the necessary subsidiary and sheltered industries for a few rich mines—and for a population of about two million people.* [112]

To support a growing population the country requires capital investment; for that it needs stability—economically, politically and policy-wise. The automotive industry has not had that in Australia. Successive governments have failed to recognise:

- *The concept of a level playing field in international trade is a myth, a concept for the naïve.*

In a keynote address to the Committee for Development of Australia, Bill Dix, then Managing Director of Ford Australia, reminded them that in 1957, Australia exported more vehicles than Japan.[113] The Japanese government then embarked on an aggressive program of promoting vehicle manufacture using quota restrictions, foreign exchange controls, high tariffs, discriminatory commodity taxes and registration controls of vehicle sizes, while promoting quality and efficiency. They ensured the competitive struggle took place at the international marketplace and not in their domestic market. Even today, old Ford hands shake their heads in disbelief that Australian governments of the day could not understand the idea that overseas companies do not necessarily use a cost plus concept to arrive at a market price, but one of cost down, to give them pricing flexibility in the marketplace. Even in 1995 the permissible vehicle imports, expressed as a percentage of local manufacture for the following countries, were as follows:

United States	25%
France	3%
Italy	3.3%
Spain	1.2%
Brazil	excluded—none permitted
Australia	no limit

Free trade negotiations and agreements have substantially removed many of these barriers and reduced or eliminated import duties and tariffs, but hidden taxes and charges under FTAs still operate. Higher sales tax on imported vehicles to discourage sales and artificial limits to engine capacity of imported vehicles are but two examples.

But successive governments ignored the warnings from others, not only the industry, on the concept of free trade. Senator Xenophon, in an address to the Senate in December 2013, said,

We have to stop being mugs. Other countries are laughing at us for being such purists about free trade.

- *International companies, not only automotive companies, will go to the source that offers them the lowest cost base or pricing structure, including indirect or 'hidden' benefits.*

In an address to employees and retirees of Ford Australia in 2013, Bob Graziano compared the cost structure of vehicles made in Australia, Thailand and Europe. Using the manufacturing and marketing cost of a Ford Falcon in Australia as a base of 100, the cost of an equivalent vehicle from Europe was 60, from Thailand, 40. In 2013, Ford Australia declined further support from the Australian government; manufacturing in Australia had been a lost cause for fifteen years. So how has the country got it so wrong? Senator Button, in his Motor Vehicle Plan-Stage Two, news release on April 13, 1988 said;

...the Automotive Industry Authority found while the car industry has made considerable progress in its drive for greater efficiency, there was room for improvement...the competitive pressure has been considerably reduced with the devaluation of the Australian dollar. The Government intends, while maintaining the essential elements of the plan to reassert that pressure...We expect reducing protection levels this will create the potential for price stability in the car industry...

The grand plan and vision died when there was no offsetting action by any Government when the currency later revalued by 30%. Instead, the whole country went on a spending spree and the world welcomed us with open arms. Writing of Toyota's planned 2017 closure, Joshua Dowling wrote;

> *Domestic car sales are no longer enough to sustain an assembly line because the Australian market is the most congested in the developed world, with 60 brands competing for 1.1 million sales. By comparison, in the US, 38 brands compete for more than 15 million sales.*[114]

Because of our open market policy, Australia is now seen as a test market for vehicle manufacturers. Novated leasing and market fragmentation completed the job; the 2014 top-selling vehicle in Australia, the Toyota Corolla, managed just over 44,000 sales. It is ironic that in September 2015, exchange rates had reduced to a level that is viable for manufacturing to continue. Too late. Soon there will be no manufacturing industry to speak of in the country. So where does Australia go from here?

It is contended that, like other essential industries, some subsidies are essential for manufacturing industry. The question is of degree. If unemployment is to fall, jobs for these people must be found, or created. The protection of a viable manufacturing industry should be weighed against the social problems and welfare costs of a whole underclass of disenfranchised and unemployed groups in society.

Dennis Glover, in his book *An Economy is not a Society,* relates his experiences of his early life in Doveton Victoria, from where the nearby factories of GMH, International Harvester and H.J. Heinz drew their labour; where once these industries alone employed 7,450 workers, now they employ a paltry 540. In 1970 there were three jobs for every Doveton family; now there is one job for every five families. Unemployment in Doveton in 1966 was less than 1%. Now it is 21.1%, where the national average is 6.1%. It is a similar story for the Broadmeadows area. Anecdotal evidence in 1970 was that Broadmeadows had one of the highest incomes per household and car ownerships per household in Melbourne. Of course, everybody in the family worked at Ford, Ericsson or Nabisco and drove to work. Now, according to Glover in 2015, unemployment at Norlane, Geelong, Broadmeadows and Elizabeth, South Australia is 20.7%, 25.7% and 32.6% respectively.

If the dire predictions of Ian Porter, former business editor of *The Age* [115], come true, the knock-on effect of between 137,000 and 200,000 workers losing their jobs in the automotive industry and their Tier one and Tier two level suppliers, will reduce the income tax take to government by over A$1.3 billion per year.

To visit a Ford site today is haunting. At BMO, the front office facing Geelong Road is locked and barricaded off, the floor rotting and unsafe. The North Shore Road office, once filled with the clatter of typewriters, the ring of telephones, the chatter of three hundred engineers with layout tables and offices has been replaced by office cells, each originally for four workers and their desks. The chest-high partitions are now a barrier between the remaining employees who sit, isolated and alone, one to every fourth cell. The stamping plant, whose heavy timber and concrete floor once vibrated with the thump of hundreds of presses, fork lifts and air guns is now so quiet one can hear an individual press as it strikes, a forlorn thump. The tool room is closed and barricaded off, the area leased to another company.

Stand in the middle of the cross-aisle of the Broadmeadows assembly plant, where once you did not dare for fear of being run down by forklifts, buggies or pushbikes, unable to hear for the cacophony of traffic, conveyors, the rattle of air-guns and the flash of arc welders. Now there are only the echoes of workers some distance away, building one of eighty vehicles for the day, a fraction of the 400–plus capacity.

Head Office is now the Ford Sales Company, located in far off Richmond, a world away from Geelong or Broadmeadows. The signage in front of the original Head Office building now announces its new position in Australia: the Product Development Centre for Ford Asia Pacific. The third floor of the building, a miniature of World Headquarters at Dearborn, is now vacant, access restricted. The ground floor and first floors are rapidly emptying, as renovations commence in preparation for the new occupants. Ford has retained the Design and Product Development functions in Australia. With more than fifty years' experience, Ford designers and engineers now design and test vehicles for the world using technology, systems and equipment unheard of in 1960, let alone 1925.

Perhaps the final word should come from a small publication issued in June 1953, to celebrate the fiftieth birthday of Ford Motor Company, *Fifty years of Watching the Fords go by*:

> *The Future? We've by no means reached the end of the Ford story. For throughout the world Ford experts are forever laying new plans, beginning new operations—forever seeking improvement on improvement. They firmly believe, as did the first Henry Ford, that 'good enough' is not good enough. They're determined that for the Ford owner 'the best is yet to be'. And they're making sure that the world, with ever–widening eyes, will continue to 'Watch the Fords go by'.*

ABOVE Main BMO site, Geelong, looking east, prior to the construction of the ACART centre in 2006

LEFT Aerial view of the Broadmeadows site, looking west, with Plant 1, Plant 2 and Paint facility. The Training Centre, Head Office and Research Centre are just north of the main plants. Plastics and Customer Service Centre are further north but not shown.

GLOSSARY

AAE Advanced Assembly Engineering.
ABS Anti-lock braking system.
ACART Advanced Centre for Automotive Research and Testing.
ACG Automotive Components Group.
ACI Australian Consolidated Industries
ACTU Australian Council of Trade Unions.
ADAPS The department, part of the Bureau of Statistics, charged with recording and publishing vehicle registrations nationally.
ADR Australian Design Rule.
AEU Australian Engineering Union.
AIA Automotive Industry Authority
ACI Australian Consolidated Industries.
APAO Asia Pacific Assembly Operations
AWD All wheel drive – 4 wheel drive.
BMO Basic Manufacturing Operations, Geelong. The division incorporating the Engine, Stamping, Chassis and Casting Plants.
BPC The British Purchasing Commission. The British Government purchasing authority in wartime, located in Washington, USA.
CAC Commonwealth Aircraft Corporation.
CAE Computer aided design and engineering.
Cd Drag coefficient, the measurement of aerodynamic efficiency of a vehicle.
CEO Chief Executive Officer.
CHOGM Commonwealth Heads of Government meeting.
c.i.d Cubic inches displacement.
CIG Commonwealth Industrial Gases.
CKD Completely knocked down. Disassembled vehicles in packing cases for export.
COTY Car of the Year.
CTC Computer torque control.
CSIRO Commonwealth Scientific and Industrial Research Organisation.
CVRM Ford corporate vehicle review manual.
DIRD Directorate of Industrial Relations.
DIVIMPRO The Division of Import Procurement. The Australian Government authority controlling imports into Australia during wartime.
DLP Democratic Labour Party.
DOHC Double overhead cam.
DSC Dynamic Stability Control
DSM District Sales Manager.
DSO Distinguished Service Order.
EAO Ford European Assembly Operations.
ECE European Community vehicle design rules, similar to Australian ADR.
EI Employee involvement.
EPDM PP EPDM rubber modified Polypropylene.
4WD Four wheel drive.
FAO Ford Assembly Operations.
FAPM Federation of Automotive Product Manufacturers.
FASPAC Ford Asia-Pacific.
FCAI Federal Chamber of Automotive Industries.
FOA Ford of Australia.
FOB Ford of Britain.
FOE Ford of Europe.
FOJ Ford of Japan.
FOP Ford of Philippines.
FPV Ford Performance Vehicles.
FUS Ford of United States.
FWD Front wheel drive.
Gaijin Japanese word for foreigners, or outsiders.
GFC Global financial crisis.
GM General Motors.
GM-H General Motors – Holden.
HDC Hill descent control.
IRS Independent rear suspension.
JAL Japan airlines
Kan-Ban Japanese term for the just-in-time philosophy of manufacturing, literally 'calling card'.
KD Knocked down, see CKD
k.p.h. Kilometres per hour
LCD Liquid crystal display
LHD Left hand drive
LPG Liquified petroleum gas
LLC Limited Liability Company in the US. Similar to a UK Plc, Proprietary limited company, or an Australian Pty Ltd company.
LWB Long wheel base.
MC Military Cross.
MITI The Japanese trade and export authority.
MM Military Medal.
MMBCL Melbourne Motor Body Company Ltd.
m.p.g. Miles per gallon
m.p.h. Miles per hour.
NAAO Ford North American Assembly Operations.
N.I.H. The not invented here syndrome. 'If we didn't make it, it's no good.'
NPD National Parts Distribution centre
NRMA Roadside assistance organization in NSW and the ACT.
NVH Noise, vibration and harshness.
OPEO Overseas Product Engineering Office

PEO Product Engineering Office, Australia. The Geelong based design, engineering and test centre.
PPP Plus Payment plan, the over-award payments for punctuality and attendance.
PI Process intent.
PM Participative management.
PU Polyurethane.
Q1, Q101 Ford Quality Standards, equal or superior to Australian Standard ISO 9001.
R/C, RC Research Centre. The FOA Design studio, now named the Design Centre.
RDO Rostered day off.
RHD Right hand drive.
RIM Reaction injection moulding. A process for manufacturing polyurethane products.
ROI Return on investment.
RWD Rear wheel drive.
S.H.E.D. test Sealed housing evaporative determination test.
SI Statistical inference.
SIDO Single Item Dealer Order, the document used to order a vehicle, which becomes a travel document on the vehicle as it is built.
SLALS Short and long arm, long spindle front suspension.
SMC Sheet moulding compound. Fibreglass supplied in a sheet form and moulded by heat and pressure in dies.
SMM&T Society of Motor Manufacturers and Traders, the body representing a group of companies which what would later become British Motor Company, including Austin, Morris, Leyland etc.
SQA Supplier Quality Assurance. The department in Ford charged with assuring Suppliers component quality.
Stillage(s) Standard size containers for storing and moving components, i.e. Large Box Pallet (LBP), Small Box Pallet (SBP) etc.
TCS Traction control system
TVE Tickford Vehicle Engineering
TK Toyo Kogyo, now Mazda Motor Company.
UAP United Australia Party. The predecessor of the Liberal Party of Australia.
UAW United Auto Workers union, the US equivalent of the VBU in Australia.
UK United Kingdom.
ULP Unleaded petrol
UPD Units per day.
VBEF Vehicle Builders Employees Federation.
VBU Vehicle Builders Union, successor to the VBEF.
VCT Variable camshaft timing.
VIC Vehicle industry training Certificate.

BIBLIOGRAPHY

The bibliography is arranged in four sections:

Books, catalogues and pamphlets
Unpublished documents
Journals, magazines and newspapers
Interviews, transcripts and notes

BOOKS, CATALOGUES AND PAMPHLETS

Australian Bureau of Statistics Year Book: 1927

Australian Bureau of Statistics Year Book: 1932

Australian Bureau of Statistics Year Book: 2009-2010, *The GFC and its impact on Australia*

Australian Dictionary of Biography: *Hubert Charles French*, Vol 14, MUP, 1996.

Australian Dictionary of Biography: *Sir Laurence Harnett*, Vol.17, MUP, 2007.

Australian Dictionary of Biography: *Essington Lewis*, Vol.10, MUP, 1986.

Brigden, Professor James, *The Australian Tariff: An Economic Enquiry*, May 1929.

Cockington, James, Oastler, Mark, et.al, Holden, *The great years, the great cars*, Rockpool Publishing, 2014

Darwin, Norm, *The History of Ford in Australia*, Eddie Ford Publications, Newstead, Victoria, 1986.

Easdown, Geoff. *A History of The Ford Motor Company in Australia*, Golden Press, 1987

Glover, Dennis. *An Economy is not a Society*, Redback, and Schwartz Publishing P/L, Collingwood, Victoria, 2015.

French, Hubert Charles: Reports and papers, Ford Motor Company of Australia archives.

Lacey, Robert. *Ford, The Men and the Machine*, Pan Books Ltd., 1987.

Nevins, Allan, & Hill, Frank Ernest. *Ford: The Times, the man, the Company*, Charles Scribner's Sons, 1954

Potts, David, J. *The Myth of the Great Depression*, Scribe Publications, Carlton North, 2006

Queensland Chamber of Manufacturers Year Book, Volume 21, 1967, printed by H. Pole & Co. Pty. Ltd, 1967

Stathis, Stephen. *Bathurst GT-HO Falcons–A Photographic Story*, Phase Three Posters, Sydney, 2005.

Wallace, Doug. *Ford Plastics – A story of manufacturing in Australia*, privately published, 2013

Wilkins, M, & Hill, F. E. *American Business Abroad - Ford on Six Continents*, Cambridge University Press, 2011

Wright, John. M. *Special – The untold story of Australia's Holden*, Allen & Unwin, Sydney, 2008.

Seidler, Edouard. *Let's call it Fiesta: The Auto-biography of Ford's Project Bobcat*, Patrick Stephens Ltd, Cambridge and Edita, Lausanne, 1976.

------, Strong Grows the Future, Ford Motor Company Australia Publication, 1950.

UNPUBLISHED DOCUMENTS

Barber, Graham, The Automotive Industry Industrial Mobilisation Course, 1988, Ford Motor Company archives, 1988

Burela, Marin: Address to AMCHAM (American-Australia Chambers of Commerce) luncheon, December 4, 2009, Ford Motor Company Australia archives.

Dix, Bill: Keynote address to the Committee for Development of Australia, Protection, Export and the Future of Manufacturing, February 2, 1985, Ford Motor Company Australia archives.

Fewchuck, David, Dealer Presentation Meeting, May 18, 1989. Ford Motor Company Australia archives.

Fewchuck, David: The Australian Capri, unpublished manuscript, 1988, Ford Motor Company Australia archives.

Ford II, Edsel: Speech to Geelong Management, September 19, 1978, Ford Motor Company Australia archives.

Gillitzer, Peter: TD Cortina Black book, pp 24, 31/1/1977, Ford Motor Company Australia archives.

------, Major competitors, Master Binder Study Plan, October 1958/1, Ford Motor Company Australia archives

McAllister, Olwen: letters to Adrian Ryan (3), 1998-2000, Ford Motor Company Australia archives.

McConnell, Stan; memoir, June 10, 2002, Ford Motor Company Australia archives.

McConnell, Stan: letter to The Editor, Ford News, June 11, 2002, Ford Motor Company Australia archives.

Vaughan, Ian: A Marathon Effort, unpublished manuscript, 1993, Ford Motor Company archives.

JOURNALS, MAGAZINES AND NEWSPAPERS

------, A Ford Celebration, *Geelong Advertiser*, July 29, 1995

Butler, Mark; Car theft crisis, *Herald Sun*, November 24, 2015

Carey, John, et.al: Ford Territory, *Wheels Magazine* Special Edition, Bauer Media, 2004

Creer, Brian: Yes there is a Cortina Fastback, *Australian Motor*, September, 1966

Dickens, Barry: People Business, *The Sunday Age*, November 22, 1998

Dowling, Joshua: Toyota to cease production by 2017, News Corp Australia Network, February 10, 2014.

Dunstan, Eddie: Ask Les–He'll know the answer, *Australasian Post*, June 21, 1951

------, End of the road for Ford veteran, *Sydney Telegraph*, September 2, 1994
Fogarty, Mark: Road Test-XD Falcon, Motoring Reporter, 1977
------, Ford to get A52m to help design new vehicles, *The Age*, May 7, 2006
Glover, Dennis: It's not working and we'll all pay, *The Age*, August 1, 2015
Goyne, Rohan: The sea mine story – from production to deployment an entirely Australian affair?
Hellenbeck, Tod: EL breaks Loose, *Wheels Magazine*, Bauer Media, November 1996
------, Hit for six, *Sydney Morning Herald*, Friday November 11, 2006
Leigh, Andrew: Trade Liberalisation and the Labour Party, Australian Journal of Politics and History, Vol. 48, Number 4, 2002.
McGregor, Craig: The man who saved the Falcon, *The Australian Financial Review*, April 12, 1996.
Porter, Ian: Here's who to blame for our coming recession, *The Age*, Monday September 7, 2015
Robinson, Peter: We get first drive: New XA Falcon, *Wheels Magazine*, Bauer Media, April 1972.
Robinson, Peter: Australian Motor Sports and Automobiles 1968, Bauer Media, April 1972.
Robinson, Peter: Cautious Kudos, *Wheels Magazine*, Bauer Media, February, 1988.
Sanidas, Elias and Jayanthakumaran, Kankesu, Trade reforms and the survival of the Passenger Motor Vehicle Industry in Australia, University of Wollongong, 2004.
Scott, Phil: Henry and the General…The Great fight for Number one, *Wheels Magazine*, Bauer Media, March 1983.
Scott, Phil: $700m Falcon keeps Ford in Australia, *Sydney Morning Herald*, July 13, 1995
Sorell, John: There he was on St Patrick's Day in best suit, *The Herald*, March 30, 1966.
Stahl, Michael: 1960-2010 – Falcon's 50 Fabulous Years, *Wheels Magazine* Special Edition, Bauer Media, 2010.
-----, The Downsizing of Australia, *Sydney Morning Herald*, October 20, 1997.
-----, The Holden Australia Story, unique cars and parts, October 14, 2014.
-----, War of the Wheels, *The Age 'Good Weekend'*, July 11, 1992.
Whitburn, James: Burners, *Wheels Magazine*, Bauer Media, May 2012.
Whitburn, James: EcoBoost Falcon, *Wheels Magazine*, Bauer Media, June 2012.

INTERVIEWS, TRANSCRIPTS AND NOTES

Lewis, Professor David L and Ryan, Adrian:
Interviews with Dave Block, Brian Dummett, Bill Dix, Sir Brian Inglis, 'Tunner' Kenworthy, David Letford, Jessie Pittman, Charlie Simpson, and Grace Tuck, *Ford Corporate History Project*, Ford Motor Company of Australia Archives, 1988.

Cook, Michele & Wallace, Margaret and Doug:
Interviews with Mike Alves, Fred Bradd, Ray Brewster, Bill Cotter, Dave Cox, Ian and Pam Craven, John Crew, Tom Davison, Lindsay Dawson, Bill Dix, Brian Dummett, Don Dunoon, Brian Egan, Dennis Flentje, David Ford, Peter Fry, Alec Hand, Frank Inturrisi, Mike Jarvis, Malcolm Johnson, Phil Jones, Max Kenworthy, Phil Jones, David Lamb, John Marshall, Don McAllister, Ken McDonald, Ern Millard, Stephen Mustica, Terry O'Brian, Noel Pritchard, Ron Rau, Peter Robinson, Jim Rose, Phil Scott, Lindsay Sheppard, Phil Spender, David Stobart, Alan Thompson, Peter Watson, Ian Vaughan, and Tad Zyppel, Ford Motor Company of Australia Archives, 2015

NOTES

1 H. C. French Report to Ford Canada, December 14, 1923 and
2 H.C. French memo to W.R. Campbell, December 24, 1923
3 American Business Abroad - Ford on Six Continents.
4 HC French memo, November 12, 1923
5 HC French memo, November 12, 1923
6 ibid
7 HC French memo, November 12, 1923
8 HC French report November 14, 1923
9 HC French memo, November 12, 1923
10 HC French report December 14, 1923
11 HC French report December 14, 1923
12 HC French memo, November 14, 1923
13 HC French memo, November 14, 1923
14 H.C. French memo, January 27, 1924
15 HC memo to WR Campbell, December 24, 1923
16 HC French report on Distributors' Convention, April 17, 1924
17 HC French report on visit to Perth, April 24, 1924
18 HC French memo to WR Campbell, December 24, 1923
19 WR Campbell memo to Edsel Ford, September10, 1924
20 BJ Craig memo to Wallace Campbell, October 1 1924.
21 Geoff Easdown, A History of The Ford Motor Company in Australia, p 34
22 The Geelong Advertiser, March 31, 1925
23 Australian Bureau of Statistics Year Book 1927.
24 Ron Phillips, Strong grows the Future, 1950.
25 Australian Bureau of Statistics Year Book 1932
26 Ibid
27 The Holden Australia Story.
28 Lew Bandt notes, May 1983
29 'Tunner' Kenworthy interview, Ford Corporate History Project, 1988
30 Lew Bandt notes, May 1983
31 Ron Phillips, Strong grows the Future, 1950.
32 H French memo to W.C. Campbell, December 13, 1933
33 George Wilden, Strong grows the Future, 1950.
34 Ibid
35 Nevins & Hill, Ford: The Times, the man, the Company.
36 Australian Dictionary of Biography, MUP, 2007
37 Essington Lewis, Australian Dictionary of Biography, Volume 10, 1986
38 L.J. Hartnett memo to H. French, July 8, 1940
39 Notes from meeting at Ministry of Munitions, May 22, 1941.
40 Geoff Easdown, A History of The Ford Motor Company in Australia, p 53
41 Rohan Goyne, The sea mine story from production to deployment an entirely Australian affair?
42 Appendix 2 contains a summary of war products, by assembly plant.
43 RW Griffiths memo to GV Cornwell December 13, 1946
44 Refer Appendix 2 for the complete list.
45 RW Griffiths memo to GV Cornwell December 13, 1946
46 Westman memo to L Hartnett, August 5, 1940
47 Geoff Easdown, A History of Ford Motor Company in Australia, p. 53
48 RW Griffiths memo to GV Cornwell December 13, 1946.
49 French memo to Tariff Board, December 15, 1942.
50 Geoff Easdown, A History of The Ford Motor Company in Australia, p 61
51 Australian Dictionary of Biography, Vol. 14, 1996, Jensen, Sir John
52 Miliken memo to French, March 22, 1945, Ford archives
53 French notes, September 18, 1945
54 Sir Brian Inglis interview, Ford Corporate History Project, 1988
55 Ford News, May 1989
56 Sir Brian Inglis interview, Ford Corporate History Project, 1988
57 Stan McConnell memoir June 10, 2002 and letter to The Editor, Ford News, June 11, 2002
58 Master Binder Study Plan, October 1958/1 – 'Major competitors'
59 Master Binder Study Plan, October 1958/1 – 'Major competitors'
60 The actual cancellation costs vary by source and may never be known. The source considered most reliable is Geoff Easdown's A History of The Ford Motor Company in Australia, p 85.
61 Dave Brock interview, Ford Corporate History Project, 1988
62 Brian Dummett interview, Ford Corporate History Project, 1988
63 Sir Brian Inglis interview, Ford Corporate History Project, 1988
64 Balance out; matching components into complete vehicle sets and disposing of excess components, often as Parts and Service

components.
65 Sir Brian Inglis interview, Ford Corporate History Project, 1988
66 David Letford interview, Ford Corporate History Project, 1988
67 ibid
68 Geoff Easdown, A History of the Ford Motor Company in Australia. p 93
69 Sir Brian Inglis interview, Ford Corporate History Project, 1988
70 Bare bodies, built, unpainted and unassembled.
71 Peter Robinson, Australian Motor Sports and Automobiles, 1968
72 Cubic inch displacement
73 *Wheels Magazine*, April 1972
74 CKD, Completely knocked down or unassembled.
75 SKD, Semi knocked down or semi-assembled.
76 Confederation of Australian Motorsports
77 Supplier Quality Assurance
78 Sheet Moulding Compound, a form of fibreglass supplied in sheets.
79 Peter Gillitzer, TD Cortina Black book, January 31, 1977, pp24.
80 Edsel Ford II Speech to Geelong Management September 19, 1978.
81 The Red Book describes the new vehicle in detail, in words, and is used for program costing and project preparation.
82 Geoff Easdown, A History of The Ford Motor Company in Australia, p 123.
83 Vehicle Builder Employees Federation
84 SIDO – Single Item Dealer Order.
85 Asian Pacific Automotive Operations
86 David Fewchuck, The Australian Capri.
87 ibid
88 David Fewchuck, Dealer Presentation Meeting, May 18, 1989.
89 Ford Corporate Vehicle Requirements Manual
90 Overseas Product Engineering Office
91 Federated Chamber of Automotive Industry and Federation of Automotive Product Manufacturers
92 Sealed Housing Evaporative Determination Test
93 Non-recurring charges incurred in cancelling the Capri program and remediation of the site after the closure of the Homebush plant of A$133.3 million, allowed Ford to report a A$79 million profit for 1993.
94 'War of the Wheels', *The Age* 'Good Weekend', July 11, 1992
95 North American Assembly Operations
96 Employee Involvement, Statistical Inference and Process Intent
97 A Marathon Effort, Ian Vaughan, 1993
98 North American Assembly Operations, European Assembly Operations and the Automotive Components Groups
99 Interview with Phil Scott, *Sydney Morning Herald*, July 14, 1995.
100 Phil Scott, *Sydney Morning Herald*, July 13, 1995
101 Interview with Craig McGregor, *The Australian Financial Review*, April 12, 1996
102 Todd Hellenbeck EL breaks loose, *Wheels*, November 1996
103 Computer Aided Design and Engineering
104 Double Overhead Cam
105 Ani-lock Braking System, Traction Control system, Dynamic Stability Control, Hill Descent Control.
106 Wheels special edition Ford Territory, 2004
107 Hit for six, *Sydney Morning Herald*, November11, 2006
108 Australian Bureau of Statistics Year Book 2009-10, The GFC and its impact on Australia, contributed by the Reserve Bank of Australia.
109 Marin Burela speech at AMCHAM luncheon, December 4, 2009
110 Joshua Dowling, News Corp, February 10, 2014, Toyota to cease production by 2017.
111 The Automotive Industry Industrial Mobilization Course, Graham Barber, Government Affairs Manager Ford Motor Company, 1988
112 The Australian Tariff: An Economic Enquiry, Brigden, May 1929
113 Bill Dix, Protection, Export and the Future of Manufacturing, February 2, 1985
114 Joshua Dowling, News Corp, February 10, 2014, Toyota to cease production by 2017.
115 Ian Porter, Here's who to blame for our coming recession, *The Age,* September 7, 2015

FORD AUSTRALIA STATISTICS

FORD AUSTRALIA PRODUCTION MATRIX—by Vehicle Group and Assembly Plant

Total Vehicle Production—to end of manufacturing, October 2016

	Falcon								
Plant	**Sedan**	**Wagon**	**Tudor**	**Ute (inc. Navarra)**	**Van**	**Fairlane**	**LTD**	**Landau**	**Group Total**
Plant 1 (to end 2015)	2,155,974	677,319	27,085	355,774	83,199	171,933	18,898	1,385	**3,491,567**
Estimated 2016 production	4,147			2,532					**6,679**
Plant 1 total	2,160,121	677,319	27,085	358,306	83,199	171,933	18,898	1,385	**3,498,246**
Plant 2 (a.k.a. Truck plant)				81,935	20,696				**102,631**
B/M Site subtotal	2,160,121	677,319	27,085	440,241	103,895	171,933	18,898	1,385	**3,600,877**
Brisbane	103,917	37,663		27,948	1,224	69,080	13,452		**253,284**
Grand Total	**2,264,038**	**714,982**	**27,085**	**468,189**	**105,119**	**241,013**	**32,350**	**1,385**	**3,854,161**

Last Update: 4/13/2016

Plant	Falcon Group Total	Canadian Group Total	English Group Total	Territory and Japanese Group Total	Commercial Group Total	War Years Automotive	SUMMARY FORD AUSTRALIA PRODUCTION GRAND TOTAL
Plant 1 (to end 2015)	3,491,567	8,453	286,719	288,604	5,291		4,080,634
Estimated 2016 production	6,679			7,873			14,552
Plant 1 total	3,498,246	8,453	286,719	296,477	5,291		4,095,186
Plant 2 (a.k.a. Truck plant)	102,631			66,662	92,520		261,813
B/M Site subtotal	3,600,877	8,453	286,719	363,139	97,811		4,356,999
Adelaide			13,964		1,944	29	15,937
Brisbane	253,284	6,375	25,875		25,501	5,365	316,400
Fremantle		2,484	9,283		1,919	1,981	15,667
Geelong		149,593	137,715		146,213	38,058	471,579
Renault			17,649				17,649
Sydney		14,795	279,218	349,006	57,657	14,018	714,694
Grand Total	3,854,161	181,700	770,423	712,145	331,045	59,451	**5,908,925**
Tractors - ALL (records incomplete)							140,442
GRAND TOTAL INCLUDING TRACTORS							**6,049,367**

War Years Products— (Memo Items Only)

Automotive	Cars, Utes, Vans, Trucks & Semitrailers and Speciality vehicles etc	59,451
Comp'ts, Mods, Convers'ns	Benches, C'boards, Kits, Conversions, Water tanks, Wheels, Winches	288,617
Marine—Vessels	Vessels, Barges, Workboats, Tugs, Lighters and Pontoons	502
Marine—Mines	Mines	12,987
Aeronautical	Aircraft Bellytanks, Oxygen Cylinders and Reconditioned Aero Engines	79,859
Machine Tools	Presses, Lathes, Gun Barrel Boring Lathes, Boring Machines	203

FORD AUSTRALIA PRODUCTION BY YEAR, RANKED BY VOLUME (Total Vehicles)

Rank	Year	Falcon Sedan/ Wag Tudor	Falcon Ute/Van	Fairlane / Ltd	Canadian Vehicles	English Vehicles	Australian Japanese	Commercial Vehicles	Military Special Vehicles	FOA Total Vehicles
1	1985	80,398	11,399	11,049			48,944	3,464		155,254
2	1984	69,576	8,266	7,998			58,156	3,690		147,686
3	1974	72,378	16,537	12,123		34,038		7,244		142,320
4	1982	70,025	7,958	9,155		0	46,251	5,248		138,637
5	1976	57,640	13,632	11,962		40,730		9,752		133,716
6	1989	66,124	14,728	10,628			35,694	5,703		132,877
7	1990	62,054	8,305	6,404			51,446	4,580		132,789
8	1972	65,775	12,042	9,668	597	37,692		4,574		130,348
9	1979	62,351	8,448	9,373		41,437		8,115		129,724
10	1977	55,526	12,008	9,627		41,462		9,173		127,796

NOTE: As Military Special Vehicles were not recorded by year, they have been included as one number in 1945

TOP 10 FALCON & DERIVATIVE MODELS—ALL PLANTS

Rank	Sedan, Wagon, Tudor	Volume
1	XD Total	178,713
2	XB Total	174,487
3	XE Total	172,681
4	BA 1 Total	156,078
5	EL Total	140,795
6	XC Total	139,518
7	AU 1 Total	119,380
8	EA 1 Total	118,859
9	XA Total	111,082
10	FG Total	109,931

Rank	Ute/Van	Volume
1	XF 2 Total	59,283
2	BA 1 Total	43,225
3	XB Total	37,494
4	AU 2 Total	32,570
5	XC Total	31,562
6	FG Total	34,656
7	XG Total	24,592
8	XD Total	22,136
9	BF 2 Total	21,167
10	BA 2 Total	19,335

Rank	Fairlane, LTD	Volume
1	ZH/P6	28,878
2	ZG/P5/P6	26,831
3	ZJ/79	24,866
4	ZK/82	20,332
5	ZF	17,306
6	ZL/84	13,693
7	NA/DA	13,468
8	ZD	12,797
9	ZC	12,513
10	ZB	10,708

Rank	Total Falcon Sedan, Wagon, Tudor, Ute, Van	Volume
1	XB Total	211,981
2	XD Total	200,849
3	BA Total	199,303
4	XE Total	191,174
5	XC Total	171,080
6	EL Total	153,791
7	XF 2 Total	144,750
8	AU 2 Total	133,047
9	AU 1 Total	130,451
10	XA Total	129,473

Top 10 Models

Rank	Model	Volume
1	AU (1, 2, 3) Total	322,838
2	XF (1, ADR37, 2) Total	322,778
3	BA (1 & 2) Total	281,197
4	XB Total	211,981
5	EA (1 & 2) Total	209,936
6	XD Total	200,849
7	XE Total	191,174
8	XC Total	171,080
9	EL Total	153,791
10	BF (1 & 2) Total	136,473

INDEX

G

H

I

J

K

L

M

N

O

P

U

V

W

X, Y, Z

VIC
PONY·19

Ford

ACKNOWLEDGEMENTS

This book could not have been written without the enthusiastic assistance of the many Ford employees, past and present, as well those involved in the industry. In particular, we would like to thank the following;

The late John Marshall, Manufacturing Director, Ford Australia for his knowledge, advice, encouragement, and sparkling conversations over many years. Peter Robinson and Phil Scott, retired editors of *Wheels* magazine for providing objective, outsider views of Ford, its products and its people. To Glenn Butler and Barry Park, current editor and Production Manager respectively of *Wheels* magazine, for allowing unlimited access to the *Wheels* magazine archives. Peter Fry, for his information on vehicles, components, terminology, his copious notes and extensive list of contacts, to which one e-mail enquiry can elicit twenty responses and an interesting debate. Ian Vaughan, Vice-President, Product Development, for his insightful and thoughtful comments on Government Affairs, the AU Falcon, Product Planning and the two London-Sydney marathons. Ian Craven for organizing the 'Sydney Crew' interviews, follow-up correspondence, and John Allardice for information on staffing of the Sydney Plant. Phil Jones, for his encyclopaedic knowledge and photographs of the construction of the many plants in which he was involved in Australia and the Asian-Pacific region. Peter Gillitzer for his comments on the Cortina, and US research clinics. Colin McKenzie, Sales Manager, Trucks, for explaining the U.S. term 'tractors.' Kathie Fewchuk, for permission to use quotes from David Fewchuk's unpublished manuscript. Cristian Brunelli, for permission to use his fantastic images, without them the book would not nearly be as interesting.

We are indebted to the following for their advice, help and assistance in tracking down those rare early photographs of the motoring industry; Daryl Meek and Helen Stitt of the Royal Automoblile Club of Victoria Archive, Mathew Lombard of the Australian National Motor Museum, David Chantrell for his research work with Duncan and Fraser.

Specifically, we would also like to thank all those who participated in interviews with the authors and contributed to the writing of this book. We have listed you in alphabetical order only because we haven't been able to work out a better system of thanking you. You are part of the history of Ford Australia and made it the company it became. Mike Alves, Fred Bradd, Ray Brewster, Bill Cotter, Dave Cox, Ian and Pam Craven, John Crew, Tom Davison, Lindsay Dawson, Bill Dix, Brian Dummett, Don Dunoon, Brian Egan, Dennis Flentje, David Ford, Peter Fry, Alec Hand, Frank Inturrisi, Mike Jarvis, Malcolm Johnson, Phil Jones, Max Kenworthy, David Lamb, John Marshall, Don McAllister, Ken McDonald, Ern Millard, Noel Miller, Stephen Mustica, Terry O'Brian, Noel Pritchard, Ron Rau, Peter Robinson, Jim Rose, Phil Scott, Lindsay Sheppard, Phil Spender, David Stobart, Alan Thompson, Don Thompson, Peter Watson, Ian Vaughan, and Tad Zyppel.

The interviews conducted and recorded as part of the creation of this book will join those of Adrian Ryan and Professor David Lewis to form a living, oral history of Ford Motor Company of Australia in the archives.

The authors are grateful to Ford Motor Company of Australia Limited, for allowing unconditional access to the extensive Australian archives, including the financial records, papers, media releases, Ford News, *Austra-Ford Gazette*, Us, and the various other in-house magazines and library, which date back to 1923. This book could not have been written without them. We are also grateful to Dave French, Programs Director, Asia Pacific, for his efforts in ensuring the accuracy of many of the photographs and captions. We acknowledge and thank the councilors and staff of the City of Greater Geelong for their assistance in the writing of this book, as well as the staff, directors and volunteers of The Geelong Museum of Motoring and Industry.

Most importantly, to Margaret Wallace and Robert Cook, our long-suffering spouses and support team for over two years; for your editing, research and clerical assistance and support.

And lastly, to the brave team at New Holland Publishing, Fiona Schultz, Alan Whiticker, Gordana Trifunovic, Andrew Quinlan and James Mills-Hicks, for helping make the dream come true.

This Paperback Edition published in 2016 by New Holland Publishers

First published in 2016 by New Holland Publishers
Sydney

Level 1, 178 Fox Valley Road, Wahroonga, NSW 2076, Australia

newhollandpublishers.com

A record of this book is held at the National Library of Australia.

ISBN 9781742579214

Managing Director: Fiona Shultz
Publisher: Alan Whiticker
Editor: Gordana Trifunovic
Designer: Andrew Quinlan
Production Director: Arlene Gippert
Printed in China

10 9 8 7

Keep up with New Holland Publishers:
NewHollandPublishers
@newhollandpublishers